PRAISE FOR

LET US TALK OF MANY THINGS

"William Buckley does indeed talk here of many things, with deft mention of the many cabbages and kings that he has addressed politically over these years. As ever, sheer delight from humor and prose, whatever the political faith."

—JOHN KENNETH GALBRAITH

"Mr. Buckley has a rare advantage over—well, over almost anyone else who might contemplate a project like this: It is impossible to read these speeches without hearing Mr. Buckley's famous voice. That adds to the pleasure."

—MICHAEL KINSLEY

"Reading Bill Buckley's collected speeches is an exhilarating experience. The cogency of his arguments and his delivery are so extraordinarily persuasive that if this collection is as widely read as it should be, it will cause havoc in liberal salons. This is one of the few books devoted to the thoughts of one person that will be read from cover to cover."

—EDWARD KOCH

Also by William F. Buckley Jr.

Nonfiction

God and Man at Yale

McCarthy and His Enemies
(with L. Brent Bozell)

Up from Liberalism

The Committee and Its Critics
(editor)

Rumbles Left and Right

The Unmaking of a Mayor

The Jeweler's Eye

The Governor Listeth

Odyssey of a Friend (editor)

Did You Ever See a Dream
Walking?

American Conservative Thought in
the Twentieth Century (editor)

Cruising Speed

Inveighing We Will Go

Four Reforms

United Nations Journal:
A Delegate's Odyssey

Execution Eve

Airborne

A Hymnal: The Controversial Arts

Atlantic High: A Celebration

Overdrive: A Personal Documentary

Right Reason

Keeping the Tablets
(editor, with Charles Kesler)

Racing Through Paradise

On the Firing Line: The Public Life
of Our Public Figures

Gratitude: Reflections on What We
Owe to Our Country

In Search of Anti-Semitism

WindFall

Happy Days Were Here Again:
Reflections of a Libertarian
Journalist

The Blackford Oaks Reader

The Right Word

Nearer, My God

Fiction

Saving the Queen

Stained Glass

Who's on First

Marco Polo, If You Can

The Story of Henri Tod

See You Later Alligator

The Temptation of Wilfred
Malachey

High Jinx

Mongoose, R.I.P.

Tucker's Last Stand

A Very Private Plot

Brothers No More

The Redhunter

Spytime: The Undoing of
James Jesus Angleton

WILLIAM F. BUCKLEY JR.

Let Us Talk
of
Many Things

THE COLLECTED SPEECHES

FORUM

AN IMPRINT OF PRIMA PUBLISHING

Published by Prima Publishing, Roseville, California. Member of the Crown Publishing
Group, a division of Random House, Inc.

Random House, Inc. New York, Toronto, London, Sydney, Auckland

PRIMA PUBLISHING, FORUM, and colophons are trademarks of Random House,
Inc., registered with the United States Patent and Trademark Office.

Library of Congress Cataloging-in-Publication Data

Buckley, William F. (William Frank)
    Let us talk of many things : the collected speeches / William F. Buckley Jr.
        p. cm.
    Includes index.
    ISBN 0-7615-2551-3
    ISBN 0-7615-3409-1 (pbk.)
    1. Speeches, addresses, etc., American.   I. Title.

PS3552.U344 L48 2000
815'.54—dc21

00-025551

01 02 03 04 05 HH 10 9 8 7 6 5 4 3 2 1
Printed in the United States of America

First Edition

Visit us online at www.primaforum.com

CONTENTS

———

THE EIGHTIES

THE NINETIES

ACKNOWLEDGMENTS

THIS BOOK HAS been compiled at the prompting of the publisher, Mr. Steven Martin of Prima Publishing.

I remember rather offhandedly agreeing to undertake the job. I knew it would be onerous but did not guess quite how much would be involved.

Apart from debates and talks at Yale, I began speaking publicly when my first book, *God and Man at Yale*, was published. Requests from myriad groups, mostly colleges, came in, and soon I retained a lecture agent. For many years I gave seventy or more lectures a year; I continue to lecture now, but less often.

The compiling of the talks for this book was a huge endeavor. My debt—complete, prostrate, eternal—is to Linda Bridges. Miss Bridges, a graduate of the University of Southern California, where she specialized in French literature and modern English, had served as managing editor of *National Review*, the magazine that I founded and served as editor for thirty-five years. Miss Bridges devoted the better part of one year to putting together this material.

The very first job was to collect the speeches. A few were with my other papers in archives at the Yale University library. Many were in office files. And many more were on computers.

The next step was to eliminate repetitions. This proved difficult because a talk substantially repeated would be slightly and sometimes critically different in different situations; always different in introductory sections, and sometimes in the body of the speech as well.

Every repeated speech set to one side, Linda (I can't continue with "Miss Bridges") listed one hundred eighty-four speeches, all different. To have published the lot would have meant a book(s) with three hundred fifty thousand words. *Gone with the Wind* is two hundred fifty thousand words. On no account, Mr. Martin said sternly, could the book come to more than one hundred seventy-five thousand words.

That was when I got the bright idea. Why not include, at the end of the book, a CD in which the whole shebang would repose, in the event that students, friendly or unfriendly, wanted access to the oeuvre? That idea, popped onto Mr. Martin's desk, proved what the French call a *fausse idée claire*—a terrific idea that doesn't work. Mr. Martin said that to enclose the CD would mean adding ten dollars to the price of the book, making it unmarketable. This is not a collection of talks opposing the working of the marketplace; and so I yielded. The CD idea may flower in a future special edition suitable for libraries and for readers especially curious to go on beyond where they are taken here.

Linda then graded the talks according to her judgment of their vitality and variety. Blue ink meant Necessary; green ink, Qualified; and red ink, Can do without. The blue-inked, plus one or two of the greens, added up to two hundred thirty thousand words. We cut, in some cases with some sadness, seventeen more speeches, leaving us with the present number. I have introduced each entry with a few words designed to give the reader information I think useful.

The initial talk is included primarily because of its auspices. It was the Class Day Oration of the 1950 graduating class of Yale University. I wince a little on reading what I wrote as a twenty-four-year-old, but that's good, they say—the perspective that makes you critical of yesterday's work. The final talk in this volume is introduced by my son, Christopher Buckley, the talented humorist, novelist, and editor. We attempted, in the ninety-odd speeches in between, to achieve a balance. Some of the weightier material, some of the lighter material; a great many oriented to one person, testimonials and eulogies.

I thought to begin the book with the essay I wrote a few years ago for *The New Yorker* on some of the trials of public speaking—a useful few pages, lighthearted and informative, about what it is actually like to travel from city to city, college to college, as has been done for so many centuries by poets, politicians, ideologues, and promoters. And then I thought to ask David Brooks to do me the honor of a formal introduction, which, as of this writing, I have not seen. Mr. Brooks, who serves as an editor of the *Weekly Standard,* was an undergraduate journalist at the University of Chicago at the time my book *Overdrive* was published. His hilarious putdown of it, in the Chicago undergraduate daily, was so funny that I reprinted the whole of it in the introduction to the paperback edition. We have since forgiven each other.

I swore I would mention only Linda Bridges in this introduction, but I can't omit mention of Frances Bronson, who since 1968 has looked after me, my papers, my articles, speeches, problems, deadlines—here is another mention of my gratitude and my indebtedness.

—WFB
Stamford, Connecticut
November 1999

FOREWORD

By David Brooks

THERE'S ONE QUESTION I have always longed to ask Bill Buckley, but I've never worked up the nerve: Are you content? Millions of people set off on their lives hoping to build some lasting legacy, to make some immortal impression upon the world. They're driven hour upon hour, day upon day, to write the next essay, or do the next deal, or paint the next painting. But only a few people in the world actually can sit back knowing beyond doubt that they have succeeded; they have altered the course of events and surpassed all realistic expectations. Bill Buckley is one of those few. No Buckley, no conservative movement; no conservative movement, no Ronald Reagan. You fill in the rest.

I'd like to think that at least for those few there is some sort of cosmic payoff. I'd like to think they experience a grand and delicious sense of tranquillity that serves as an oasis after all the years on airplanes, in meetings, or in front of the keyboard. But maybe one of the reasons I've never asked Bill Buckley this question is that I sense he'd tell me there is no sublime contentment. There are always more speeches to be given, more controversies to be addressed, more points to be made. After all, even today, in what in some senses is a retirement, Buckley continues to give more talks, write more columns, and attend to more disputes than most people do in their prime. There's obviously some spur still driving him on. And maybe he'd add that the kind of oasis I'm talking about isn't to be found in this fallen world, which, literally, is a shame.

There are a lot of speeches in the book you hold in your hands. And they reveal a lot about Bill Buckley. But they also reveal a lot about world history over the past fifty years. These are primary documents that take you straight back to the atmosphere of the Cold War, the 1960s, Watergate, the Reagan years. Suddenly, you are back in the audience in 1950, when a twenty-four-year-old William F. Buckley Jr. challenges the powers at Yale University; in 1960, when he addresses a rally at Carnegie Hall gathered in protest of Nikita Khrushchev's American visit; in 1962, when he faces off against Norman Mailer in a packed amphitheater in Chicago. These are thrilling confrontations, but if you are like me you will read them with a sense of *tristesse*. The debates in those early days seemed so much more dramatic. The issues were fundamental. And, without question, there was a wider gulf between Left and Right.

Liberalism was then at its most outrageous, and Buckley was a little outrageous himself. Debating the *New York Post*'s James Wechsler in 1959, Buckley assailed: "I cannot think of a single word James Wechsler, a spokesman for American liberalism and a product of it, has ever uttered, or a deed he has done, that could be proved to have given comfort to slaves behind the Iron Curtain, whose future as slaves would be as certain in a world governed by James Wechsler as the future of slaves in Atlanta would have been in an America governed by Jefferson Davis." He doesn't tell us whether they shook hands after that exchange.

A few pages further on, the reader comes to that Mailer debate, and what fun it must have been to see. The topic for the evening was the meaning of the American right wing, and Buckley doubts the subject will be of much interest to Mr. Mailer: "I am not sure we have enough sexual neuroses for him. But if we have any at all, no doubt he will find them and celebrate them." But Buckley goes on to hope that Mailer will show some contempt for conservatism: "I do not know anyone whose dismay I personally covet more; because it is clear from reading the works of Mr. Mailer that only demonstrations of human swinishness are truly pleasing to him." This is not genteel analysis on the *Charlie Rose* show. Nor is this a couple of pundits cross-talking on *The Capital Gang*. This is debate at a much higher

level, at once funnier, more serious, and more vicious. This is incivil-
ity with a purpose.

Especially in the 1950s and 1960s, Buckley was a provocateur. But
he was not only that, for mixed in here you will find theological orations, often in the form of commencement addresses, in which
Buckley talks seriously about serious things. He was certainly not
playing to the crowds. There are a few talks in this book I could never
have followed while sitting on some folding chair on a sunny spring
afternoon in my cap and gown. Buckley clearly wasn't going to go
down to the level of his audiences; he was going to force them up to
his. Maybe you can't be the leader of a movement unless you possess
this instinctive force of will.

And as the pages roll by, you see Buckley emerging as the leader
of the conservative movement. There is the striking talk he gave on
September 11, 1964, to the national convention of the Young
Americans for Freedom. Barry Goldwater is going to lose the coming
election, he tells them. But, he continues, the Goldwater campaign
and the conservative efforts that will follow are parts of the decades-
long assault on the walls of fortress liberalism. On the day after the
election, he says, "we must emerge smiling, confident in the knowledge that we weakened those walls, that they will never again stand so
firmly against us." As prophecy, not too shabby.

In the late 1960s and early 1970s, we see Buckley engaged on
different battlefields. The New Left spread a poisonous anti-
Americanism. It even infected the Right. And so Buckley set about
defending America—assailing a little less and celebrating our national heritage a little more. Buckley emerges in the 1970s as a calming
influence. He seeks to defuse the passions that threaten to blow
libertarians apart from their conservative allies. He seems to become
more interested in the ideas of the American Founders. The 1980s
brought Buckley's friend Ronald Reagan to the White House.
Buckley's talks become more engaged with issues of day-to-day governance. There are even speeches on economics, as Buckley sets out
to defend Reaganomics. One can see the influence of George Gilder.

In 1984, a new character enters the scene: Blackford Oakes.
Buckley gave a speech on the hero of his best-selling novels. And in

his description of what makes Oakes a hero, one begins to perceive another shift in Buckley's field of interest, from public virtue to private virtue. Many of the talks in the latter part of this book are given in honor of some friend or hero: Clare Boothe Luce, John Simon, Jack Kemp, Andrei Sakharov, Vladimir Bukovsky. None of these talks is solely about private character because none of these are private individuals, but Buckley seems to be exploring what it means to lead a noble life. Some will say he mellows as he gets older. It's hard to dismiss that. As you read his remarks to the fortieth reunion of the Yale class of 1950, reflect back on the remarks he made to that same class four decades before, the first speech in this book. But saying that Buckley has mellowed does not explain away the evidence we have before us. The world has changed, for the better.

In the latter part of the book, Buckley addresses audiences at conservative societies and think tanks that came into being during the course of his career and that he himself inspired. He is not a lonely fighter anymore; it would be odd if he continued to behave like one. Some conservatives seem to grow more sour even as conservative ideas are more widely accepted—even as Communism dies and capitalism triumphs. They insist on their own marginalization, and savor it. But Buckley, though a controversialist, seeks pleasure, not pain. If he seems less offended in the later speeches in this book, maybe there is less to be offended by. The country has gone through many changes over the past five decades, and one of the revelations of this book is how Buckley has changed too.

In the later speeches, in particular, we see the trait that makes him distinctive. When people learn that I worked briefly at *National Review* and ask me what Bill Buckley is like, the thing I always mention first is his capacity for friendship. We all see the energy he puts into his speeches and columns and television appearances. But lots of people work hard. What is distinctive about Buckley is the energy he puts into his friendships. The world might be different if he didn't have this gift.

By the time I got to *National Review* in 1984, it was a convivial ship. We were all so wrapped up in admiration for managing editor Priscilla Buckley that we weren't in a mood to feud. But in the early days, apparently, *NR* was like a crowded valley in the Appalachians, with rifle fire from shed to shed. It must have been Buckley's talent for companionship that kept the brilliant but ornery editors together. And a friendship that threads its way though this book is drawn from that era, the one with Whittaker Chambers. Buckley quotes Chambers several times in these speeches. Each quotation is a gem, and each is introduced with an unmistakable tone of devotion.

Perhaps this talent for friendship has something to do with Buckley's prolific speechifying. Think of it: thousands of speeches over dozens of years. Tens of thousands of listeners. Hundreds of thousands of airplane miles. Why give so many speeches? And why do we show up for speakers like Buckley? After all, if it is mere information and argument we want, a magazine article is a more efficient way to get it. An article is on the page, so you can go over it again if your mind wanders, and you can save it for later reference. And if it's simply Buckley's locutions you want to hear, you can sit at home and watch him on TV.

But live encounters offer something more, a personal connection that is the seed of friendship. For all Buckley's contributions to conservative ideas, his most striking contribution is to the conservative personality. He made being conservative attractive and even glamorous. One suspects that more people were inspired by his presence at these events than were converted by the power of mere logic. It would be wonderful if we could go back and watch these clashes firsthand. It would be even more wonderful if we could go back armed with the knowledge we now possess: that in most cases, subsequent events have proved that Buckley's tormentors were wrong, and he, it transpires, was right.

NOTES FROM
THE LECTURE CIRCUIT

A Veteran's Complaints, Delights, Concerns
By Wm. F. Buckley Jr.

A GENERATION AGO Bernard De Voto, Harvard historian, novelist, and wit, resolved to give up public lecturing. After so many years of it, he had had enough. Besides, there were those books he wanted to get written, those books still left to read. But he had a valedictory in mind on the subject of public lecturing, and he devoted his column "The Easy Chair" in *Harper's* magazine to it. He gave the reader an instructive and amusing account of pitfalls in the trade. Much of what he wrote lingers in the memory of the present-day lecturer, which is not surprising, because the basic arrangements are unchanged.

For instance, you have agreed to lecture six times during the month of May. Your agent discloses a few months ahead where the lectures will take place. A week or two before each event, you receive detailed marching orders. Up until then, though, you will find yourself putting off specific attention to mainstream lectures, i.e., those where one isn't asked to address special, ad hoc concerns. The reason for this, I suppose, is that one generally puts off thinking about any sort of heavy duty ahead; you tend to avoid looking down the calendar when you know it is heavily stocked with looming obligations, whether professional or social. If you project that inertia a step or two, you will, I hope, understand why, as often as not, I do not actually examine, until the plane has set down, the page in the folder that describes my exact destination and the name of the sponsoring body. I tend to do this when, upon landing, I rise from my seat, pull out the folder from my briefcase, and fall, at the end of the gangway, into the arms of my host or his representative.

Now vagueness of that order can get you into trouble when successive economies of preparation accumulate. A few years ago I left my hotel in St. Louis, where I had spoken the night before, to go to the designated hangar at the airport where a little chartered plane waited to take me to a college a few hundred miles away, where I would speak that evening. I had been counseled to travel light on the four-seater Cessna and accordingly brought along only a book and my clipboard with my speech, leaving my briefcase at the hotel, to which I'd return late that night.

When I arrived, two charming students, a young man and a young woman, whisked me off to a restaurant for a quick pre-speech dinner. I was suddenly confronted with the fact, as we chatted merrily along, that I had no memory of the name of the college whose guest I was. I attempted to maneuver the conversation in search of the institution's identity.

When was "the college" founded? I tried. I got from my hosts the year, some of the history, some of the problems, the year coeducation was introduced—but never any mention of the college's name. And so it went, right through the crowded evening. To this day I don't know where I lectured that night, other than that it was a couple of airplane hours north (I must have looked at the compass) of St. Louis, Missouri.

I assume that my experiences, over the forty years I have been on the circuit, are fairly typical, though there is of course this difference: as a conservative controversialist, I could not reasonably expect to be greeted onstage as, say, Jacques Cousteau would have been. In pursuit of my apostleship, and the attendant revenue flow to *National Review*, I used to do seventy engagements a year; I now attempt to limit myself to twenty. There are several motives for lecturing. One of them is the redemptive impulse: you feel you have to get your message out there. Another is the histrionic bent: some wish always to lecture, to teach. Then of course there is the economic factor. Most successful lecturers will in whispered tones confide to you that there is no other journalistic or pedagogical activity more remunerative—a point made by Mark Twain and by Winston Churchill. Yes, one can find exceptions. James Clavell and James Michener no doubt earned as much in a day spent on their new novel as they would have giving a lecture. But forget the half dozen exceptions. The working professor or journalist will spend two or three days reading a book and reviewing it for the *New York Times* for $450; or—at the most lucrative level—three or four days writing an essay for *Playboy* for ten times that sum. A night's lecture will bring in better than commensurate revenue. And sometimes the host at this college or that convention—for whatever reason—wants you and no one else, and the offer proves irresistible.

To De Voto's reflections, in any case, I append my own, starting with Buckley's Iron Law of Public Lecturing. It is that no matter what they tell you, between the time when they pick you up at your motel and the time when they return you to your motel, five hours will have elapsed. How so? Didn't the initial contract call simply for a forty-five-minute address, followed by a fifteen-minute Q&A? Forget it. Well no, it isn't exactly an Iron Law, because there are exceptions; the dream dates. These happen when you are asked to lecture between 11:00 and 11:45 and please do not go over your time period, Mr. Buckley, because the next lecturer comes in at noon and there must be a coffee break for the convention subscribers between you and him. You arrive, as requested, fifteen minutes before the hour; the host/hostess leads you to an anteroom of sorts in which, by closed-circuit TV, you can hear the tail end of your predecessor's speech and get some sense of the audience. Promptly at 11:00 you are introduced, and promptly at 11:50—the master of ceremonies had said there was time for just three questions—you leave the stage, shake hands with somebody or another, go out into the street, and rejoin the free world. But interaction at such a mechanical level is rare.

A few performers we get to know about on the circuit are abrupt in their dealings with their hosts. Evelyn Waugh was the Great Figure in this regard. It is said that his agent would shrug his shoulders and warn the prospective lecture host that there was simply no shaking Mr. Waugh from his ways. No, he would give no press conference. No no no, no dinner before the lecture. No! No! Absolutely no signing of books. No-receiving-line-no-questions-after-his-speech. If that sounds awfully austere, it is absolutely convivial in contrast with what Mr. Waugh would proceed to do, which was remain in his limousine outside the hall until after he had been introduced. Only then would he lumber onstage, deliver his speech, and return to his limousine, whose door, one supposes, was held open for him. We do not know whether he paused to say good night to his host.

To behave that way and somehow get invited to deliver more lectures, you need to have a reputation as a grouch so entrenched as to become mythogenic—indeed, in a way, endearing, like the temperament of the Man Who Came to Dinner in the famous movie. The lecture public is titillated before such a character's appearance by tales of his eccentricities and would be disappointed if he were other than as advertised.

Those who aren't given to misanthropy, natural or cultivated, simply can't get away with it and wouldn't want to if they could. They oblige—both because good nature impels you to do so and because it is, in the long run, easier to comply than to resist. Your agent tells you that the sponsors who put up the money for the engagement are having a private dinner at which your presence is . . . expected. A letter comes in, a week or two before the event, from the student who has led the threadbare conservative movement at the college, and life and death—the future of the Republic!—hang on your agreeing to meet with his group for a mere half hour some time before or after the engagement. After the lecture, there is to be a public reception—it is a fixed part of a hundred-year-long tradition at the Xville Forum, and any failure by you to attend it would quite shatter the evening and demoralize the dozens of people who had a hand in making it a success. The lecture will be so widely attended that there won't really be a proper opportunity for the twenty brightest students at the college to interrogate you, so surely you wouldn't mind an hour's seminar at five, well before the lecture? It would mean so much to the students to have this opportunity.

Most people, as I have suggested, are good-natured. We give in, up to a point, and what finally makes it difficult to protest is the attentiveness and kindness of most of one's hosts and hostesses, who have spent fifteen hours of hard work for every hour's work of the visiting speaker. Notwithstanding good intentions, however, the speaker's priorities aren't always intuited, let alone observed. I have mentioned the ancillary activity with which you will inevitably become involved. That is a burden. So also is the absolutely distinctive fatigue that goes with the experience. This doesn't, I think, have anything to do with stage fright (I don't get this). And it is not alone a product of anfractuous travel schedules (flight to Louisville, feeder flight to Canton, car meets you, hour-and-a-half drive to lecture site; reverse procedure the following morning, which means you will need to leave your motel at 6:15 in order to catch the only flight that will get you securely to where you are headed).

What sets in, and I think my experience is not unique, is a quite situation-specific exhaustion. You are back at the hotel at 10:30. You are not a television watcher, so that form of decompression doesn't work on you. You have a briefcase bulging with undone work, but reading manuscripts at that hour induces only a conviction that nobody who writes manuscripts can hold your attention in your current mood. If it had been fifty years ago and you were reading Hemingway's "The Killers," you'd probably have wondered, after page two, why in the hell he hadn't got to the point. You pour yourself a glass of wine from the bottle provided by your thoughtful host, nibble at a cracker, and read the back-of-the-book of *Time* or *Newsweek*. You then get around to calling the hotel operator. You tell her that the world itself hangs on her dependability in waking you at 5:15. That is too early for coffee, so you will use your wife's hot-wired hair-curler type thing, which brings a cup of water to the boil in a minute. You might pop a sleeping pill, read two or three pages from your current book, and go to sleep.

What can happen then is a lecturer's nightmare. When your escort, often an undergraduate, tells you he/she will be there at 7:30, about one-half the time no one is there at 7:30. "Dear Josie," I began my letter to my student hostess at the University of Colorado a few years ago. She had been incensed, on arriving at my hotel, to find me in a cab, about to drive off. "Let me explain the events of yesterday morning so that you will not think me rude to have acted as I did," I wrote. "You had said the night before that you would pick me up at 7:30 to drive me to the Denver airport. You weren't there at 7:30. At 7:35 you still were not there. What passes through the mind in such situations is this: If Josie is not there at 7:30, when she contracted to be there, when in fact will she be there? It is possible that she overslept. Or that she has had a flat tire. In which case she might not be there for a half hour—which would mean missing your plane. Precious time, dear Josie, is slipping through your fingers, so you go to the porter and say, Can you get me a taxi to drive me to the airport at Denver? He calls, and the lady driver arrives, and the two of you have just completed loading the luggage when Josie drives up, at 7:41. Now the point you made—that there was still plenty of time to get to the airport at Denver—isn't what goes through the mind of the lecturer. If I had absolutely known that you would materialize at 7:41, I'd have waited. But if you weren't there when you said you'd be there—at 7:30—how could I absolutely know that you would be there in time for me to make my plane? Having brought in the lady driver, negotiated the fare to the airport, and put all my luggage in her cab, I thought it would be unseemly to pull out the bags, dismiss her, and go with you. I do hope you understand."

Josie never acknowledged my letter. I guess she's still mad. Make it a point to say two things, ever so gently, to the people who are going to pick you up. First, make it clear that punctuality the next morning is very important to you. Second, stipulate an offbeat time for a rendezvous. Never an easygoing 7:30. Rather, 7:25. Or 7:35. If you were back with the CIA, you'd say 7:33. Nobody is ever late if told to be there at 7:33. Dear Josie would have been on time at 7:33, but she would have thought it positively weird.

The whole operation is, as I say, strangely fatiguing. The compensation, however, lies not alone in the fee and the satisfaction of passing along the Word but also in the relative ease of preparation. For some of us, writing out an entire speech is intensely laborious work, in part, I suppose, because most journalists are accustomed to writing thousand-word bites, or else three-hundred-page books. But if your lectures come in orderly sequences, the major effort is made once a season, either a calendar season or a political season (the inauguration of Bill Clinton, for example, constituted the beginning of a political season). I have a half dozen offbeat speeches in my portfolio: "The Origins of Conservative Thought," "The Case for National Service," "The Genesis of Blackford Oakes"—that kind of thing. If the scheduled engagement calls for a debate (there are about five or six of these per year), that requires hard hours of ad hoc study, but there is no need to write out anything—debates call for extemporaneous handling.

Otherwise, I give out as my title (it is always the same) "Reflections on Current Contentions." The advantages are manifest. There are always current contentions, and pundits always reflect on them—indeed, as in the troubles of Mr. Clinton, revel in them. Every weekend during the two lecture seasons (fall and spring—I do not lecture in the summer), I pull out last week's speech and go over it line by line—search out anachronisms; insert fresh material; add or subtract a proposition; decide which contentions to analyze at a college, which at a business meeting or civic association. It makes for a busy few hours on Saturday or Sunday, but then you have in hand a speech that, as far as the audience is concerned, might have sprung full-blown from your imagination that very morning.

Some professionals frown on reading a speech. Mine now are mostly read. It requires experience to do this without appearing to be glued to the text. I have that experience. But I also know that there is going to be a question-and-answer period and that during that period I will establish to the satisfaction of the audience that I can handle myself (and my interrogators) extemporaneously. The statement "Mr. Buckley has graciously agreed to answer a few questions," which inevitably precedes this part of the program, would more correctly be put as, "Mr. Buckley demands that there should be time for questions." Sometimes a Q&A is necessarily excluded—the hall is too large, the occasion too ceremonial (for instance, a commencement)—in which case you simply make do. But you are left feeling both underexploited and underappreciated; a singer of great range whose upper and lower registers were never tested.

And then whether there is to be a Q&A can depend on the hour,

and here is a Great Grievance. I speak of the dinner that begins at 8.
At about 9 o'clock you start looking down at your carefully drafted
forty-five-minute speech. As the clock moves relentlessly on, you
start fidgeting with your text. Got to cut something! Maybe cut that
section? Contract the beginning? Maybe eliminate it? Got to do *something*, because it's getting very late.

The enemy of the after-dinner speaker is identified with remarkable ease. Yes, sometimes there are too many cards to be played:
awards given out, accounts of activity during the preceding year. But
most often, the enemy is—the salad course. I can think of fifty salad
courses that came close to ruining an evening, and that is because
serving a salad, waiting for it to get nibbled away, removing it, and
coming in with the main course is going to consume a half hour.
During that period (a) everybody is eating up finite reserves of energy, and some people are getting a little sleepy; (b) many are assuaging
their anxiety/ennui/irritation by drinking more copiously than they
otherwise would; and (c) the speaker is sitting there knowing that
every minute that goes by is a minute that increases the natural torpor of active Americans at the end of a working day, inevitably affect-
ing the keenness of their disposition to listen to his subtleties. And it
is a law of nature that when something goes on for too long, management tends to chop off that which can be chopped off. If a Q&A was
unscheduled, forget it; if a Q&A was scheduled, the master of ceremonies is likely to eliminate it ("Due to the lateness of the hour, we
will need to do without the question-and-answer period Mr. Buckley
had so graciously agreed to").

Speaking of booze, I am reminded of one of Professor De Voto's
major complaints, namely, the dry host. In 1980, many years after
reading De Voto's jeremiad, I had Harold Macmillan on my *Firing
Line* program. He insisted on a half hour's preparatory interview the
day before, designed to explore the ground I intended to cover. After
touching on Winston Churchill's disappointments, on the perils of
the Normandy landing, on the winds of change in Africa, Mr.
Macmillan got down to business: he would expect some champagne
in the room to which he would be conducted before going into the
studio. Harold Macmillan was a pro.

There are several stratagems for dealing with The Problem. Entering senior citizenship, I have become blunter than I was as an apple-checked circuit rider. So, on the way from the airport to the motel, I will say to my escort, "I see dinner is at 6. Will they be serving wine?"

The chances are about six out of nine these days that the answer will be yes. But it might well be no, especially if you are eating in a dining hall located on the premises of a state college, or if you are in a dry county, or, of course, if you are in Mormon country. Some hosts/hostesses instantly understand, and those who do will vary their responses all the way from inviting you to the president's house for "a little wine" before the dinner, to inviting you to their own house, to delivering a bottle of wine to your room. People really are kind and obliging. But the trouble with any of these expedients is that some of us are indisposed to have a drink at 5:30 when dinner is scheduled for 6 and the lecture for 8. The kind of stimulation one is looking for won't keep for two and a half hours; and then, too, however happy you might be to find yourself with extra moments of unscheduled privacy, you desire privacy least during the cocktail hour, which is inherently convivial.

Might a lecturer abuse the cocktail hour? Rarely, I believe, and I am aware only of the lurid exception of Truman Capote. Arriving in New Orleans twenty years ago, I was picked up by the chairman of Tulane's annual Academic Week, during which the college sponsors five different lectures or debates on consecutive nights. On the way to the hotel from the airport, I found my young host in high dudgeon. He and other members of the undergraduate committee had put hundreds of hours of work into planning the Academic Week, and what was the fruit of it all last night? he asked dramatically, as we threaded our way through New Orleans traffic.

"We knew Mr. Capote had this problem," the tall, angular, blond pre-law student explained, shaking his head slightly. "So during the cocktail hour I handed him a drink that was about one-half jigger bourbon and one gallon of soda water. It didn't work. Mr. Capote said, 'Heh heh, lit'l man, you cayan't get away with that, no sir, not with Truman Capote!' He handed me back his glass, and I had to give him a regular drink. Then another. Then another. And he was already bombed when he arrived. By the time he got to the seminar, he couldn't even talk! We had to rely on the other lecturer, Edward Albee, who carried the whole ball. And then . . . and then"—my driver was throbbing with indignation—"after the main talk, you know from the last time you were here, we all go over across the street for the informal talk. Well, Mr. Capote's aide came to me and said, 'Mr. Capote is too tahhred out to engage in the second pahht of the proceedings.' So I said to him, 'Well, you tell Mr. Capote if he doesn't come to the second part of the engagement, he's not going to be paid for the first part.'"

What happened? I asked.

"He made it. But there wasn't much for him to say, I mean, nothing much he *could* say."

I consoled him. "Ten years from now," I promised him, "the Tulane audience will remember only one thing about your Academic Week. It was the week in which Truman Capote got tanked and couldn't speak." I was right, as usual.

Then there is the matter of the introduction. A few months back I listened with mounting horror to an introduction of me that Demosthenes would not have merited. I wish I had it in my power to restrain the enthusiastic introducer—particularly the one who wants to justify the special pains the committee went to in getting you there by dwelling on the discursive dreamland that lies ahead for the audience. He (or she) might feel that to do less than advise the audience to expect the wit of Oscar Wilde, the eloquence of Abraham Lincoln, and the profundity of Aristotle would suggest that he held you in less than the esteem owed ex officio to any guest selected by the Lackawanna Annual Forum Series. The thing to do—it works about one-third of the time—is to write out a suggested introduction to yourself, making the usual high points sufficiently to justify your presence there and the audience's, but carefully refraining from hyperbole. Having said this, I have to add that some hosts take extraordinary pains in composing their words and indite truly elegant introductions.

If the beginning of your talk is unchanged and you have given it to a dozen audiences in the past ten weeks, you will know very quickly the speed of this assembly, as also something of its disposition. Audiences are generally a little nervous, starting out: they don't quite know what they will make of you, and they often fear that their reaction may be ploddish. If you are talking to undergraduates, they will wish to be wooed; but they are nicely disposed, except for those whose fidelity to antithetical politics is a matter of deep principle. I remember lecturing at noon at Long Beach State University during the Vietnam frenzies of the late 1960s. Two thousand students lay stretched out on the lawn (that was the convention at the weekly lectures). A few months before they had permitted Senator Vance Hartke of Indiana to get through only ten minutes of his speech unmolested, notwithstanding that the senator was against the war and had been from the beginning. After that, the students began talking to one another, laughing, walking about. I had no problem, none at all, getting through my talk, some of it stoutly defending the policies of Lyndon Johnson. After it was over, I said rather complacently to my host, a professor from the department of psychology, that it was reassuring that I had the power to compel a college audience to listen to me on so excitable a subject. His comment was wonderfully deflating: "Don't you understand, Mr. Buckley? When you speak, they treat you as they would a man from the moon. They don't care what you say. They are just biologically curious."

Most people who wonder about the subject at all (mostly, press interviewers writing about a talk, past or scheduled) wonder whether I have been given a hard time for taking positions usually (especially when speaking at colleges) at variance with those of my audiences. But the shock to the listeners was always reduced by the foreknowledge that they would be listening to a conservative. At the beginning, in the 1950s and 1960s especially, college students, and of course faculty, were surprised, not to say aghast, at the heterodoxies they were hearing from the Right. But there was never (almost never) disruption.

The demands of courtesy tend to prevail. But sometimes someone just can't take it. And sometimes a public point is intended. Last May in Wilmington, Delaware's governor sat on the dais, and I devoted the whole of my time to the problems that had arisen from the Lewinsky–Clinton business. My analysis was sharply to the disadvantage of the president. When I finished speaking, the governor rose and walked swiftly from the dais, manifestly in order to avoid social contact with the speaker after the evening's formal closing.

If the ambient mood is doggedly skeptical, then waste no time in giving out your conclusion unless you have extraordinary diplomatic balance wheels. I have seen Hubert Humphrey, and indeed Bill Clinton, draw blood from a stone in public speeches, attacking the skeptics in the manner of Jimmy Durante, who would, if necessary to entertain his audience, take an axe to the piano. Such as these have very special skills. The other way is to strive to communicate to your audience that if they exhibit the curiosity and the attentiveness to hear you out, their favors in attending will match yours in appearing; and both parties will leave the hall with a sense that neither wasted its time.

It is a grueling business, though obviously easier on those who are happiest when operating from a podium. The late Max Lerner, a learned evangelist who was truly contented when instructing others how to think and what to believe in, told me that a perfect life for him would involve lecturing every day of the week: the rabbinical itch. Others cherish their afflatus but are more happily engaged when sweating over blank sheets of paper. What would be ideal for us would be an audience of people who sat there while you wrote and told you, after every paragraph or so, whether you were succeeding in reaching them.

THE FIFTIES

TODAY WE ARE EDUCATED MEN

The Class Day Oration at Yale University; New Haven, Conn., June 11, 1950

A senior is tapped to give the Class Day Oration, elected to do so by Yale Class Council. There was some apprehension when my name was announced because earlier that year I had been selected by the administration to be the student speaker at the annual Alumni Day festivity on Washington's birthday. For that occasion I wrote a talk critical of what I believed to be the bias in thinking in the faculty—collectivist in political and economic orientation, secular and humanistic in other studies. There was much alarm over the prospective ventilation of such views to a thousand visiting alumni; and for the sake of decorum, I withdrew the speech. (It was published as an appendix to my first book, God and Man at Yale.*)*

My Class Day Oration, although otherwise pretty conventional, hints at such concerns against the historical backdrop. Five years earlier we had won the world war, but the struggle for the world was at high pitch. The Soviet Union had gobbled up Eastern Europe, exploded a nuclear bomb, and encouraged the Communists in China who overthrew the Nationalist government, exiled now to Taiwan. Two weeks after Class Day the Korean War would break out, involving the United States in a three-year-long military campaign. On the home front President Truman was adamantly encouraging an expansion of the New Deal.

A YEAR AGO, the orator for the class of 1949 stood here and told his classmates that the troubles of the United States in particular and of Western democracy in general were attributable to the negativism of our front against Communism. His was not a lone voice jarring smug opinion in mid-twentieth-century America. Rather he is part of the swelling forefront of men and women who are raising a hue and a cry for what they loosely call positivism, by which they mean bold new measures, audacious steps forward, a reorientation towards those great new horizons and that Brave New World.

It is natural at this point to realize that (although we must be very careful how we put it) we are, as Yale men, privileged members of our society, and to us falls the responsibility of leadership in this great new positivist movement. For we have had a great education, and our caps and gowns weigh heavy upon us as we face our responsibilities to mankind.

All of us here have been exposed to four years' education in one of the most enlightened and advanced liberal-arts colleges in the world. Here we can absorb the last word in most fields of academic endeavor. Here we find the headquarters of a magazine devoted exclusively to metaphysics, and another devoted entirely to an analysis of French existentialism. And here, for better or for worse, we have been jolted forcefully from any preconceived judgments we may have had when we came. Here we can find men who will tell us that Jesus Christ was the greatest fraud that history has known. Here we can find men who will tell us that morality is an anachronistic conception, rendered obsolete by the advances of human thought. From neo-Benthamites at Yale we can learn that laws are a sociological institution, to be wielded to facilitate the sacrosanct will of the enlightened minority.

Communism is a real force to cope with only because of the deficiencies of democracy. Our fathers, who worked to send us to Yale, their fathers and their fathers, who made Yale and the United States, were hardworking men, shrewd men, and performed a certain economic service, but they were dreadfully irresponsible, y'know, in view of today's enlightenment. . . .

And so it goes: two and two make three, the shortest distance between two points is a crooked line, good is bad and bad is good, and from this morass we are to extract a workable, enlightened synthesis to govern our thoughts and our actions, for today we are educated men.

NOTHING, IT IS true, is healthier than honest scrutiny, with maybe even a little debunking thrown in. When a dean tells us that our task is to go out and ennoble mankind, we nod our heads and wonder whether the opening in the putty-knife factory or in the ball-bearing works will pay more. When we are told that Lincoln was totally unconcerned with politics, we might ponder the occasion in 1863 when he could not focus his attention on the questions of a distinguished visitor because he was terribly worried over what Republican to appoint postmaster of Chicago. In 1913 Charles Beard wrote his *Economic Interpretation of the Constitution.* It was banned in seven state universities and brought almost nationwide ostracism for the author. Today a study of this analysis is a prerequisite to a doctoral degree in American history.

Certainly civilization cannot advance without freedom of inquiry. This fact is self-evident. What seems equally self-evident is that in the process of history certain immutable truths have been revealed and discovered and that their value is not subject to the limitations of time and space. The probing, the relentless debunking, has engendered a skepticism that threatens to pervade and atrophy all our values. In apologizing for our beliefs and our traditions we have bent over backwards so far that we have lost our balance, and we see a topsy-turvy world and we say topsy-turvy things, such as that the way to beat Communism is by making our democracy better. What a curious self-examination! Beat the Union of Soviet Socialist Republics by making America socialistic. Beat atheism by denying God. Uphold individual freedom by denying natural rights. We neglect to say to the Communist, "In the name of heaven look at what we *now have.* Your standards don't interest us." As Emerson threatened to say to the obstreperous government tax collector, "If you pursue, I will slit your throat, sir."

The credo of the so-called positivists is characterized by the advocacy of change. Republicanism, on the other hand, is negativism because conservatives believe that America has grown and has prospered, has put muscle on her bones, by rewarding initiative and industry, by conceding to her citizens not only the right and responsibilities of self-government, but also the right and responsibilities of self-care, of individually earned security. The role of the so-called conservative is a difficult one. A starry-eyed young man, nevertheless aggressive in his wisdom, flaunting the badge of custodian of the common man, approaches our neat, sturdy white house and tells us we must destroy it, rebuild it of crystallized cold cream, and paint it purple. "But we like it the way it is," we retort feebly.

"Rip 'er down! This is a changing world."

IS OUR EFFORT to achieve perspective all the more difficult by virtue of our having gone to Yale? In many respects it is, because the university does not actively aid us in forming an enlightened synthesis. That job is for us to perform: to reject those notions that do not square with the enlightenment that should be ours as moral, educated men, beneficiaries of centuries of historical experience. Yale has given us much. Not least is an awesome responsibility to withstand her barrage, to emerge from her halls with both feet on the ground, with a sane head and a reinforced set of values. If our landing is accomplished, we are stronger men for our flight.

Keenly aware, then, of the vast deficiencies in American life today—the suffering, the injustice, the want—we must nevertheless spend our greatest efforts, it seems to me, in preserving the framework that supports the vaster bounties that make our country an oasis of freedom and prosperity. Our concern for deficiencies in America must not cause us to indict the principles that have allowed our country, its faults notwithstanding, to tower over the nations of the world as a citadel of freedom and wealth. With what severity and strength we can muster, we must punch the gasbag of cynicism and skepticism, and thank providence for what we have and must retain. Our distillation of the ideas, concepts, and theories expounded at Yale must serve to enhance our devotion to the good in what we have, to reinforce our allegiance to our principles, to convince us that our outlook *is* positive: that the retention of the best features of our way of life is the most enlightened and noble of goals. Insofar as the phrase "For God, for Country, and for Yale" is meaningful, we need not be embarrassed to mean "For God as we know Him, for country as we know it, and for Yale as we have known her."

THE TROJAN HORSE
OF AMERICAN EDUCATION?

A Baccalaureate Address at St. Joseph's College; Collegeville, Ind., June 8, 1952

This address to a conservative Catholic college reflected an emphasis in God and Man at Yale, *which had been published the previous fall, stirring up much controversy. I remained grateful to my supporters (see my reminiscences concerning Henry Regnery, April 12, 1972, and John Chamberlain, November 9, 1978). In this address I challenged the views of the president of Harvard, Dr. James B. Conant, who had expressed himself as opposed to education in private schools. I emphasized the encroachments of secular perspectives on learning and stressed the importance of conventional Christianity.*

A s I LOOK about me, I see that you have made no particular effort to disguise the proceedings here this afternoon. Lots of people are in attendance—parents, alumni, benefactors, the leading citizens of Collegeville. The ceremony will probably receive generous mention in the local press. All in all, quite a to-do.

Yet if James B. Conant, dean of American college education and president of Harvard University, has right on his side, the ceremony we are participating in today ought to go underground. There shouldn't be anything brassy to commemorate the intellectual puberty of a regiment of young men who, by virtue of their education in a private school, promise to introduce into our society divisive and undemocratic influences.

That's what you're going to do, gentlemen of the graduating class. Dr. Conant says so. He spelled out his misgivings last April. True, he spoke specifically of private preparatory schools; but logic requires that private colleges—most especially denominational colleges like this one—fall under his indictment. We can only achieve unity, Dr. Conant insists, "if our public schools remain the primary vehicle for the education of our youth, and if, as far as possible, all the youth of a community attend the same school irrespective of family fortune or cultural background. . . . There is some reason to fear," he continues, "lest a dual system of secondary education . . . come to threaten the democratic unity provided by our public schools. The greater the proportion of our youth who attend independent schools, the greater the threat to our democratic unity. . . ."

Less prominent men, but important men just the same, gleefully took up the cry. A Dr. Oberholtzer, speaking at the same conference, said, "It is the ideas or philosophy behind the nonpublic schools that are dangerous." The executive secretary of the American Association of School Administrators, a branch of the National Education Association, Dr. Worth McClure, added, "The denominational schools build prejudices, they build little Iron Curtains around the thinking of the people."

Now the American people are not, as a general rule, given to talking back to educators. We have been taught better. Education is good. More education is better. Still more education is better still. The more education we have, the sounder will be our judgment and the less we ought to be contradicted. Mr. Conant has had great gobs of education. His advice, generally speaking, ought to be worth many times our own.

Still, some undisciplined folk are inclined to tell Professor Conant to go take a ride on Charon's ferry. They simply don't agree that private education is necessarily divisive and undemocratic, and even to the extent that private education is not socially cohesive, they're not particularly concerned to foster the sort of unity Mr. Conant is interested in. In short, they want to know why Mr. Conant is attacking private education—especially since the record is clear that graduates of private schools, Mr. Conant included, have made and continue to make striking contributions to our society.

To understand Mr. Conant, it doesn't help to read his full statement, which treats mostly of the advantages of mixing rich and poor, Catholics and Jews, artists and farmers. All of us agree that the tolerance generated by mixing with people of diverse backgrounds and interests is all to the good—while perhaps rejecting Mr. Conant's intimations that this is the highest value of education. Yet none of us have spotted any marked intolerance coming out of private schools—

no more, certainly, than comes out of public schools. Nor are we convinced that there is less stratification within a public high school, or a state college, or a value-anarchistic private university like Harvard (where groups with common intellectual, cultural, racial, or religious interests tend to stick together) than there is in the private school or in the private denominational college. So why should a man whose most casual asides shake the foundations of the educational world come out and say such unreasoned and unfriendly things about the men and women who support private schools and send their children there?

The answer is that Dr. Conant, along with some powerful educational confreres, is out to fashion society in his own mold. The most influential educators of our time—John Dewey, William Kilpatrick, George Counts, Harold Rugg, and the lot—are out to build a New Social Order. And with a realism startling in a group of longhairs, they have set about their job in the most effective fashion. They don't dissipate their efforts on such frivolities as national elections (though they do this incidentally); they work with far more fundamental social matter, the student.

The chagrined and frustrated parent has very little luck opposing the advances of the New Social Order. "The consumer has no rights in the educational marketplace," Professor Henry Steele Commager puts it. Translated, this means that a parent has no right to seek reform regardless of the extent to which he disapproves of the net impact of the local school. The educator, in short, has consolidated his position as the exclusive, irresponsible regent of education. *L'école*, he says, *c'est moi.*

There is not enough room, however, for the New Social Order *and* religion. The New Order is philosophically wedded to the doctrine that the test of truth is its ability to win acceptance by the majority. Economically, the New Order is egalitarian; politically, it is majoritarian; emotionally, it is infatuated with the State, which it honors as the dispenser of all good, the unchallengeable and irreproachable steward of every human being.

It clearly won't do, then, to foster within some schools a respect for an absolute, intractable, unbribable God, a divine Intelligence who is utterly unconcerned with other people's versions of truth and humorlessly inattentive to majority opinion. It won't do to tolerate a competitor for the allegiance of man. The State prefers a secure monopoly for itself. It is intolerably divisive to have God and the State scrapping for disciples.

Religion, then, must go. First we must expose religion as a not-very-serious intellectual and emotional avocation (see the famous 1945 Harvard Report's dismissal of religion: ". . . we did not feel justified in proposing religious instruction as a part of the curriculum. . . . Whatever one's views, religion is not now for most colleges a practicable source of intellectual unity.").

Next, we must prove that to allow religion to be taught in public schools imminently commits us to uniting Church and State (see the *McCollum* decision of the Supreme Court). Having paved the way, we can rely (always barring divine intervention) on the results. If religion is given no place at all—or just token recognition—in the intellectual diet of the school, the growing generation will probably come to think of it, as Canon Bernard Iddings Bell puts it, as "an innocuous pastime, preferred by a few to golf or canasta." When this happens, religion will then cease to be a divisive influence.

The fight is being won. Academic freedom is entrenched. Religion is outlawed in the public schools. The New Social Order is larruping along.

But there remains an enemy. An implacable Trojan Horse that threatens the uniform evolution towards the New Order. The private schools (outnumbered ten to one by public schools) are still measurably independent. And many of them are straightforwardly religious. So long as these schools survive, the public-education monolith is threatened.

How best to do away with them? The modern mind turns automatically to the State to do a job. Why not outlaw private schools? Dr. Conant is too realistic. The American mind is not yet conditioned to such heavy-handed federal action. Other means must be found.

Private schools are supported by private money. So why not expropriate private money? This campaign of attrition is already succeeding. The private colleges are in desperate shape. And many of them are masochists of the first order: for the most part, they urge upon their students the evils of private property and the glories of egalitarianism. Quite predictably, these students graduate to urge higher and higher taxation on their political representatives, who comply by absorbing a greater and greater percentage of individual income, thus making less and less of it available for the maintenance of private colleges. The next step, clearly, is for our government to rush in with various species of federal grants to keep the schools from perishing.

But if "public" money is used to support an educational institution, certain requirements must be fulfilled. No classes on religion, of course, else you marry the Church to the State. And nothing too unkind about the State itself. Nor may the school indulge itself in its own admissions policy. In short, the acceptance of federal grants means the surrender of the school's independence.

Alongside an economic war against the private schools, a propaganda assault must be staged against them. The movement to discredit the private schools began, indirectly, a long time ago. The philosophers of egalitarianism and class hatred started to hack away at "private schools for young fops." The psychological groundwork has been laid, and the time is ripe for the direct onslaught.

Gentlemen, the enemies of private schools, the champions of academic freedom, refuse to think through the implications of education. Whereas they constantly talk about the search for truth, they refuse to face the implications of *finding* truth.

Dr. Charles Seymour, ex-president of Yale University, is often quoted as stating, "We shall seek the truth and endure the consequences." What, indeed, are the consequences of finding truth?

Presumably, they are twofold: The truth must be embraced, and its opposite must be scorned. Students must be encouraged to recognize and honor truth and to reject and battle its opposite.

Again, we must ask: How do we know when we have discovered truth or when we have, at least, discovered the nearest available thing to truth? The answer is that we can only know after canvassing alternatives and bringing our reflective faculties to bear on them. But once we have selected our truths—and each individual is entitled to select his own truths—it becomes our duty to promote them as energetically as we can.

The overseers of the denominational schools, the patrons of our private nonsecular schools and colleges, believe they have found the truth in God and through God. It is their privilege and their duty to promote this truth as efficaciously as possible, through the medium of the classroom. When educators say that denominational schools "build little Iron Curtains around the thinking of the people," they really mean that in their opinion the overseers of these denominational schools have selected not truth but error. Surely if they believed that denominational schools were teaching the truth, they would not brand them as Iron Curtain hangers. In short, gentlemen, after you strip away the circumlocutions and casuistry, you find yourself at point-blank range with what the proponents of the New Social Order really mean. They really mean that those people who disagree with their version of truth, who disagree that pragmatism, positivism, and materialism are the highest values, are in error. And, with characteristic intolerance towards differing creeds, they seek to liquidate their opponents by talking about such things as democracy and divisiveness.

You graduate into a turbulent and confusing and perverse world situation which, because so many men have forgotten the lessons of Christ and because so many men have turned their back on Him, seriously threatens the international ascendancy of evil: a physical war against Christian civilization, and an intellectual war against the foundations of our spiritual faith.

Leadership in the movement against the Antichrist is sorely needed; and yet the sternness and sacrifice and singleness of purpose which we must show to win the fight seem to be lacking in a good many of us. They are lacking, mostly, because of the easy and lazy optimism that has developed as a result of seeing over the centuries individual after individual, tribe after tribe, country after country discard their pagan beliefs in favor of Jesus Christ. We have come to feel that the truths of God are so intellectually and emotionally compelling that they are certain to triumph in the contest of ideas. And because of our faith in the organic attraction of Christianity, we are no longer fired with the resolution and zeal which characterized the small band of men whose willingness, nineteen hundred years ago, to sacrifice, to proselytize, and to teach is responsible for the fact that on Sundays we worship at the altar of Jesus Christ rather than at the altar of twentieth-century counterparts of Zeus and Athena and Apollo and Pluto.

Too many of us have fallen prey to the spurious logic best typified by a recent statement of Max Eastman, who labeled it "silly that two-legged fanatics should run around trying to look after a God whom they at once consider omnipotent and omniscient."

Gentlemen of the graduating class: It is not sacrilege to state that God needs your help. It is not vainglory to state that you can help God. It is not empty rhetoric to state that insofar as you help man, you help God; that insofar as you serve God, you serve man, and you serve yourself. And it is not Commencement Day bombast to remind you that knowledge of truth carries with it awful consequences, as well as sustaining joys.

THE ARTIST AS AGGRESSOR

An Address (excerpted) to a "Welcome to New York" Rally Sponsored by Aware; the Ballroom of the New Yorker Hotel, New York, August 15, 1955

Until National Review *came into being, my papers were scattered, and no speeches survive from 1953–54. During that time the Korean War had ended (in stalemate), General MacArthur had been fired (and was now a diffident candidate for president), Senator McCarthy had risen and fallen. The anti-Communist movement had suffered from McCarthy's disgrace but wasn't moribund. In New York an organization called Aware was formed to give support to the House Committee on Un-American Activities and to a Hollywood group that sought to identify and resist fellow travelers. This speech was to a rally welcoming the chairman of the House committee, Francis E. Walter, and members of*

*the committee to New York City, where they would be continuing their
in vestigation of Communists and fellow travelers in the entertainment
industry.*

M R. WILLIAM SCHLAMM wrote a year ago that "the
essence of what we have learned in five thousand years
about the nature of man is that the inviolable sovereignty
of the person presupposes his inseparable responsibility for the positions he takes, even wrong ones." Yet now the liberals are in effect
insisting that "man is morally a vegetable and intellectually an eternal
child. The intellectual scandal" of the day centers on the "frightening frivolousness" of the position "which holds that man's choices
signify nothing; that on his walks through the valley of decisions man
picks and discards commitments with the abandon of Peter Pan picking daisies."

In dealing with artists, the liberal is particularly dogmatic in his
insistence that men be not taken seriously. If a politician or a professor should be lightly let off for joining Communist fronts, an artist is
almost to be commended for doing so. The artist is entitled to espe-
cial immunities given the fact that his interest in politics is avoca-
tional, and his knowledge of politics correspondingly inexpert. On
top of that, any liberal will tell you, it is unfair to retaliate against an
artist in his capacity as an artist for what he does after hours, so to
speak, in his capacity as a citizen.

That is an appealing argument—but irrelevant. The fellow-trav-
eling artist upon whom anti-Communists train their sights has not
generally been the man who is content to indulge his political passions discreetly, in his capacity as a private citizen. Rather he is the
man who trades upon his artistic reputation to advance his political objectives. When Paul Robeson emerges as a high official in the
National Council on Soviet Friendship, or Larry Adler comes up
sponsoring the Joint Anti-Fascist Refugee Committee, it is a brazen
fact that Robeson has not been selected for so high a position because
of his renown as a master of Soviet-American diplomatic history, and

that Adler cannot be assumed to know with a precision that sets him apart from other men just what fascism is all about. In other words, it is clear to those who gave Paul Robeson and Larry Adler their posts, and it is clear to the community at large, and it should be very, very clear to Mr. Robeson and Mr. Adler, that their occupancy of politically significant positions arises exclusively from the fact that the one is a very able singer and the other a very able harmonica player. More precisely, their occupancy of those positions arises from the fact that in the course of singing and playing these men acquired a public reputation and hence a public following; and in splashily joining a political organization, the artist is inviting the community, which honors him as an artist, to give sympathetic attention to the objectives of the organization.

What is the community to do? How is it to resist the aggressors? Yes, the artist is the aggressor: he initiated a political gesture that cannot, if human beings are to be taken seriously, be ignored but must be accepted or rejected. The politician who announces his support of Communism meets up with professional political opposition backed by those in the community who reject Communism. Pro-Communist publicists—newspapermen, radio commentators, columnists—are replaced by newspapermen, radio commentators, and columnists who are, at least ritualistically, anti-Communist. But what is to be done with the artist who consciously commits his artistic self to a partisan political cause? The orthodox resistance measure—the backing of the competitor—is only sometimes applicable. In the nature of things, some artists are irreplaceable. Who is to replace Charlie Chaplin, one legitimately and even apprehensively asks? No one, is the somber answer. Hence we must ask ourselves: Do we abhor the aggressive political identity of Charlie Chaplin enough to deny ourselves the pleasures of his genius? The answer is not an easy one. Decisions must be individually made. Many artists back political causes which, while we may disapprove of them, are not in themselves morally objectionable. With such artists we can agree to co-exist. But with others, with men and women who ally themselves with a movement which aims at overturning the bases of society, we cannot negotiate. There are higher values than art. The Sistine Chapel is not as valuable as a single human life. The pro-Communist artist, as the willing or unwilling agent of a revolutionary system, must, if he insists on it, be dealt with as a human being rather than as an artist. . . .

ONLY FIVE THOUSAND COMMUNISTS?

An Address to a Rally Sponsored by Aware; New York, May 7, 1958

The chairman of the House Committee on Un-American Activities was again in New York City in pursuit of the committee's business, and again a rally of welcome was organized. As the speaker, I defended the work of that committee and of the Senate Internal Security Subcommittee, argued with the proposition that the word "un-American" was indecipherable, and took on several of the committee's critics, notably Professor Arthur Schlesinger Jr., the noted historian, and James Wechsler, then the editor of the New York Post. *In that period the* Post, *under Wechsler and owner-publisher Dorothy Schiff, was the flywheel of the liberal Left.*

HALFWAY THROUGH THE second term of Franklin Roosevelt, the New Deal braintrusters began to worry about mounting popular concern over the national debt. In those days the size of the national debt was on everyone's mind. Indeed, Franklin Roosevelt had talked himself into office, in 1932, in part by promising to hack away at a debt which, even under the frugal Mr. Hoover, the people tended to think of as grown to menacing size. Mr. Roosevelt's wisemen worried deeply about the mounting tension . . . And then, suddenly, the academic community came to the rescue. Economists across the length and breadth of the land were electrified by a theory of debt introduced in England by John Maynard Keynes. The politicians wrung their hands in gratitude. Depicting the intoxicating political consequences of Lord Keynes's discovery, the wry cartoonist of the *Washington Times Herald* drew a memorable picture. In the center, sitting on a throne in front of a Maypole, was a jubilant FDR, cigarette tilted up almost vertically, a grin on his face that stretched from ear to ear. Dancing about him in a circle, hands clasped together, their faces glowing with ecstasy, the braintrusters, vested in academic robes, sang the magical incantation, the great discovery of Lord Keynes: *"We owe it to ourselves."*

With five talismanic words, the planners had disposed of the problem of deficit spending. Anyone thenceforward who worried about an increase in the national debt was just plain ignorant of the central insight of modern economics: What do we care how much we—the government—owe so long as we owe it to ourselves? On with the spending. Tax and tax, spend and spend, elect and elect . . .

Why do we need the House Committee on Un-American Activities, in the year of our Lord 1958? Imagine the reaction of *New York Post* editor James Wechsler when he read, a few months ago, that enrollment in the Communist Party was down to five thousand members! Joy floods down upon him. Not because he learns that there are fewer Communists; he doesn't attach much importance to that: there never were enough Communists in America either to please or to bother James Wechsler—not enough to please him when he was engaged in recruiting members to the Communist Party, which he did with the same zeal with which he nowadays recruits anti-anti-Communists; nor enough to bother him when he broke with the Party, even though there were enough to control, among other enterprises, the newspaper for which James Wechsler went to work. No, the joy that came to the House of Wechsler lay in the potential of this magic incantation: *There are only five thousand registered Communists in America!* What do we need congressional investigating committees for? What do we need the anti-subversive division of the FBI for? Why the Smith Act? The McCarran Act? The loyalty oaths? *Where is the clear and present danger?*

Ladies and gentlemen, that is the new look in the struggle to rid America of anti-Communism. Liberals have fallen in love with numbers—provided they are not used to describe victims of Soviet concentration camps. Quantitative analysis, you beautiful doll! Accordingly, we are destined to become as familiar with the intoxicating datum attesting to the negligibility of Communist strength as we are with the fact that, if the news is fit to print, the *New York Times* will print it. The opinion makers will not only emphasize the sheer numerical weakness of five thousand people (there are twice as many anti-vivisectionists, you know); before long, we will be left with the distinct impression that those five thousand are every one of them arthritic, so that even on the wild hypothesis that they chose to plant bombs all over the Capitol, probably among them they couldn't muster the physical strength to throw the switch.

Internally, however, the argument of numbers does not really satisfy the Wechslers or the Joseph L. Rauhs or the Arthur Schlesingers. When there were twenty times as many members of the Communist Party as there are today, they were not stressing the *importance* to the nation of a House Committee on Un-American Activities. Their basic quarrel has very little to do with the size or strength of the enemy. It has to do with the idea that anybody has the right to decide what is "un-American."

What *is* un-American about Communism?

Well yes, violent overthrow of the government is un-American, all right; but we have laws against that, so why do we need House committees and additional laws? And if the Communists, when they talk about the necessity for violent overthrow of the government, are talking only in a fanciful sort of way—in the way, for example, that Dante talks about the physical dimensions of Hell—then can you, in a democratic society, punish them for what amounts to nothing more than the exercise of free speech?

What are these terms? What is to be "subversive"? "Subversive" of what? What is "treason," or "treasonable"? What, when you come down to it, is "un-American"? Lots of people think Franklin Roosevelt was un-American. Should he have been investigated by the Committee on Un-American Activities? Isn't it a law of life that what is considered un-American today is due to become established national doctrine tomorrow? Doesn't a congressional committee on so-called un-American activities in effect ask a society to stop in its tracks, blocking to an anxious people access to security in the womb of the Brave New World?

The liberals, ladies and gentlemen, are, and let us never forget it, in control of events; so that—like bears on Wall Street—they have the raw power to justify their own predictions and their own analyses. They appear to have done so in this case; something a great many people would have deemed un-American ten years ago—standing up for the Soviet national anthem—now happens at the Metropolitan Opera House every night before the Moiseyev Ballet.

The vision of our thought leaders is not of an America of unchanging basic attributes, the kind of America that we dreamed about one hundred eighty years ago when words like "inalienable" and "immutable" and "indefeasible" were so freely used. *Their* dream is a shifting dream. *Our* dream is of an America whose essential characteristics must never change, however violently time and tide pound upon our shores. Our vision is not of the Open Society of an Oliver Wendell Holmes or an Alan Barth or a Henry Steele Commager, but of an America of fixed landmarks. *Their* America prepares for a measured surrender to socialist ideology. *Our* America is evoked by the great theorists and poets of our past, who used a language which moves us even now and permits us, even now, to know what is subversive, and un-American; that what was subversive of the American dream yesterday will be subversive tomorrow; what was beautiful then will be beautiful tomorrow, if it survives the ministrations of the Deweys and the Holmeses.

I do not believe there was ever a time when there was more for a congressional Committee on Un-American Activities to do. The challenge is not so much, at this moment, to rescue America from five thousand Communists, as to rescue America from the national delirium that gives to five thousand Communists the power of five million. We are in danger of going mad, and I take the liberty of declaring madness to be un-American. We are becoming not a peaceful but a pacifist people—and to go from peacefulness to pacifism is like going from thrift to miserliness. Many of our opinion leaders clamor for retreat, at every level. The lighthouses of anti-Communist resistance are, by the enveloping darkness, being blotted out from sight.

All this a congressional committee, with its unique facilities, might successfully dramatize. A big job for so small a committee, to

be sure. But the few have saved the many before. For a few exhilarating moments, Mr. Eugene Lyons wrote after the Hungarian uprising,
it almost looked as if Hungary would liberate the United States. The
committee must never lose sight of the fact that it is our leaders,
above all, who need to be educated. By his own admission, the President of the United States does not know how to argue the superiority of the West against a champion of Communism. Assuming Radio
Free Europe were an effective propagandist for the truth, I would recommend that it beam its message not at the Iron Curtain but at
America, directing its strongest impulses towards 1600 Pennsylvania
Avenue.

Perhaps it is romantic to assume that the House Committee on
Un-American Activities can adhere to a position so very much different from that of the President of the United States and the majority
of the Congress. But I do not think so. It was done before—by this
same committee, bucking very strong tides, in the late 1930s and early
1940s. It must be done again, and fast. There may be only five thousand Communists left in America. But they threaten to outnumber
the anti-Communists.

SHOULD LIBERALISM BE REPUDIATED?

The Opening Statement in a Debate with James Wechsler at a
National Review Forum; Hunter College, New York, April 9, 1959

A half dozen times a year, National Review *sponsored public meetings at
Hunter College—lively affairs, this one a debate with James Wechsler on
the proposition: Resolved, That liberalism should be repudiated. The
opening statement adduced central affirmations of the contemporary liberalism which I thought at best vulnerable, at worst wrong and even dangerous. Many allusions were of topical interest to a highly partisan and
expressive audience, especially the ones to a confidence man named Paul
Hughes, who, it was revealed, had for months posed successfully as an
employee of Senator McCarthy, collecting, and relaying to his sponsors*

at the Washington Post *and the Americans for Democratic Action, the fruit of his supposed discoveries in McCarthy's offices. He had confided to his patrons that the cooking editor of the* New York Post *was a clandestine McCarthyite.*

I WISH TO DISTINGUISH sharply between the question, *Should* liberalism be repudiated? and the question, *Will* liberalism be repudiated? The differences are obvious, just as, a century and more ago, it was generally conceded that there was a significant difference between the question, *Should* slavery be abolished? and the question, *Will* slavery be abolished? Abolitionists had been active for many years, making effectively the case for the abolition of slavery, before it came to be said that slavery *had been* abolished.

I say it "came to be said" that slavery had been abolished because, lo and behold, there are more slaves in the world today than there were one hundred years ago, though indeed slavery has taken a different form from that familiar to the antebellum South. As to slavery of the earlier kind, I think it safe to assume that against it my distinguished adversary, Mr. James Wechsler, would have joined forces with the Abolitionists, as I hope I should have done. But in the current phase of the eternal struggle against slavery, I fear we shall continue to limp along without Mr. Wechsler's support. I cannot think of a single word James Wechsler, a spokesman for American liberalism and a product of it, has ever uttered, or a deed he has done, that could be proved to have given comfort to slaves behind the Iron Curtain, whose future as slaves would be as certain in a world governed by James Wechsler as the future of slaves in Atlanta would have been in an America governed by Jefferson Davis.

Not only do the voices of liberalism strike despair in the hearts of millions of slaves; they do more: they chill the hearts of potential slaves in the Free World. Every time I go through an issue of the *New York Post*, I make it a habit to calculate roughly how much freedom I would lose if all the measures advocated in that issue were to become law. On a typical day I count myself lucky to lose a mere 10 percent.

When Mr. Wechsler is feeling extremely liberal, I can count up to 25 or 30 percent. And of course there are the days, for example when Mr. Wechsler calls upon us to surrender Quemoy and Matsu, in which he disposes of 100 percent of some people's freedom.

As I say, there is no strain of the abolitionist remaining in the modern liberal, the mantle having fallen completely on the shoulders of conservatives. That development was spotted early by the philosopher George Santayana, who commented that the only thing the modern liberal is interested in liberating is man from his marriage contract.

So I cannot predict when liberalism *will* be repudiated. But I can maintain that liberalism *should* indeed be repudiated and pray that the moment will not forever be postponed.

Mr. Wechsler, who is a superb journalist, is fond of focusing on little incidents of a workaday sort and placing them in proper focus, in order to expose the black reaction of those who drag behind his own liberalism, the black reaction of, say, the *New York Times*. It is a perfectly legitimate device, for we do indeed have the best view of the universe from the study of a grain of sand, though of course it makes a considerable difference what prism you use. For example, for years Mr. Wechsler and his associates have made great sport of the proposition that if a man is a loyalty risk—that is to say, if there are grounds for questioning his loyalty to the government of the United States— he should not be employed by the government of the United States, even in a nonsensitive position. I doubt if a week has gone by in the history of the *Post* under its present steward that Mr. Herblock, or Mr. William Shannon, or Miss Doris Fleeson, or someone else, has not regaled us with the story of the persecution of some poor Communist working innocently in the Post Office, or the Bureau of Wildlife and Fisheries, who has been wrested from his job by the violent hand of hysterical American conformism. Mr. Joseph L. Rauh Jr., co-founder with Mr. Wechsler of the Americans for Democratic Action, led the fight in Washington against the dismissal of employees working in nonsensitive positions in government and most recently won a notable victory in the case of *Cole v. Young,* in which the Supreme Court was persuaded that the relevant loyalty and security legislation really intended to reflect the views of Mr. Rauh and Mr. Wechsler, rather than those of Senator McCarran, who was principally responsible for drafting the bills.

As I read the glowing tribute to Mr. Rauh in the *New York Post*, I was persuaded to take another view of that grain of sand. Three years ago a confidence man, Mr. Paul Hughes, was brought to trial in New York. He had successfully conned the editor of the *Democratic Digest*, the editors of the *Washington Post*, and Mr. Joseph L. Rauh Jr., extracting from them $12,000 in return for lascivious accounts of the venalities of Senator Joseph McCarthy, on whose staff he pretended to be serving as a secret investigator. The unfortunate Mr. Hughes then turned and tried to con the Federal Bureau of Investigation, an encounter which led to his present embarrassment.

In the course of his trial, Mr. Hughes described his relationship with Mr. Rauh, to whom he had sold his fabricated secrets. Mr. Rauh is now on the stand and has been reminded that one of the secrets Hughes "stole" from Senator McCarthy was that McCarthy had a sympathizer on the staff of the *New York Post*. Mr. Hughes had found out, he said—a complete fabrication, I remind you—that McCarthy's spy on the *Post* was the cooking editor.

"Did you call Mr. Wechsler," asked Hughes's lawyer, "and tell him?"
Rauh: Yes, sir.
Q: You didn't feel that the cooking editor was going to slant any recipes in McCarthy's favor, did you?
A: That wasn't the purpose. [The purpose] would have been to have somebody there.
Q: What was the purpose of McCarthy having a spy as the cooking editor?
A: Because a cooking editor like anybody else has access to all the records, files, and clips and other matters on the paper and to all discussion. It doesn't matter who the person is. I didn't feel [McCarthy] should have *anybody* on the paper.

I give Mr. Wechsler back his grain of sand, having now understood that it is all right for agents of the Soviet Union to occupy nonsensitive jobs in the United States government, not all right for a sympathizer of Senator McCarthy to stay on as cooking editor of the *New York Post*.

This considerable facility of which I speak, to view a grain of sand in different ways, depending on the light, is indispensable to the successful operation of liberalism; it is the reason why, for instance, liberals can call for massive expenditures—and reduced taxes; for equal treatment for all persons—except wealthier persons; for an impartial receptivity to all points of view—except the conservative point of view; for rule of law—except when the Supreme Court decides to go in for a little sociological pioneering.

The economic philosophy of liberalism is, every bit of it, reflected in a grain of sand—one of those that escaped Mr. Wechsler's attention.

In the tense closing hours of the 1958 gubernatorial campaign in New York, Averell Harriman, grown desperate, loosed on his opponent the three most sinister imaginable political imputations. The first had to do with Nelson Rockefeller's alleged inconstancy to Israel, but this quickly backfired when friends of Rockefeller were able to show that he had given barrels of money to the United Jewish Appeal dating back even to before Israel existed. The second two charges evidently worried Rockefeller so much that he spent virtually all his talking moments, right through to election day, denying he had ever entertained such heinous thoughts. Under no circumstances would he (1) permit a rent rise in rent-controlled New York City or (2) stand by while the subway raised its fares.

It is tempting to dig out the root economic assumptions of liberalism by examining its attitude towards the New York City subways. In a discussion of subways, moreover, one does not bog down with that old devil profit, for the subways belong to the people of the City of New York.

The calumny Mr. Harriman attempted to pin on Mr. Rockefeller was that he would permit the Transit Authority to do the only thing the Transit Authority is permitted by law to do when it is losing money, namely, raise the fares. But raising subway fares is a politically explosive business, which is why Mr. Rockefeller went to such pains to express himself as horrified at the very thought. What must be done, both he and Mr. Harriman agreed, is to meet the subway deficit out of general funds.

This involves, of course, a net imposition on non–subway riders, for the benefit of subway riders. So be it. If all goes according to plan, Cayuga County apple pickers will soon be making it possible for Manhattan elevator operators to ride to work for 15 cents even though it costs the Transit Authority 20 cents to provide the service. In due course, the political representatives of Cayuga County will appeal for increased off-season benefits for apple pickers, whereupon it becomes necessary to increase the taxes of subway riders. Keep this up, and the skies are black with crisscrossing dollars. A dispassionate accountant, viewing the purposeless pell-mell, would surely wonder, What on earth is this all about?

What is wrong with the economy of the crisscrossing dollar?

Well, for one thing, there is the well-known fact that any time a Cayugan sends a dollar down to New York City, it is going to stop at Albany for an expensive night out on the town. But aside from the leakage, what is wrong with the political economy of liberalism, in which dollars are exchanged by political negotiation?

What is principally wrong is that it is an economics of illusion. What is secondarily wrong is that the system permits profiteering by politically mobilized groups. The third way in which it is wrong is that it diminishes the influence of the individual in the marketplace, transferring the lost power to politicians and the ideologues who stir them up.

In the last days of 1958 Senator Jacob Javits wrote his constituents a glowing year-end report. From the middle of 1952 through 1958, he wrote, the federal government spent the enormous sum of $28 billion in New York State. The statistic was jubilantly reported, and the senator further uplifted his constituents by reminding them that the expenditure of "federal funds in New York generated additional public and private spending which might not otherwise have benefited New York."

What was the senior senator from New York trying to tell his constituents, if not that New York, thanks to the acumen of New York's political representatives, was getting an outsized slice of the federal pie? But what did Senator Javits *fail* to report to his constituents? That during the period in question the federal government received in taxes paid by New York citizens and corporations the sum of $83.6 billion, or about three times the sum of money that found its way back. The facts are these: projecting the average figures over the past seven years, New York State can expect to pay 18.5 percent of any future national tax levy, while the percentage of any federal aid program it is likely to receive is 6.9. In other words, New York senators and congressmen anxious to spend, say, $100 million of "federal money" on New York education will find themselves voting to tax New Yorkers about $250 million to make that possible By contrast, Mississippi puts up 0.22 percent of the federal tax dollar—and gets back $2.07. So that the Mississippi senator or congressman can assume that for every $1 million of extra taxes he loads down on his fellow Mississippians for federal aid projects, he can return them $10 million.

In its elusiveness, liberal economic theory lends itself to political deviousness. There is considerable sentiment in New York, for the most part stimulated by the indefatigable dissemination of liberal superstitions, in favor of federal aid to education. Now I am convinced that there are residents of New York State who are concerned with the depressed level of education in Mississippi to the point of wanting to contribute New York dollars to the advancement of Mississippi education. And I am just as convinced that they do not number one-tenth of 1 percent of the population of the state— indeed, not one-tenth of 1 percent of the readers of the *New York Post*. Federal aid programs are, for New Yorkers, a form of autotaxation in behalf of non–New Yorkers; but the voters do not know this, and Jacob Javits is not going to tell them, any more than Nelson Rockefeller did—or Averell Harriman, whose silence on the subject aroused the antagonism of neither James Wechsler *nor* Dorothy Schiff.

Forget everything I have said. Let us assume that schools rise up out of the cornfields, great big beautiful air-conditioned schools, staffed by teachers who have each spent ten years at a teachers college on a federal John Dewey Fellowship and have passed examinations in all the works of Max Lerner [a prolific columnist for the *New York Post*]. Education today claims to emphasize the development of the critical faculties—but to what purpose is not clear, and that it is not clear is the central revelation of the contemporary critique of education. Although it is tacitly agreed that graduates of our schools must be molded in liberalism, to recall the injunction of Senator Joseph Clark in *The Atlantic Monthly*, it is not really clear what liberalism is. Mr. Wechsler constantly bemoans in his paper the listlessness of the people and their failure to rally behind a more aggressive liberalism, and Professor Arthur Schlesinger, writing in *The Reporter* a year ago, spoke deeply and eloquently about our absent discontents. The readers of the *New York Post* have not felt deeply since the days of the Reign of Terror, back when Bertrand Russell—a fountain of wisdom out of which American liberals regularly drink—was telling Englishmen that Senator McCarthy had made the reading of Thomas Jefferson a criminal offense.

Beyond the savage response of the liberals when their orthodoxy is threatened—a common psychological reaction; ask Mr. Max Lerner—liberals do not feel deeply because liberalism has no fixed, acknowledged norms by which, taking the measure of our deviation, we feel deeply the need for reform. The big excitement at Yale University in the fall of 1958, in connection with a protest addressed to Khrushchev against the handling of Boris Pasternak, was over the question whether Americans were morally licensed to issue such an objection! If the Soviet Union persecutes its intellectuals for writing the truth, the students assembled concluded, it is no different from a congressional committee's persecuting an intellectual for writing error. Truth? Error? These are strange words, atavistic words. Granted, most students can be counted on to smell out the phoniness of the argument that America is as guilty as the Soviet Union in the matter of bringing intellectuals to heel; left to their own devices they would come to an acknowledgment of a qualitative difference between, say, Columbia's handling of Gene Weltfish and Russia's of Shostakovich.

Still, they wonder, what is the theoretical base from which to talk back to the proposition that persecution is persecution, and that's all there is to it? They grope because prevailing preoccupations are with method, not substance; and so by a little dialectical artfulness one can group together the treatment of Pasternak and Lattimore under the classification "The Showing of Displeasure by an Agency of Government towards an Intellectual."

If evil and good are merely conventional words, the student is left only with the fact of harassment to weigh, not the provocation of it. How can one feel passionately about method? And what other than method is one encouraged to feel passionately about? There was much more excitement over Senator McCarthy's methods (Did he or did he not, in the case of Civil Servant Jones, observe approved methods of interrogation?) than over his putative revelations (Did Civil Servant Jones in fact whisk away that atomic secret?). There are many more allusions, on college campuses, to the fact that Salazar governs Portugal undemocratically than to the fact that he governs it well.

Democracy has no eschatology, no vision, no point of arrival. Neither does academic freedom. Both are merely instruments, the one supposed to induce a harmonious society, the second supposed to advance knowledge. But let me say that I, for one, would not willingly die for "democracy," any more than I would willingly die for "academic freedom." I do understand the disposition to die for the kind of society democracy sometimes ushers in; and I do understand the disposition to die in behalf of some of the truths academic freedom may have been instrumental in apprehending. *There* is the difference. It is not lost on the undergraduate that there is no liberal vision. And so long as there is not, there is no call for the kind of passionate commitment that stirs the political blood. What is the liberal millennium? As far as I can make out from reading the pages of the *New York Post*, it is the state in which a citizen divides his day equally among pulling levers in voting booths (Voting for what? It does not matter so much; it matters only that he votes); writing dissenting letters to the newspaper (Dissenting from what? It does not matter; just so he dissents); and eating (Eating what? It does not matter, even to the cooking editor of the *Post*, though one should, of course, wash the food down with fluoridated water).

I advise my friend Mr. Wechsler that he will have to make Max

Lerner write columns twice as long if, in the years to come, he is to succeed in drugging his constituency with the superstitions of liberalism. He knows that. Every New Dealer knows that; every socialist knows it: the dose must get stronger and stronger, or there is the danger that one will come out of it, stupefied by one's long lapse into a state of intellectual and moral idiocy. When the day comes that the drug no longer works, we will properly celebrate the twentieth-century equivalent of the Emancipation Proclamation. That is the day when liberalism *will* be repudiated. That it *should* be repudiated has been evident to the editors of *National Review* from the moment our publication was launched. We stand ready to take over the *Post*— and are prepared on this occasion to announce the identity of its next editor. You've guessed it: the cooking editor.

THE SIXTIES

In the End, We Will Bury Him

An Address to a Rally Protesting the Visit to the United States by Nikita Khrushchev; Carnegie Hall, New York, September 17, 1960

When Premier Khrushchev came to New York for his visit to the United Nations, to be followed by a trip to Washington, there was some consternation at the hospitality he would need to be shown and the implications of it for the anti-Communist struggle, which depended so heavily on protest and corresponding public attitudes. Carnegie Hall was sold out, and eleven speakers held forth.

THE DAMAGE KHRUSHCHEV can do to us on this trip is not comparable to the damage we have done to ourselves. Khrushchev is here, and his being here profanes the nation. But the harm that is done, we have done to ourselves; and for that we cannot hold Khrushchev responsible.

I deplore the fact that Khrushchev is traveling about this country, having been met at the frontier by our own prince, who arrived with his first string of dancing girls, and a majestic caravan of jewels and honey and spices; I mind that he will wend his lordly way from city to city, where the Lilliputians will fuss over his needs, weave garlands through the ring in his nose, shiver when he belches out his threats, and labor in panic to sate his imperial appetites. I mind that Khrushchev is here, but I mind more that Eisenhower invited him. I mind that Eisenhower invited him, but I mind much more the defense of that invitation by the thought leaders of the nation. Khrushchev cannot by his presence here permanently damage us, I repeat, and neither could Mr. Eisenhower by inviting him. But we are gravely damaged if it is true that in welcoming Khrushchev, Eisenhower speaks for America, for in that case the people have lost their moral equilibrium; and we cannot hope to live down the experience until we have recovered it.

I mind, in a word, the so-called reasons why Mr. Eisenhower

issued the invitation. I mind first that "reasons" are being put forward, but mostly that they are being accepted. Khrushchev's visit has been successfully transmuted into a "diplomatic necessity," and many speak of it as a stroke of diplomatic genius. When President Eisenhower extended the invitation in his capacity as principal agent of American foreign policy, the deed was explosive enough. But the true dimensions of our national crisis became apparent with the concentric ripples of assent that followed the issuance of the invitation. *A splendid idea*, said the chairman of the Senate Foreign Relations Committee, having presumably first consulted the editorial columns of the *New York Times* to make sure his compass was properly oriented. In a matter of days, we were being solemnly advised by the majority of the editorial writers of the nation that (a) the invitation was bound to meet with the approval of all those who favor peace in the world and goodwill towards men and (b) in any event, those who opposed the invitation have no alternative save to abide by the spirit that moved the president—as a matter of loyalty. "If you have to throw something at him," said Mr. Nixon upon touching down after his visit to Moscow, "throw flowers." And then Mr. Gallup confirmed the popularity of the president's decision—which, it turns out, exceeds even the popularity of the president himself. I do not recall that six months ago Mr. Gallup canvassed the American people on the question whether Mr. Khrushchev should be invited to this country. But I doubt that anyone would dispute my guess that an emphatic majority would then have voted *against* the visit.

What happened? The sheer cogency of the invitation evidently struck the people as forcibly as the superiority of round over square wheels is said one day to have struck our primitive ancestors. *Obviously* the visit is in order, the people seem to have grasped, giving way before the analyses of their leaders. How mischievous is the habit of adducing reasons for everything that is done! I can, happily and unassailably, delight in lobster and despise crabmeat all my life—as long as I refrain from giving *reasons* why the one food suits and the other sickens. But when I seek rationally to motivate my preferences, I lose my authority. If only the publicists had refrained from shoring up the president's caprice with a Gothic rational structure! But no. We are a rational people. There must be reasons for the invitation; and so the reasons are conjured up.

I have not heard a "reason" why Khrushchev should come to this country that is not in fact a reason why he should not come to this country. *He will see for himself the health and wealth of the land.* Very well; and once he has done so, what are we to expect? That he will weaken in his adherence to his maniacal course because the average American has the use of one and two-thirds toilets? One might as well expect the Bishop of Rome to break the apostolic succession on being confronted with the splendid new YMCA in Canton, Ohio. Does Khrushchev really *doubt* that there are 67 million automobiles in this country? What is he to do now that he is here? Count them? And what will he do if there is a discrepancy? Fire Alger Hiss? If Khrushchev were a man to be moved by empirical brushes with reality, how could he continue to believe in Communism? He cannot turn a corner in the Soviet Union without colliding against stark evidence of the fraudulence of Marxist theory. Where is the workers' paradise? In the two-room apartments that house five families? In the frozen reaches where he commits to slavery the millions upon millions who fail to appreciate the fact that under the Marxist prescription they have been elevated to a state of total freedom? In the headquarters of the secret police, where files are kept on every citizen of the Soviet Union on the *presumption* that every citizen is an enemy of the proletarian state?

Any man who is capable of being affected by the evidence of things as they are need not leave Russia to discover that the major premises of Karl Marx are mistaken. Dante cultivated a love of heaven by demonstrating the horrors of hell. It did not occur to him that the Devil might be converted by taking him around the glories of the court of the Medici. What reason have we to believe that a man who knows Russia and *still* has not rejected Marx will be moved by the sight of Levittown?

But even if Khrushchev fails to readjust his views after witnessing the economic miracles wrought by capitalism—in which connection it is relevant to recall the amazement of American industrial leaders on learning last winter that Mikoyan [the Soviets' deputy premier] knew more about Ameri-can industrial accomplishments than they did—even if Khrushchev finds out that Mikoyan was right all along, will he learn that other great lesson which the president advanced as a principal "reason" why Khrushchev should come? Is he going to encounter that firmness of American resolution which will cause him, when he returns to Russia, to furrow his brow in anxiety on resuming the war against us?

I suggest that this brings us to the major reason why Khrushchev should *not* have been invited. If indeed the nation is united behind Mr. Eisenhower in this invitation, then the nation is united behind an act of diplomatic sentimentality which can only confirm Khrushchev in the contempt he feels for the dissipated morale of a nation far gone, as the theorists of Marxism have all along contended, in decrepitude. That he should be invited to visit here as though he were susceptible to a rational engagement! That he should achieve orthodox diplomatic recognition not four years after shocking history itself by the brutalities of Budapest; months after endorsing the shooting down of an unarmed American plane; only weeks since he last shrieked his intention of demolishing the West; only days since publishing in an American magazine his undiluted resolve to enslave the citizens of free Berlin—that such an introduction should end up constituting his credentials for a visit to America will teach him something about the West that some of us wish he might never have known.

What is it that stands in the way of Communism's march? The little homilies of American capitalism? A gigantic air force which depends less on gasoline than on the pronouncements of the Committee for a Sane Nuclear Policy to know whether it can ever be airborne? *Is this indeed the nature of the enemy?* Khrushchev will be entitled to wonder exultantly, after twelve days of giddy American camaraderie. Will he not return to Moscow convinced that behind the modulated hubbub at the White House, in the State Department, in the city halls, at the country clubs, at the economic clubs, at the industrial banquets, he heard—*with his own ears*—the death rattle of the West?

It is the imposture of irrationality in the guise of rationality that frightens. The visit is timely, we are told. Why? State one reason. If it is timely now, why was it not timely a year ago? If Eisenhower is correct today in welcoming Khrushchev, then was he not wrong yes-

terday in *not* welcoming him? But we were all pro-Eisenhower yesterday—when he declared that he would not meet with the Soviet
leaders while under pressure of blackmail in regard to Berlin. And
yet we are pro-Eisenhower today—when he proceeds to meet with
Khrushchev, with the threat still hanging over us. If it is so very
urgent that we should acquaint Khrushchev with the highways
and byways of the United States, why did Eisenhower wait seven
long years after he first had the opportunity? The social history of
the White House under Mr. Eisenhower will after all record only
one exclusion and one addition during his tenure. Khrushchev was
added, Senator McCarthy was ejected. And both times, the thousands
cheered.

This afternoon Mayor Robert Wagner danced attendance upon
Mr. Khrushchev. Did he do so because Premier Khrushchev is head
of a foreign state and so entitled, ex officio, to the hospitality of New
York's mayor? It isn't that simple, as we pointed out last week in the
National Review Bulletin. Last year Mayor Wagner ostentatiously announced his refusal to greet Ibn Saud—on the grounds that Ibn Saud
discriminates against Jews in Saudi Arabia, and no man who discriminates against Jews in Saudi Arabia is going to be handled courteously
by Bob Wagner, mayor of New York. Now, as everybody knows, what
Nikita Khrushchev does to Jews is kill them. On the other hand, he
does much the same thing to Catholics and Protestants. Could *that* be
why Mr. Wagner consented to honor Khrushchev? Khrushchev murders people without regard to race, color, or creed, and therefore
whatever he is guilty of, he is not guilty of discrimination? Is *that* the
shape of the new rationality?

LADIES AND GENTLEMEN, we deem it the central revelation of
Western experience that man cannot ineradicably stain himself, for
the wells of regeneration are infinitely deep. No temple has ever been
so profaned that it cannot be purified; no man is ever truly lost; no
nation is irrevocably dishonored. Khrushchev cannot take permanent
advantage of our temporary disadvantage, for it is the West he is fighting. And in the West there lie, however encysted, the ultimate

resources, which are moral in nature. Khrushchev is *not* aware that the gates of hell shall not prevail against us. Even out of the depths of despair, we take heart in the knowledge that it cannot matter how deep we fall, for there is always hope. In the end, we will bury him.

Scholar, Fighter, Westerner

Remarks Introducing Jacques Soustelle at a *National Review* Forum;
Hunter College, New York, December 1, 1960

This was another event at Hunter College, the guest of honor a brilliant anthropologist and hero of the French Resistance, a socialist and an intimate of President Charles de Gaulle who, however, staunchly opposed a French withdrawal from Algeria. That was then the greatest enthusiasm of the anti-colonialist movement.

An interesting sequel: An official of Hunter College sat in on Soustelle's speech, and a week later we received notice that Hunter College would no longer provide its facilities for our forums. The New York Civil Liberties Union championed our cause (Hunter College is city property) and forced a reversal by the Hunter administration.

WHAT CUBA IS for us, Algeria is for Europe. As it goes in Cuba, so is it likely to go in Latin America. As it goes in Algeria, so is it likely to go in Europe.

The question is no longer whether this is so but whether the relevant people can be made to realize that it is so. We see in Venezuela a classic confutation of the dream-theory that all we need, to bring social serenity and progress in Latin America, is to elect a good socialist to power in a democratic election. We know now that it is not so simple, that nations cannot be run by local chapters of the Americans for Democratic Action. Every nation is different; yet every nation is individually subject to a universally insistent pressure, generated by the wildness in the human spirit and organized by the Communist movement, which aims at ferment and the collapse of the civil society. Our oracular opinion makers are at home in their Houses of Abstraction: but they have not proved able to rule the world because they are not of this world. They cannot understand the composition of society as far away as Little Rock or New Orleans, let alone Cuba or Venezuela. For Algeria, they say simply: "Colonialism must end. If you doubt us, look under 'Colonialism' in the *Columbia Encyclopedia of the Social Sciences.*"

Jacques Soustelle knows all about abstractions, and about the great ideas that have illuminated our civilization. In behalf of the idea of freedom he risked torture and death, day after day, week after week, year after year, organizing the French Resistance movement, coordinating its intelligence aspect, evading the Gestapo by hairsbreadth escapes, thrilling his countrymen, as, next only to de Gaulle, he emerged as the most visible, and exciting, symbol of continuing French vitality. He fought then for ideals, but he knew the social terms that framed the context within which he worked. To such an understanding, indeed, he was educated: for Mr. Soustelle is by training an anthropologist, with impeccable academic credentials, who might, but for the call of duty, have continued happily his explorations of prehistorical civilizations in Mexico, writing about them, as he had already done, as definitively as anyone before or since.

Precisely that training to observe led him to know with confidence that Algeria cannot be surrendered, never mind the abstractions of colonialism and democracy. He came to know that the effect of the weight of atmospheric pressure on French policy would be to deliver Algeria over to wild and barbaric forces, which would be sure to do for Algeria what Fidel Castro has done for Cuba, and, in strategic terms, worse: for the loss of Algeria would dispose the African land bridge in favor of the great Communist thrust that aims at the social cordite to the south and to the west, to Latin America, and our own backyard.

The crucial distinction today is between men who accept history and men who make it. We are told—often by the same people who want for all the world a single government—that one government is not enough for France and Algeria. We are told—often by the same people who thought it altogether feasible to establish a little Jewish enclave in the bosom of Arabia—that a great nation *cannot* remain in an area it has nurtured with its blood and sweat and culture for one hundred years, if it is surrounded by men of another race. Cannot? Mr. Soustelle begins by asking. Why? It was harder, surely, to eject the Nazis from France. Harder, in point of fact, to learn to detonate an atomic bomb. Much, much harder to learn, as we did over the course of the centuries, how necessary it is to work, day and night, to stay civilized.

You will hear now from a singular man, a scholar, a fighter, and a Westerner. There is not in all American public life a man combining those qualities in so generous measure. We shall hear from the man who was the closest intimate of Charles de Gaulle until February of this year, when they broke over the issue of Algeria. What conversations must have passed between them! Rich in the knowledge of history, profound in the knowledge of man, passionate in their differences as only men can be who have shared so closely their lives and fortunes. One shudders at the contrast with the great American debates of last fall.

Herewith the former minister-delegate of France, the former governor-general of Algeria, former head of the Free French resistance movement, author of *The Daily Life of the Aztecs on the Eve of the Spanish Conquest,* Mr. Jacques Soustelle.

THE LONELY PROFESSOR

Remarks at a Testimonial Dinner for O. Glenn Saxon; the Taft Hotel,
New Haven, Conn., May 22, 1961

---

*This testimonial speech is one of a dozen that will be included in this col-
lection. It was given at a small dinner honoring Professor Saxon, the lone
active free-market economist at Yale in the late 1940s and the 1950s.
Yale did not exercise the option to continue him active after he reached
retirement age. A few undergraduates put the dinner together and invited
me and other speakers to record our feelings about Glenn Saxon.*

P ROFESSOR SAXON WAS the nearest thing to an omnipresence
I ever knew. He made Yale unsafe for economic presumption.
You could never tell just when one of the current economic
myths, traveling about the campus drawing applause from all the little apprentice social magicians, would turn a corner, bump into Glenn
Saxon, and die a miserable death. Occasionally, our beleaguered conservative forces needed a massive display of strength, and we would
summon forth our Big Bertha, and put Mr. Saxon publicly on display
before, say, the Political Union. There he would pronounce the verities, and, as it was said of Timothy Dwight doing battle against
paganism in the early days of his tenure at Yale, infidelity would skulk
and hide its head: and, reanimated, those of us who were convinced
of the interrelationship of economic freedom and freedom could go
about our business with the unique confidence that comes from
knowing that the champion of your ideas has met the challenger and
is still champion.

During those years it was fashionable to call Mr. Saxon a long list
of derogatory names, usually calculated to stress the anachronism of
his ideas. It was far safer to say simply that Saxon was a troglodyte,
whence it follows that his ideas have not seen the daylight, than to put
up the opposing ideas side by side with his, to see which in fact
reflected the greater light. Some students, I grant, were afraid of Mr.
Saxon. For one thing, there is that face. When it is tense, there is no

face in the literature of determination to match it: Michelangelo's depiction of Hercules writhing in his labors, Rodin's Perseus slaying the monster: mere milquetoasts by contrast with that face, standing up to economic heresy.

I never knew a student who complained of being treated meanly by him (I wish I could say I never knew a student who treated him meanly). In argument he was intense, but not unyielding. I once heard a student ask him, "Don't you admit the New Deal was right in setting up the SEC?" To which he retorted grandly, "Even a stopped clock is right twice a day."

His truths are his truths, his demonstrations his demonstrations, his experiences his experiences: and the question was less whether these were valid truths, profound demonstrations, relevant experiences than whether a great university would have the generosity to treat a scholar, a gentleman, and a dissident generously. I think Yale— if I may use a collectivity in Mr. Saxon's presence—failed: but not, thanks largely to the students who organized this dinner, wholly. A part of Yale is here tonight to say to him: For so long as we live, we shall not forget your courage or the force of your devotion, or the arena in which you fought.

AN ISLAND OF HOPE

A Speech at a Rally in Behalf of the Republic of China (Taiwan), Sponsored by the Committee of One Million; Carnegie Hall, New York, September 21, 1961

The Committee of One Million (Against the Admission of Red China to the United Nations) was a very active lobby during the 1950s and 1960s. In the fall of 1961 is organized a rally to register opposition to the admission of Peking (which was finally done ten years later—see my speech to a conference sponsored by the American-Asian Educational Exchange, October 29, 1971). General Edwin A. Walker, mentioned in the final paragraph, had been stationed in Germany and was called back when he gave a vitriolic speech deriding various Establishment figures. On his return to the United States he joined forces with Billy James Hargis in radical-right activity. In April 1963 an attempt on his life was made by a rifleman who missed his head by a few inches. The failed assassin was Lee Harvey Oswald, who seven months later assassinated John F. Kennedy.

WE MEET HERE tonight to raise our voices on a matter of great importance to the survival of freedom, hoping that the reverberations from this gathering will cause a fresh wind to blow in the United Nations, to give it courage to resist its increasing colonization by the Soviet Union.

The crises man faces are of two kinds. Some we cannot avoid, as we cannot avoid a flash flood or a prairie fire. Others we see approaching with a dreadful clarity of vision, and these we can hope to do something about. True tragedy is man-made. Hurricane Carla was a catastrophe; it was not a tragedy. Tragedy results from a flaw in the human character, a weakness in the human will, an imperfect moral understanding, a failure of courage. The overarching tragedy for the past fifteen years has been the failure of the West's strategic vision— a moral failure, essentially. It has led to a long series of defeats. It led to Korea, and to Suez, and to Cuba. The failures there were human, not natural. In refusing to win the war in Korea, and thus to pursue the opening that events had given us, we lost the opportunity to speak back to history and reclaim China. In failing to support the English and French and Israelis in Suez, we failed to say to Africa what needed to be said, that our retreat from colonialism would be phased with the great strategic imperatives of freedom and justice. In Cuba, at the Bay of Pigs, we faltered, and so made known that we would tolerate an enemy beachhead in the Western Hemisphere. We showed, by our deeds, that we would sooner appease the neo-democratic divinities of world opinion than follow the imperatives that come from the planning boards of Western survival.

I count as no less important the crisis that impends in the United Nations. There, not a man stands to be shot: there, there is no Yalu, no Port Said, no Bay of Pigs, but only file upon file of wooden desks and paper clips and earphones; the actors are not soldiers but diplomats. Yet it is a great battlefield all the same, and what hangs in the balance is the hopes of good men in the Far East and everywhere else.

There are those in America who make a religion of pragmatism, who say that ours is not, never was, and never should be a nation wedded to abstract ideals: that the genius of American politics is not utopian stargazing, not the pilgrim's search for great metaphysical realities, but rather the search for the practical thing, the do-able thing, the thing that works for the United States.

I have philosophical disagreements with that school of thought, but I am ready, as perhaps you are, to tell the pragmatists that we are willing to wage the fight on Red China on their terms. Three short years ago we were told by the doomsayers that unless we surrendered Quemoy and Matsu, we would bring on a regional war whose sympathetic detonations would explode right on our own hearths. John Foster Dulles stood firm, and he prevailed; and lo and behold, the thousand persons who met in Harvard Square to denounce his policy of firmness as a death warrant pronounced upon their invaluable selves are with us yet—and so too are the fifty thousand Chinese who continue to enjoy the freedom of their beleaguered little islands. Indeed, Mr. Richard Rovere of the *New Yorker,* concertmaster of the doomsayers at the time of the crisis, has had the courage to say that the turn of events proved that Mr. Dulles was correct: that by refusing to yield Quemoy and Matsu, we did not detonate a world war but rather vouchsafed a continued liberty to Quemoy and Matsu and breathed into the free peoples of the Far East a deep and revivifying lungful of life. The United States, the free peoples of the Far East learned, was alive after all, and from our life, they drew breath.

Our action was not a reflexive act of moral rectitude. If I must die a violent death—I speak only for myself—I do not choose to die for Quemoy or for Matsu, or for Berlin, or for Formosa. I would die willingly only for my country, for my family, or for my faith. The decision to hang on to Quemoy-Matsu was a strategically intelligent decision designed to protect not Quemoy-Matsu but America: it was a pragmatic decision, based on the correct presumption that in our shrunken globe freedom from Communism *has* become indivisible—not for metaphysical reasons but for strategic reasons. We Americans are prepared, if necessary for our own survival, to give over to darkness the fifty thousand Chinese who live on Quemoy and Matsu. But experience shows us that this would not be the isolated consequence of such a default: such a surrender would be no different from passing the ammunition to our enemy, to make him grow stronger and more terrible, and capable of advancing more menacingly not only upon his neighbors but upon those who live and work and worship and laugh right here in the United States.

I do not need to make to this audience the strategical demonstration. We know that, as it is true that on the fate of Berlin hangs the fate of Europe, on the fate of Formosa hangs the fate of those counterrevolutionary forces in the Far East on which we rely to keep the enemy at bay and to keep kindled the hope that, God willing, the sun will shine again on quarters of the globe which are under the long shadow of the dark and dusty corner of the British Museum where Karl Marx worked, developing his spite against humankind.

My motives, then, and let me speak frankly to my friends in China, are not altruistic. I would not commit the United States to a course of perpetual war in behalf of perpetual peace: I choose rather to wage war against the appeasers in our midst because that war, bloody as it sometimes appears, is infinitely less so than the war we shall have to fight if we continue to appease the enemy and to give him, as already we did in those three great crises in Korea and Suez and Cuba, grounds for believing that there is not left in the bourgeois world the will to withstand the presumptions of international Bolshevism.

THIS CRISIS IS distinguished from others we have faced by the singular amount of time providence has given us to meditate on the consequence of our deeds. Other speakers have cogently demonstrated the emptiness of the argument that we must, in order to face the reality of Communist control of Mainland China, permit her entry into the United Nations. We have had ten years' experience, and no indication whatever that recognition would have done for us any more than it has done for Great Britain or for other Western powers that rushed unthinkingly into it. A few months after Red China chased the elements of civilization from the Mainland, we might have justified diplomatic recognition by abstract reasoning. But for ten years now we have seen that there is not a single advantage to be gained from recognition, whereas the disadvantages are striking.

Is it seriously believed that by recognizing Red China we would subject her to the pressures of International Togetherness and bridle her appetites, mitigate her ideological lust? How have we fared with Russia, after twenty-eight years of recognition?

Recognition would serve not to teach Red China table manners, but to fortify her in the abiding Communist belief that the West is too frail, too rotten, to be able to resist her most conceited demands; that notwithstanding her studied career as principal desperado among nations, she can force her way into the chambers of an assembly whose charter—in words plain and simple, the text of which was approved in four major languages—qualifies for membership only those nations of the world that seek to keep the peace. If the world were sane, and if the leaders of the United States could rise up from liberalism, the debate in the United Nations this fall would not be on the question whether to accept Red China for membership but on the question whether to expel from membership the Union of Soviet Socialist Republics.

THIS AUDIENCE KNOWS the relevant realities. We know that the persons who press for appeasement in the Far East tend to be the same persons who press for appeasement in all the other theaters of the world. The men and women who call for the recognition of Red China tend to be the same men and women who called for what they termed moderation—what one might call, with a sense of poetic satisfaction, ultramoderation—in Korea. Who abominated the efforts of England and France and Israel to repress the arrant nationalism of Nasser. Who call for the abandonment of the outposts of civilization in Africa. Who deplored America's brief flirtation with resolution in Cuba. Ultimately their arguments must, by logical necessity, come down to surrender. And indeed, this exactly is the naked word that is finally being used by a few brave cowards. "For the first time in America," writes Mr. Joseph Alsop, "one or two voices are beginning to be heard, arguing that what ought to be done is to surrender."

"Mr. Kennedy says Berlin is not negotiable," writes Mr. John Crosby [a fire-breathing columnist for the *New York Herald Tribune*]. "Why isn't it? Why isn't anything negotiable rather than thermonuclear war? . . . Are we going to wipe out two and a half billion years of slow biological improvement in a thermonuclear war? Over what—*Berlin*? I agree with Nehru that to go to war under any circumstances for anything at all in our world in our time is utter absurdity. . . . I certainly think Berlin is negotiable and, as a matter of fact, Khrushchev is not even asking very much. . . . [And after all] Communism . . . is not that bad, and some day we're going to have to face up to that."

And Mr. Kenneth Tynan, the English critic, agrees. "Better Red than dead," he writes, "seems an obvious doctrine for anyone not consumed by a death-wish: I would rather live on my knees than die on my knees."

Well, assuming it is death towards which we are headed as a result of our determination to stay free, let it be said that Mr. Tynan would not need to die on his knees. He could die standing up, like those of his ancestors who died at Runnymede, at Agincourt, at Hastings, at Dunkirk, fighting for the freedom of their descendants to exhibit their moral idiocy. Mr. Crosby appears to have substituted for the American slogan "Give me liberty or give me death" the slogan "John Crosby is too young to die." Let them live. There remain impenetrable corners of the Soviet Union where Messrs. Crosby and Tynan could store up their twenty-five hundred calories per day and remain absolutely free from the hounds of radioactivity, if not from the horrors of Bolshevism. But let them not contaminate the air that free men breathe. We seek not to start a war but to *avoid* war, and the surest way to avoid war is by asserting our willingness to wage it, a paradox that surely is not so complex as to elude the understanding of professional students of drama. The appeasers and collaborationists in our midst seek to pour water into our gunpowder and lead into the muzzles of our cannons, and to leave us defenseless in the face of the enemy's musketry. There is no licit use for a nuclear bomb, they are saying in effect, save possibly to drop a small one on General Walker. These are in fact the warmongers, for they whet the appetite of the enemy as surely as a stripteaser whets the appetite of the lecher. "However I survey the future," writes Kenneth Tynan, "there seems to me nothing noble" in dying. "I want my wife to have another child, and I want to see that child learn to walk." Those in the West of civilized mind and heart are engaged in making just that possible, the birth of another child to Kenneth Tynan, always assuming he has left the virility with which to procreate one. Ours is the way of *life*—with freedom. Without freedom there is no life. Let us now in the name of life on earth extend our hands to the free Asians and say to them the same words that baptized this nation: that we pledge, together, our lives, our fortunes, and our sacred honor.

NORMAN MAILER AND THE AMERICAN RIGHT

The Opening Statement in a Debate; Chicago, September 22, 1962

Two young entrepreneurs thought to stage a big theatrical event, Norman Mailer versus WFB, to argue the meaning of the American right wing. The huge amphitheater was packed, SRO, because what seemed the entire heavyweight-boxing community was present for the championship match three days later between Floyd Patterson (defending champion) and Sonny Liston. Mailer arrived with his retinue and demanded cash up front before stepping onstage. It was not easy to raise $1,000, in $20 bills, from ambient friends and stagehands. Both opening speeches were reproduced in Playboy *magazine.*

I WELCOME MR. MAILER'S interest in the American right wing. On behalf of the right wing let me say that we, in turn, are interested in Mr. Mailer and look forward to co-existence and cultural exchanges in the years to come. I hope we can maintain his interest, though I confess to certain misgivings. I am not sure we have enough sexual neuroses for him. But if we have any at all, no doubt he will find them and celebrate them—if not here tonight, then perhaps in a sequel to the essay in which he gave, to a world tormented by an inexact knowledge of the causes of tension between the Negro and the white races in the South, the long-awaited answer, namely, that all Southern politics reflects the white man's resentment of the superior sexual potency of the Negro male. Mr. Mailer took his thesis—easily the most endearing thing he has ever done—to Mrs. Eleanor Roosevelt, to ask her benediction upon it. She replied that the thesis was "horrible," thus filling Mr. Mailer with such fierce delight that he has never ceased describing her reaction, commenting that he must be responsible for the very first use of that overwrought word by that lady in her long, and very talkative, career.

"Oh how we shall *scarify!*" the dilettante Englishman reported exultantly to his friends a hundred years ago, on announcing that he had finally put together the money with which to start a weekly magazine. How Mr. Mailer loves to scarify!—and how happy I am that he means to do so at my expense. Not only do I not know anyone whose dismay is more fetchingly set down, I do not know anyone whose dismay I personally covet more; because it is clear from reading the works of Mr. Mailer that only demonstrations of human swinishness are truly pleasing to him, truly confirm his vision of a world gone square. Pleasant people, like those of us on the right wing, drive him mad and leech his genius. Recently he has confessed that it is all he can do to stoke his anger nowadays, and he needs that anger to fire his artistic furnace. The world must be a cad; how else will Norman Mailer get to be president? For Mr. Mailer, to use his own phrase, has been "running for president for ten years." He means by that he wants the world to acknowledge him as the principal author of our time—*número uno*, the unchallenged, unchallengeable matador, the biggest bullkiller since Theseus; and so those of you who wish him to be president must confirm his darkest thoughts and suspicions about you, so that he may give birth to that novel of outrage which, he gloats, will be, "*if I can do it*, an unpublishable work." It would be a novel so great—so great that Marx and Freud themselves would want to read it; for they would recognize in it, says Mr. Mailer, a work that "carries what they had to tell another part of the way." Those few of us who are not needed to preserve the hideousness of this world, so as to fatten Mr. Mailer's muse, are assigned by him the task of cultivating "the passion for socialism," which Mr. Mailer finds "the *only* meaning I can conceive in the lives of those who are not artists." They will want a socialist world not because they have the conceit that men would thereby be more happy, but because they "feel the moral imperative in life itself to raise the human condition even if this should ultimately mean no more than that man's suffering has been lifted to a higher level, and human history has only progressed from melodrama, farce, and monstrosity, to tragedy itself."

Not very long after writing that sentence, Mr. Mailer and a dozen others, including several other presidential candidates, signed an advertisement in papers throughout the country under the sponsorship of a group which called itself the Fair Play for Cuba Committee. "The witch-hunting press," the advertisement said in almost as many words, "is suggesting that Castro's great democratic revolution is contaminated by Communism. That is hysterical and fascistic nonsense." One or two signers of that petition—Kenneth Tynan, the English critic, was one—were subsequently called before a congressional investigating committee and asked what they knew about the sponsorship of the Fair Play Committee. To Mr. Mailer's eternal mortification, he was not called, thus feeding what *Time* magazine has identified as Norman Mailer's subpoena envy. Anyway, it transpired that the organizer of that committee was a paid agent of Fidel Castro, who even then was an unpaid agent of the Soviet Union. The insiders no doubt found it enormously amusing to be able to deploy with such ease some of the most conceited artists in the world behind the Communists' grisly little hoax. There is melodrama in Norman Mailer rushing forward to thrust his vital frame between the American public and a true understanding of the march of events in Cuba; there is even farce in the easy victimization of Mr. Skeptic himself by a silent-screen ideological con man; and it is always monstrous to argue aggressively the truth of the Big Lie. But I think the episode was less any one of these things than an act of tragedy with dire consequences, not for the players—they are strikingly impenitent, insouciant—but for others. The people of Cuba are also writing a book that carries forward the ideas of Marx and Freud, a truly unpublishable book. Their suffering, for which Mr. Mailer bears a part of the moral responsibility, they must endure without the means to sublimate; they are not artists who count their travail as a stepping-stone to the presidency.

Consider this. Last spring a middle-aged Cuban carpenter, known to persons I know, received notice at his three-room cottage on the outskirts of Havana at five o'clock one afternoon that at nine the next morning his twelve-year-old son would be taken from him to be schooled in the Soviet Union during the next six years. The father, who had never concerned himself with politics, asked if his son might not, as an only child, be spared. The answer was no. The father spent the evening talking with his wife and sister, and on his knees praying. The next morning he opened the door to the escort who had come to fetch his son, put a bullet through his head, turned and shot his wife and child, and then blew out his own brains.

That is not merely a personal tragedy, any more than the story of Anne Frank was merely a personal tragedy. It is part of a systemic tragedy, just as the annihilation camps in Germany and Poland were part of a systemic tragedy: the tragedy that arises not out of the workaday recognition of man's capacity for brutality but out of the recognition that man's capacity for good is equal to the task of containing systemic horror but that we are nonetheless frozen in inactivity. The horror spreads, leaping over continents and oceans and slithering up to our shoreline, while those whose job it is to contain it grind out their diplomatic nothingness, and the nation's poets wallow in their own little sorrows. The American right wing—of which I am merely one member, clumsily trying to say what Norman Mailer with his superior skills would be saying so very much better if only he would raise his eyes from the world's genital glands—is trying to understand why; is trying to understand what is that philosophy of despair and who voted to make it the law of nations, that we should yield to it; that philosophy which teaches us to be impotent while fury strikes at the carpenter's home ninety miles from the greatest giant history ever bred, whose hands are held down by the Lilliputian solipsists of contemporary liberalism.

CUBA IS A symbol of American liberalism's failure to meet the challenges of the modern world. If such a thing as Castro's Cuba were not possible, such a thing as the American right wing, as it exists today, would not be possible; as things are, the American right wing is necessary, and providential.

Why are we now threatened with Castro? Why should Castro ever have arisen to threaten us? That is a question, I dare suggest, which the Right alone has been asking. If the President of the United States desires a clue as to the answer to that question he might reflect on a scene enacted three and one-half years ago at his alma mater. It was a brilliant spring evening, and Harvard had not found a hall large enough to hold the crowd. The meeting was finally held out of doors. And there ten thousand members of the Harvard community—teachers, students, administrative officials—met in high spirits to give Fidel Castro a thunderous, prolonged standing ovation.

That is why the United States has not been able to cope with Castro—nor, before him, with Khrushchev, or Mao Tse-tung, or Stalin; or, for that matter, with Alger Hiss. We have not understood. The most educated men in our midst and the most highly trained—including those who trained the Kennedys—have not been understanding the march of history, in which Castro is a minor player, though at the moment great shafts of light converge on him to give him a spectacular brilliance. When Castro arrived at Harvard he had been five long, hectic, flamboyant months in power. He had kept the firing squads working day and night. He had reduced the courts to travesty; he had postponed democratic elections until a day infinitely distant; he had long since begun to speak stridently about world affairs in the distinctive accents of Bolshevism; he had insulted our ambassador; his radio stations and newspapers were pouring out their abuse of this country and its people. Things would become worse in the next months, and the more offensive Castro became, the madder we were all instructed to get at General Trujillo. Castro would not get such a reception at Harvard today. But today is too late. Today is when President Kennedy labors over the problem of how to contain Castro. Now, having waited so long, Mr. Kennedy must deal with the doctrine promulgated by Khrushchev on September 11 which states that "the Soviet Union will consider any attempt on the part of the Western Hemisphere powers to extend their system to any portion of the Communist world as dangerous to our peace and safety"—what we have identified at *National Review* as the Monrovsky Doctrine.

No one in power seems to know exactly how to deal with Castro. But there is a much larger problem: we don't know how to deal with Harvard University. If Harvard couldn't spot Castro for what he is and show us how to cope with him, who can? And yet Harvard, so dulled are her moral and intellectual reflexes, cheered while Castro was accumulating the power to engross the full, if futile, attention of President John F. Kennedy, B.S. 1940, LL.D. 1956, even while another of her illustrious sons, Norman Mailer, B.A. 1943, was propagandizing for a Committee to Hasten the Unmolested Communization of Cuba.

Of Cuba, the right-winger concludes, it can truly be said that she was betrayed. That melodramatic word is not being used only by the founder of the John Birch Society. It is the word—"*la gran estafa*"—being used by most of Fidel Castro's former closest associates, who had thought they were struggling all those months in the Sierra Maestra for freedom, only to find that at a mysterious political level, arrangements were being made to use their hunger for freedom and reform as the engine to create a slave state. They, the earliest associates of Castro, were not really to blame. They fought bravely, and one must not fault the working soldiery for a lack of political sophistication. But there were others whose business it was to know, who did not know, and their ignorance resulted in the betrayal of those men who followed Castro blindly, only to find that they had dug a ditch out of their cell into a torture chamber.

The United States was caught by surprise? The right wing suggests there are reasons why we were caught by surprise, and that we can never be done exploring what those reasons were, and how to avoid them in the future: but all inquiries of this nature are denounced as McCarthyite. President Kennedy has told us the government was caught completely by surprise by the East Germans last August when the great wall was erected. I *believe* him—though it strikes me as strange that so massive an accumulation of brick and mortar could have escaped the notice even of our CIA. The result of our failure to anticipate that wall has been to freeze the dreams of one-half of Germany and chill the hopes of free men everywhere. In Laos we were *surprised* by the militancy of the thrust from the north and the intransigence of the insurrectionary force—whereupon we yielded, midwiving a government whose archetype we saw in Czechoslovakia just after the war; we know, but haven't learned, that coalition governments become Communist governments; that who says A must say B.

So it has gone, throughout the history of our engagement with the Communist world; and only the Right, and honorable and courageous but unrepresentative members of the Left, have had the compassion to raise their voices in sustained protest. "Never fear," our leaders sought to pacify us in 1947: "We have established a policy of containment." On the fifteenth anniversary of the policy of containment we can peer ninety miles off the Florida coast into Soviet-built muzzles. And on the other side of the world, in Laos, those who fumble trying to define the New Frontier learn that it has crept five hundred miles closer to us since Mr. Kennedy undertook to set this nation to moving again.

IT IS SAID of the American right wing that we do not trust our leaders. Nothing could be closer to the truth. Our leaders are not Communists, or pro-Communists, and are not suspected of being so, notwithstanding the gleeful publicity which has been given to the aberrations of a single conspicuous member of the right wing, who made a series of statements which I would put up alongside some of the political commentary of Herbert Matthews, Gore Vidal, and Norman Mailer, as qualifying for the most foolish political prose published during 1961. If you were a Cuban who believed in freedom, would you trust the leaders of America? Or if you lived in East Berlin? Or Laos? Or China, for that matter? Our leaders are not Communists, but they have consistently failed to grasp the elementary logic of nuclear blackmail.

Disintegration is what we conservatives see going on about us. Disintegration and acquiescence in it. History will remark that in 1945, victorious and omnipotent, the United States declined to secure for Poland the rights over which a great world war had broken out; and that a mere sixteen years later—who says B must say C—we broke into a panicked flight from the responsibilities of the Monroe Doctrine, which had been hurled by a fledgling republic in the face of the powers of the Old World one hundred forty years ago, back when America was a great nation, though not a great power. It is the general disintegration of a shared understanding of the meaning of the world and our place in it that made American liberalism possible, and American conservatism inevitable.

For the American Right is based on the assumption that however many things we don't know, there are some things we do know; on the assumption that some questions are closed, and that our survival as a nation depends on our acting bravely on the answers, without whose strength we are left speaking like Eisenhower, which is to say speaking organically unintelligibly; rhetoricizing like Kennedy, which is to say putting Madison Avenue to work making nonaction act; or writing like Mailer, which is to say writing without "beginning to know what one is, or what one wants"—the criticism of Mailer made by his friend, my enemy, Gore Vidal.

TO WIN THIS ONE, ladies and gentlemen, it will take nerve, and courage, and a certain kind of humility, the humility that makes man acknowledge the demands of duty. But it takes also a quiet and unshakable pride, the pride of knowing that with all its faults, with all its grossness, with all its appalling injustices, we live here in the West under a small ray of light, while over there is blackness, total, impenetrable. "You have to care about other people to share your perception with them," Norman Mailer has written. But nowadays, he confesses, "there are too many times when I no longer give a good goddamn for most of the human race." It is tempting to observe that nothing would better serve the good ends of the goddamn human race than to persuade Mr. Mailer to neglect us; but I shall resist the temptation, and predict instead that those liberating perceptions that Mr. Mailer has been wrestling to formulate for lo these many years are, like the purloined letter, lying about loose in the principles and premises, the organon, of the movement the Left finds it so fashionable to ridicule.

There in all that mess he will, for instance, run into the concept of duty. Why our great retreat from duty? Because our leaders are, when all is said and done, scared. "We will take Berlin," Khrushchev told an American cabinet officer a few weeks ago, "and *you* will do nothing about it." Why *won't* we do anything about it? Because we might get hurt, and so we rush to the great comforting bosom of unreality, who strokes our golden locks and tells us nothing will happen to us if only we will negotiate, keep sending lots more foreign aid to India, lots more sit-ins to Georgia, and lots more McCarthyites to Coventry.

The true meaning of the American right wing, Mr. Mailer, is commitment, a commitment on the basis of which it becomes possible to take measurements. That is true whether in respect of domestic policy or foreign policy. For those on the radical Left with Norman Mailer, and for so many Americans on the moderate Left, the true meaning of our time is the loss of an operative set of values—what one might call an expertise in living. For them, there is no ground wire, and without grounding the voltage fluctuates wildly, wantonly, chasing after the immediate line of least resistance—which, in Cuba, is *Do nothing.* For those, like Norman Mailer, who have cut themselves off from the Great Tradition, it is not truly important that Laos has been dismembered, or that a great wall has gone up through Berlin, or that Cuba has been Communized: Mailer's world is already convulsed at a much higher level, and he has no ear for such trivia as these. For he views the world as groaning under the weight of unmanageable paradoxes, so that Euclidean formulas, Christian imperatives,

Mosaic homilies become, all of them, simply irrelevant; worse, when taken seriously, they get in the way of that apocalyptic orgasm which he sees as the objective of individual experience.

How strange it is that all the Establishment's scholars, all the Establishment's men, have not in the last half dozen years written a half dozen paragraphs that probe the true meaning of the American right wing. They settle instead for frenzied, paranoid denunciations. There is no enormity too grotesque, too humorless, to win their wide-eyed faith. I have seen some of them listen respectfully to the thesis that Americans belong to the right wing out of resentment over their failure to get their sons into Groton; and I remember the rumor that swept the highest counsels of the ADA and the *Washington Post* in 1954, that Senator McCarthy was accumulating an arsenal of machine guns and rifles in the cellar of the Senate Office Building.

"Therefore they took them and beat them and besmeared them with dirt, and then put them into the cage, that they might be made a spectacle to all the men of the fair." And the charge was brought against them by the principal merchants of the City: "that they were enemies to and disturbers of their trade; that they had made commotions and divisions in the town." Thus John Bunyan wrote about the town of Vanity, and how it greeted those in the city who came to buy the truth.

"I am frankly all but ignorant of theology," Norman Mailer writes. If he wants to learn something about the true nature of the American right wing, I recommend to him the works of Presidents Matthew, Mark, Luke, and John.

WHAT COULD WE LEARN
FROM A COMMUNIST?

The Opening Statement in a Debate at the Yale Political Union;
New Haven, Conn., October 24, 1962

---

*The circumstances were unusual. The undergraduate chairman of the
Yale Political Union, David Boren (not so many years later a United
States senator), invited me to address the Union. I accepted. A few weeks
afterwards I saw a clipping which listed the Union's fall series. The next
speaker after me was to be Gus Hall, the head of the Communist Party,
U.S.A. I telephoned Boren and told him I always declined to appear in
any series that included the head of the Communist Party. I agreed to
proceed if he would agree to a debate on the topic: Resolved, That
Communists should not be invited to speak under university auspices.
Boren consulted his colleagues, and they agreed that if I carried the
house, the invitation to Hall would be rescinded. After a tumultuous
debate, the invitation was in fact rescinded.*

I AM HAPPY to be at Yale, and to speak before the Political Union,
where once I held the highest office. May I take two minutes of
your time to reminisce? A little story utterly irrelevant to tonight's
grisly proceedings, but of historical interest, perhaps, to members of
the Political Union.

Easily the most tempestuous meeting the Union presided over
during those strenuous days [in the late 1940s] was a debate between
a graduate student and an undergraduate. A few weeks before this
meeting, in the spring of 1948, Pasquale J. Vecchione, a graduate student in Far Eastern affairs, had, as moderator, looked down from the
lectern of the Yale Law School Auditorium after the applause died
down and invited those who wanted to address questions to the speakers to raise their hands. During the next half hour hands went up, but
never more than one or two at a time; and for long, embarrassing
periods, during which Vecchione virtually begged for more questions,
no hand at all. That is, except one, a hand that had gone up the

moment the question period began, and had stayed up, continuously. It had begun to look almost like a fixture of the auditorium. But even when it was the only hand held high, standing out like a lighthouse in a black night, it was ignored by Pasquale Vecchione, president of the Progressive Citizens of America and Students for Wallace for President, who on that occasion was host to three distinguished fellow travelers who had reported to the assembly on the consuming iniquities of the West.

The moderator declared the meeting adjourned, whereupon the neglected student, Brent Bozell, rose to his feet and accused Mr. Vecchione of deliberately ignoring him, of suppressing the ventilation of opposing points of view at an allegedly open meeting; indeed, of employing tactics characteristic of "the group it is my opinion the Progressive Citizens of America supports—i.e., the Communists."

A long and bitter and significant dispute developed. Defending his organization against the suggestion that it was influenced by Communists, Vecchione published a long statement in the *Yale Daily News* calculated to establish beyond peradventure that "Mr. Bozell's charges are unfounded, unfair, malicious, and the product of a line of reasoning characteristic of fascists."

Bozell, in turn, prepared a document pointing to the long record of the national directors of the PCA as apologists for Soviet Russia.

The Political Union brought the principals together, and they collided before an overflow audience in the same auditorium in which Bozell had been snubbed. Vecchione began his address by insisting that the issue before the house was not whether the Wallace movement was infiltrated by Communists—no reasonable man could believe that, he said. The issue was how could society protect itself against the likes of Brent Bozell, whom he identified as "an unabashedly egocentric, warmongering smear artist." Bozell spoke quietly, but with a near-horrible precision. He did not, he said, challenge Vecchione's loyalty; he wished merely to point out that he was aligned with a party which manifestly was following the Communist line. By the time he was through, so was Vecchione: the PCA never fully recovered at Yale. Scores of students and some faculty rallied to the defense of Vecchione, but it was too late. Suffering a bad case of diminished prestige, he gradually yielded the generalship of the Wallace movement to a fellow graduate student, Robert Crane. Imperiously and with great diligence, Crane supervised the activities of the Wallace camp. His lieutenant, in charge of the salvation of the undergraduate body, was an energetic, scholarly young man who was the president of the Labor Party of this Union. His name was James Kelly. Backing them up on the faculty were the three furies of Progressivism, Professors David Haber, Fowler Harper, and Thomas Emerson.

After the Political Union debate, the order went out, statewide, from Professor Emerson, that no member of the Progressive Citizens was to condescend even to discuss the question whether there was Communist infiltration in the Wallace movement, so obviously was that a smear. Professor Willmoore Kendall said over the radio, in a debate with a law student, that those who were preparing to vote for Henry Wallace were "in effect transferring their allegiance to the Soviet Union." And two days later he was sued by that student for $50,000. Fifty thousand dollars is a lot of money; more money, even, than Yale University subsequently paid to Professor Kendall to transfer his allegiance to some other college, any other college. The year's activities were capped with a spectacular demonstration on the New Haven Green against the emergent militarism of the West (the draft), the division of Europe into armed camps (the Marshall Plan), and America's program to abolish humanity (atom-bomb tests).

Ten years later an inconspicuous television repairman, testifying in connection with a government prosecution, said that between 1947 and 1950 he had been a member of the Communist Party, New Haven branch, which he had joined in order to forward information to the Federal Bureau of Investigation. Yes, there had been some Yale students who were members of the Communist Party during that period, he testified. Among the members he had known were James Kelly, Robert Crane, and Pasquale Vecchione. Well, you could have knocked me over with a feather.

Some of you may imagine I am insinuating that David Boren, who thought to issue the invitation to Gus Hall, is a secret member of the Communist Party. What infinitely intriguing possibilities could be built on that theme! Comrade Boren, Gus Hall's man at Yale!

Buckley Calls Invitation to Hall Communist Plot, Citing Communist Infiltration at Yale Fourteen Years Ago. At Battell Chapel next Sunday the Reverend Mr. Coffin would offer up prayers of joy more fervent than any since the days when he was driven into a trancelike state of exultation by the vision of men with bayonets in Little Rock. It is interesting—have you noticed?—how deeply disappointing it is to so many critics of the American Right when members of the Right decline, however politely, to act irresponsibly. They ask us to be reasonable and restrained, by which they mean really that we should abandon our positions and accept theirs; otherwise, they'd rather we spoke in the accents of Robert Welch. I sometimes get the feeling about Mr. Coffin that he would hear the voice of the prodigal son only if it spoke of having come back home via Albany, Georgia.

But time moves on. Saints Peter and Paul set out one day to play golf. Peter swung and hit a miserable little slice, but lo, suddenly the ball soared up and went down the fairway, two hundred fifty yards, for a hole in one. Paul stepped up, swung mightily, and missed the ball altogether. Notwithstanding, it ascended solemnly from the tee, zoomed down the course—another hole in one. Saint Peter turned to Saint Paul: "What do you say we cut out the crap and play golf?"

Last spring, Dr. John Meng addressed a letter to his faculty. Dr. Meng is the president of Hunter College, a political scientist by training, and a man well known for his liberal views. "Ladies and gentlemen," he wrote, and I quote the letter almost in its entirety, "a properly chartered student organization . . . has organized a series of . . . forums under the general title 'Out of the Mainstream.' The first two of these forums, scheduled for April 11 and May 2, are to be addressed by George Lincoln Rockwell, self-styled Commander of the American Nazi Party, and by Gus Hall, General Secretary of the Communist Party, U.S.A. Student sentiment on the . . . campus . . . with regard to the propriety of these invitations is sharply divided. Students on both sides of the controversy agree in expressing detestation for the doctrines professed by the two invited speakers. What the students are arguing about is whether they have properly assumed the responsibility which is theirs as a result of the freedom accorded them by the College. . . . Those of us who remember the Second World War, the horrors of Nazism, and the cruelties of Communism on the march tend to forget that these memories are not a part of the mental equipment of most of our present student body. Their knowledge of those events is largely knowledge transmitted by an older generation or through the medium of historical accounts. It is not surprising that many of them should evince some intellectual interest in listening to a living, avowed Nazi or to an openly dedicated Communist speaking in the American idiom.

". . . I am completely confident that neither the staff nor the students of Hunter College will permit the foul mouthings of a pipsqueak Hitler, or the delusive dialectic of a Khrushchev in knee pants, to persuade them to abandon their intellectual integrity. To accord these undistinguished visitors anything more demonstrative than a shudder of polite disgust would be to attribute to their presence a totally fictitious importance.

"Those of you," Dr. Meng concluded, "who prefer love to hate, beauty to bestiality, and freedom to bondage may join with others of us among the staff and students of the College in attending the Passover Assembly at Park Avenue at the time [the Fuehrer and the Commissar are] scheduled to speak in the Bronx."

Dr. Meng thus expressed himself, movingly, on what he understands to be the moral question involved in inviting a Nazi or a Communist to speak on a college campus: To do so, he is saying, is to put curiosity above other values, communicating a kind of callousness, an aloofness from the suffering caused by those who practice their ideologies on whole peoples all over the world. But moving though his words are, they seem not to be at the center of Dr. Meng's analysis. What Dr. Meng is saying to his faculty is this: Those who issued these invitations are undergraduates. They do not know what Nazism was and do not, apparently, know what Communism is. Therefore they deem it necessary to their intellectual experience to hear out a Nazi and a Communist, in "the American idiom." But Dr. Meng, by declining to examine more closely the unarticulated premises of this summary, yielded that point which I most earnestly cherish, and wish tonight to stress.

Dr. Meng says that the students of Hunter have not experienced Communism; more specifically, that they have not heard a defense of Communism, delivered by a Communist, in the American idiom. Conceivably, Dr. Meng himself, and many members of his faculty, have never heard a live Communist defend Communism, or a live Nazi defend Nazism: but, he implies, it is not necessary that they should have this experience in order to know what they need to know as educated and responsible members of the academic and civil communities. He did not say to the faculty: Those of you who have not heard a Communist should make it a point to attend this lecture, to fill out an otherwise incomplete educational career. He speaks on the assumption that the faculty know quite well enough what is the Communist position and how it sounds articulated in the American idiom; that, by implication, it is not the ends of education that are served by listening to a Communist who comes on campus to speak; but rather—but rather what?

What is served, other than extrinsic points—an affirmation of the students' administrative right to invite whomsoever they please to address them? But Dr. Meng does not challenge that right. No more have the authorities of Yale University: it was never in question. What then? What does one come to know, that one did not know before, on listening to an American Communist speak?

Nothing, presumably, if one is qualified to participate in a political union, concerning either Marxist analysis or Communist rhetoric. It is inconceivable, Dr. Meng would presumably say, that a thirty-minute address by an official of the Communist Party would add to an understanding of the theory or nature or strategy of the Communist Party. Every official of the Communist Party ruthlessly observes the discipline of his calling; over four decades, when has it *ever* been reported that a Communist official, addressing a college gathering or any other non-Communist gathering, said something unexpected? When last did an official of the Party speaking to a college audience let himself improvise, speak ad libitum, vouchsafing us, for even one instant, a sunburst, illuminating the dark mysteries of the Communist pathology? Communists do, sometimes, speak their minds, but never to bourgeois gatherings: here they are on duty, fighting men on the march; they come to recapitulate their dogmas, to press their drive to co-opt the moral slogans of the West, to seek legitimization, and to practice the science of confusion. Not that they succeed in confusing. They do not confuse the proletariat, for heaven's sake, in whose name their slogans are forged; they are hardly likely to confuse an audience of college students: they are not likely, in Dr. Meng's phrase, to "persuade [the students] to abandon their intellectual integrity."

Might they, then, these Communist speakers, contribute as much factual, or even human, knowledge about the current Communist program as a single copy of the *Daily Worker?* Less, by far, one would think, considering that the average issue of the *Worker,* which takes no more than thirty minutes to read, covers a wide range of issues, giving the Communist view of the day on everything from Cuba to Ross Barnett to the New York Giants.

Is this enough of an argument, one might ask? That an individual's views are well known, and that it is known that he adheres to them rigidly? No, that argument is not sufficient. If it alone were relevant it might be used by the protectionists among you to shield the Political Union from, say, a typical spokesman for the Democratic or the Republican Party.

The argument broadens here in many directions, and one needs to draw breath deeply, for to go from here to there we must tread on highly delicate ground, must step right over one of the most highly cherished dogmas of the modern age, namely, the notion that all ideas are created equal. Even so, the reason why a Democratic bore might be acceptable while a Communist bore would not is not emotional, but intellectual. Fiercely though the archetypal Democrat or Republican will resist the opportunity to respond to the challenge of public debate as a human being rather than as an automaton, there is in his heart and mind, calcified though they may have become out of long and unthinking and unquestioning service to his party, a disposition to think of himself as a member of our community, possessed of a point of view which is held by the community at large to be, within the widest limits of toleration, reasonable. Some views are unreasonable and tolerable. Some views are unreasonable and intolerable, especially insofar as they are systemic rather than merely personal. The Democrat and the Republican will regularly exaggerate in behalf of their causes; sometimes they will consciously lie; they will feign concern where none is felt; they will decry the manners and morals of the opposition, knowing well that those are indistinguishable from their own manners and morals: but they remain, flesh and blood and heart, a part of America.

The Communist has of course renounced our institutions, which is perhaps all right, but he has done something very much more: he has renounced the bond—and fragile though it is, it is there, make no mistake about it—that holds together Republicans and Democrats, socialists and Manchesterians, syndicalists and elitists, pacifists and warmongers, civil libertarians and McCarthyites, Townsendites and Coughlinites, Southerners, Westerners, Easterners, Northerners. The Communist has renounced the bond explicitly and intentionally—renunciation in the first degree—and for the duration of that renunciation he cannot speak to us and we cannot speak to him, because however deep we reach, we cannot find a common vocabulary: we can no more collaborate with him to further the common understanding than Anne Frank could have collaborated with Goebbels in a dialogue on race relations. Until that trance is broken, formal communication is impossible, for the Communist speaks to us in a language whose utter unrelation to reality rules out any possibility of meaningful discourse. There is no idiom available to us for simultaneous usage. Certainly the American idiom will not do. We all abuse the instruments of discourse, but we seek, under the massive superstructure of point and counterpoint, to say things to each other that come truly out of our minds and our hearts, because we feel that in deeply significant ways we are related by that highly elastic, but not infinitely elastic, bond.

Such a man, then, whose explicit message we know beforehand, which message he must deliver undeviatingly, cannot communicate to us orally anything of political interest, the subject with which the Political Union properly concerns itself. He is a fit object of curiosity for students of certain other subjects than politics. A Communist might with good reason be called upon to address serious students of sociology, seeking some accidental insight into the social causes that might have led a man to ideological mania; or to serious students of psychology, who seek to examine the reflexes of a man who, for the sake of his Truth, will utter and defend every necessary untruth. The courtroom in Jerusalem was crowded with professors of the specialized social sciences: but they were not men who would have invited Adolf Eichmann to their college to defend the regime of Adolf Hitler.

The Communists are of concern to nonspecialists, I am trying to say, primarily as human beings suffering from the most exotic and the most mortal illness of our time, the mania of ideology, which in one of its excrescences in our time, while you were living, blithely stoked the ovens of Germany with Jewish flesh; which, without the hesitation a normal man feels about running over a dog, committed millions to death by starvation in the very breadbasket of the Soviet Empire; which, as we speak here tonight, commits dozens of millions of people to death in pursuit of a lunatic delusion in China. The servants of these ideologies are dislodged from the human situation and yet—

And yet they are human beings themselves, for no one has the power formally to renounce his membership in the human race. And it is over their plight *as human beings* that we must, it strikes me, pause; for that is the problem supremely that you face, above all others; certainly above the political problem, it being conceded that you are immune to seductive passes at your intellectual and moral integrity and that the words, the wooden words, are words you knew before. The problem is human. What will you do when Gus Hall, the human being, comes here to defend the cause that you know ahead of time to be the cause of organized inhumanity? Will you give that "shudder of polite disgust" recommended by Dr. Meng? How does one give shudders of polite disgust? Is this a new social skill we need in fact to cultivate in our time? A part of the social equipment conferred upon us in virtue of our great good fortune as recipients of a Hunter or Yale education? Or will you applaud him when he is introduced? Yes, there will be applause—in recognition of his courage in facing a hostile audience. But the applause will be confused, will it not? Because you know that objective courage is not necessarily admirable: the man who threw acid in the face of Victor Riesel in the middle of Times Square was courageous, as was Khrushchev when he ordered the tanks to run over your courageous counterparts in Budapest. Is it not likely that among those of you who applaud there will be those who are in fact applauding their own courage in applauding a real live apologist for human atrocity? But the applause, no matter how frenetic it sounds, is likely to be of that special metallic quality which issues out of the ambiguity in your unpossessed souls. Some of you may feel the obligation to externalize your knowledge that Gus Hall is here to defend the indefensible. You may jeer him, as he has been jeered by those who wrestle for their livelihood with their hands, who especially despise him because he claims to speak for them; some of you may treat him with that terrible coldness that is the sign of the intellectual foreknowledge that you cannot, at your level of attainment, take seriously the man who speaks and works for a kingdom which it is the very purpose of your education to teach you to despise. Why then bring him here, if no purpose can be served, and if it can only result that you will humiliate yourselves, and him. Fight him, fight the tyrants everywhere; but do not ask them to your quarters, merely to spit upon them: and do not ask them to your quarters if you cannot spit upon them. To do the one is to ambush a human being as one might a rabid dog; to do the other is to ambush oneself, to force oneself—in disregard of those who have *died* trying to make the point—to break faith with humanity.

WHO DID GET US INTO THIS MESS?

The Opening Statement in a Debate with Murray Kempton on the Topic
"Who Got Us into This Mess?"; the University of Pennsylvania, Philadelphia,
April 16, 1963

---

*Murray Kempton was a poet-journalist, and it was he who suggested the
topic for this debate. The first paragraph of my opening statement
is a nice example of topical badinage. The key: (1) Professor Arthur
Schlesinger Jr. and I debate in Boston. (2) In high sarcasm he tells the
student audience, "Mr. Buckley has a facility for rhetoric which I envy,
as well as a wit which I seek clumsily and vainly to emulate." (3) A collection of my work is published in the fall, and I print as a blurb these
words from Schlesinger, as if they were solemnly intended. (4) He hires
the massive firm of Greenbaum, Wolff & Ernst to sue me and the publisher unless I agree to remove the tribute intended as caricature. (5) I
decline to do so, and the tribute lives on in all editions of the book,*
Rumbles Left and Right. *Kempton and I were close friends, and he dedicated his last book to me.*

I T IS A pleasure to meet with Murray Kempton. He has a facility
for rhetoric which I envy, as well as a wit which I seek clumsily
and vainly to emulate. He can quote me. I shall not sue. Mr.
Kempton would probably construe my decision not to sue him as an
anti-social refusal to redistribute my wealth among Messrs. Greenbaum, Wolff, and Ernst. For Mr. Kempton is nothing if not complicated. Indeed, his views are so complicated that sometimes, as you
may have observed, they are sound.

That can get him into trouble. On one occasion we appeared
together on a television program. By concerted effort we managed to
interrupt Mr. David Susskind just long enough to make our simple
points, which happened to converge—on what subject I am not
absolutely sure now; whether it was our common admiration for
William Butler Yeats, or for Westbrook Pegler. There was, in any case,
a quite general dismay, upon which Mr. Susskind, reaching for a word

adequate to express his consternation, remarked that what he had just heard was "gallimaufry."

Did you know that Murray Kempton has a mean streak? Because he thereupon said, right to Mr. Susskind's face, and before the billion-odd people who were listening, "What does 'gallimaufry' mean, Mr. Susskind?" Now Kempton knew exactly what the word meant—he knows what all the words mean, and how to use them, even if he doesn't know for what purposes to use them, which is the root cause of his Johnsonian melancholy—but for an instant Mr. Susskind's face was frozen in horror. And who should come gallantly to his rescue? The Department of Health, Education, and Welfare? The Peace Corps? No, a conservative—yours truly; whose job it is, some of you may have noticed, to mediate the harsh effects of liberal behavior whenever it manifests itself. Where was I? That was a rhetorical question. I know exactly where I was: I was saying that I have the honor of sharing some of Mr. Kempton's opinions, and that he runs the risk of sharing some of mine, and I go on to say that there is nothing, I hope, that the polarizing tug of our public quarrels will do to cause him to relinquish certain of his opinions merely in order to disagree with me, and vice versa.

Well, who *did* get us into this mess? The contest appears to be close, in intellectual circles, between the reactionaries, who hold Adam and Eve responsible, and the progressives, who blame the John Birch Society. The only thing the liberals appear *absolutely* certain of is that *they* did not get us into this mess.

But then of course we need to ask the prior question: How do you define a mess? Albert Jay Nock once thought it would be amusing to write an essay on how to go about discovering that you are living in a Dark Age. But that is the kind of question that invites the still prior question: How do you define *anything*? And that, of course, is the point at which liberals and conservatives frequently separate, the former, using the terminology of the academy, tending towards epistemological pessimism, the latter towards epistemological optimism.

What is a mess? Not Jackson Pollock. Not Kandinsky. Not William Burroughs. That, after all, as Malraux has told us, is how our painters paint and our writers write; and by what other standards can we judge them?

The pitch of human life, that surely is a mess. Or is it? Is it really so that the materialist criterion governs? How many of you arrived here hungry tonight? Or are we to assume that what messes exist, do so outside of the University of Pennsylvania? Malcolm Muggeridge says that culture is those few moments when we, who are essentially pigs, lift our heads from the trough and look about. Really? By that standard Marx, whose mouth was seldom at the trough but whose mind never left it, was a cultured man. Was he a mess, who dreamed of mess making on a cosmic scale?

Can we agree that Castro's Cuba is a mess? Oh no we can't. Richard Rovere of *The New Yorker*—whose role as chief messologist for the Establishment has led him for years to identify as messes any ambiguous phenomena that emerge on the starboard horizon, and to see absolutely nothing at all over on the port side, not even if it is a hurricane blazing in—Richard Rovere reported recently that in fact it is a considerable blessing that Castro occupies the island of Cuba, that things are much better for us and for anti-Communism in Latin America on account of the closeness of a Communist-dominated state than they were when the nearest Communist state was four thousand abstract miles away. By an extension of that thinking we'd be better off still if, say, Ohio went Communist.

The Law of the Left appears to be: If there is a mess, the Right created it. The Right does not blame everything on the Left, believing as we do that all human beings are to a dangerous degree mess-inclined, and that any plans for us made by human beings with super-duper ideas had better take this fact into consideration, as also this other fact, that their idea of what is super-duper may not appeal to me at all, and that I count, ex officio, as a human being. So that paradoxically the conservatives see man, because of his penchant for mess making, as the conclusive argument against utopian social craftsmanship; and we see the very same man, because of his innate worth, as the principal argument against victimization by grandiose social manipulations. It makes no difference that, in a democracy, a

man visits these schemes upon himself; they are no less noxiou[s]
their popularity. It is all we can hope for that a few people, i[n]
age, can truly be thought of as housebroken, i.e., non–mess ma[
the majority of us—Plato's "many," Jefferson's "herd," Or[
"masses"—are properly the object of the best and most urgen[t]
cern of the spiritual and intellectual aristocrats: but these last [
not, at the risk of losing their station, invite us, by sycophantic
advances upon the majority, to prescribe false standards, depose reality and crown surreality, and debauch the moral patrimony. We must
all cooperate in the maintenance of standards. The messes, to return
to the original question, cannot be located, let alone removed, if we
cannot distinguish, to begin with, between a daffodil and a dung heap.
And our failure to perceive the difference ("If you had to, if somebody said you've got to live in America or live in Russia for the rest of
your days," asked the interrogator of C. P. Snow, "which would you
choose?" "Well," answered Sir Charles, "that is very difficult; I think
to be honest I could be very happy in either of them")—our failure to
perceive the difference is the best index of the mess we are in.

LET ME SUGGEST who got us into this mess by a drastically simplified account of a few of those things that this conservative, at any rate,
cares deeply about, so that we can then ask, How are we faring?

I care deeply about religion. There are obvious shortcomings in
the exasperated disjunction of Charles Péguy. But I quote his statement not to emphasize its transparent failings, but to acknowledge its
suggestive vitality. He said, "There is as much difference between a
Christian and a pagan as there is between a pagan and a dog." Now
there are, by Péguy's standards, probably fewer Christians in America
than there are entries in the *Social Register,* and any correspondence
between the two is purely coincidental. But our age strains to cut the
cord altogether—in our public philosophy (it was eighty years ago
that Nietzsche announced the death of God, but the celebrations
continue riotous to this day); in our educational institutions (witness
the longknifemanship in the academic world directed against the

believer); in our jurisprudence (the First Amendment, conjoined with our system of public education, has become an instrument of secularism); and even in our theology (early this month the Bishop of Woolwich vouchsafed to his flock the news that they need not, in order to be Christians, believe in any kind of God).

I care for the freedom of the individual. We live in a straitened world and so must accept dutifully the impositions of technology, the demands of order in an increasingly interdependent society, the necessity for continence in those situations where individual agitations can lead to decisions that affect not merely the agitators but many others; yet I say that the question that precedes any consideration of any piece of legislation ought still to be, Will this measure augment or diminish the individual's freedom? And up against this criterion most of our coercive legislative measures would fail, as would clearly, e.g., the immunities conferred upon our monopoly labor unions; as would the farm subsidies and the protective tariffs; as would such measures as in recent days have authorized the federal government to collect taxes to pay 60 percent of the cost of a bridge vaulting the richest business district in America, in Hartford, Connecticut, and to study the problem of juvenile delinquency in New York City.

And yet I care not merely that men should be left free to make their own decisions, but also that we should have every opportunity to learn to make them wisely, and to cultivate the desire to make them wisely; and so I care deeply about the corruption of words and ideals, by which, for instance, we deceive ourselves into believing that freedom consists in closed shops, in coercive Social Security, in FTCs and ICCs, FPCs and NLRBs. I care about the efforts of those ideologues who feed and then live off the economic illiteracy of the people by promulgating the myth of the spontaneously generating dollar in Washington, D.C.; whose programs call for every man's shouldering of others' concerns but never his own; who are always shooting down the U-2 planes we conservatives seek stealthily to launch, which might from great heights observe, and relay to the people, the crazy traffic in crisscrossing dollars that is blackening the skies.

I care about the strategic imbecility (I use the phrase of Adolf Berle) and the moral imbecility (I use the phrase of Peter Viereck) of those who failed to recognize the nature of the Communist thrust, and who therefore proved incompetent to contain it before it had ravaged what is sometimes spoken of casually as a billion or so people, which I ask that we think of not in the macrocosmic terms that are fashionable among the mess makers, the only food their IBM machines will tolerate, but in individual terms, you, me, him, her, and say it again, until you count to one billion.

I care about the loss of the intellectual and moral apparatus by which purposive communication is possible. Murray Kempton is a good man, better I am sure than most who oppose him, certainly including myself; but for all his knowledge and for all his wit, he does not know, appears not to be capable of knowing, what is the nature, let alone the dimensions, of the threat; so that he can continue to worry more about the House Committee on Un-American Activities than about the Soviet Union; to consider himself a partisan of freedom while enrolling as a member of the Socialist Party; to pitch for the common man while celebrating the outrages of monopoly labor unions; to address a gathering of Communists as "brothers" as though he were Francis of Assisi—which he comes close to being, come to think of it, but not close enough to call Communists his brothers under klieg lights. St. Francis could hardly have talked to the birds while serving as an editor of the *New Republic.*

I say to the would-be mess removers: (1) fear the Lord and love Him, and laugh gently in the faces of those who disdain Him; (2) resist kindly, but no less firmly, the ministrations of those who would reach into your very shower to adjust the temperature of the water according to their most recent afflatus; (3) reinstruct men, in the maxim of William Osler, that their freedom ends where the freedom of others begins; (4) study the ways of the enemy and learn to outwit him; and (5) read Murray Kempton, but don't relax. And (6), in moments of despair, read Murray Kempton, who, at least, will usher you sweetly into the Dark Age, and numb your great pain.

THE IMPENDING DEFEAT OF
BARRY GOLDWATER

An Address to the Young Americans for Freedom's National Convention;
New York, September 11, 1964

This was the fourth anniversary of the Young Americans for Freedom, founded in 1960 at Sharon, Connecticut, at the home of my father and mother. It was the first of an encouraging new wave of conservative organizations—which by 1964 included the New York Conservative Party and the Philadelphia Society—that rose to join the libertarian Intercollegiate Society of Individualists (see my speech on November 29, 1988) and Foundation for Economic Education (April 11, 1996).

YAF grew rapidly and was substantially responsible for organized support for the nomination and then the candidacy of Senator Barry Goldwater. The fourth meeting of the national council was held off the record, at my request. I intended to predict that Goldwater would lose the election and to attempt words that would keep fired up the spirit of disillusioned young people.

O NCE AGAIN YOU have done me the honor of inviting me to address you. I am greatly flattered by this attention. I sometimes feel like the old movie that stands by for service at one in the morning, in the event that nothing more alluring comes along. But I am glad that some of you are so kind as to sit still for a rerun of Captain Blood, who, it is said, was quite a blade in his day, back in the dimly remembered 1940s, when, at Yale, God and man were locked in mortal conflict, and the script required, as is the mood in modern drama, a surprise ending.

A great many of you have done me, and the beloved journal I serve, a great many public and private favors, and I take the opportunity to thank you kindly, in behalf of myself and my colleagues. You may think that the hauteur of our editorial tone suggests a total independence of spirit, a total aloofness from any need for human and compassionate sustenance. *That is a front.* We need you every bit as urgently as you need us. We have no other function than to help you, and no greater necessity than to be helped by you. If we fail you, we fail ourselves, and any infidelity to the cause we hope to serve—and no doubt we commit those infidelities frequently—is a cause for mortification. I do not know of any purpose for *National Review* if it is not to serve as a lightning rod for the best thought, and the best expression of that thought, by which to pierce the surrounding gloom and remind ourselves of the necessity to hurl back what I called a year ago, at your meeting in Fort Lauderdale, the effronteries of the twentieth century. We do not believe in platonic affirmations of our own little purities. Our intention is to take the clay God gave us and mold it into a better world. If we do not help to fire your imagination or your zeal, we might just as well retire into the night, and bury that fingernail of a saint that Whittaker Chambers said might yet be the only recourse for sensitive men, "against the day, ages hence, when a few men begin again to dare to believe that there was once something else, that something else is thinkable, and need some evidence of what it was, and the fortifying knowledge that there were those who, at the great nightfall, took loving thought to preserve the tokens of hope and truth."

My debt is to you in general, but in particular to your chairman, Robert Bauman, for his incessant courtesies and for his manly and courageous leadership of this organization, which has seen dark days, most of them the making of our insensate society, which so hotly resists the nurturing of any tokens of hope and truth; some of them the making of our own flawed natures, which are so greatly attracted to our petty vanities as to interrupt grievously the progress we need to make in order to stay alive, and to prosper, and to justify ourselves.

I wish to speak on two subjects. The first has to do with the role of the conservative movement at this juncture in American history, when, to no one's surprise more than our own, we labor under the visitation of a freedom-minded candidate for the presidency of the United States. I say labor, because the nomination of Barry Goldwater, when we permit ourselves to peek up over the euphoria,

reminds us chillingly of the great work that has remained undone. A
great rainfall has deluged a thirsty earth, but before we had time
properly to prepare the ground.

I speak of course about the impending defeat of Barry Goldwater.

That it impends is an objective judgment. That it will happen is
of course not certain: it was not after all certain that the French would
defeat King Harry at Agincourt, though defeat most certainly im-
pended. I shall not attempt to fire you on to superhuman endeavor,
for three reasons, the first being that any charge by me to go forward
and fight would be tautological; the second, that I am not William
Shakespeare; the third, that I view this as an intimate occasion, a conversation among those who are determined to live to storm the gates
of Agincourt another day, in the likely event that this time we do not
succeed.

My words are not intended for public currency. They are intended for your ears, and for my own edification. The beginning of
wisdom is the fear of the Lord. The next and most urgent counsel is
to take stock of reality. Reality, during a political campaign, sometimes suggests the advisability of dismissing strategic considerations
in favor of tactical imperatives, which call for cultivating, in the
Goldwater camp, the morale of an army on the march. Our morale is
high, and we are marching. But the morale of the army on the march
is that of an army that has been promised victory. It is wrong to
assume that we shall overcome; and therefore it is right to reason to
the necessity of guarding against the utter disarray that sometimes
follows a stunning defeat. It is right to take thought, even on the eve
of the engagement, about the potential need for regrouping, for gathering together our scattered forces. After all, we take it as established
that even after November 3, although you will have aged you will still
be young; and although you will have been discouraged you will still,
God willing, desire to pursue freedom; and by your persistence you
will prove, as King Harry sought to do, that if it be a sin to covet
honor, you are the most offending souls alive.

I have on a few public occasions ventured to predict that Senator
Goldwater will most likely lose, and I have been dismayed by the
growls of resentment at the utterance of this political truism. The

election of Barry Goldwater would presuppose a sea change in American public opinion; presuppose that the fiery little body of dissenters of which you are a shining meteor suddenly spun off nothing less than a majority of the American people, who suddenly overcame a generation's entrenched lassitude and, prisoners all those years, succeeded in passing blithely through the walls of Alcatraz and tripping lightly over the shark-infested waters and treacherous currents, to safety on the shore.

The Goldwater movement is in the nature of an attempted prison break. It is supremely urgent that the effort be made, gloriously encouraging that we are mobilized to make it: but direfully perilous to proceed on the assumption that we will succeed or to reason that if we do not, the attempt to reach safety cannot ever succeed. To those who remark the danger of demoralization by talk about an impending defeat, it is necessary to remark the danger of demoralization after November 3. I fear that the morale of an army on the march is the morale that is most easily destroyed in the event of unanticipated defeat. I do believe that Senator Goldwater would be the first to deplore the rise of any spirit of synthetic optimism which might result in a national demoralization of the conservative movement the day after the campaign ends.

The glorious development of this year was the nomination of a man whose views have given the waiting community a choice. The opportunity is golden to take the advantage we have got. It is an advantage that has been given us primarily as the result of the gallant efforts of Senator Goldwater. His disposition to sacrifice his career [by giving up his Senate seat] in order to give us these few months to take our point to the people from a national platform is an act of political nobility. The successful fight to nominate Senator Goldwater has required the opinion makers to consider more seriously, if no less scornfully, the substantive alternatives that a freedom candidate offers, and has required the American people to think through the conservative alternative.

Now is precisely the moment to labor incessantly to educate our fellow citizens. The point is to win recruits whose attention we might never have attracted but for Barry Goldwater; to win them not only for November 3 but for future Novembers: to infuse the conservative spirit in enough people to entitle us to look about, on November 4, not at the ashes of defeat but at the well-planted seeds of hope, which will flower on a great November day in the future, if there is a future.

If God should grant us a victory at this moment there is time enough to count our unexpected blessings and to exult greatly. But we dishonor the Goldwater movement if we permit ourselves to speak to those recruits we gather as though the walls of Agincourt were hollow eggshells which will come crumbling down under the pressure of our heroic rhetoric. We have in mind, do we not?, a counterrevolution. Counterrevolutions are not accomplished by defeating Nelson Rockefeller or William Scranton. The enemy is made of sterner stuff. So are we, and we must prove it by showing not a moment's dismay on November 4 in the likely event that the walls have stood firm against our assault. On that day we must emerge smiling, confident in the knowledge that we weakened those walls, that they will never again stand so firmly against us.

On that day we must be prepared to inform Lyndon Johnson that we too will continue.

A GROWING SPIRIT OF RESISTANCE

An Address (excerpted) to the New York Conservative Party's Second Anniversary Dinner; New York, October 26, 1964

The Conservative Party of New York was founded in 1962 in protest against a state GOP governed by Nelson Rockefeller, who had oriented the party in a liberal direction. The Conservative Party made a decent showing in its first two years; it steadily grew in importance and remains a swing element in tight New York political races. This speech attempted to say that great movements were under way that challenged many liberal assumptions and gave heart to conservatives. I slightly changed the talk a few months later and gave it to the senior class at Yale, greatly dis-

tressing my friend the Reverend William Sloane Coffin Jr., a leading liberal figure on campus and nationally.

I N THINKING ABOUT the election, I suggest only that we bear always in mind that a conservative is concerned simultaneously with two things, the first being the shape of the visionary or paradigmatic society towards which we should labor; the second, the speed with which it is advisable to advance towards that ideal society, in the foreknowledge that any advance upon it is necessarily asymptotic: that is, that we cannot hope for ideological home runs and definitive victories; not, at least, until the successful completion of the work of the Society for the Abolition of Original Sin.

How Mr. Goldwater, considering the contrary tug of history, has got as far as he has got is something that surpasses the understanding of natural pessimists like me. Even so, I detect myself yielding, from time to time, to the temptation to overstress the ideal, and precisely at the moment when the prudential should weigh more heavily. Let those of us who feel the temptation to express conclusive exasperation over any thought, word, or deed of Senator Goldwater's reflect on the exasperation we have felt with the occasional thought, word, or deed of pure old incorruptible us—the editors of *National Review*, the officers of the Conservative Party, you and your friends—and let us judge him at least as kindly as we would want ourselves to be judged. . . .

Enough on that point; I wish to look tonight at some of the impersonal causes that made possible the rise of Senator Goldwater's candidacy.

I was recently in Europe, where the phenomenon of the rise of conservative thought in America is only more baffling than it is here. Remember that it is generally believed in Europe that the principal contribution America can make to Western thought is not to think at all. I grant the generality that the world would probably be better off, not worse, if a lot of people who are currently hard at work thinking desisted from doing so and spent their time, instead, cultivating the elevated thought of others. Not long ago an editor of *National Review* remarked, on hearing the news that $600,000 had been allocated to bring together in seclusion for one year at Santa Barbara a dozen top American philosophers just to think about thinking, that the expenditure of $50,000 apiece towards the withdrawal of the average modern philosopher from public life was a price America could ill afford not to pay.

But the fashionable view in Europe about American intellectual activity is, I should say, oversimplified. It is generally thought there that America, in the modern era, has taken the place of Rome in the ancient era: that it is we who have successfully organized the resources of nature in order to guard the peace, and who have produced the greatest share of the world's material goods, in order that others should indicate how best they might be enjoyed in usufruct. But unlike ancient Rome, it is said sadly—truthfully—America has not acquired the mien, let alone the habit, of great power. We have not even acquired *gravitas*. Nor has America shown a proper veneration for the values of the Old World, to compare with the Romans' humility before the civilization of Greece. America, it is generally agreed, can contribute to Western thought only the physical shelter under which Westerners can continue their dialogues; but even then—hark the dissent—it is altogether possible (altogether likely, in the opinion of some; altogether predictable, if we are to listen to such as Bertrand Russell) that in an excess of zeal, out of the fatuous idealism which distinguishes our exuberant moralism, we will end up by triggering a conclusive holocaust, which would forever interrupt that purposive intercourse among the blither spirits of the West, the continuing hope of an upwardly mobile mankind, the dialogue between C. P. Snow and Yevgeny Yevtushenko.

The existence of the American conservative movement, and the causes that spawned it, is a phenomenon of which European intellectuals are in a state of innocence. They do not know that there really is growing in America a spirit of resistance to the twentieth century: for this is indeed what it is.

You will note that I am implicated in an uneasy figure of speech. It is hardly possible to "resist" the twentieth century, any more than it is possible to "resist" gravity, or death. But the figure is useless only insofar as it invokes a mechanistic view of history, which presupposes that it is the inescapable destiny of the twentieth century to codify certain trends, social and philosophical, economic and organizational, trends which are irresistible even as the passage of time is irresistible.

It is a common way of dismissing someone whose views are out of fashion, as you and I know, to say that he "resists the twentieth century." There are any number of lively polemical variations on the theme. Senator Goldwater, it has tirelessly been said, entered the twentieth century kicking and screaming. Russell Kirk, it has been said one thousand times—mostly by those who are unfamiliar with the Middle Ages—"has a brilliant fourteenth-century mind"; and so on.

The friction arises, of course, when two essentially different attitudes towards history are rubbed together. We of the Right do not doubt that the vectors of social thought and action nowadays point to monolithic government and the atomization of norms. And it is certainly true that most of the intellectuals in America seem disposed to submit to the apparent imperatives of the twentieth century. Apocalypse is in the air; and the cost of hitchhiking along with the century, in Europe, in Asia, in America, is tacitly acknowledged to be the surrender of the self. The older intellectuals in America in particular grew into a world which seemed to be headed inescapably towards social self-destruction; and then, when the Bomb came, towards physical self-destruction. Ten years ago Whittaker Chambers drew my attention to a note in the journal of the Goncourt brothers, one of whom had been taken by Madame Curie to see radium, in the laboratory in which she had discovered it. "On being shown radium this morning," he wrote, "I thought I heard the voice of God, ringing out as clearly as the doorkeeper's at the Louvre at five o'clock every weekday afternoon, and uttering the same solemn words, 'Closing time, gentlemen!'"

Indeed, no one of those who would resist the twentieth century would be so foolish as to say that it is the ideal arena in which to make the struggle. "If you wish to lead a quiet life," Trotsky once said, "you picked the wrong century to be born in." "And indeed," Chambers commented, "the point was finally proved, when a pickaxe mauled the brain of the man who framed those words."

So it is not an escapist's ignorance of the distinctive darkness of this century's shadows that makes possible the spirit of modern conservatives. The spirit of defiance doesn't issue from a romantic American ignorance of the gloomy composure of the times we live in; but it does, I think, issue in part from distinctively American patterns of thought, from the essence of the American spirit.

The European observer is entitled to believe, on the basis of the evidence which marches out of the submissive ghettoes of many American universities, that all America has come to terms with the twentieth century of the determinists; yet I suggest that his eyes are not properly focused.

In America there are those who are *dragging our feet*; resisting, kicking, complaining, hugging tightly to the ancient moorings.

What do we cling to? Among other things, the individual, and the individual's role in history. We hope for the individual to survive the twentieth century. We bank our faith on the individual's resources, guided by eternal lights; and we venture to predict that, in Conrad's words, America will spit back at the gale, giving it howl for howl, and in the end will assert our mastery over the seething elements.

These are heroic words, mere rodomontade, many will think, but consider the facts.

(1) It is essentially the modernist view that only the state can negotiate the shocks that lie ahead of twentieth-century man. Yet even though the statists have lulled the general public into accepting the state as a genial servant, the state has not been truly integrated as a member of the American household. The majority of Americans are still reluctant to accept the state as a sacramental agent for transubstantiating private interest into public good.

Have you reflected on the course of postwar American history?

- The call for the nationalization of basic industries, so insistent in the immediate postwar years, has been stilled; droning away only in the fever swamps of the dogmatic Left.

- With all his power, with all his popularity, with all his prestige, the last president of the United States failed in his efforts to ease over to the federal government the primary responsibility for education, or health, or even housing; and his successor tacitly acknowledges similar difficulties.

Through inertia we might indeed end up, as Tocqueville predicted we would, as minions of an omnipotent government; but it may yet be seen that the resistance by the American minority is more remarkable than the acquiescence by the American majority.

(2) Probably no country in the history of the world was ever so devoutly secularist as our own in its practical affairs; and yet the spiritual side of life, which the twentieth century is here to anachronize, is an unshakable part of us. The worst failure in America is the man who aspires to true cynicism. Let the lushest bloom of the twentieth century stand before a typical nonacademic American audience and declare his fidelity to materialism, and the audience will divide between those in whom he has aroused pity, and those in whom he has aroused contempt. It is as fashionable in America as in Europe to declare that truth is not knowable, that the freedom of inquiry is the nearest we can hope to come to the truth; and yet, although the American people tolerate and even support universities dedicated in effect to the proposition that no truth is knowable, still, the majority of the universities' supporters organize their lives with reference to certitudes, certitudes which for reasons sometimes of humility, sometimes of laziness, sometimes of awe, they decline to identify; but that these certitudes are there, they do not seem to doubt; and this—the faith of our fathers, it is sometimes called—gives the distinctive cast to our, to be sure equivocal, foreign policy. The utter failure of the collaborators in our midst to engage the public in a trauma of self-doubt over the issue of Red or Dead finally suggests the incorrigible resistance of the American people to the twentieth century.

And finally (3) what most interests me, and perhaps some of you. There is in America a renaissance of thought, a grinding of wheels, an ongoing commotion. What is coming, I think, is the intellectualization of the spirit I speak of. Modern formulations are necessary even in defense of very ancient truths. Not because of any alleged anachronism in the old ideas—the Beatitudes remain the essential statement of the Western code—but because the idiom of life is always changing, and we need to say things in such a way as to get inside the vibrations of modern life.

For years Americans seemed woefully incapable of speaking for themselves. The great apostles of the twentieth century are not American. With perhaps the exception of Oliver Wendell Holmes and John Dewey, no matter how hard they practice in the American idiom, our own intellectuals speak in European accents. Adlai Stevenson is, for reasons perfectly clear to me, a greater hero in England than in America. So are John Kenneth Galbraith and David Riesman. So—dare I say it?—is Franklin Delano Roosevelt, notwithstanding the genius with which he seemed to be fashioning indigenous American ideals, though all the time he used alien clay. In the past ten years in America—can you appreciate the great excitement of it all?—a new class of intellectuals has risen and stormed the ramparts of the academy, with ideas, elaborations, insights, the sum of which challenge, root and branch, the presumptions of the twentieth century. American scholarship has recently recaptured Edmund Burke, has shown that his great voice was tied to eternal ideals, that he spoke from a belief in the natural law. The seemingly invulnerable John Maynard Keynes has been exposed as an economic poet, not a scientist, who left more questions unanswered than answered. The intuitive wisdom of the founders of the American Republic, and of the European giants from whom they learned the art of statecraft, has been rediscovered. The shallowness of the nineteenth-century social abstractionists has been penetrated, and their followers are thrown on the defensive. The meaning of the West is being exhumed; impulses that never ceased to beat in the American heart are being revitalized.

Will, then, America save itself and then save Europe? Or will the European revival overtake our own? I care not who saves whom, caring only that we be saved from that dreadful century whose name stands for universal ignominy in the name of equality and, in the name of freedom, a drab servitude to anonymous institutional idealisms. I hope and pray that as time goes by, the twentieth century will shed the odium that clings to its name, that it may crystallize as the century in which the individual overtook technology, the century in which all the mechanical ingenuity of man, even when fired by man's basest political lusts, proved insufficient to sunder man's relation to, and dependence on, his Maker. The movement is of you, as American conservatives, by you, and in you. In wishing you luck, I am wishing for myself, and my family, and my country, good fortune, peace, and freedom.

THE FREE SOCIETY—WHAT'S THAT?

Remarks on Henry Hazlitt's Seventieth Birthday; New York, November 29, 1964

The emphasis at the celebratory dinner was on Henry Hazlitt's accomplishments as an economist, and the speakers included Ludwig von Mises, Milton Friedman, and Larry Fertig. Hazlitt had also had a lively career as a journalist, which included a fortnightly essay in Newsweek *magazine. We wished him a long life, and providence obliged. I spoke again at his seventy-fifth birthday and at his eightieth and eighty-fifth.*

O N THIS HAPPY occasion I join with you in saluting an old friend and mentor, Mr. Henry Hazlitt, and his incomparable and gifted wife, Frances. I was greatly frightened when our host, Mr. Larry Fertig, asked me to speak, and especially after I saw the list of speakers and realized that this was designed as a Festschrift, to which I was presumably expected to contribute an economic pearl, thereafter to be known as Buckley's Diminished Return.

I am left with the difficult job of sounding other than trivial and idiotic after the profundities of Professor von Mises, and in anticipation of those to come from the other speakers. I surrender. For those of you who, like myself, so often despair of following the cadenzas that these men play in the abstruse world of economic theory, I bring you this consolation: only a fortnight ago Professor Milton Friedman confessed to me that he does not altogether understand the last work of Professor William Hutt. We must assume that this is not because Mr. Hutt is absolutely unintelligible, in the sense that Mr. Hazlitt proved that Lord Keynes so often was; but because in the spheres in which these men move, reciprocating wheels become a prerequisite to understanding one another's most elusive works. It is surely the genius of Henry Hazlitt that he is totally at home in the ether of the most abstruse economic theory, and yet has never failed to communicate his analysis and his findings to the layman. The force of his arguments and the special discipline he has imposed on himself to make those arguments public are a part of the patrimony of all of us who are concerned for the free society.

The free society. What's that? It is, let us face it, and notwithstanding the great labors of the men and women who are here tonight, a concept increasingly elusive.

What is a free economy? Christopher Hollis, the English Catholic journalist and historian, came to the United States just after the election in 1960 to do a piece on the first Catholic family in the White House and found himself interviewing one of the Kennedy ladies, to whom he put the question, "Have you found it very difficult as a wealthy person to find daily challenges of the kind that is said especially to commend the poor to God?"

"Not at all," she said, "not at all."

Mr. Hollis, making notes, murmured pleasantly, "Then you don't believe it's harder for a rich man to get to heaven than for a camel to pass through the needle's eye?"

"What a quaint saying," said the lady. "Where did you pick that up?"

The sister of the first Catholic president apparently had not heard that saying; as, we warrant, her brother's successor as the leader of the Free World, President Lyndon Johnson, has not heard of the book *Economics in One Lesson*, although its worldwide circulation probably is the only rival to that of the Bible. Better, perhaps, *not* to have read it, than to have read it and disregarded it. "I approve of the Index," Evelyn Waugh once wrote. "I find it a convenient excuse for not reading Sartre."

But so dazzling are Mr. Hazlitt's accomplishments in economics that we tend to forget some of his other extraordinary feats. In the summer of 1960, for instance, during the period when the Russians had taken to announcing, several days after the event, spectacular feats of orbital acrobatics, Mr. Henry Hazlitt, the epistemological skeptic, felt the time had come to put aside his modesty, and so he wrote a letter to the *New York Times:*

Dear Sirs:

On August 17, two days before the Russians sent up the dogs, I was shot into orbit inside a 12-ton space ship. After 17 revolutions around the earth I tilted my retro-rocket and landed safely within 7 inches of a pre-selected target.

This means that I have scored a first, ahead even of the Russian claims. Reasons of military security prevent me from saying anything really informative about the mechanism of the satellite, or revealing the place from which I was shot into orbit or the place of landing, or any other such detail. Nor did I give out any advance notice of the intended time of the shot so that tracking stations could satisfy an idle curiosity. I may reveal, however, because of its extreme scientific interest, that my wife could distinctly see me through a television camera taking orange juice, toast, and coffee.

If either Russian or American scientists are malicious enough to ask for the evidence that this took place, they have my word, which is at least as good scientific evidence as an announcement by TASS. Besides, here is the clincher: I am alive and healthy, show no ill effects from my trip, and can be visited and photographed by skeptics. If I had not been recovered safely from the capsule, how would all this be possible?

And now, at seventy, Mr. Hazlitt has turned to ethics. Indeed, what field, one wonders, could he not have mastered? One day years ago, when he was editor of *The Freeman* magazine, the suggestion was made at an editorial conference that perhaps something appropriate should be said on the occasion of the death of King Carol's consort.

Within moments Henry Hazlitt had jotted down a proposed obituary.
It read:

> *Said the beauteous Magda Lupescu*
> *As she rushed to Rumania's rescue,*
> *"It's a wonderful thing*
> *To be under a king.*
> *Can democracy beat it, I ask you?"*

I know you will join me in wishing the very happiest birthday to
an economist, philosopher, historian, poet, and astronaut, our friend
Harry Hazlitt.

BUCKLEY VERSUS BUCKLEY

A Self-Interrogation (excerpted) before the National Press Club;
Washington, D.C., August 4, 1965

---

*I had accepted the Conservative Party's nomination to run for mayor of
New York City against the Democratic Abe Beame and the nominal
Republican John Lindsay. When I later wrote a book about the experience (*The Unmaking of a Mayor, *Viking, 1966), I introduced it with
this talk, in the form of a self-interview explaining my purposes in running. I got 13 percent of the vote. The preceding Conservative Party candidate had scored 2 percent. Five years later, James L. Buckley, my
brother, would be elected to the Senate on the Conservative ticket.*

*(Footnote: In 1971 John Lindsay, eyeing the presidency, formally
left the Republican Party. But even as a Democrat he proved to be an
unsalable commodity outside New York City.)*

Q: Mr. Buckley, why are you running for mayor of New York?
A: Because nobody else is who matters.
Q: What do you mean, "who matters"?
A. Who matters to New York. New York is a city in crisis, and all the

candidates agree it is a city in crisis. But no other candidate proposes to do anything about that crisis.

Q: What is it that distinguishes you from these other candidates?
Why should only great big brave you consent to run on a program
that would really liberate New York, while the other candidates
do not?

A: Because the other candidates feel they cannot cope with the
legacy of New York politics. That legacy requires the satisfaction
of voting blocs, with special attention given to the voting bloc or
blocs most fractious at that moment.

Q: Would you mind being specific?

A: As far as New York politicians are concerned, a New Yorker is an
Irishman, an Italian, or a Negro; he is a union member or a white-
collar worker, a welfare recipient or a City employee, a Catholic or
a Protestant or a Jew, a taxi driver or a taxi owner, a merchant or
a policeman. The problem is to weigh the voting strength of all
the categories and formulate a program that least dissatisfies the
least crowded and least powerful categories, while most greatly
satisfying the most crowded and most powerful categories: and
the victory is supposed to go to the most successful bloc Benthamite in the race.

Q: What's the matter with that?

A: What is the matter with it is that New York is reaching the point
where it faces the marginal inutility of bloc satisfaction. The race
to satisfy the bloc finally ends in dissatisfying even the individual
members of that same bloc. If, for instance, you give taxi owners
the right to limit the number of taxis available in the City, people
who need taxis to get from where they are to where they want to
go can't find taxis when they most want them. If you allow truck
drivers to double-park because it is convenient for them and for
the merchants whose goods they are unloading, traffic is snarled
and taxi drivers can't move fast enough to make a decent living.
When traffic is snarled, people stay away from the City and the
merchants lose money. If the merchants lose money, they want to
automate to save costs. But if the unions don't let them automate,
they want to leave the City. When they leave the City, there are

fewer people to pay taxes to City officials and to the unemployed. The unemployed aren't allowed to drive taxis because the taxi companies have monopolies. Taxes have to go up because there are fewer people to pay them. The unemployed grow restless, and breed children and crime The children drop out of school because there isn't anyone at home to tell them to go to school. Some of the children who go to school make school life intolerable for other children, and they leave and go to private schools. The teachers are told they mustn't discipline the schoolchildren; otherwise they will leave the schools and commit crime and unemployment. The unions don't want the unemployed hired because they will work for less money, or because they are Negroes or Puerto Ricans and obviously can't lay bricks or wire buildings like white people can, so they are supposed to go off somewhere and just live, and stay out of the way. But they can't live except in houses, and houses are built by plumbers and electricians who get eight, ten, twelve dollars an hour, which means that people can't afford to buy houses or rent apartments at rates the City can afford to pay to its unemployed, so the federal government has to build housing projects. But there aren't enough housing projects, so there is overcrowding, and family life disintegrates. Some people turn to crime, others to ideology. You can't walk from one end of New York City to the other without standing a good chance of losing your wallet, your maidenhead, or your life; or without being told that white people are bigoted, that Negroes are shiftless, that free enterprise is the enemy of the working class, that Norman Thomas has betrayed socialism, and that the only thing that will save New York is for the whole of the United States to become like New York. Bloc voting is all the more dangerous, potentially, with the advent of the contemporary democratist mania. The illegitimization of any state legislature in which representation is based other than on one man, one vote, brings the possibility that the big cities will dominate entire states, that New York City politicians will, if not successfully challenged in their own lair, control both houses of the New York

State legislature and impose upon the state their own neuroses and taboos.

Q: What would you do, if you became mayor of New York?

A: I would treat people as individuals. By depriving the voting blocs of their corporate advantages, I would liberate individual members of those voting blocs.

Q: What would the individual stand to gain, if you were mayor of New York?

A: (1) The security of life and limb; (2) an opportunity to find gainful employment without the artificial hindrances now imposed by monopoly labor unions and minimum-wage laws; (3) the hope of finding decent living quarters without paying profits to land speculators or oligopolistic construction companies; (4) the opportunity to be educated without weekly litmus tests to determine whether the composite color of every school is exactly the right shade of brown; and (5) the internal composure that comes from knowing that there are rational limits to politics, and that one tends to be better off when government is devoted to dismantling, rather than establishing, artificial privileges of the kind New York has been establishing for years, following the lead of Washington, D.C.

Q: What does Washington, D.C., have to do with this?

A: Many of the reforms that New York needs, New York cannot effect unless Washington grants it the authority to proceed. For instance, New York can't guarantee newspaper service [there was at the time a citywide newspaper strike] or shipping service to New Yorkers unless national legislation is passed which would permit the prosecution of monopoly union practices in restraint of trade. New York can't finance its own reforms so long as the money it needs to effect them is drained down to Washington to be spent watering the caliche country surrounding the Pedernales River. New York can't do anything about its structural unemployment problem unless the minimum-wage laws are eased. That kind of thing.

Q: Why didn't you run in the Republican primary?

A: Why didn't Martin Luther King run for governor of Alabama?

Q: For one thing, he isn't a resident of Alabama.

A: That could be arranged.

Q: Are you comparing yourself to Martin Luther King?

A: No.

Q: Why haven't you availed yourself of the two-party system in New York, and fought your fight with John Lindsay in the primaries?

A: Because in New York the Republican Party is dominated by the Liberal Party. Besides, if I had entered the Republican primary and lost to John Lindsay, I'd have felt obliged to support him in the election. But I could not in good conscience have endorsed Mr. Lindsay. To avoid this dilemma, I am running as a Conservative, on a platform that is wholly congruent with the Republican National Platform of 1964.

Q: If the Republican Party in New York City is oriented towards Democratic principles, then isn't that because New York Republicans wish it to be so, and don't New York Republicans have the right to shape the character of their own party?

A: Barry Goldwater, in 1964, got 800,000 votes in New York City. If there are 800,000 people in New York City willing to vote for Barry Goldwater, you have to assume that the Republican Party, understood as a party reflecting an alternative view of government to that of the Democratic Party, isn't dead in New York City. The question, then, is whether to try to double those 800,000 votes, to the point sufficient to win an election, by evangelizing, or, as John Lindsay is doing, by unsexing the Republican Party and flitting off with the Democratic majority, for the purpose of achieving a Republican victory that would be purely nominal and would ultimately convince the voters that the Republican Party offers no genuine alternative.

Q: Isn't John Lindsay engaged in revitalizing the Republican Party?

A: No, he is engaged in devitalizing the Republican Party. A party thrives on its distinctiveness. John Lindsay's decision, made years ago, to bestow himself upon the nation as a Republican rather than as a Democrat was clearly based on personal convenience rather than a respect for the two-party system, let alone a respect for the Republican alternative. The two-party system, if it is meaningful, presupposes an adversary relationship between the parties. John Lindsay's voting record and his general political pronouncements put him to the left of the center of the Democratic Party. As such he is an embarrassment to the two-party system. . . .

Q: What does Barry Goldwater think of all this?

A: Ask him. But I can tell you what it is reasonable that he should think. It is reasonable that he should think it time that responsible elements in New York City organize to liberate New York from the one-party system.

THE HEAT OF MR. TRUMAN'S KITCHEN

Remarks (excerpted) at *National Review*'s Tenth Anniversary Dinner;
the Imperial Ballroom of the Americana Hotel, New York, November 11, 1965

It was a very big affair, with 1,500 people in attendance. Clare Boothe Luce was the chairman of the event, and on the dais were Henry Luce, John Dos Passos, Lewis Strauss, and Barry Goldwater. The mayoral campaign had concluded nine days before, and John Lindsay had been elected mayor. An endless list of guests sought out the signatures of Mrs. Luce and Senator Goldwater.

The speakers were amusing, and confidence was in the air. My own talk reintroduced a kind of historical despondency that many were feeling about politics, at home and abroad. More and more American troops were being sent to Vietnam, Defense Secretary McNamara manifestly had no persuasive plan to win the war, student activism had metastasized to campus disruptions, and there was reason to expect the growth of President Johnson's Great Society to intrusive proportions.

L ADIES AND GENTLEMEN, Mr. Harry Truman once remarked that if you can't stand the heat, you should get out of the kitchen. I think he implied by that something a little different

from the truism. He implied that no normal man—no virile man—
would *want* to get out of the kitchen. I should like humbly to question Mr. Truman's planted axiom. I do not, to begin with, understand
why any normal person should enjoy the heat of the kitchen, and
especially I don't understand why anyone should desire to expose
himself to a heat which he cannot, under the terms of Mr. Truman's
metaphor, insulate himself against. The normal thing for a normal
person to do is to step outside the kitchen, and let the political heat
rage on within it. And an effective person takes matters into his own
hands, and reduces the heat to a point of tolerability. Politics, it has
been said, is the preoccupation of the quarter-educated, and I do
most solidly endorse that observation, and therefore curse this century above all things for its having given all sentient beings very little
alternative than to occupy themselves with politics. It is very well to
say we will ignore the Great Society. But will the Great Society repay
us our courtesy by ignoring us? How is it possible nowadays for a normal young man to go to school in, say, Berkeley, California, and *not* be
occupied with politics? He cannot walk across the hall to the bathroom without having to step over the bones of a classmate protesting
in the prone position. How is it possible for a sensitive human being
on the dark side of the Iron Curtain to avoid politics, when he cannot
visit an art gallery or read a textbook without the heat of the kitchen
reaching out to scorch him, lest his mind should stray from the dog-
matical reservation? And therefore how is it possible on the happier
side of the Iron Curtain for a man sensitive to the suffering of others
to retire from the kitchen in order to devote himself wholly to his or
his family's private concerns? To retreat from the kitchen is surely
not undesirable but altogether the most desirable of things to do: but
where can we go, always provided we have to take our consciences
with us, and be free of the heat? Where can we go and feel free not to
read the *New York Times?*

No such freedom exists nowadays, which is the conclusive reason,
surely, to deplore this century's most distinctive aggression, which is
against privacy, publicly understood. Move your ashtray from here to
there, and in this century there are vibrations caused that rattle the
bones of other men far, far away. Fail to bestir yourself in foreign pol-

icy, and you fail to bring hope to desperate people. Decline to talk back to the editor of your newspaper, and you will find before long that he is reaching into your very living room to regulate the temperature. Accept passively the strictures of your textbooks, and you will find that you are indulging not abstract arguments relating to other people in other times, but terribly concrete arguments binding on your own life and thought. There is no refuge, in our world, from Mr. Truman's kitchen. Mr. Jack Kerouac can counsel us to go on the road; but to do that is right away to acknowledge that we are refugees, seeking the privacy of the Flying Dutchman. Mr. Norman Mailer can counsel us to adopt an existentialist permissiveness; but soon we recognize that thrill seeking is a tedious substitute for the homelier, and headier, pleasures of duty and restraint, of order and peace, of self-discipline and self-cultivation. . . .

It is undoubtedly necessary, every now and then, to bare one's teeth; and we do so, preferably, in the course of smiling. But the smiles have a way of freezing, as the sadness rolls in. The joys of war-making presuppose the eventual stillness of victory; and that, so far as I can see, is beyond our reach. Perhaps it was meant to be so. T. S. Eliot observed that there are no lost causes because there are no gained causes. Perhaps providence has decreed that the price of a soaring gross national product is perpetual servitude in the kitchen. I don't know. I know only this, and I know it as a certitude, that you are the finest company in all the world, and that on the tenth anniversary of *National Review* I celebrate, above all things, yourselves.

On Selling Books to Booksellers

An Address (excerpted) to a Convention of the American Booksellers
Association; Washington, D.C., June 7, 1966

---

*The invitation was to take twenty minutes of the hour shared with author
Ralph Nader and author Louis Auchincloss. I had just completed* The
Unmaking of a Mayor *and thought to tell the book merchants something
about what was in store for them in the book, scheduled for publication the
next winter. I engaged in a few I-told-you-so's, which is the habit of all
politicians who did not win an election; and, I now established, of non-
politicians who did not win the election.*

AS YOU UNDOUBTEDLY know, you have an awful capacity to
terrify. A few months ago I was in Switzerland, awash in
sheets of blank yellow paper, incommunicado in a compound manned at its four corners by agents of Viking Press, each of
them with a machine gun trained on me, a huge stopwatch counting
down the minutes before the deadline, a horrible, imminent ninety
days away. I couldn't change my typewriter ribbon without seeing
their eyebrows rise and their trigger fingers twitch. But in that heat
one messenger was ceremoniously piped aboard my quarantined
quarters—bearing an invitation to address the American Booksellers
Association. The monitors, ever after, occasionally smiled at me.
Indeed, on two or three afternoons they gave me the liberty of a
trusty and permitted me to go skiing with John Kenneth Galbraith.

"You're not writing a serious book, are you?" Mr. Galbraith asked
me as we were going up the lift.

"Not really," I said. "It's not about you or your doctrines."

We skied down the top slope together, and I was greatly pleased
to observe that he had certain difficulties in negotiating it which I
hadn't had, and so I thought to say to him—a dreadful error, to
patronize Ken Galbraith—"How many years have you been skiing?"

"Thirty," he replied.

I was tempted to observe that that was about as many years as he had studied economics. I didn't yield to that temptation, since after all I was no longer running for public office, and a ruthless candor in the style of my political campaign was no longer imperative.

Some of you may be aware that over a period of years conservatives have complained that American booksellers are too heavily influenced by reviews, predictably unfriendly, of books by conservative-minded authors. Of course, it is always easy for a conservative to plead that his book did not go because the Establishment denied, *a priori*, its merit; but, I know you will understand, it is hard for every conservative author to reconcile himself to the proposition that he writes the way Professor Galbraith skis. Several books ago, my sainted mother decided to wage a personal campaign to ensure that all the booksellers in New York City kept my book in stock. At nine in the morning she would begin tramping down the streets of Manhattan, stopping at every bookstore, and asking the same question: "Do you have *McCarthy and His Enemies* by William F. Buckley Jr.? I understand he's a *very* interesting young man." To her increasing dismay she found herself frequently presented with a copy of the book—whereupon, paying cash, she was forced to come up with the name of somebody to send it to, without using the surname Buckley and tipping off the clerk. She was getting, by the third day of her campaign, to the furthest reaches of family and friends. Towards the end of a very long day, wan and haggard, she limped into a bookstore and asked the routine question, and the bookseller produced a copy. "To whom would you like it sent, Madam?"

Probing her memory for the name of a relative who had yet to be afflicted by a copy of the book, my mother remembered a remote second cousin: "To Mrs. C. V. Perrier."

"How do you spell Perrier?" asked the bookseller patiently.

"B-u-c-k-l-e-y," said my mother absentmindedly.

A month or so later I ran into a bishop who told me that he had lunched with a priest on leave of absence from his post in Latin America who professed an interest in the controversy involving Senator McCarthy. The bishop promised there and then to present him with a copy of my book, and after lunch they walked to a tiny little bookstore across the street from the downtown restaurant, and the bishop asked for a copy of *McCarthy and His Enemies*. "Sorry," said the clerk, "we have no copies."

"What do you mean, you have no copies?" the bishop asked. "There's one on display right there in your window."

"Bishop," the clerk replied wearily, "that's the only copy we have left. And if I let you have it, so help me God, Mrs. William F. Buckley Sr. will materialize within one hour and say, 'Why don't you have my son's book in your window?'"

I banter on, ladies and gentlemen, because I do not know that I could hope to compete, in the discussion of substantial matters, with Mr. Ralph Nader, who so eloquently demonstrates the undesirability of cars running into each other if both are traveling at high rates of speed. Or with Mr. Louis Auchincloss, whose great talents I so enormously admire, and who gave me as recently as a fortnight ago the timeless pleasure of reading the life of the Rector of Justin. My own forthcoming book is, in a way, as concretely concerned as Mr. Nader's with the future safety of Americans, though not only those of them who drive automobiles. And concerned, or at least I naturally believe so, with the preservation of such values as the Rector of Justin sought to maintain, though he died uncertain of whether he had succeeded in his mission—however certain he was that Mr. Auchincloss's description of his efforts would always survive. I have written, in my current book, about certain social and political and human dilemmas as they emerged in the course of a municipal campaign whose setting happened to be New York City. The cast of characters features three men, of whom I cast myself as the hero. In the role of a hero, you will find, I am not absolutely convincing; which, however, you are to understand as signifying the failure of my literary skills, rather than any uncertainty respecting my communion with the saints. *The Unmaking of a Mayor*, as I gloomily entitle my book, concerns the efforts of an amateur to describe some of the dilemmas of municipal politics. . . .

I don't pretend that I went on in the course of the campaign to offer the only conceivable solutions to those dilemmas. I recommended last summer, in recognition of the frightening advance of dope addiction in New York, the forcible sequestration of drug addicts in medical centers. I was promptly accused of recommending concentration camps. ("What group will he want to put in concentration camps next?" asked one candidate darkly. "Lepers," I replied.) A few months later, Governor Rockefeller introduced a bill calling for compulsory segregation for drug addicts.

I acknowledged during the campaign the clear necessity of raising the subway fares in New York City, for which I was roundly denounced by the gentleman who, having become mayor, now concedes the inevitability of a fare rise. The notion that, in situations of water scarcity and water waste, water metering is the indicated solution was denounced as demagogic; but water metering is now on the agenda. I observed the necessity of an additional tax, and the new mayor, having during the campaign denounced a City income tax, now recommends it. I cite these examples not only to exercise my vanity, but also because I am interested, and hope that you are too, in the recurrent and, I judge, intensifying disparity between the requirements of successful politics and the requirements of successful government. Mr. Kennedy was forced, by the realities, to acknowledge that the missile gap was in fact the other way around. He was forced to acknowledge that taxes were too high. Mr. Johnson was forced to acknowledge that the Vietnamese crisis called for more vigorous intervention. One has to conclude that the final resources of right reason were not reached by them, any more than they have, as regards some of the issues of the New York campaign, been reached by Governor Rockefeller or Mayor Lindsay. But the gap seems to widen between what you can talk about in election campaigns and what you need to do as a public official if you want to stay abreast of reality. This disparity, growing more acute, raises questions about the evolution of democratic procedures, the integrity of which is a matter of concern for all of those who commit our destinies to them.

Enough. Talking about destinies, I suppose Mr. Nader and Mr. Auchincloss and I would at least agree that ours are in your hands.

THE AIMLESSNESS OF
AMERICAN EDUCATION

An Address (excerpted) to the Council for the Advancement of Small Colleges;
Los Angeles, September 15, 1966

---

*I revert to my complaint about the theory of academic freedom and take
note of the practice of it, e.g., at Harvard. I hold that colleges should,
however broadly, feel free to define civilized goals and to urge their student bodies to share their cultivated wisdom. I argue that the smaller colleges are the best suited for experimentation and reform.*

THERE IS A sameness, both dreadful and reassuring, in the
statements one is pelted with these days, mostly by the presidents of the larger colleges and universities, on the aims of
American education. John Barrymore once said he could induce a
severe case of delirium tremens by reckoning the amount of whisky
he had drunk during his lifetime and imagining it all in a single glass,
about the size of a small movie theater, poised for him to start all over
again. The young college president, freshly in office, must pale at the
thought of the miles and miles of clichés that stand between him and
that final baccalaureate address, twenty years hence, when he will say:
essentially the same thing. . . .

But why do we weary even of the relatively enlightened statements that are being made by those who reject progressive education?
Why does the very eloquent president of UCLA sound so much like
the very eloquent president of Sarah Lawrence, who sounds so much
like the very eloquent president of Swarthmore, who—alas—sounds,
allowing for differences in syntactical resourcefulness, like an hour at
the hearthside of a cliché factory?

The answer has to do with the incompleteness of their position.
No matter how pleasing the fugue is as it rolls along, the final satisfaction is denied until all the individualistic, though harmonious,
strands come together to establish their essential unity. The critique

of progressive education absolutely establishes many things; we are finally airborne—but we never land.

I think that for the most part our educators (and we are talking now about the good guys among them), while they are coming to know what education is not, do not know for sure what education is. The principal reason why they do not know and cannot know is that they are restrained from seeking educational ends by a mystique, academic freedom, which is all promises and no delivery. Perpetually hovering, it remains, in its own exalted way, as anti-intellectual, as destructive, as the precepts of progressive education. . . .

We are, to be sure, agreed on an important postulate, namely, that for personal and social reasons it is desirable that human beings exercise their distinctively human faculties (principally the power to reason and the power to apprehend beauty). But what is it about the aims of education as commonly set down that leaves us with a sense of incompleteness? The kind of incompleteness that leads, ultimately, to frustration and boredom?

Certainly we are not told how to account for the profound conflicts that sunder the educated world. If education is a civilizing experience, then we should be entitled to correlate education and civilization. Yet it does not work out that way, does it? Educators know or are expected to know, writes college president Dr. Herbert Lowry, "how vital colleges and universities are in giving leading ideas to . . . national life—all down the line. They know that education is eventually a kind of dynamite." Which exploded in our day, in various parts of the world, in socialism, fascism, and Communism. Dr. I. L. Kandel has conceded the lamentable truth that "education is the most Fascist aspect of the Fascist Revolution, the most Communist feature of the Communist Revolution, and the most Nazi expression of the National Socialist Revolution."

The correlation, in other words, doesn't automatically work. It is *not* safe to say: Knowledge is wisdom. In terms of sheer knowledge, sheer book learning, Lenin and Trotsky had few peers. Yet it would greatly have relieved the world had everyone concerned with cultivating the powers of these men been persuaded to desist from his labors.

It may be argued that in worrying about Communists and Nazis and Fascists, one is worrying about aberrants—intellectual mutations who should not be allowed to distract us from the formulation of general laws. Let us suppose that this is so and move over to a part of the world governed by more conventional political and philosophical ideas. Let us put down in London.

In London there is Bertrand Russell. Lord Russell knows more about more things than, quite possibly, anyone else now living. What has it done for him? Or for us? Apart from his technical philosophical contributions, of great but specialized significance, what has he done to ease, or to direct into productive channels, the labors of society? What has he done to refine the understanding? What has he done for *himself*? He had more than the *two* educations that Mr. Robert Hutchins [former president of the University of Chicago] once suggested were requisite to marital felicity: and he has had five wives. He has taken a very wide range of iconoclastic positions over the past thirty years, challenging at the root the basic Western convictions on theology and ethics. And now, in the plenitude of his wisdom, he advises us to yield to the Soviet Union: to yield to barbarism, rather than fight to save our institutions. "The civilized world will be destroyed!" The Great Scholar trembles, repeating the words that undermined the Romans' will to resist *their* barbarians fifteen hundred years ago, a moral failure described more vividly than almost anywhere else in one of Lord Russell's own books. Was it the aim of the education of Bertrand Russell that he should learn to so instruct us? To be sure, there is a consistency in his advice. He has devoted his life to challenging the validity of Western convictions; it follows that they are not worth defending at the risk of war.

We put down again, this time in Cambridge, Massachusetts, and wander about the halls, listening for the wisdom that true education will make us privy to. There, having returned from the Indian wars, is Professor John Kenneth Galbraith [who had served as ambassador there] insisting that the premises of our economic organization are outmoded, are merely sustained by the "conventional wisdom." Perhaps he is right, for he is an educated man who did not while away his high-school hours on driving lessons and life-adjustment courses.

But if one travels to the University of Chicago and listens there to Professor Friedrich Hayek, at the very least as well educated a man, one is told that the way of Galbraith is the way to (1) serfdom and (2) poverty. Mr. Hutchins, a highly educated man even by his own exacting standards, terms nonsensical some of the views of Dr. James Conant, a highly educated man by anyone's standards. Professor Sidney Hook, a highly educated man, tells us we must emancipate ourselves from the thrall of religion, and Professor Reinhold Niebuhr, a highly educated man, tells us that through religion we find truth, freedom, and perhaps even salvation.

What is to be done about all those modern problems we hear so much about, ranging from armed conflict to proliferating slums? To answer those questions, we keep on being told, we need bold solutions; revised, renewed, upgraded, modernized thought, of the kind that will occur only to a society that has been to schools of the kind Dr. Hutchins would operate. But what *are* these solutions behind which a truly educated public could be expected to rally? Why not ask those men who have *had* the kind of education of which Dr. Hutchins approves? What do *they* want the nation to do? Well, of course, in asking that question, we turn on Babel. Everybody is speaking, and in different tongues. There are schools of thought, to be sure. One says the time is ended when major social problems can be settled by individuals or voluntary associations: that we must turn to the state. There is the conflicting view, that the state is, for reasons metaphysical and prudential, precisely the wrong agency through which to attempt social reform. There are multifarious views, many at daggers drawn, on colonialism, states' rights—everything.

I am saying, very simply, that the educated elite are not agreed as to what are the central problems which education aims to settle, let alone what is their solution; that among the elite there are radical and irreconcilable differences which have nothing whatever to do with the size of the brain or the length or breadth of the education. I go further and say that when the educational elite do appear to be taking a position almost unanimously, it is often impulsive, wrongheaded, and superficial, as when, for a while, it was sweepingly accepted that Darwin had buried God.

I myself am persuaded that a good education is sufficiently justified by what it renders to the individual who receives it and that no
external justification for it is needed. But I do not believe we will ever
be convincing in our effort to mobilize the nation in behalf of good
education until we state the aims of that education more intelligibly.
And this we cannot do, so far as I can see, until we free ourselves of
the superstitions of academic freedom. So long as academic freedom
is understood to mean the right of the researcher to pursue knowledge without being hindered by the law, the doctrine is unassailable.
But it does not make sense to suggest, as is done on so many campuses, that academic freedom should constrain an institution to keep
a teacher on even if he devotes himself to undermining the premises
of the school at which he teaches, or the society in which he lives.
Such a teacher may properly be deemed incongruous, and any college
that so finds ought to be as free to replace him as a community is free to
replace a public servant for whose services there is no longer a demand.

It is especially urgent that academic freedom be abandoned in its
capacity as keeper of doctrinal parity, as guardian of the notion that
all ideas are equal. Under academic freedom, the modern university
is supposed to take a position of "neutrality" as among competing
ideas. "A university does not take sides on the questions that are discussed in its halls," a committee of scholars and alumni of Yale
reported in 1952. "In the ideal university all sides of any issue are
presented as impartially as possible." To do otherwise, they are saying, is to prejudice the race which, if all the contestants are let strictly
alone, truth is bound to win.

That is voodoo. The aims of education are to forward knowledge
and right conduct—at the *expense* of some points of view. The educated man, Russell Kirk has said trenchantly, is the man who has
learned how to apprehend ethical norms by intellectual means. He
has come to know, in a word, what is right conduct, and why one
should conduct oneself rightly, and he has come to know this by
understanding the rational basis for such conduct. As long as the faculty and officials of a center of humane learning take the position that
they will not affirm one idea over another, they are saying that they do

not know what right conduct is. They are, moreover, saying that they never will know, for academic freedom is not conceived as a self-terminating device to be discarded after the Grand Discovery. Academic freedom is conceived as a permanent instrument of doctrinal egalitarianism: it is always there to remind us that we can never know anything for sure—which I view as another way of saying we cannot really know what are the aims of education.

To say a college should not take sides because it cannot take the chance of choosing the wrong side is to sentence colleges to a destiny of intellectual and moral futility. To assume, as academic freedom implicitly does, that every student should in nonscientific matters begin afresh, as if Plato and Aristotle and St. Augustine and St. Thomas had among them reached not one dependable conclusion, is to doubt the very structure of learning; is to doubt that there are any aims at all, aside from purely utilitarian ones, to education.

If it can be said that the education of Lenin produced an aberrant, then it is tacitly conceded that standards exist by which aberrancy can be judged. It must follow, then, that there are standards by which we judge whether Lenin or Hitler—or Leninism or Hitlerism—deserves equal attention and respect from our students: whether a university should be "impartial" to them. And if there *are* standards, they ought to be accounted for in any theory of education. Such a theory might aver something like this:

There is a purpose in life. It is known what that purpose is, in part because it has been divulged, in part because man is endowed with a rational mechanism by which he can apprehend it. Educators should pass on the truths that have been discovered and endow students with the knowledge of the processes by which these truths are recognized as such. To do this is the single greatest contribution a teaching institution can make: it is the aim of education, to which all else is subordinate. If education can endow students with the powers of ethical and rational discrimination by which to discern and give their allegiance to the great certitudes of the West, we shall have a breed of men who will discharge truly the responsibilities that face them as the result of changing conditions.

I ADVOCATE INDOCTRINATION? That is a devil word, with lots of power left in it to tyrannize over any discussion of academic theory. In fact, it is literally impossible to act on the abstract directives of academic freedom. Just as it is almost impossible for an individual to be entirely neutral, so it is impossible for a department within a college to be entirely neutral, or even for a college to be entirely neutral. "Indoctrination," in the sense of the urging of one doctrine over another, goes on all the time; indeed, some of the most vociferous academic-freedomites are themselves the premier indoctrinators.

Recently at Harvard the editors of the student newspaper, *The Crimson,* conducted an extensive survey of undergraduate political and religious attitudes, and uncovered by scientific means what has been clear to any sensitive intelligence for many years, namely, that Harvard, like so many other great universities, has become an engine for the imposition of secular and collectivist values. One out of two Protestants who go through Harvard lose their faith, in considerable part as the result of the secularist stamp of the faculty and curriculum. Jews and Catholics do not appear to go quite so easily, but a considerable percentage of them also turn from religion. In politics and economics the call is for centralization and more centralization. The editor summarizes: "within the College . . . Federal aid is rapidly gaining the status of a magic word. Surrounded by a climate of liberalism, most Harvard undergraduates seem ready to accept increased Federal activity in almost any area of national life—from housing developments to theatres, and from farms to factories."

In international affairs, the impact of Harvard education is measured by this datum: one-third of the student body would sooner surrender to the Soviet Union than fight a nuclear war.

How did the students get that way?

"For the most part," the *Crimson* report states, "the College students did not arrive in Cambridge with these beliefs; they picked them up at Harvard. Over half admit that their political views have been strongly influenced since Freshman Registration, and of these, seven-tenths have changed either 'from conservative to liberal' or 'from liberal to more liberal.'"

Now it may be that to indoctrinate students in political liberalism and philosophical agnosticism is to lead them towards the truth—certainly Harvard appears to be acting on that assumption. But what is relevant in this discussion is not *what* direction Harvard is taking, but the fact that, in violation of the precepts of academic freedom, it is taking any direction at all; what is remarkable is that, contrary to the dictates of the theoretical literature that continues to pour out of Cambridge, Mother Harvard is not "impartial" or "neutral." The fact that some of us disagree with the political tendencies of Harvard education has no bearing on the meaning for all of us of a very clear departure from the doctrinal imperatives of academic freedom.

Surely the small college and the individual student must emerge as the principal agents of educational reform. The small college because there uniquely is the organizational mobility, the residue of faith, the preoccupation with the individual student and his intellectual and spiritual needs, the independence of spirit to resist the shibboleths of mass education. The small college, with its small group of devoted scholars who look not for prestige or desks in the White House: there, I expect, is where the regeneration will come.

And the student too is bound to be an agent of that reform. How can he contain the moral energy that every man is born with, when he surveys the world he lives in and reflects that this is the world that education built—not, mind you, the world that poverty, or illiteracy, or sickness built. Our principal afflictions are the result of ideology backed by the power of government. It takes government to translate individual vices into universal afflictions. It was government that translated *Mein Kampf* into concentration camps. The morally sensitive student is bound to revolt, and he will find, I think, that it is in the small private college that his views will have the greatest leverage.

I SAY ONLY that the wisdom is *there,* and that educational theory ought to adjust to that fact. The changing conditions we hear so much about do not affect the validity or applicability of the central directives concerning human conduct. If those who are always shouting at us that we need brave new solutions to our problems seem to be giving more time to clamoring for new solutions than to looking for them, do not judge them harshly; they have no alternative. Edmund Burke would have treated them with tolerance, as he did his own contemporaries when he said, speaking for all the men of his age, "We know that *we* have made no discoveries, and we think that no discoveries are to be made, in morality; nor many in the great principles of government, nor in the idea of liberty, which were understood long before we were born, altogether as well as they will be after the grave has heaped its mould upon our presumption, and the silent tomb shall have imposed its law on our pert loquacity."

"YOU HAVE SEEN TOO MUCH IN CHINA"

Remarks on Accepting an Award from the American-Jewish League against Communism; the Hotel Biltmore, New York, December 2, 1966

The principal speaker was Republican Senator Everett Dirksen, the Senate minority leader and a renowned orator. The news was everywhere about the enormities in China in pursuit of Mao's Cultural Revolution. I asked a question, never answered then or in ensuing human-rights crises in Russia, Rwanda, Bosnia, Kosovo, China, Indonesia: What are the responsibilities of the civilized world?

I THANK YOU greatly for this honor, which I accept on behalf of my colleagues at *National Review*, for whom I am only a single spokesman. I share the evening's honors with Senator Everett Dirksen, which is presumptuous enough. To escalate the effrontery, I am supposed to orate from the same platform as Senator Dirksen. Three days after Pearl Harbor, one day after Germany joined Japan in declaring war on the United States, an agitated State Department messenger brought President Roosevelt the news that Bulgaria had just declared war against us. "Did you ever," commented Mr. Roosevelt, "hear an ant pass wind in a hailstorm?"

Bulgaria salutes you.

My friends, a year or so ago, in a widely quoted speech, much of it perversely irrelevant, Senator William Fulbright wisely observed that "insofar as a nation is content to practice its doctrines within its own frontiers, that nation, however repugnant its ideology, is one with which we have no proper quarrel." Thus, even though it is clearly within our power to do something about it, we do not interfere with, say, Papa Doc in Haiti, or whoever it is that is currently in charge of carnage in Nigeria. But there are nations in the world which very much desire to practice their doctrines outside their own frontiers, and our interest in those doctrines is accordingly other than abstract.

The West German correspondent Jürgen Dennert is quoted in *Life* magazine. He has been in China, observing the activities of the Red Guards. "In Wuhan," he writes, "I saw—I could almost touch him—a Christian priest surrounded by the Guards. They had put a white robe over his clerical vestments and tied a piece of wood around his neck so that his head was forced down at an angle of almost 90 degrees. The top of the dunce cap pointed ahead like an arrow. Behind him were a group of 10 or 12 people, probably part of his parish. I could see their faces very clearly—an expression of despondency, visible even beneath the black lacquer which the Communists had smeared on their faces. . . . I counted more than 60 victims being led past in less than two hours. I asked one of my interpreters: 'What happens to the people who are taken out of the city?'

"He smiled courteously and said, 'They will return in the evening.'

"'And those who leave at night?'

"'I guess they will return the next morning.'

"'I have never seen any come back.'

"'But I have.'

"'And when they return, where do they live?'

"'In their houses, naturally.'

"'How do they enter their houses if the doors and windows are sealed up and nailed?'

"'Only such houses are sealed as have second entrances.'

"'But if they are not where they live—could they possibly be in prison?'

"'Impossible. We do not have prisons for millions of people.'

"'But if they are not in their houses and not in prison, where are they?'

"'You have seen too much in China.'"

An estimate of the victims of the great purge that followed the taking of the Mainland by the Communists in 1949 was made by a commission retained by the AFL. The appalling figure it came out with was twenty million people.

The Free World did nothing.

Meanwhile, the Chinese Communists developed an atom bomb, and then a missile to deliver it. And now they have begun a purge that some observers believe will be the most massive in Red Chinese history. Again we do—nothing. Nothing except, in some quarters, to urge admitting Red China into the United Nations and to whisper about the alleged delinquencies of Pope Pius XII in failing to rally sentiment to relieve human suffering twenty-five years ago in Germany.

It might be contended, taking into account the limits—which Senator Fulbright points out—of any single country's ability to order the workings of other countries, that we were justified in interfering with Hitler's viciousness not merely because he was tormenting Germans and killing German Jews but because he also threatened the peace of the world. At any rate, one must agree that the satisfaction we took in overthrowing Hitler was more acute than the satisfaction we had taken in overthrowing the Kaiser: because in the war against Hitler, self-defense and the ethical impulse to help one's fellow human beings brilliantly fused.

But many men are at best perplexing in their handling of Red China. We are simultaneously told that the world can never forget nor forgive itself the callousness it showed towards the persecution of the Jews in the late 1930s—a judgment with which I tend to agree. And so we continually berate ourselves. To what purpose? Surely to remind ourselves that we should not permit such a thing as happened to the Jews to happen again—and certainly not to victims of an aggressive power that seeks to "practice its doctrines" outside its own frontiers.

"The helpful time," writes Mr. Jack Jones, "for assessing the morality of the Nazis was before, and not after, it was too late. Our main ethical task at the moment is to prevent the repetition of such things, if that is possible. . . . Mao Tse-tung, who is in a better position than I am to force his ethical views on the world, may be quite right in his prophecies of more of the same for the human race, especially the hapless portions of it that lie in his path.

"When asked about those totalitarian powers which were not defeated, which survive today, Dr. [Karl] Jaspers [who recently excoriated the world for its lateness in coming to the rescue of the persecuted peoples in Germany] takes refuge in an uncertain and evasive tone. This," Mr. Jones concludes, "is intolerable, for precisely the crime—against all mankind—for which he indicts the whole German people without exception is silence; the refusal to see, to understand, the horrors in front of them. All conventional and practical considerations, all custom and all law, become irrelevant and even positively evil, by his way of it, insofar as they stand in the way of open and violent warfare against crimes of such terrible scope."

The American-Jewish League against Communism is, I judge, a symbol of hope for those who believe that some at least learn from history, that genocidal suffering is genocidal suffering whether it occurs in the East or in the West, and that those who suffered most a generation ago have not forgotten what it is to despair and will not, to the extent that they can prevent it, permit others, despairing, to go into the night.

THE DUTY OF THE EDUCATED CATHOLIC

An Address at the National Honor Society Exercises at Stamford Catholic High School; Stamford, Conn., April 7, 1967

What follows, I now think, would have been more appropriate for graduate students than for high-school students, but Stamford is my hometown, and one does one's civic duty. It is an attempt to urge young people not to be overwhelmed by the contradictions so often disabling to religious faith.

I AM ENVIOUS of your accomplishment, and grateful for your existence. You have, through hard labor, distinguished yourselves. You will proceed with a very special cachet which marks you not merely as young members of the intellectual community, but as young men and women whose credentials are especially meaningful because they are touched by grace. You are entitled, at least today, to feel more keenly the joys of achievement than the burdens of duty. Though as a reminder that the world is filled with the latter, you must pause and listen to me—the final ceremonial encumbrance between you and the consummation of the honors which are your due. You are right to be impatient, I to be awed. We are both right to be thankful—you, that the clock moves ineluctably, athwart my proven incapacity to set it back; I, that I should figure, however briefly, in the calendar of your arduous but glorious academic career.

Briefly, then, I meditate on some of the pressures you will undoubtedly feel along the way to becoming highly educated Catholics. The vector of intellectual forces during the past century has been in the direction of provoking an intellectual uneasiness in the Catholic mind.

There is no doubting that speculative and positivist learning has battered the traditional Christian faith. Darwin gave us a naturalistic explanation for the biological evolution of the world; Freud gave us a psychological explanation for the arrangements of our appetites and emotions; Marx gave us a historical explanation for the dialectical progression of social forces. Indeed it was confidently predicted a century ago that the engines of scientific achievement were closing the gates on Christian faith.

Something has kept them ajar. I mean something other than the adamant foot of the Holy Spirit. Some say it had largely to do with the social modernism of Leo XIII. Others, that Christianity profiteered from the hubris of scientism. Some would say that it has been the collective exertions of great individuals that have kept the hounds at bay: the poetical-metaphysical insights, not to say the spirit, of G. K. Chesterton; the hard analytical intelligence of George Tyrrell, God bless his excommunicated soul; the work of such skeptical skeptics as the physicist Pierre Duhem or the scientist-philosopher Pierre Le Comte du Nouy. And, in the world of the indirectly engaged, there is the force of Graham Greene, the literary Manichaean; of Evelyn Waugh, the serene Christian pessimist; of T. S. Eliot, the subtle Christianizer; of C. S. Lewis, the advocate of the beleaguered miracle; of Eric Voegelin, the historical transcendentalist. And then of course the dozen theologians who have withstood wave after wave of assaults, finding that their arguments are, miraculously, as plentiful as the loaves and the fishes turned out to be when they were so sorely needed.

But then we have always known, have we not?, that the day has never been when the sum total of man's available resources was insufficient to cope with skepticism, one of those resources, in the earliest days of our faith, having been an obligingly ubiquitous God. In respect of apologetics we are better off in the twentieth century than we were in the first. St. Peter would have had a more difficult time engaging a Sophist than, say, John Courtney Murray would have today, replying to Bishop Pike. Even so, notwithstanding our intellectual resources, notwithstanding our moral and spiritual resources, we are on the defensive. And it is the excruciating irony that the more highly educated we are, the more keenly we tend to feel the pangs of exclusion from the dominant intellectual hustle and bustle of the age. Our faith is more severely buffeted, now that we move easily in the world of knowledge, than it was when we were illiterate. The more we know, the more we have reason to sense how infinite are the rational and spiritual reserves of the Christian faith. And yet the more we know, the more tempted we are, by the tug of our common bonds with the regnant intellectual community, to empathic twitches of impatience with those features of our faith which the secularist world deems most anachronistic: which is to say, the Faith itself.

What is it that causes this great uneasiness? One cause, one obvious cause, is the interminable war between the self-justifying flesh and the forlorn spirit, a war in which all baptized human beings are eternally conscript as double agents. Another cause is the lure of rationalism: If we can perfectly understand how to split the atom, why can't we know how to fuse the Trinity? Surely another cause is the friction between fundamentalist and transcendent understandings of scripture. The skeptical world was convulsed with mirth when Clarence Darrow asked William Jennings Bryan, How did the serpent manage to get about, before being cursed by God to move on his belly? It requires a special weakness for the pretensions of rationalism to believe that Darrow actually reified a Christ-sundering dilemma. It requires an act of faith in the power of Clarence Darrow to repeal the metaphor; which is to say to repeal poetry; which is to say to repeal one of the principal means by which God has sought to instruct His prosaic flock.

The appeal of literalism has done much to shake the faith of the literate, as has the appeal of those who, because they have succeeded—and nothing is easier to do—in identifying the discrepancy between Christian behavior and Christian idealism, go on to suggest that Christian idealism is organically tainted. Because there are wars and fornication, we are asked to believe in the irrelevance of Christianity. As long as there are wars that we approve of, Christianity is deficient; as long as there is fornication, which we disapprove of, Christianity is unrealistic. It is not only, in our time, the secularist literature that hungers to conform to the standards of contemporary humanism, urging us towards the position that no wars are just, and no fornication unjust. There is also the Christian, or at least the self-understood Christian, literature which, overcome by the chic of the modernists, grovels in self-doubt. Is it possible truly to understand Pope John's encyclical *Pacem in Terris* outside the context of Christian dogma? There are those, yet they are bewilderingly few, who do not believe so; but the critical Christian community, by and large, permitted that document, sucked dry of its sanctifying blood, to serve as a social paradigm for a meeting of intellectuals convened in New York two years ago—the desecration of a document which, abstracted from Christian teaching, is nothing more than an agglutination of sentimentalist banalities. Charity without the crucifixion, Whittaker Chambers reminded us, is liberalism.

Catholic higher education is a heavy cross. It is blessed only in the sense that the cross is blessed, in that it gives us the heavy opportunity to do our duty. As members of the educated elite, you are greatly exposed to importunate winds. You are asked to penetrate Darrow's dilemmas, to account exactly for the role of mythology in biblical history, to accept the responsibility for Jim Crow in a Baptist community, to reconcile the gentleness of Christ with the thunder of Hiroshima, the love of God for little children with the incidence of polio, the overlarded table of a Christian in Connecticut with the hunger of his Christian brother in New Guinea.

The anomalies sometimes seem overwhelming, as if we had learned nothing from the primal anomaly: that God sent His own Son to earth to be tortured and killed. Yet in current circumstances the wider our eyes are opened and the more diligently our ears are unwaxed, the more seductive is the call of modernism: the more readily we are drawn to the rationalist heresy that the imperfections in ourselves and in our world are imperfections that grow out of the natural order—which, because it is of God's making, suggests to some the unbelievability of God rather than the believability of our own ungodliness. It is the temptation of many educated Christians to doubt that the God who gave us the latitude to behave as we behave is a God we can worship as wholeheartedly as we do those human divinities who labor to abolish Jim Crow, or dissipate the mushroom cloud, or comfort the unwed mother.

It is more than a decade now since Monsignor [John Tracy] Ellis criticized the failure of Catholic education to breed a class of triumphant scholars. The immediate reaction to Monsignor Ellis's exhortation was an altogether healthy resolution to work harder to hone the Catholic mind. The tendency of more recent years, it sometimes seems to me, is to measure the achievements of Catholic education by exclusively secularist standards. The anxiety to compete for intellectual favor sometimes seems to argue for kicking over our spiritual traces, those encumbrances which hinder our competitive standing. Thus we have lately seen Catholic scholars appear before congressional committees to argue the wisdom of the judicial ruling which forbids the acknowledgment of God in public-school classrooms, thereby to establish, one supposes, that Catholics are every bit as sensible as the most distinguished pagans of the desirability of totally separating church and state. And, sure enough, we hear now the voices of certain Catholics who question even the *relevance* of Catholic education; education being, one is asked to infer, either Catholic or educational. In an age so greatly afflicted by its own failures, by the manifest shortcomings of a liberal culture which seems above all to have succeeded in creating self-disgust, the moment is surely at hand to draw on the special reserves of Christianity—patience, self-denial, understanding, faith, joy—and to recognize that all that we have learned in the super-sophisticated years of our intellectual maturity is of minor consequence alongside what is revealed to us in the homilies of our faith; that we are equipped by our faith to stand up against the effronteries of this or any future century; that the experience of our age must, on reflection, serve to recertify the relevance of Christianity.

"I see it as one of the greatest ironies of this ironical time," writes Malcolm Muggeridge, "that the Christian message renouncing the world should be withdrawn for consideration just when it is most desperately needed to save men's reason, if not their souls. It is as though a Salvation Army band, valiantly and patiently waiting through the long years for Judgment Day, should, when it comes at last and the heavens do veritably begin to unfold like a scroll, throw away their instruments and flee in terror."

Ladies and gentlemen, I do not doubt that our Father is proud of you today and that, in the years to come, you will justify Him, and be justified. The Church asks us to love the Lord with all our heart, and all our soul, and all our mind. You have gone as far as you can at your age to prove that you love Him with all your minds. Love Him also with all your hearts, as He loves you.

DID YOU KILL MARTIN LUTHER KING?

An Address to a Convention of the American Society of Newspaper Editors; Washington, D.C., April 19, 1968

For many reasons, personal and historical, a special encounter. Newspaper columnists, addressing newspaper editors, are addressing their patrons. The columnist's fate depends on their interest, disposition, assessment. I had been six years a columnist, and I had many clients. I addressed directly the delicacy of such an encounter and gave the audience the single funniest paragraph ever written on the subject of columnists' sycophancy, a paragraph from the unique Murray Kempton. I went then to a matter of immediate and urgent interest, the assassination, two weeks earlier, of Martin Luther King. I had found myself the day after the assassination in a seat of special anxiety and turmoil, addressing six thousand people at a convocation of students and VIPs assembled by Vanderbilt University. Word had got out that the unknown assassin had left Memphis the day before, heading towards Nashville, where Vanderbilt is located. The other guest that morning was Julian Bond, the young and impressive black leader, who exclaimed that he had lost all confidence in America. I answered him defiantly. The exchange with the students remains in the memory.

ALTHOUGH I WAS carefully coached by my devoted friend Harry Elmlark [who handled my syndicated column], I did neglect to ask him what is perhaps the critical question, namely: Am I supposed to make a good impression on you, or are *you* supposed to make a good impression on *me*? As a conservative, I suppose that I should adopt the prudent alternative.

We column writers are, I am led to believe, the original Toms.

Murray Kempton recently observed that the Communist *Worker,* on announcing its intention of becoming a daily publication, could get all the favorable publicity it needed merely by announcing that it was in the market for daily columnists. Mr. Kempton, although in some respects he is innocent beyond the imagination of Walt Disney, is as a columnist the noblest of us all. "Columnists," Mr. Kempton reminisced, "have attacked Albert Schweitzer, the Pope in Rome, Mrs. Roosevelt, and even J. Edgar Hoover, but I can think of only one who ever attacked his publisher. That, of course, was Westbrook Pegler, who disappeared. A more typical case is that of Joseph Alsop, a man whose pride towers at least as high as Pegler's ever did. I remember when we trailed into Indianapolis with Eisenhower in 1952 and Joe Alsop said he was going to dinner with Eugene Pulliam, publisher of the *Indianapolis Star.* Now Alsop is a man I would expect to be unable to look at Indianapolis without retiring to his hotel room with the sheets over his face; he has been known to send the hollandaise sauce back at Maxim's; he would not normally endure twaddle at dinner from Dean Acheson. From what I know of Eugene Pulliam's generosity, he was probably paying Joe $20 a week for the column; from what I know of Pulliam's charm, I would sooner dine with Senator Hruska; I know nothing of his table, which must be unimaginable. Yet Joe Alsop spoke of the prospect of dinner with Pulliam not with alarm but with delight. If Malcolm X had been a columnist he would have Tommed to D. Tennant Bryan of the *Richmond News-Leader.*"

Now of course Mr. Kempton, in order to make his point, is saying a lot of unjust things about some very nice people, a technique any editor will understand. But it never *has* been all that clear what are the ideal relations between the columnist and the editor. I think of Conrad's idea of the proper relations between the sailor and the sea. The sea, Conrad observes—and he is not lightly dismissed by any philosopher of the sea—is the enemy. But it is the irresistible enemy. The sea is the creature which, at the margin, can drown the sailor. But however tempestuous, however arbitrary, however sullen the sea can be—however much like an editor—the sea maintains its basic integrity: and if the sailor observes the rules, if he maintains his guard, he is permitted to survive: and the experience is sublime.

Imagine the thrill of negotiating successfully a passage across the editorial page of the *New York Post?*! I feel a kinship with Sir Francis Chichester. I am certain that, upon approaching the Horn, he asked himself, agonizingly, "What, what is Dolly preparing for me?"

I had a curious experience, which I presume to mention to you only because you are, visibly, on your best behavior. I wrote a syndicated column for eighteen months before meeting a single editor or publisher of any of the newspapers that carried the column. At first I thought this healthy, in a perverse sort of way—a means of proving something about the essential integrity of the whole process. But two unruly thoughts stalked that romantic notion. One was that many of my generous patrons were probably patronizing not me but the undeniable Harry Elmlark; the other was that, in fact, I was feeling a little lonely. I yearned—I still do occasionally—to begin a column by saying, "Hi! Say, Boston, how do you like Teddy's latest nomination to the federal judiciary? Pretty off-putting, no? How's the weather up there, by the way? Good for a little weekend rioting? Good morning, Mr. Manchester, and what do you propose to do *now* about the state of New Hampshire? Offer it to the Vietcong as a part of a general settlement? Look here, L.A., if you think that by cutting my last three pro-Reagan columns you are succeeding in telling me something, you are absolutely correct." But no, the conventions always seem to close in on us, don't they? The same conventions that keep us from telling a man to his face what we are willing—indeed anxious—to say about him when he is gone, and we are writing his obituary or speaking his eulogy. As you can see, I do not know what is, finally, the way in which the columnist and the editor can approach each other to their mutual advantage. I know only that here I am, and there you are, and it would be nice if we managed to touch each other.

I prefer, as you might expect, to ponder the delinquencies of editors, over against the delinquencies of columnists. Mr. Howard K. Smith recently resigned from our profession, complaining that editors are irresponsibly attracted to the reporting of irresponsible people. I remember being in Africa a few years ago and picking up an English-language newspaper whose headline read, "American Negroes to Be Deported to Africa in 1972." That, I thought, was a scoop if ever I saw one. I read on, and the story, datelined Arlington, said, "George Lincoln Rockwell, commander of the American Nazi Party, announced today that he expected to win the governorship of Virginia in 1970 and the presidency in 1972, and that he would instantly undertake to remove all American Negroes to Africa." That of course is parody, the kind of news story Mr. Herblock most easily festoons. But the thought sticks with me that the decision of the editor of that newspaper in Liberia to give such prominence to such a story is not so easily explained as by suggesting that he is an agent of the Communist Party of Monrovia, or that he was educated in America and was refused admission into Delta Kappa Upsilon at the University of Pennsylvania. What caused that headline, the sensationalism aside, was at least in part related to the general disposition to think ill of America.

I grant two contributing factors. One of them is neurotic. The theologians of yore identified the sin of scrupulosity, from which people suffer who believe that they are unclean. The other factor is virtuous, altogether noble, reflecting that simple, eternal concern with one's shortcomings which one associates with the dogged discomposure of the saints. But I do believe that some of the reactions a fortnight ago to the slaughter of Dr. Martin Luther King reflected the first rather than the second disposition. Christians acknowledge that all of us—those who are dead, those who are alive, and those who are as yet unborn—conspired to make necessary the sacrifice of Christ. But that metaphysical communion in sin hardly commits us—or does it?—to the murder of Martin Luther King. I found myself, twenty-four hours after the tragedy in Memphis, Tennessee, debating on the subject of civil rights, before an audience of six thousand, against Mr. Julian Bond—in Nashville, Tennessee. I shall not soon forget the solicitude of the chancellor of Vanderbilt University, who brought Mr. Bond and me together in a corner of the cafeteria moments before the debate and whispered to us, "My men went over every square inch of the gymnasium late this afternoon"—he beamed triumphantly—"and we didn't find a *thing*." Mr. Bond and I registered our gratitude; what other response is appropriate? And the chancellor continued, still sotto voce, "And in addition, I want you to know that I have distributed 95 plainclothesmen throughout the audience." *That* is Southern hospitality.

Mr. Bond, who began the evening's discussion, punctuated his manifesto against America with the heroic trope: "All of this was killed last night at Memphis." By "all of this" he meant all that America has ever claimed for itself. Any pretensions that we have to justice. Any that we have to the rule of law. Any that we have to equality, compassion, mutual esteem, love. The audience cheered him. That young audience thus sought to atone for the crime against Martin Luther King—once again for reasons both pathological and sublime—by offering its body, prostrate, in expiation. Its own innocent, virginal body, unflexed, to the scourges of Julian Bond.

There is a sense in which that was a chivalrous reaction, young and generous. But I do not understand that as an adequate explanation for the more considered reaction of older America. *Time* magazine is able to orchestrate whatever response it desires to any American crisis, and the editors choose in the current issue to feature letters which raise doubts about the worthwhileness of the American Republic. The lead letter, from California, says, "Martin Luther King was murdered because he was our uncomfortable conscience. I am filled with shame and loathing for our race." The correspondent here betrayed genocidal convictions of the kind Dr. King fought against. Never mind. Again: "When statesmen look to give aid to the uncivilized and underdeveloped countries of the world, please let ours be first on their list"—a moving letter from a lady in New Jersey who, perhaps understandably, does not go on to list the countries so manifestly qualified to instruct us in the ways of civilization. And a gentleman from Arizona says, "The land of the free and the home of the brave—and probably the only civilized nation on earth where a winner of the Nobel Peace Prize, holding no political office, can be assassinated while serving on his mission"—an objurgation so vastly confused and confusing as to require hours to unravel; any attempted response would begin patiently with the observation that, for instance, Mr. Pasternak was not even permitted to accept the Nobel

Prize, that the subsequent moral assassination of Pasternak was a collective undertaking, coolly executed by a killer state. But no, the mood is: Hate America.

That isn't, needless to say, the mood of the majority of the editors of American periodicals: their attitude is not merely part of the general Weltschmerz; it has more to do—as I understand it—with a sense of shared responsibility.

I judge this reaction, even when the intention is to harness it to ends that we approve of, to be philosophically dangerous. Bloodguilt is the matrix of genocide. I asked the audience of six thousand people at Vanderbilt University whether they were representative of America. Were there rich men in the audience? Poor men? Old, young? Southerners, Easterners, Westerners, Midwesterners? Catholics, Protestants, Jews? College graduates, high-school dropouts? Yes; yes; yes; yes . . . All right then, raise your hands, those of you who consider yourselves implicated in the assassination of Martin Luther King.

"*I am filled with shame and loathing for our race,*" says the featured correspondent of *Time* magazine. Why? There in Nashville not one person could be got to profess satisfaction from the great perversion at Memphis. Who is it that we Americans are so busily engaged in blaming? Not—when you pose the question directly to six thousand members of the community in Nashville, Tennessee—not them. Not, one may be sure, the editors of *Time* magazine—they are surely blameless. It is always . . . those other people—those people whose ranks yield forth the John Wilkes Booths and the Lee Harvey Oswalds.

Me, I say this: that more significant by far than the ghastly murders of John Kennedy and Martin Luther King, acts committed by isolatable and isolated men—more significant by far is the spontaneous, universal grief of a community which in fact considers itself aggrieved. That is the salient datum in America: not that we bred the aberrant assassins of John Kennedy and Martin Luther King, but that we bred the most widely shared and the most intensely felt sense of grief: such grief over the loss of Mr. Kennedy and Mr. King as is felt over the loss of one's own sons.

That is what I judge to be the newsworthy datum; a point I stress not because I feel the need to flatter the United States of America, but because I feel the need to reassure the United States of America, which is the land where I was born and choose to live, which is the land where you were born and choose to live; which land, I feel increasingly, needs us all as her devoted bodyguards, even as Messrs. Kennedy and King needed more bodyguards than they had, at the crucial moment in *their* histories. She needs us, however quarrelsome we are; however disparate our views; however pronounced our separations. I feel that we should be grateful, whatever our differences, to be facing the sea—this sea; this enemy—in this bark. I do believe that the time is overdue to profess our continuing faith in this country and in its institutions—including its press.

LIFE WITH A METICULOUS COLLEAGUE

Remarks at a Testimonial Dinner for William A. Rusher; the Baroque Room of the Plaza Hotel, New York, April 10, 1969

A dinner in honor of the publisher of National Review. *William Rusher received his B.A. from Princeton and his law degree from Harvard, where he founded the Young Republican Club. He practiced law in New York City for a few years and then went to Washington as assistant counsel to the Senate Internal Security Subcommittee. I had lured him to leave and become the publisher of* National Review *notwithstanding that we were, and continued to be, an indigent publication dependent on the philanthropy of our readers. Rusher was/is an irresistibly mythogenic figure, right out of Dickens, mutatis mutandis.*

I JOIN WITH Marvin Liebman and Clif White in welcoming you on this happy, and expensive, occasion. It is seldom that I am called on other than to denounce someone; so that it requires a reorientation, the strain of which you may find visible in my rhetoric, when I announce that we are here to celebrate, rather than to deplore, Bill Rusher.

Clif White has known him much longer than I have, although I daresay not so intimately. To know anyone intimately it requires that he have the authority to question your expenditure of money. In this respect I am certain that you will all be glad to know that the guest of honor is the quintessential Republican. I don't mean to say that he is tiresome about it, merely that he is thorough. And unrelenting. Even on Sundays. I remember the legend of Congressman Rich of Pennsylvania, who was elected to the House of Representatives sometime before the First World War, and served there until his death, approximately forty years—should we say long years?—later. During the first thirty-nine of those years he uttered only a single declamation—the same declamation, on a dozen or more occasions each year. The debate on a spending measure would take place and, after it became obvious that it would be approved, Congressman Rich would raise his hand and, recognized, would say, "Gentlemen, where are we going to get the money?" and sit down. It is recorded that in his declining years, following a debate which had gone on for three weeks and kept his colleagues at their desks night after night, the moment finally came for a vote on the controversial measure, at which point, nearing midnight, Congressman Rich raised his hand. The entire chamber groaned. But under the rules the Speaker was powerless. Grumpily, he recognized the member from Pennsylvania, who, struggling against his great age, rose to his feet, looked around at his colleagues, and said, "April fool!"

Bill Rusher is not that versatile. But as publisher of a journal which holds out great promise of being the longest, most consistent money loser in American publishing history, he is at once badly cast, and well cast. Badly cast in that it strikes anyone who views him coming jauntily to his office every morning, not sooner than three minutes to ten nor later than two minutes to ten, that he could not be other than the president or vice president of a prosperous house of usury; well cast in that his serene and self-confident mien easily belies the probability that the first person he will encounter on entering his office is an irate creditor; and the second, his secretary giving notice.

Our friend is a man of most meticulous habits, and it is a miracle, of the kind which providence less and less frequently vouchsafes us, that he should have endured for so long the disorderly habits of his colleagues. When so many years ago, in 1957, I asked him timidly whether he would consent to accept the responsibilities of publisher, he instinctively reached into his pocket and pulled out his notebook, presumably to see whether his notebook had any objections. Having passed that hurdle, *National Review* was subjected to a methodical probing over a period of three or four weeks. A few very close friends were directly consulted, among them Clif White, and in due course the decision was reached. Our old friend, providence, cooperated with us in keeping Bill Rusher away from the offices of *National Review*, which had he examined them he would no doubt have returned without faltering to the relative tranquillity of the Senate Internal Security Subcommittee. But he was trapped; and he began to impose order on our affairs.

To this end he began his famous graphs. We have graphs at *National Review* charting every quiver in the organization's metabolism. We have graphs that show us how we are doing in circulation, in promotion expenses, in political influence. We have graphs that chart the fidelity to conservative principles of most major, and all minor, public figures in America. We have a graph that will tell you at a glance whether Lauren Bacall is more or less conservative than Humphrey Bogart. Our late friend and late colleague, the late Professor Willmoore Kendall, once dumbfounded Bill Rusher by telling him, "Bill, there is no proposition so simple that it cannot be rendered unintelligible to me by putting it on a graph." But the graphs go on: and, for those who have the stomach for it, they will give you a synoptic understanding of the financial record of *National Review* over the last twelve years.

His fastidious habits give him an enormous advantage over the rest of us. There is, for instance, no such phenomenon as an unanswered memorandum from William A. Rusher, and if you think it works to say absentmindedly, "I never *got* that memorandum, Bill," forget it, as I did after trying it once ten years ago, only to be reminded that I had received the memorandum in the presence of fourteen editors and three photographers. So much is our publisher the creature of habit that, he once confessed to me, on entering the washroom he reaches up to pull the light cord, and if it should happen that by mistake the previous patron of the washroom had left the light on, why Mr. Rusher turns it off before he can control his reflex action, thus finding himself, as he does several times a year, in total darkness, and without practical recourse to his secretary.

Occasionally his admirers show their envy of him, as when, while he was away on a lecture tour, we tiptoed into his office and exactly reversed every reversible physical accoutrement. Thus the picture of Lincoln hung now, at our mischievous hands, where the picture of Washington had hung from time immemorial, and the picture of Washington hung where the picture of Lincoln had hung. Thus when he depressed Button One, instead of his secretary, the bookkeeper would answer; and when he depressed Button Two, instead of the bookkeeper, his secretary would answer. When he turned over the leaves of his calendar, he would find himself moving not towards the end of the month but towards the beginning of the month; and when he opened the drawer where his graphs were kept he would find not his graphs but his pills; and so on.

On entering his office and exposing himself to the pandemonium, he quickly decided that he had had enough. We had tried hard to substitute the door leading into his bathroom for the door leading out of his office but found that the problem was metaphysically insoluble. So he left, returned to his apartment, telephoned his secretary on the outside line, issued a few crisp instructions, and retired to his club for the rest of the day, pending the restoration of order.

Such have been his tribulations at *National Review*, in spite of which, I suspect, it could not have come as a great surprise to him that tonight his colleagues have rallied so enthusiastically to the idea of coming together to celebrate his achievements and his person. The most exasperating people in the world are so often the most beloved, and he is no exception. Sometimes, at the weekly editorial conference, to which he descends with his notebook and his clippings, to pour vitriol on the ideologically feeble—sometimes he looks about him and no doubt feels as Congressman Rich felt surveying the expressions of those whom he would summon to fiscal rectitude. But his performance at those meetings is one of the great running acts on the ideological stage.

His scorn is not alone for those in public life whose activities during the past week he finds contemptible, but also for those who lag a bit behind in exhibiting a similar scorn. For them, for his colleagues, his scorn is especially withering. "I notice," he wrote me recently after enduring an editorial conference during my absence and running hard into the opposition of some of our younger colleagues, "I notice the difficulty in planting my views against the opposition of Merrill Lynch Pierce Fenner and Smith sitting at the opposite side of the table. I find that Merrill seldom disagrees with Lynch, who seldom disagrees with Pierce, who always disagrees with me. Perhaps you will find an opportunity to suggest a good basic reading list to our younger members." Such a reading list, I gathered, as would be everywhere useful nowadays, including in the White House.

But all is not lost; all is never lost. There is always next week's editorial conference, next month's financial crisis, next year's election: and on he marches, gyroscopically certain, ever in command of himself, whether communicating his pleasure, or registering his doubts, or metronomically tut-tutting his disapproval. Always a presence, always a performance; and always—I speak for myself and for those who know him best—a friend. I give you Bill Rusher.

On the Perspective
Of the Eighteen-Year-Old

A Commencement Address at the Chapin School; New York, June 4, 1969

---

*Chapin is a sophisticated and exclusive girls' school in New York City.
In June 1969 there was much turmoil in the colleges. It was the year of
the Woodstock festival, of continuous bloodshed in Vietnam, of student
takeovers of campus buildings from Brandeis to the University of
Minnesota to San Francisco State. I addressed a few propositions about
the responsibilities of the student that I developed, subsequently, into
commencement addresses that I gave widely.*

YESTERDAY EVENING I rang Mrs. Berendson and asked, "How
long should I speak?"

"Twenty, twenty-five minutes."

"What should I say?"

"Anything you like." Pause. "Anything you think appropriate."

This is in the permissive tradition of the Chapin School, so that
I find that I arrive here unencumbered by any instructions or prohibitions. Oh, I mean almost unencumbered. One of my agents told me
that I am not to say anything critical of Mayor Lindsay in the presence of Mrs. Gordon, nor anything favorable to Mayor Lindsay in the
presence of Mr. Gordon. Since they are both here, I shall manage to
go through the morning without mentioning Mayor Lindsay at all.
Wouldn't it be splendid if the voters discovered so diplomatic a solution to our vexed political problems?

I thought to take my few minutes in discussing the responsibilities of the student on reaching college. I reject, as perhaps many of
you reject, the notion that the "relevance" one hears so much about
as justifying education is determined by education's usefulness in life
adjustment. Mr. Scott-King, the classics teacher, after his tour
through Evelyn Waugh's modern Europe, comes back to school, and
there the headmaster suggests that he teach some other subject in
addition to the classics—economic history, say—because the classics

are not popular. "I'm an old Greats man myself," the headmaster says. "I deplore it as much as you do. But what are we to do? Parents are not interested in producing the 'complete man' anymore. They want to qualify their boys for jobs in the modern world. You can hardly blame them, can you?"

"Oh, yes," Scott-King replies. "I can and do." And, deaf to the headmaster's entreaties, he declares, shyly but firmly, "I think it would be very wicked indeed to do anything to fit a boy for the modern world."

WHAT, THEN, ARE the responsibilities of the student in the modern world? My list is not comprehensive, but any list should, I think, touch on the following points.

(1) In his book *The Revolt of the Masses,* Ortega y Gasset identified the distinguishing feature of modern man, which is his utter incomprehension of the extent of his indebtedness to other people. Ortega's point is platitudinously recalled here and there, mostly in an economic context, as when the local nag from the ACLU reminds us of the iniquitous reliance by the few on the sweat of the many—a point worth making, mind you, but a point so often made without reference to the fuller implications of it. There is every reason for the weak relying on the strong. Who else are they expected to rely upon? But why is it that the strong feel the need to rely upon the weak? In purely economic terms that is what the monopoly labor unions do when they drive up wages at the expense of those who are not competitively equipped to rise with the union scale. At an economic level this touches on education; you see the students in New York and California angrily denouncing proposals that they contribute to the cost of their own education [Governor Ronald Reagan had proposed a modest tuition fee in the California state college and university systems in place of the traditional no-fee policy], even when it is demonstrated that taxi drivers and elevator operators would be thus relieved of a part of the burden of supporting them. At another level, a law student at the University of Minnesota has written, "Too often we

have thrust upon us the notion that society owes us something, the notion that we must do nothing, accomplish nothing to justify our existence."

That is to finger, surely, the first responsibility of the student: to give something back. Not as good as he gets—in this sense he is, providentially, the eternal beneficiary. We repay not by suggesting that what we can contribute to our culture is equal to what our culture has vouchsafed to us. We contribute most by recognizing the extent of our patrimony. The chances are that students cannot return to their college, even if they should devote their lifetimes to the effort, what the college makes available to them in a single shelf of its library. In a single shelf they have access to the work of Aristotle and Plato; of Milton and Shakespeare; of St. Augustine and St. Thomas and Eric Voegelin. How can any of us expect to repay in kind?

The principal contribution to the commonweal we are in a position to make as individuals is the recognition of other individuals' superiority to ourselves. The mere acknowledgment of that superiority sets us apart, paradoxically, from our bumptious fellow men. It gives us the vantage point whence, simultaneously, to judge our own limitations, our own potentialities, and the acutest needs of the world we live in.

(2) Concerning their teachers, students owe them, I think, the respect which is due them in virtue of their academic achievements; and a courteous skepticism concerning their ideological pretensions, or at least the ideological pretensions of those who have ideological pretensions. The best way for a student to treat an arrogant teacher is to patronize him. The teachers who most need patronizing are those who patronize the ideals of this country. I do not suggest that the thing to do, when you hear your country criticized, is to bounce up from your seat and launch into a rendition of "The Star-Spangled Banner." I do suggest that you train your ears to distinguish between criticisms which are reformist in character and those others which suggest an ignorance of or even a hostility to the essential American propositions: those criticisms which are less in the spirit of Martin Luther King than in the spirit of Lee Harvey Oswald, whose hatred

of America is finally justified only by the ineradicable fact that America did, indeed, produce Lee Harvey Oswald.

The point I make should be stressed, if only because (3) I do think it is among the responsibilities of American students to meditate on the fact of their being Americans—as distinguished from, say, Chinese, or Yugoslavs, or even Frenchmen. This pre-supposes a knowledge of history. James Thurber once remarked, "Women are taking over the world because they are blandly unconcerned about history. I once sat next to a woman who asked: 'Why did we have to purchase Louisiana, when we got all the other states free?' I explained to her that Louisiana was owned by two women, Louise and Anna Wilmot, and that they sold it to General Winfield Scott, provided he'd name it after them. This was called the Wilmot Proviso, and his closing of the deal was the *Dred Scott* decision. She answered, 'Never mind the details. Why did we let them talk us into it at all?'"

The abstraction that, in search of higher education, students are catapulted from any bonds to their fellow Americans and graduated into a supranational elite is UN-talk, i.e., silly. Our culture is not a drag upon our intellectual development. It is the likeliest source of our intellectual animation. It isn't parochial for us to proceed with the conviction that it makes a *difference* that the blood of Thomas Jefferson and James Madison, of Lincoln and Emerson, of Thoreau and Theodore Roosevelt and George Washington Carver runs through our veins, as indeed it does even for those of us who arrived only yesterday as immigrants from Transylvania. There is no such thing as a universality of outlook so total as to deprive us of the meaning of our own experience as Americans. The more we know, the more greatly relevant we will discover our nationhood.

(4) It is the students' responsibility, I think, to insist as best they can that reason be reintroduced to all discussions, especially those most highly vexed by passion, lest they too wind up at Santa Barbara [the most recent site of student anarchy]. It might be contended that here is the principal contribution of conservatism, as formally understood, to the commonweal. . . .

And (5) I suppose my remarks must include, under the strain of the stimulations of the day, the necessity to regulate not only our political appetites, but also our other appetites. There are the conventional temptations—sex, booze, drugs, iconoclasm—each one of them potentially a killer, emotionally, physically, and intellectually, if indulged in without reference to standards defined outside the demands of our own senses. Don Giovanni died not only painfully but a nervous wreck for the knowledge that somewhere, somehow, there existed a maiden whom he had not seduced. The student pusher who wrote recently in *Esquire* magazine lives in nervous apprehension lest the drug exists which he has not tried. I lie sleepless at night worrying that I might die before having just one more opportunity to enrage the *New York Times*. It is all quite pointless, isn't it? And one has, at a university, a chance precisely, as Russell Kirk tells us, to stock up on the intellectual arguments with which to apprehend the moral norms, one of them being that self-control is the most exhilarating of pleasures. I can't say that I envy today's students—so much to do, so many confusing people, like myself, to hector them along the way.

But meanwhile it is very necessary—and this surely is a paramount responsibility—(6) to enjoy yourselves as you go. There is nothing to match the sensation of discovering one's own powers, of feeling some of the magic excitement that generated the very idea of America, of feeling a little of the spiritual consolation that comes with the knowledge that we are not alone, that the Lord of Hosts is with us yet.

WORDS TO THE COUNTERREVOLUTIONARY YOUNG

An Address to the National Convention of the Young Americans for Freedom;
St. Louis, Mo., August 28, 1969

*The atmosphere was tense, the mood fractious, even rebellious. The chal-
lenge to the leadership of YAF was from the so-called libertarian wing,
students who were attracted to anarchic attitudes towards government.
Their organizing center was in California, and their idol was Karl Hess,
who had served as a speechwriter for Barry Goldwater and was now a
vociferous advocate of total repudiation of government. My effort was to
emphasize the element of conservatism, as espoused by YAF at its founding convention nine years earlier, that stressed the collateral needs for
order and self-government and due process. The speech was tranquilizing,
but a few weeks later the California division withdrew; within a few
years, YAF had become a dead letter.*

I ASSUME THAT you know I am happy to be here. Otherwise, as a
libertarian, I wouldn't be here. Right? Wrong. I might very well be
here, even as you, and you, and you, might be here, not because
you want to be here but because you feel you should be here. What is
it that determines what one *should* do? Surely not only what one *wants*
to do, because the answer is then circular, leaving the question substantially unanswered. Duty sometimes coincides with desire, a happy
but alas unusual conjunction. Duty more often marches off in a direction independent of desire, and I do not of course mean merely
fleshly desire, but also intellectual desire.

It is fun and games to think that freedom consists alone in the
gratification of one's own, uniquely brewed desires. It is much more
complicated to understand that freedom, this side of paradise, means
not only the pursuit of one's own objectives in one's own ways—
though that is extremely important—but also a certain attachment to
common principles. That attachment we must always be free as individuals to renounce. But having renounced it, we must recognize that

we then become excommunicates, who have lost the freedom that issues from that common bond. We rightly despise the society that forbids apostasy, and pity the apostate who finds no honorable alternative to apostasy. I despise the Soviet Union among other things for forbidding apostasy, and I pity Kuznetsov [a prominent Soviet dissident] for suffering the loneliness of apostasy.

The freedom that some of our fanatics talk about is the freedom of the excommunicate. I listen to their songs, and find only disharmony. Thus the most conspicuous critic of the Young Americans for Freedom says of you that you are led astray by "false and authoritarian friends": that the leadership of your movement "would like nothing more than the return of Cotton Mather or Torquemada"; that the "F" in YAF stands for what you have "secretly stood for all along, fascism"; that "order" as you desire "order" means simply "State dictation and State-controlled property"; that the State defends itself by the hiring of "goon squads." Not only is the thought remarkable for its opacity, the rhetoric acquires the feel of the ideological meat hook. It loses balance, point, equilibrium, grace. It turns to heavy banality. "Poor Bastiat and Cobden," the critic writes, "must be"—one hopes for surcease, but the iron pull of platitude does not permit the freedom of literary imagination. Poor Bastiat and Cobden "must be turning over in their graves." Poor Shakespeare and Hemingway are surely turning over in their graves.

Another man, by nature gentle and kind, is drawn by the same cankerous muse to the fever swamps. There he writes such prose as, "This supposedly noble land"—he means this country, the second oldest republic in the world, the great fortress of freedom on a terrorized planet; the object of the affections of Thomas Jefferson and Abraham Lincoln, of Theodore Roosevelt and Barry Goldwater—"this supposedly noble land has been fed and bred on this obviously ignoble fare." "Fed and bred"? The gentleman once made a living as a professional writer. "On this obviously ignoble fare"? Is he distinguishing *obviously* ignoble fare from *surreptitiously* ignoble fare? "It seems now impossible," he continues towards his rhetorical climax, "to say that all of this horseshit is just some aberration of an otherwise perfect civil comity and economic dynamism." It certainly seems impossible now to recall that the gentleman used to write speeches for Barry Goldwater; as an alternative, it seems clearer why Barry Goldwater lost.

It is a deep and paralyzing drug, fanaticism. "To really love this land," our critic completes his essay, addressed to you here, delegates to this convention, "to really love this land one must first learn to loathe this nation and the system for which it stands." Surely if this land is to be distinguished from this nation, you can love it just as it is. There is no such thing as a Communist or a totalitarian or a democratic or a libertarian lake or mountain spring or prairie. What does he mean? Why must you *loathe* this nation? In what sense does this nation "stand for" a system? The thought is as confused as the language is extreme.

Is *this* what they call extremism in defense of liberty? I shouldn't think so. I rue the unnecessary distance this country has traveled away from freedom for its citizens. YAF was founded among other things to brood over that excess, and to keep it constantly before the mind of the public. But to assume that young Americans, or old Americans, could have any freedom at all in the absence of a measure of sacrifice towards that common affection which lifts our society into being is to assume that each one of us is omnipotent, and to prove that each one of us is omnipotent only in the capacity to fool oneself, and to make oneself a fool.

I hope it will not be thought a betrayal to observe that the fight for freedom and the fight to conserve require different emphases depending on the historical situation. Americans could hardly be enthusiastic, for instance, about the policies proposed for Czechoslovakia by Dubcek in the spring of 1968: such policies, were they proposed for the United States, would pitch this group, and quite understandably, into revolutionary resistance. But such policies as Dubcek proposed in 1968 were wildly welcome in Czechoslovakia—as an advance towards freedom.

The concerns of young and old Americans for freedom are, I judge, twofold. First, to hold out some idea of how things ought to be, ideally; second, to hold out some idea of the direction towards which our society should move, considering which are the available roads. The most conspicuous enemies of freedom nowadays are—as always—the governments that gorge themselves on human freedom. But there are other enemies. Listen, if you will, to a letter, a lengthy letter, that reached me yesterday, in whose lines is impacted almost everything that there is to worry about in our time.

Dear Mr. Buckley:

I am writing to you in a state of frustration, frustration at my own life. I do not know whom to turn to. My parents I can't bring myself to ask. My church, Grace Cathedral, was the former stomping ground of Bishop Pike. I am almost 19 and will be attending my second year at Berkeley. Last year is when what I call my "attacks of doubt" fully blossomed. I do not really know what is wrong with me, but I do feel that something is wrong with me, and I ask your advice. I am sorry for wasting your time, if I am, but I am so sad and need help.

In college last year I joined a fraternity (sex and pot among the liberal element is as frequent there as drinking beer, which is as frequent as eating, which is as frequent as breathing). And I have discovered that I am, like Dmitri Karamazov, enchanted with sensual pleasure and beauty. I eat, play music and want to sleep with every woman that arouses me in the least, and hardly study. . . .

I became confused. My English 1A teaching assistant, a most depressing young Marxist, came to the conclusion that literature, art are totally useless, frivolous. I could not find words to reply, nor reason. Then I took a philosophy course which sent me spinning. How can one learn the Truth about something when he cannot know for sure if what he is told is the truth unless he knew beforehand what it is, in which case there would be no reason to ask questions? I began to doubt reality, after a while. A painful pang of doubt clutches my heart after every word I utter anymore, and then my mind goes reeling off into a thousand thoughts. . . .

I go back to Berkeley soon. I went there to save the world initially, but now I believe alternately during the day in nothing, and sometimes, something. I was president of the revived chapter of YAF long enough to revive it officially and to set up its first pamphlet table. As I sat there, the first person to confront me was a grinning joker with red-tinted glasses, a Communist, a Marcusean. He made mincemeat of me. I could not answer him. I could do nothing. I went to a YAF conference near L.A. last Christmas, found most of them to be atheists, tried to break up a fight over a wine bottle so savagely that I frightened the guy I grabbed into attacking me, listened to a philosophy teacher comment that your magazine is malarky because it's hung up on religion, and then he ridiculed James Burnham.

When I go back to Berkeley I will be lost, and what with all the damned depression, riots, and attempts by everyone to get me on pot I am afraid I shall just flip. Please, can you offer me some advice? Forgive me for inconveniencing you.

Sincerely, . . .

How does one reply to such a letter, other than on one's knees? There is freedom abounding in America—which does not help that student. He sees the ground of truth removed from him, lowering him down into the depths of epistemological despair. At one YAF meeting he finds that the excitement is over who gets the wine bottle, and who can exceed the others in iconoclasm, as though freedom consisted in a Luddite destruction of all our carefully built ties to the past, to the present; to nature, to supernature.

How does it go for us? What are the proximate concerns of those who care for freedom? What is the new, the current conservatism?

It is correctly supposed that it is, in some respects at least, different from the old conservatism. Consider ten years ago. Conservatives in America rallied in their disapproval of the invitation to Nikita Khrushchev to visit the United States, attaching to that visit a symbolic significance which indeed it had, notwithstanding the violent reversals that were to come so soon, over the next three years, when Khrushchev successively (1) withdrew his reciprocal invitation to Eisenhower, in high dudgeon over the U-2 flight; (2) erected the

Berlin Wall; and (3) sent missiles to Cuba with which to threaten us.
But the trend had set in and when, in June 1967, Kosygin came over
to the UN and popped down to New Jersey to visit with President
Johnson, there wasn't a picketer in sight.

The incident is revealing not only for reteaching us what is after
all obvious—that that which arouses public protest on Monday becomes routine on Tuesday. It teaches us also that some connections
are forever broken by the snapping of a symbolic switch. What appeared so wrong to many people was the very idea of a state visit by
the active leader of the most highly organized totalitarian force in history. That is the force which Mr. Henry Kamm of the *New York
Times*, no doubt greatly surprising some of his colleagues, identified
two weeks ago on his return from a tour of duty in the Soviet Union
as the "most comprehensive onslaught that has ever been mounted on
the human spirit." But the moment that Khrushchev's visit was consummated, it became ever after all but impossible to restore the status
quo ante; so that an attempt to return to chastity became, in a way,
pointless. Once one is deflowered, that is it.

Thus when the invasion of Czechoslovakia took place [in August
1968] the editorial chastisements of the Soviet Union were just a little perfunctory, like an obituary notice written years ago that is pulled
out and given a fresh lead. Sub specie aeternitatis they are equally
horrifying, the rape of Hungary (as we used to call it) and that of
Czechoslovakia twelve years later. But somewhere along the line the
word went out—and its force was not lost on conservatives—that it
had become somehow vulgar to raise one's voice against the
Communists. So that when we did so in the summer of 1968, it was
like an impromptu cadenza, the climax of which was candidate
Richard Nixon's suggestion that perhaps this was not the ideal climate in which to vest our confidence in an anti-proliferation treaty.
Six months later President Nixon routinely sent the treaty through
for ratification, with an explanation as to why things were different
now from what they had been last August, an explanation which
nobody can recall with any precision.

What is the meaning of this for conservatives? It drives us, even as domestic developments do, to different positions. The major battle of the year was over ABM [the Anti-Ballistic Missile treaty]. Never mind the scientific dispute, which, after all, is neatly consigned to irrelevance by the observation that if the one group of scientists is correct we have lost five or so billion dollars; if the other is correct we might lose thirty million lives. The anti-Communism of the old days, when YAF was founded, was in part evangelistic. It held, as the Sharon Statement records, that we had an obligation to help those who could not help themselves to fend off the juggernaut. There was talk, even, of rolling back the Iron Curtain—the liberation rhetoric of the early 1950s. But the principal thrust of anti-Communism—again I refer you to the Sharon Statement—was less evangelistic than self-affirmative. Anti-Communism was a means of saying not only that we disliked Stalin, but that we liked the opposite of Stalin: represented, roughly speaking, by—us.

The debate on ABM at one level counterpoised the true conservatives and call them what you will—"the doubters" is perhaps the least provocative designation. The conservatives are reduced to insisting that the defense of our country is worth it at any cost. This was at the heart of the debate. During the four or five years preceding it, doubts about America were industriously cultivated, doubts that had never been raised before outside the camps of the neurotically disaffected. Who, for instance, listening to the public utterances of the Reverend William Sloane Coffin or of Dr. Benjamin Spock would conclude that saving what we now have—whatever its faults— is worth even the hypothetical risk of atomic war? What we have is a country (ask the Kerner Commission) deeply and passionately committed to racism; a country (ask Seymour Melman) altogether dominated by the military-industrial complex; the world's principal agent of violence and savagery (ask Martin Luther King); the apogee of materialism and hypocrisy (ask Herbert Marcuse). Why would anyone go to such lengths as conceivably might be required to preserve such a nation as that? A velleity to survive is one thing. An atomic defense is another.

I see it as the historical role of young Americans for freedom and old Americans for freedom not to abandon our traditional concerns, but to accept the necessity for gut affirmations respecting America's way of doing things. We are under the circumstances constrained to look anew at, for instance:

(1) *The democratic process.* This was never considered by conservatives as a principal responsibility of ours. There were quite enough bards of democracy floating about, even ideologists of democracy: even imperialists of democracy. So that for years conservatives thought it better to ask questions about what it was that democracy had ushered in, rather than join the chorus that made the democratic process itself the venerable thing.

It is a little different now. Because order has been challenged, and conservatives have always believed in the blessings of a rudimentary order. It was, above all, the conservatives who observed that Lyndon Johnson had been elected president by the democratic process and that, pending his repudiation, rights were vested in him to exercise. And conservatives have had to stress the democratic process at other than governmental levels. It isn't exactly democracy that designates who will be the president and the fellows of Harvard University, but the views of the relevant constituency, the alumni of Harvard, are taken into consideration. So that conservatives find themselves defending the rights of the authorities of Harvard against the mobocratic demands of students and faculty who wish to leapfrog the authorities so as to have their own impulsive way, instantly.

(2) *Due process,* the meticulous cousin of democracy. We have often looked cynically on due process—the means, along with the Constitution's commerce clause, by which the federal government has managed whatever intervention in human affairs appealed to it. Thus due process was used by the Supreme Court to revolutionize criminal prosecution, even as the Court had used the commerce clause to defend Congress's right to set the rate of pay of elevator operators. The abuse of due process was rampant: but how valuable due process becomes, up against Marcusean furies! Thus conservatives, though perhaps historically bitter over what due process was

made to do at the hands of the abstractionists and the semantical profiteers, find ourselves fighting especially hard for its survival. The guillotine is sharpened not alone for those who have been raised over us by the exercise of democratic authority—the Lyndon Johnsons, the Richard Daleys, the Nathan Puseys—but also for others—the prosperous owners of Dow Chemical (*Merchants of death, take away what they have*), the little Jewish delicatessen owner in Harlem (*Racist exploiter, vandalize him out of existence*).

(3) *Upward mobility*. Over the years the social democrats were thought of as the principal enthusiasts for it because of their social programs, which were essentially egalitarian. The conservatives insisted (quite rightly) that upward mobility was precisely what the free-market system most generously contributed to, and we had the figures to prove it. But having said as much we left it (quite naturally) to internal resources, up against the system, to take advantage of the opportunities to rise. Many many millions took those opportunities. But now the need for that mobility is more acute than ever because of such restlessness as is suggested in the letter of the despairing young man from Berkeley. So much so that many conservatives are giving the free market something of a hand, for instance, by preferential hiring of Negroes. That is helpful. Even more helpful, I think most of you would agree, is a concerted assault on institutional barriers to the rise of the poor. So? Repeal the minimum-wage laws. Destroy anti-black discrimination in the labor unions. Ease—preferably, eliminate—the graduated feature of the income tax. Adopt an altogether different attitude towards what Mr. Roger Starr [the social historian] so acutely isolates as the "disorganized poor," in contrast to the transient poor.

Here is an order of concerns for the conservatives which by no means involves the abandonment, let alone the theoretical repudiation, of some of our other concerns. But the historical responsibility of the conservatives is altogether clear: it is to defend what is best in America. At all costs. Against any enemy, foreign or domestic. That way only can we find fruitful avenues for our energies, and rediscover a way to attract the attention of the sophomores at Berkeley and elsewhere who, lacking your faith, lack your imagination. There is so much that might rescue us, that might leaven the life of the sophomore at Berkeley. You can't get it merely from an organization. But organizations have their place, and yours is a glorious place in these days of upheaval and self-doubt, when you can be seen going about your business, exercising your freedoms as individuals, but concerting to make known to the doubters that you *know*—know enough to believe in the American dream; enough to know that what we have in America is worth saving, yea even unto the consummation of the world.

THE SEVENTIES

ON THE WELL-TEMPERED SPIRIT

A Commencement Address at Curry College; Milton, Mass., May 31, 1970

Still a turbulent season, with student demonstrations and canceled college commencements; it was the year of the shooting at Kent State. I began with colloquial references to the scene and led off with the question of "the stabilization of the spirit," enjoining the graduating class to acknowledge the uses of technology, so deplored in that season, and the continuing uses of reason.

I T IS THE fashion to remark that you leave after today for the great wide world of adventure. It is more appropriate, under the circumstances, to say of those of you who are leaving the academy that you are moving into a world of relative tranquillity conducive to the stabilization of the spirit—even if one worries, in our age, whether the spirit *can* be stabilized without being totally extinguished. . . .

I discern that that is the worry of sensitive people of your age, here and elsewhere. It is also the worry of sensitive people who are older than you. A worry of those who have made it, but are still enough alive to know from the sensations in their head and in their loins that they are not hollow men, dying from Portnoy's complaint or coupling their way through an eternal wastefulness with no higher goal than to make John Updike credible. But they worry. It is always touch and go: now you're alive; now you're not quite sure you're alive.

And a worry of those who have not made it, those who fall and know that they have fallen: like John Cheever's Wapshots, who manage in their aristocratic destitution to be quite objective about it all, taking the precisionist's stock of their depleted reserves of puritan blood and their dissipated ethos—and reasoning that you can't change it, can't change the system; and anyway, if you could, who is to say that you'd even then come out alive? They worry too, some of them, about those younger than they who have not lost their spirit: worry lest they should do so, lest the young should become old.

I do not know the formula for a well-tempered spiritual adjustment that situates us somewhere between licentiousness and torpor. I do know that my Redeemer liveth, and that we are capable of being surprised by joy. But one is timid about expressing one's private formulas, because they are likely to disappoint others. Yet certain things can be attempted, obliquely.

(1) *I take it that you do not intend to repeal technology.* "I worked the hay load last night against the coming rain—by headlight, long after dark," Whittaker Chambers wrote a friend ten years ago. "I know the farmer's case for the machine and for the factory, and I know, like the cut of hay-bale cords in my hands, that [any political philosophy] that cannot find room in its folds for these actualities is a [philosophy] that is not a political force, or even a twitch: it has become a literary whimsy."

Just so. And yet the machine is nevertheless also the enemy. And we come to terms with it uneasily because we know that good machines, like tractors, can beget bad machines, like tanks: or, more exactly, we know that machines can be used not only to liberate farmers but also to enslave them. We know that the machine gives great leverage to human passions, and that such passions as fired the human spirit before the machine age fire the human spirit now: so that our disposition to protect ourselves against the machine requires of us in given circumstances quite inhuman activity, in which even poets and priests engage, as, for instance, thirty years ago, when we elected war over peace, because we reasoned that the machine had got into the hands of people whose possession of it we could not tolerate.

Now the machine, engorged by scientific discovery and technological ingenuity, has got so big that even though such reasoning as took us to war thirty years ago easily applies, we are, or believe ourselves to be, powerless to dispossess the current menace. And so we simply make do, as best we can: and, sometimes, to make things easier on our conscience, we persuade ourselves that perhaps the old equations have changed, perhaps the human disposition has altered: persuade ourselves, even, that nothing that can be done to us could be worse than the price we would need to pay in order to prevent its happening. The dilemma is, for some people, a real spirit crusher, and, inevitably, the public rhetoric dwells more on the explosive horror of the battlefield than on the encephalophonic hideousness of the slave state. I do not know what will be the final resolution of this great tension. The Vietnam War is an expression of one adaptation to it, but that war, so remote, so unloved, so inglorious, teaches us that the disposition to fight those who abuse the machine runs nowadays thinly in our veins, leaving us uncertain and introspective, wondering whether we are left even with the powers to distinguish the just from the unjust cause.

(2) *I take it that however caught up you are in the romanticisms which sweep the world you will not deny the occasional uses of reason.* Reason is to be sure in disrepute, because reason has been used to construct whole systems we abhor. Reason must be denied when it becomes presumptuous, which is to say, when it goes forward as rationalism. Michael Oakeshott reminds us that in the civil order, rationalism is "making politics as the crow flies." We have done a fair amount of that kind of thing in recent times in America, and have bred ourselves great frustrations. We fused rationalism with utopia, and the result was psychedelic.

There came, as there had to come, the great disillusionment. Some went so far as to drop out—and yet they seem especially sad, especially lonely. "Now that I've dropped out," says Claude plaintively in the play *Hair*, "why is life so dreary, dreary? / Answer my weary query, / Timothy Leary, dearie."

Mostly, they didn't drop out, but such disillusion as set in colored whole worldviews, rendered reason suspect—though not, curiously, utopianism. There are those who are angry because Lyndon Johnson failed to eliminate poverty, but who are unquestioning about Mao Tse-tung's incapacity to produce shredded wheat. Reason may not save us, any more than it saved the Delian League, but the absence of reason will not help us. How, for instance, without invoking reason, do we discover some very simple things? If, as Professor [Staughton]

Lynd and others are claiming, what we are experiencing in America today, on the campuses and in the cities, is revolution, how, except through the use of reason, do we discover that in that event the state is authorized to exercise counterrevolutionary powers?

And (3) *I take it that you will not want to deny the idealism of other men, who pursue other visions than your own.* It is dangerous to do so. Whittaker Chambers wrote to me on one occasion to remind me what were Bukharin's last words to the court which condemned him to death. "I do not understand," Chambers complained, "how men, knowing that, in our own lifetime, another man spoke these words at such a moment, can read them and fail to be rent apart by their meaning. Yet these words are scarcely known. I would print them bold and hang them at the front of college classrooms, not to be explained as a text, but to be seen often and quietly reflected on."

Bukharin, it must be remembered, is literally innocent. He is guilty only of the logic of his position, the fact that, in the given historical juncture, the position which he held in theory might, if pushed into the realm of practice, work against the Revolution. It is his uncommitted crime that he pleads guilty to. He says: "I shall now speak of myself, of the reasons for my repentance. . . . For when you ask yourself: 'If you must die, what are you dying for?' an absolutely black vacuity suddenly rises before you with startling vividness. There was nothing to die for if one wanted to die unrepentant. . . . This, in the end, disarmed me completely and led me to bend my knees before the Party and the country. At such moments, Citizen Judges, everything personal, all personal incrustation, all rancor, pride, and a number of other things, fall away, disappear. . . . I am about to finish. I am perhaps speaking for the last time in my life."

"Is there not," Chambers asks, "a stillness in the room where you read this? That is the passing of the wings of tragedy."

It is by the exercise of reason that one discovers the errors of the particular idealism to which Bukharin remained faithful, and for which he gave his life. But reason also reveals the symmetrical cogency of his final decision to repent, even as reason discloses the irresistible arguments for considering this impure nation of ours as the altogether proper vehicle for our hope, as a continuing source of our critical pride, as the deserving object, my accomplished friends, of your devoted attention.

RESOLUTELY ON THE SIDE OF YALE'S SURVIVAL

Remarks (excerpted) at the Twentieth Reunion of the Yale Class of 1950; New Haven, Conn., June 12, 1970

These few words were spoken at a moment of special tension at Yale University. Two months earlier students and faculty had called a strike to protest the trial in New Haven of Black Panther leader Bobby Seale. The president of Yale, Kingman Brewster, had opined that he did not believe black revolutionaries could get a fair trial anywhere in the United States; Vice President Spiro Agnew had retorted that President Brewster should resign in favor of someone more mature and responsible; and President Brewster had shot back with an invidious remark concerning the qualifications of the vice president. . . . But reunions have to have a bit of the old spirit—here attempted, before touching down on the pressure points of the day.

R EUNIONS ARE, to say the least, permissive occasions. I remember five years ago. I sat after dinner in the courtyard of Branford College, next to Charlie Taylor, who was next to Van Galbraith. Suddenly, courtesy of the greatest impresario in the history of college reunions, Dealer Clark, we found ourselves looking at first one, then a second stripteaser, both of whom obviously put their hearts into their work. I somehow found it a little awkward to continue the usual badinage with Charlie—after all, there he was, the second-ranking educational official of Yale University, sitting in Mr. Branford's courtyard, and doing what? Reading a novel by Jane Austen? Writing poetry? Drinking beer and reminiscing about the

Harvard-Yale game? No, he was studying the ecdysiast's art, with a professional concern that becomes a university official on the eve of coeducationalization. Still, the paradox was a little oppressive, and after the girls had withdrawn, the cheers of the class of 1950 ringing in their ears, Van turned and said, "Charlie, what is Official Yale's position towards this?" Charlie removed the pipe from his mouth, looked sternly in the direction of the now-empty stage, and replied, "Yale's official position is that the Second One is better than the First One."

Taking that as a Lesson, I proceed on the assumption that the prevailing good humor and toleration are such as will permit a member of this class to touch lightly on certain themes which, when taken together, do not come out as merely another chorus of "Old College Years" or, even, of "Brewster's a Jolly Good Fellow." . . .

Here at Yale the entire campus was mobilized around the proposition that justice was not being done to the Black Panthers. Then President Nixon announced the Cambodian incursion, and the demonstration proceeded—same actors, same lines; the most exacting ballet master could not have detected a missing beat. In France there is no Vietnam, no Black Panthers: and yet the students recently paralyzed France, and are today scattering bombs about the country, as routinely as they would hail a bus. . . .

Surely Yale has failed to register these points. And to note that Yale's failure is after all no greater than the failure of society at large is twice to obscure the question, because Yale's responsibilities are greater than the responsibilities of the provinces, point one, and point two, in fact the provinces seem to have done much better than Yale at registering the essential points. Mr. Agnew's suggestion that Mr. Brewster be replaced was certainly presumptuous, even as it would be presumptuous for Mr. Brewster to suggest that the class of 1950 designate a different speaker. But the provenance of a suggestion does not define the merit of it.

And anyway, the replacement of an individual does not in and of itself assure that the policies one desires to replace will accordingly be replaced, which after all is the complaint we hear from those who understood themselves to be voting for Mr. Nixon in order to alter the policies of Mr. Johnson. Mr. Agnew's suggestion that Mr. Brewster's replacement would transform Yale is as romantic as Mr. Brewster's suggestion that abandoning Vietnam would compose Yale. Mr. Agnew's interest in the policies of Yale no doubt reflects his assessment of Yale's importance in the polity, which assessment in no sense differs from that of Mr. Brewster. Mr. Brewster no doubt rues the fact of his living in a society governed by such as Mr. Agnew, even as Mr. Agnew rues the prospect of living in a society governed by those who are being taught by Mr. Brewster to be skeptical about the ability of American institutions to behave justly. There are no ready resolutions to these problems, my very old friends, but I hope we can control the snobbish impulse to observe, as was indirectly done by one champion of Mr. Brewster, that a man with the limited educational background of Spiro Agnew isn't fit to advise so finished an educator as Mr. Brewster. Because, of course, that way *tu quoque* lies; and before you know it, you have Mr. Agnew observing that anyone who cannot control the Students for a Democratic Society on the campus of Yale ought not to instruct the President of the United States on how to control the Communist armies on the Asian continent. If you see what I mean.

I do think this: that five years from now when we meet again, it will have become clear whether Yale will survive as a private institution devoted to her old ideals. I can only say in defense of my remarks, and others that I have made about Yale during the preceding twenty years, that I hope I have made it clear that I am, most resolutely, on the side of Yale's survival. I extend to you all my thanks, and my most affectionate greetings.

THE REPUBLIC'S DUTY TO REPRESS

A Luncheon Address at a Conference of New York State Trial Judges,
Sponsored by the Judicial Conference of the State of New York;
Crotonville, N.Y., June 25, 1970

---

*The dissent that had begun with a call for civil rights and gone on to insist
on a withdrawal from Vietnam was now showing signs of "the anarchic
passion to smash," characterized in another context fifty years before by
Herbert Agar. The revolutionists were adamant in their claims. They
insisted that the Constitution and its judicial and theoretical evolution
guaranteed them absolute rights to proceed with their pursuits, which here
and there even involved deaths, but at the least involved disturbances
that interfered with others' civil rights. I undertook to make the case that
the maintenance of order had high constitutional sanction.*

I SHOULD LIKE to record a few impressions of the contemporary
scene, some of them obviously related to each other, others less
obviously so; all of them, I think, impinging in some way on an
understanding of what is going on. Accordingly, I attempt a few
propositions.

Proposition 1: *The opinion-making community misunderstands the
usefulness of repression.*

I mean by this proposition to draw attention to the great success
the recent mentors of American civilization have enjoyed when they
suggest that repression is the kind of thing practiced only by Storm
Troopers and rationalized in *Mein Kampf*, or, in other situations, by
such as Lester Maddox in his chicken restaurant, driven by theories
of white supremacy.

I am indebted to Professor Harry Jaffa for an essay which in my
judgment forever destroys the dilettante's notion that it is the theoretical burden of the tolerant forever to endure intolerance.

It is his conclusion that there is no evidence in early American
history to suggest that the men who wrote the Constitution believed

that all thought was in some way equal, simply because they went on to devise a Bill of Rights that forbade the Congress to enact any laws abridging the freedom of speech or of the press. When Thomas Jefferson spoke about the virtue of tolerating even those who seek to repeal our republican form of government, it seems clear from his other writings, and from the lapidary record of his own activities, that what he meant to say was that the toleration of certain kinds of dissent is a tribute to the majority of the people, who can be counted on to reject the blandishments of an anti-republican minority. It is, after all, a form of democratic self-indulgence to allow oneself to stroll peacefully through Hyde Park listening to orators who denounce our free institutions. It puts one in mind of the cozy children's dream of waking up suddenly in a jungle surrounded by wild beasts who however are powerless to harm you, because you are surrounded by an impenetrable bubble of glass.

Abraham Lincoln the polemicist pulled a fast one, Professor Jaffa reminds us, in his Gettysburg Address. His old adversary Stephen Douglas during the famous debates had based his case on the Constitution alone—with exclusive reference to which it could indeed be argued that the *Dred Scott* decision was meticulously correct. Lincoln, at Gettysburg, cited the founding of the United States as having taken place "four score and seven years" before. That is to say, in 1776, with the adoption of the Declaration of Independence. Accordingly, said Lincoln in effect, the ideals of the Declaration of Independence animate the Constitution: so that when scholars and statesmen disagreed, as they did with increasing heat in the years that led to the explosion of civil war, it was to the Declaration of Independence that the abolitionists repaired for guidance. The Declaration spoke of self-evident truths, among them that men are born equal. The initial toleration of slavery, in the understanding of Lincoln, was a historical accommodation, the accommodation of a great weight on America's neck, to be recognized by its leaders as such, to the end that, step by step, they might direct public policy towards emancipation by attrition. Professor Jaffa reminds us that "no American statesman ever violated the ordinary maxims of civil liberties more than did Abraham Lincoln; and few seem to have been more careful of them than Jefferson Davis." And then he adds the point which is so striking in the present situation: "Yet the cause for the sake of which the one slighted these maxims was human freedom, while the other, claiming to defend the forms of constitutional government, found in those forms a ground for defending and preserving human slavery." It is instructive to meditate on this apparent paradox at a moment when so much of the liberal community is disposed to denounce such modest efforts as are nowadays being made to enhance the public order.

Proposition 2: *The absolutizers, in their struggle against what they call repression, are doing their best to make the Constitution incoherent.*

It ought to be obvious that it is impossible to absolutize any one freedom without moving it into the way of another absolutized freedom. How can you simultaneously have an absolute right to compel testimony in your own behalf (Amendment 6) while others have the absolute right (Amendment 5) to refuse to testify lest they incriminate themselves? How can you have absolute freedom of the press (Amendment 1) alongside the absolute right to a fair trial (Amendment 6)? How can you have absolute freedom of speech (Amendment 1) alongside other people's absolute right (Amendment 14) to their property, including their good name?

Oliver Wendell Holmes, asked to define a fanatic, said something to this effect: Look, everyone will agree as a matter of common sense that a house owner owns the space above his roof, so that, for example, he can prevent his neighbor from constructing a perpendicular extension reaching out from his own house to overshadow his neighbor's. The fanatic, however, will reason from his ownership of the space above his roof to ownership of a shaft of air that projects straight out into the heavenly spheres, such that no child's kite or supersonic transport can overfly him without written permission. It is ironic that it is to a famous dissent of Oliver Wendell Holmes that the absolutizers, which is to say the fanatics, turn when insisting that all ideas are to be treated with absolute impartiality. It was Justice Holmes who said that "the best test of truth is the power of the thought to get itself accepted in the competition of the market."

If that maxim were accepted, white racial superiority would long since have been accepted as truth in parts of this and other countries. In any case, the statement is hard to reconcile with the notion that some truths are self-evident. Certainly it is hard to reconcile with the attitudes of the men who urged the adoption of the Constitution.

The Federalist Papers stressed among other things the usefulness of a federal government in guaranteeing freedom within the individual states. Concerning the problem of indigenous threats to the Republic, Alexander Hamilton wrote most directly. His plea for the proposed Constitution was not merely a plea against the anarchy that every schoolboy knows he abhorred. He knew also of the dangers of despotism. "It is impossible to read the history of the petty republics of Greece and Italy," he wrote, "without feeling sensations of horror and disgust at the distractions with which they were kept in a state of perpetual vibration between the extremes of tyranny and anarchy." He went on to argue that historical advances in the science of government now permitted the granting of powers sufficient to avoid anarchy, yet insufficient to promote tyranny.

But he did insist that the government must have the power necessary to make its laws obeyed—such power, it might be argued, as the present-day revolutionists and their fellow travelers are quick to criticize, pleading an absolutized version of the Bill of Rights. Hamilton wrote in criticism of the Articles of Confederation that the government as then composed had "no powers to exact obedience or punish disobedience to [its] resolutions either by pecuniary mulcts or by a suspension or divestiture of privileges, or by any other constitutional mode." Unless that situation were changed, he warned, the United States would afford "the extraordinary spectacle of a government destitute even of the shadow of constitutional power to enforce the execution of its own laws."

So the Constitution that Hamilton and the others advocated was adopted, and inasmuch as it expressly guarantees republican government to each constituent state, we get a little historical focus on Thomas Jefferson's boast of the nation's toleration even of those who would tear down our republican form of government. But Hamilton went on in his analyses, veering towards the same sin of civic pride that Jefferson was to commit more flamboyantly a few years later, that John Stuart Mill would elevate to democratic dogma a generation after that, Oliver Wendell Holmes going to the final extreme in 1919. Hamilton wrote: "Where the whole power of the government is in the hands of the people, there is the less pretense for the use of violent remedies in partial or occasional distempers of the State. The natural cure for an ill administration is a change of men."

But what about those situations in which republican government is threatened, whether by an assertive minority or by a passive majority, or by a combination of the two? How much power should a government have to protect the Republic against insurrection? A very important question, which is being fought out today in Congress, in the courts, and among the opinion makers. On this matter the absolutists of, for instance, the American Civil Liberties Union feel perfectly at home with all the old rigidities. But they are not winning all the constitutional debates. It is currently being tested, for instance, whether the government may punish those who, in the opinion of the court, conspired to go to Chicago in order to abridge the freedom of others to transact their business at the Democratic Convention. The question arises: Is the 1968 act under which the Chicago 7 were tried and convicted constitutional? "The idea of restraining the legislative authority in the means of providing for the national defense," Hamilton ventured, "is one of those refinements which owe their origin to a zeal for liberty more ardent than enlightened." He argued that, after all, "confidence must be placed somewhere," and that "it is better to hazard the abuse of that confidence than to embarrass the government and endanger the public safety by impolitic restrictions on the legislative authority."

So, then, was Hamilton encouraging something which nowadays would go by the name of "repression"? *Precisely.* "The hope of impunity is a strong incitement to sedition; the dread of punishment, a proportionally strong discouragement to it." Over and over again Hamilton leans on the assumption that the general majority are as a practical matter going to be content with laws which are in some sense of their own devising. However, he implicitly acknowledges that irrationality could now and again raise its ugly head. To assume that the government in a democratic society will not ever have to use force to assert its laws is naive; ". . . the idea of governing at all times by the simple force of law (which we have been told is the only admissible principle of republican government)," he writes acidulously, "has no place but in the reveries of those political doctors whose sagacity disdains the admonitions of experimental instruction."

Very well then, if we concede that the right to attempt to bring down the republican form of government is not absolute, either in theory or in the historical experience of America, does it follow that we are bound to indulge, let alone applaud, such expressions of public impatience as are embodied in the 1968 act? We come to

Proposition 3: *Such self-proclaimed revolutionists as Messrs. Hoffman, Rubin, Dellinger, and Seale, and such others as, for instance, Tom Hayden and Staughton Lynd, do not appear to understand the historical, let alone the theoretical, rights of counterrevolutionists.*

In the beginning—for our current revolutionists—was the American Revolution. It is their charter, the touchstone of their thought and their action. It is as important to their defense of their dogma and their behavior as Prohibition is to the defense of the young pot-smoker who says, If the older generation could drink unconstitutional booze, why can't we smoke illegal grass? The revolutionists insist that this country was after all baptized in revolution, that revolution is genetically a part of the American way.

Although some historians have insisted that the American Revolution was not a revolution properly speaking but rather an act of secession, it is instructive to recall that whichever of the two it was, the British were, if only by contemporary standards, entitled to resist it. Edmund Burke, whose sympathies were plainly with America, never suggested that King George was violating any known canon of civilization by sending a large army to America to say *No* to the army of George Washington. If Washington had been caught and hanged, Burke would no doubt have deplored royal punctilio, but there was no higher law in plain sight to appeal to than had been available to

Vercingetorix to use against Julius Caesar. By the same token, the United States today is entitled, by conventional standards, to hang true revolutionists.

If, then, the present-day revolutionists can find no historical right to revolt against our society under immunity from repression, can they find any abstract "right" to commend their enterprise?

Mr. Jefferson's Declaration of Independence acknowledges the "right of the people" to "alter or abolish" their government and "to institute a new government, laying its foundation on such principles, and organizing its powers in such form, as to them shall seem most likely to effect their safety and happiness."

The Declaration goes on to enumerate the grievances of the colonies. It is a stirring catalogue, but it finally reduces to the matter of the source of power, i.e., Who should rule? "He [King George] has refused his assent to laws the most wholesome and necessary for the public good," says the Declaration. Who is to decide what are the laws most wholesome and necessary for the public good? Why, the people—the people who are affected by those laws. The American Revolution was about *who* should rule. Everybody? Mr. Jefferson, perhaps from tact—perhaps even from cunning—introduces into the peroration of his manifesto a subtle distinction: "We, therefore, the representatives of the United States of America . . . do, in the name and by the authority of the good people of these colonies, solemnly publish and declare . . ." The *good* people of these colonies? A ritual obeisance? Or a sly recognition that there are plenty of colonials around who oppose secession? Bad people?

Mr. Jefferson always acknowledged the existence of bad people, in a way that Oliver Wendell Holmes had difficulty in doing, so absolute was his relativism. But Jefferson's rationalist faith in the inherent power of good ideas to defeat bad ideas in the marketplace was ringingly proclaimed in his later years: "Those who wish to dissolve the union or to change its republican form should stand undisturbed as monuments of the safety with which error of opinion may be tolerated where reason is left free to combat it." It isn't of course suggested in this passage what is the indicated course of action if reason should fail in the performance of its delegated duty, but we know from Jefferson's own autocratic habits that he often gave reason a helping hand; and we know from the Declaration of Independence that he dubbed some truths as self-evident; and, derivatively, that he judged those people who acknowledged these truths as "good," and those who did not as something else. It was also Jefferson, presumably in a more skeptical frame of mind, who said, "Let us hear no more of trust in men, but bind them down from mischief by the chains of the Constitution."

From all of which one infers that in Jefferson's America (a) there is, on some very basic points, a right and a wrong position; (b) the probability is that the people will opt for the right position, prodded by reason to do so; but (c) it sometimes becomes necessary to resist the bad people, whether they are numerous, or whether they are, simply, the King of England. Abbie Hoffman [one of the Chicago 7] is not the King of England, but the point is that he seeks a kind of metaphorical accession to the throne, and the corollary point in our troubled times is, Shall we restrain him? And if so, how? How shall we protect not so much the White House from his occupation of it as lesser folk than the president—you and me and the rest—from such a denial of our rights as Mr. Hoffman and his mini-legions are capable of effecting, in their quixotic but not altogether toothless campaign for revolution? The Jeffersonian ideal continues to be exemplary: the Hoffmans and the Dellingers and the Cleavers should be laughed, or disdained, into impotence. But there is a creeping difference between, for instance, the way the whole of the American public reacted against the white racists who assaulted the civil-rights advocates during the 1960s, and the way the community reacts now to the New Left revolutionaries. Mr. Al Lowenstein recently told me that it was not a new experience for him to be silenced, and even threatened and shouted down, by those who disagree with him. But when he was given such treatment by Ku Klux types in the South, the whole of America reacted in horror and registered its solidarity with those who worked for the continuing attrition of the birthmark that the Civil War did not succeed altogether in erasing. A few months ago, at Columbia University, Mr. Lowenstein was hooted down and literally silenced for defending the right of Professor Herman Kahn to speak unmolested. Faculty members in the audience countenanced and even egged on the jacobinical furies that ruled the crowd—who needless to say went unpunished, even unreprimanded, although they most indisputably conspired together to abridge the civil liberties of two men, Herman Kahn and Al Lowenstein, who have never by word or deed disparaged the civil liberties of any American citizen.

Proposition 4: *So far have the professionally tolerant gone towards fanaticism that we stand in danger of losing the salutary force of public sanction.*

If it blurs in the mind just who are the Black Panthers, why they are an organization founded a few years ago on the doctrine that the United States is a racist-oppressive country best dealt with by the elimination of its leaders and institutions. Suggestive of its rhetorical style is the front page of its house organ, which featured on the day after his death a photograph of Robert Kennedy lying in a pool of his own blood, his face transformed to the likeness of a pig.

Do you think Robert Kennedy was a pig? I asked Eldridge Cleaver a while ago. Yes, he said. Did Cleaver believe in the elimination of pigs? Yes, he did. Well, why not begin with Nixon: surely he is the chief pig? I observed. Mr. Cleaver, who has had intimate experience with the law, advised me that he knew enough not to counsel directly the assassination of the president, but that if in fact someone did kill him, that would be one less pig in the world.

Those who believe that Cleaver, and derivatively the Panthers, have mellowed might look at the introduction Cleaver wrote to Jerry Rubin's book, published recently by the august house of Simon & Schuster, putting us in mind of Lenin's comment that when the last bourgeois is hanged, it will have been a capitalist who sold the hangman the rope. In his introduction Mr. Cleaver, an official of the Black Panthers, urges his disciples in America, black and white, to "rise up and kill pigs," and recalls as the most precious memory of his political experience a shoot-out in Oakland, California, at which he observed that after one salvo, a "pig white lay dead, deep fried in the fat of his own bullshit."

Mr. Cleaver is not in this country, his career as visiting professor at Berkeley having been interrupted by a parole court. We cannot do anything about him. So what do we do about the other Black Panthers, of whom he is the spiritual leader? Why, if we are Leonard Bernstein, we have a big cocktail party to which we invite a local representative of the Panthers.

Mr. Bernstein, in pursuit of understanding, had obviously been studying up on the idiom of the times; indeed, it is altogether possible that he staged a rehearsal or two, because a dialogue with a Black Panther is every bit as difficult to perform as a symphony of Schönberg. Anyway, the Black Panther, Mr. Cox, began by announcing that if business didn't provide full employment, then the Panthers would simply take over the means of production and put them in the hands of the people, to which prescription it is recorded that Mr. Bernstein replied, "I dig absolutely."

Mr. Cox told the gathering how very pacific he and his confederates are; that ultimately of course they desire peace, but that they have been attacked in their homes and murdered in their beds and have the right to defend themselves. "I agree 100 percent," Lenny said, neglecting to ask Mr. Cox to explain to what defensive uses his confederates intended to put the hand grenades and Molotov cocktails that were discovered in the raids. . . .

Proposition 5: *Although such as Eldridge Cleaver can be extremely specific, the vagueness of the revolutionary program of much of the New Left is its most singular strength, confronting the Republic with its subtlest challenge.*

It is a commonplace to observe that those of a rebellious spirit in our midst do not know what they want. And even that they do not know by what means to achieve the conditions they cannot specify. I consider these data rather less reassuring than otherwise. If the revolutionists were committed to an identifiable program, they might be bombarded with demonstrations that their program, or an approximation of it, is not producing the goods (in Cuba, say, or in the Soviet Union). But precisely the de-ideologization of their movement—the loose-jointedness of their approach—leaves them in a frame of mind at once romantic and diffuse, and the rest of us without the great weapon available to King Canute when he was able to contrive what would nowadays be called A Confrontation between the ineluctable laws of nature and the superstitious indulgences of his subjects. . . .

It is all very well to take the revolutionists by the scruff of the neck and show them that revolutions, as Professor Toynbee preaches, historically have not brought about the ends explicitly desired, but something very like their opposite; but the success of such demonstrations presupposes a clinical curiosity on the part of the observer, and such is not the temper of those in America who are talking about revolution. The point to stress is that the allure of revolution and the importance of revolutionary attitudes in present-day political and social affairs are bound to grow, not only because the sanctions of stability are not being pressed, but precisely because every modern irritation is transformed into yet another cause for revolutionary commitment, and the ideologists of revolution are careful to tread a line far enough on the specific side of generality to describe a recognizably American situation, yet far enough short of specificity to permit them constantly to nourish the revolutionary imagination—to stimulate the confidence that liberation lies just over there on the other side of the barricades, even as Nat Turner dreamed that if only he could make it to the Dismal Swamp, the world would begin anew.

Reason is not availing, not in the current mood. Reason cannot reach the revolutionary vapors on which the revolutionists are stoned. What is required, I think, is, among other things, a premonitory sign, a sign of firmness; such a sign as Hamilton foresaw might, from time to time, need to be shown.

That sign, my honorable friends, is above all yours to make. It is a sign—the enforcement of the law—that suggests a corporate reaffirmation of the community's ideals, the most pressing one being its decision to survive: all this keeping in mind the words of Belloc, who, observing the rise of Hitler in Europe, wrote: "We sit by and watch the barbarian; we tolerate him; in the long stretches of peace we are not afraid. We are tickled by his irreverence. His comic inversion of our old certitudes and our fixed creeds refreshes us. But as we laugh, we are watched by large and awful faces from beyond; and on these faces there is no smile."

It is your duty—your sublime duty, I judge it—to meditate on those martyrs who gave us our liberty, and on those corpses that met their bitter end because their liberties had been lost, and turn, unsmilingly, to the duty which it is your destiny, above that of any other class, to discharge, for the benefit of a grateful, dependent people.

"THAT MAN I TRUST"

Remarks (excerpted) to the New York Conservative Party's Annual Dinner;
the Waldorf-Astoria, New York, October 12, 1970

The Conservative Party dinner was alight with enthusiasm and hope. The Senate race, the polls revealed, was astonishingly close. The Republican incumbent, Senator Charles Goodell, appointed by Governor Rockefeller after the assassination of Senator Robert Kennedy in 1968, had turned hard left, alienating many voters. Democratic challenger Richard Ottinger was fighting hard, but the Conservatives' choice of James L. Buckley had actually suggested the possibility of a third-party victory, which would be the first since Robert La Follette went to the Senate in 1907 on the Progressive Party ticket. There was special excitement because Vice President Agnew had intimated support for Buckley, manifestly a rebuke of the incumbent by President Nixon, without whose consent Agnew would not have supported a non-Republican candidate. The preliminaries dispensed with (random railleries), I spoke a tribute to the candidate, as his younger brother.

I PROPOSE FROM this moment on to go nonpolitical. Or rather, to put it fairly: to be quite personal. My reason is that my political views are well known to you all; or if they are not, then I am the greatest failure in modern communications. The one thing I know better than anyone else on the platform tonight is not political or economic theory, or philosophy, or history; it is—Jim.

Will anybody listen to me? Would anybody take seriously advice given by Laurel about Hardy, or Gilbert about Sullivan?

I take the opportunity to recall that Gilbert and Sullivan couldn't stand each other; indeed (if my memory is right), they ended up refusing to have any personal dealings with each other, so that in fact their wonderful collaborations were coordinated through an agent, and they were spared, except perforce on opening nights, the pain of laying eyes on each other. So has it been, under the surface, with a number of figures, historical and current, who had close biological or professional ties, but who never got along offstage.

The thing about Jim is: he is out of this world. I mean by this that he is the only person I have ever known who has no enemies. It is extraordinary to be able to say this about Jim, because he is a very steadfast human being. He is, although always tactful, absolutely resolute about what he thinks. But there is something about him that has always persuaded everyone with whom he has contact that his fairness is, in a sense, a tribute even to those who are the immediate victims of that fairness. If Jim were a witness to an accident in which an automobile driven by his very best friend collided with an automobile driven by Eldridge Cleaver, and Jim saw that Cleaver had the green light, the testimony would be very direct on the matter, and Jim's good friend would—somehow—bear no resentment at all against Jim, even if he really and truly believed that at the moment of impact the light had turned against Eldridge Cleaver, which, come to think of it, lights would if the muses were at their proper stations.

Jim does that to people. It was so even when he was very, very young. Jim cared, always, for nature, so that, at age fourteen, he could not wait to enter Millbrook School, because he had heard about the fabulous zoo that the biology teacher there had founded. My father indulged him and, if I may say so, rather overdid it. I mean by that that Jim persuaded Father to invite the biology teacher and his wife to come to our home in Sharon, Connecticut, to spend the summer, in order to teach the rest of the family Everything There Is to Know about Biology and Animal Husbandry. When my father got a sniff of life with the biology teacher morning, noon, and night, he discreetly left, with my mother, to spend the summer in Ireland, leaving us poor victims helpless at the hands of Jim's favorite teacher. The result was a summer in which our free time was spent either in discussing the singular virtues, natural and moral, of leaving snakes unmolested; or in making graven images in plaster of Paris out of leaves taken from innocent trees; or in helping to build cages for what would become, before my father came back and promptly liquidated it, the largest zoo north of the Bronx.

Now the point of this story is that, notwithstanding the sheer torture of that summer inflicted by Jim on his eight brothers and sisters, somehow it didn't occur to any of us—not even to me, whose spleen, even at age ten, was hungry for objects of antipathy—to blame Jim for those two miserable months. Nevermind that I and my brothers and sisters had probably spent the most useful summer of our lives. The important thing to remember is that gruesome though it was, somehow we didn't blame it on Jim, though there was never any doubt that he was *personally and with malice aforethought responsible.*

Jim was a sophomore at Yale when the Japanese struck Pearl Harbor. He had been majoring in English literature and, on the side, watching birds and keeping snakes. Yes, snakes, or at least one snake. I hesitate to reveal this datum, since it is not likely that many voters in this election incline to herpetology, notwithstanding the *New York Times*'s political tastes. But it is a fact that Jim had a pet boa constrictor, left over from that summer zoo, which he used to take with him to class. Martha, as she was called, wound round his neck, then down his sleeve to the shirt cuff, where, one supposes, she would sleep, or listen, depending on the professor. The master of Jim's college in due course got wind of all this, and ordered the expulsion of Martha forthwith. It was not in those days known that the thing to do with obnoxious university officials is throw them into the river; hence Jim complied, and a big party was given for Martha, who was offered her fortnightly ration of one white mouse. Ladylike, she declined to gobble him down in the company of so many oglers.

Mind you, Jim did not then give up Martha. Martha was his Israel. He brought her to South Carolina for the vacation with his family. A few minutes before train time to go back to Yale, Jim, greatly distressed, reported that Martha had got out of her cage and disappeared. Distress does not do justice to the state of mind of those of us, young and old, who were *not* leaving in order to go back to the safety of Yale. We had to live in that house in the constant fear that one night Martha might take one of us for Jim, snuggle up, and give us a rapturous embrace, which might well have been our last. It was several months later that the local paper reported, in a tiny item, on a farmer who had shot an enormous snake, seven feet long. "If I didn't know better," the farmer was quoted as saying, "I'd have thought it was one of them bore constrictors they grow in Africa." Even after *that,* we didn't hate Jimmy.

At college he was on the newspaper, for which he wrote a thrice-weekly column on the affairs of the world, which didn't read his column, which is why the affairs of the world are in such bad shape. In the navy he served on an LST in the Pacific, and I remember receiving a letter from him when I was in basic training, I having complained about this or that. "Don't worry," he said. "Things go slowly in any bureaucracy, even in times of war. I am tempted to write an autobiography, which will be called: *My Meteoric Career in the Navy: From Ensign to Lt. J.G. in 39 Months.*" But by the fortieth month he was back, having survived a great deal of war, and having laid eyes on Peking. He went to law school and practiced in New Haven; then to New York, the home base for his travels, which included many months in the Philippines, Canada, Latin America, and Israel. His interest in public affairs was always marked, but he adopted, as so many people do, the idea that public affairs are for *other* people to take on. From this happy state I guess I bear some guilt for wrenching him, when I asked him to serve as my campaign manager in 1965. He consented to do so only because he will do anything any friend asks him to do, not because the life of politics engrossed him. Then, a few years later, the 1968 election. . . . And now?

Why do I prattle on about this kind of thing? In part because it would be unnatural, under the circumstances, not to dwell on Jim's personal characteristics. In part for other reasons. I had a conversation, a few years ago, with a very interesting and very well informed Englishman. He is the editor of the Sunday *Telegraph,* and he was in this country when John F. Kennedy was assassinated. He is considered, in England, the compleat Tory. During the years when he lived in Washington he was steadfastly pro-Kennedy. A few days after the assassination he visited with me, and I remarked on the anomaly of his being at once a conservative and a great enthusiast for a liberal Democrat. He replied that increasingly he thought less about ideology, more about human beings. His judgment was that John Kennedy was an exceptional human being, and that exceptional human beings would, in due course, come forward with desirable policies.

I let the matter drop, in part because I do not like to wrestle with guests, in part because I wanted to think through, a bit, what Mr. Peregrine Worsthorne meant. Well, I have done so, and have come to the conclusion that there is a transideological attraction to my brother Jim, something that causes people to believe that, notwithstanding explicit differences on explicit issues—like having to share quarters with Martha—somehow, they believe in him. I do not think that is necessarily an anti-intellectual impulse. I agree with Mr. Worsthorne that sometimes one comes, by whatever road, to the conclusion: *That man I trust.* I think that that quality in Jim has been his principal asset in this extraordinary contest. There are other people— you, me, thousands of others—who advocate the positions he advocates. But I do not think that many of us would have attracted, so quickly, so much general support. I think that many people who listen to Jim come to feel: Well, the issues are very complicated, and I know that there are very complicated reasons for saying yes or no on this or that question, and so I am going to vote for Jim Buckley. Because I believe that he is less tied than others to political fashions, less enslaved than others by ideological abstractions.

Jim wrote me a couple of years ago, when it had been suggested to him that he should run for the Senate, to say with his instinctive modesty, "I can't imagine why I'd be useful to the public, still less why the public should want me." I liked that then, and I like it still more now, in the light of the overwhelming evidence, given by New Yorkers, that they *do* want him to speak for them, on so many of the problems, so very vexing, that are coming up. We used to tease Jim that he was never available for any family function on Saturday, because Saturdays are when people tend to get married, and Jim was always away at weddings, usually as best man, sometimes as usher. His friends felt, instinctively, that they wanted him around at critical peri-

ods in their lives. I think that the voters of New York feel the same
way about Jim, wanting him in the Senate at this critical period in our
lives.

THE WORLD THAT LENIN SHAPED

A Lecture (excerpted) at Tulane University; New Orleans, La., April 21, 1971

---

*Word had got out that I had just visited the Soviet Union, and the invi-
tation was to talk about the trip, which I did in the narrative mode—as
it happened, almost exactly a year before a trip to an even more forbidden country, China. I told of the atmosphere in the Soviet Union under
Brezhnev and of the adventures of, not exactly a tourist (I was there on
an official visit as a member of the U.S. Advisory Commission on Information, which oversees the U.S. Information Agency), but a visitor who
looked with a tourist's wide eyes, seeing a great sadness.*

I T WASN'T SO long ago, to answer directly a question put to me by
my hosts at dinner, that one simply didn't travel to Russia as a
routine thing. Years and years ago distance was the problem. It is
fifteen hundred miles from Paris to Moscow, and historical ac-counts
leave permanently in mind how long it took, how hard it was, and how
unprofitable was the journey for the most publicized nineteenth-
century traveler from Paris to Moscow, who barely made it back, leaving most of his army behind. More recently, the casual traveler was
simply not permitted to go to Russia: tourism was one of those few,
blessed subjects upon which V. I. Lenin did not pronounce, and
therefore the presumption—during the 1920s and 1930s—was: *No.*
To enter Stalin's Russia you had to be a journalist, preferably friendly; or a scientist; or Paul Robeson. After Stalin died, little by little, the
curtain was shiftily parted, and a trickle of disinterested Americans
came in.

I had been briefed in Washington and would be briefed again in

Moscow on how to keep out of trouble in Russia. No sex (the cameras are ubiquitous); no drunkenness (beware the Mickey Finn); no compassion for the stranger who approaches asking would you please mail this letter to her daughter when you reach New York (entrapment); no rubles bought in Paris (where you can get them at, approximately, seven for one versus the one-for-one official rate); no provocative ideological literature, even if it is for your own use (a novel by Solzhenitsyn is not the ideal thing to carry in your briefcase).

I was told about a recent case, an English M.P., a lovely fellow, brimming over with the milk of cultural exchange, who dutifully undertook at a ceremonial lunch to match his Soviet hosts drink for drink, toast for toast, to the point where, his vision having blurred a bit, he did not notice that the Russians who were now raising their glasses of vodka were not in fact the same Russians who had excused themselves a few moments before to use the sanitary facilities. They were what we imperialists call ringers, and they drank heartily, until the point of conviviality was reached beyond which our friend could not express himself except by lurching forward to the only window in the little banquet hall, and there relieving himself of every good wish he had so ceremoniously ingested in honor of Mother Russia and her contemporary leaders. By utter coincidence, exactly across the street was a Russian photographer with telescopic lens, who instinctively recorded the plight of the guilty, sick Englishman. Which photograph the Soviet press published widely, suggesting, ever so delicately, the incontinence of the typical English official visitor to the Union of Soviet Socialist Republics.

MOSCOW. THE AIRPORT. (Which, along with military installations, you are forbidden to photograph. Especially you must not photograph bridges. *Never* photograph a bridge. Don't even bring along with you a picture of your favorite bridge back home.) The terminal we landed at is strangely unmenacing in appearance, and would be thought inadequate as the municipal airport for Bridgeport, Connecticut. There is Muzak, and I heard "Home on the Range"! I had completed the Customs Declaration Form, answering "No" to the question did I have with me "gold, silver, platinum, metals of the platinum group, coins, bars, unwanted scrap, precious stones, pearls, and articles thereof." Then the drive into Moscow. It's late afternoon, during the equivalent of the Western rush hour. I didn't count, but I am certain we did not see twenty passenger cars along the twenty-five-mile route. It was a Vlaminck sky, dark grey, white white.

Moscow is at latitude fifty-five, abreast roughly of Copenhagen, so that during the late spring the day yields grudgingly to the night, and at 10:30 we could still make out the Prussian blue in the sky, giving the background for the golden domes and spires of the Kremlin, where at Ouspensky Cathedral eighty years ago, young Nicholas II was crowned emperor of Russia, and the people, in an excess of enthusiasm, stampeded over each other during the attendant celebration, killing one hundred of the celebrants. Their grandchildren, in *their* enthusiasm, line up day after day, by the thousands, to walk into the tomb of Lenin, who, through his minister Sverdlov, executed the czar and his empress and their children and every other Romanov he could get his hands on. They do not stampede, the present-day pilgrims, because queues in the Communist world are orderly, except where, as in East Germany up until 1961 and in today's Cuba, the frontier abuts on another world, in which case the queues are quite uncontrollable, so much so as to require, finally, huge walls, and paralyzed airports, and gunboats foraging in the fishing boats for human cargo, to stanch the flow of pilgrims who yearn to get away from the world shaped by the little bald brawny fanatic lying in state fifty years after his death, whom time has scarred so very much less than the world he had a hand in shaping.

But in Red Square, even as four hundred years ago they worshiped Ivan the Terrible, today they file into the squat, austere mausoleum on the terrace of which we can see the inscrutable officialdom of Red Russia lined up on ceremonial occasions, the Kremlinologists dangling over them with their calipers, to measure the telltale differences that might suggest who is closer today, who is further removed, from the power to catapult the world into one more war, the final war, perhaps. Behind Lenin's tomb is the Kremlin wall, on the grassy border of which the heroes of the Soviet Union are buried, or in any case memorialized, the least of them first on the northern end of the wall, their names written on stone slabs. Then, proceeding south, the greater figures, who merit bronze busts and pediments. Directly behind Lenin's tomb we saw the simple slab beneath which are the remains of Josef Stalin, removed from alongside Lenin after his disgrace in 1956. But Stalin is gradually rising from the dead. Only a month or so after we dallied over his perfunctory slab, a bust sprouted up from the ground—an enterprise which could not have required less official attention than the launching of a Skylab. Just this year, the Soviets managed to publish an official history of the Second World War and its aftermath without mentioning Stalin after 1945—one of those breathlessly humorless accomplishments of which they are so singularly capable, reminding us again and again and again of the undeniable vision of George Orwell.

THE AMERICAN AMBASSADOR had invited me to a biggish lunch with Soviet officials. And so, at 1300 Moscow Mean Time, on May 11, I walked down from my room into the great reception hall of Spaso House and, for the first time in my life, found myself surrounded by officials of the Soviet Union, each of them with a drink in his hand.

The gentleman on my left was afflicted with a fine sense of humor, which he turned uniformly on all matters, except of course that he would never turn it on the Soviet Union. I mean, if you had said to him, "Didja hear the one about what was the most important historical event of 1875? Lenin was *five years old*!!!!" he *might* have laughed, but there was enough ideological steel there to cause you not to go in for that kind of thing; so we talked about his avocations, the most important of them being canoeing. Canoeing. Hmmm. That made him a canoeist. I told him that not long ago Premier Trudeau of Canada had been accosted by a lady who, seizing his lapel, asked him, "Is it true that you were once a Communist?" Trudeau had answered, "No, madam, not a *Communist, a canoeist*"—and proceeded there and then to relate to her, at a length most distracting to his appointment keepers, his last memorable experience canoeing down some

Canadian river or another. "How long is that river?" my companion asked. I don't know, I said; very long. "Well," he smiled, "the river I went down on my last vacation was eighteen hundred kilometers long—and not one human being did I see the whole length of the passage!" I told him that that was quite extraordinary, which it certainly is, and promised to send him James Dickey's novel *Deliverance*, and we agreed that we both looked forward to our meeting tomorrow at the Institute of the U.S.A. and Canada. (The institute, run by Georgi Arbatov, is a fairly new, Kremlin-sponsored organization, composed of scholars, journalists, scientists, and diplomats—one hundred fifty of them in all—whose job it is to concentrate on North America.) I asked him how many would be present at the session scheduled to interrogate me, and he said a half dozen or so, a half dozen being exactly how many in fact were there, when I arrived at the haughty mansion that the fabulous Prince Bolkonsky, introduced to the non-Russian world by Leo Tolstoy in *War and Peace*, once lived in, and dominated. . . .

The phone rang early in my room at Spaso House. *Pravda* had published that morning an extensive and rather extraordinarily bitter attack on the United States Information Agency, on its director, Frank Shakespeare, and on myself, calling us "werewolves." A few hours later, at the U.S.A. Institute, I was cordially, if formally, greeted—certainly I was not made to feel like a werewolf—and found myself seated at a table opposite my Stakhanovite canoeist friend of the day before, surrounded by his colleagues.

The chairman-canoeist began with a ritual denunciation of our move into Cambodia, in which his Rockettes concurred (I do not mean to suggest that they were not bright, and learned, and resourceful in their arguments: merely that they played together like the Budapest String Quartet), and I replied, Look, let's save time. The United States, belatedly, is treating the Cambodian frontier like the geographical fiction you people have been treating it as ever since the war began, so what is the point in accusing us of escalation, simply because we behave like you?

We traversed the frontiers of the Cold War, at military, political, and even—ever so lightly—philosophical levels. What interested my interlocutors most, however, was clearly economics. Only a week or so before, Henry Ford had come to town. The Soviet Union was after him to build a great big truck complex, and the reception given to him was, by all reports, the most fabulous since Marco Polo arrived in China. Anyway, the chairman wanted to know how could I account for the *stupidity* of those Americans who opposed Henry Ford's setting up a truck plant in the Soviet Union when, after all, if we didn't, all the Russians would have to do was invite *any* old other country to do the same thing, like say Japan, or Italy, or Germany, or France, or England—and what would *that* do to our balance of payments? I murmured something about Americans' resentment of the number of trucks currently being sent by the Soviet Union to North Vietnam, which were being used to bring down ammunition to kill Americans with, whose parents might, under the circumstances, look darkly at the prospect of the Ford Motor Company's supplying the Soviet Union with those trucks it was short of, on account of its commitment to North Vietnam—get it? I was dealing with enormously sophisticated people, and gradually it became clear to all of us, but it would have been very impolite to recognize the hovering fact, which was that just any old country could *not* in fact supply Russia what the Ford Motor Company could supply it. A few days later, in Leningrad, I heard the news that Henry Ford, back in Detroit, had said: No, he would *not* build the new plant in Russia. I thought of my friends at the U.S.A. Institute and the blast they would surely receive the next day from the Kremlin. Well, at least they hadn't got the bum steer from me.

THE FOLLOWING DAY, a trip to Zagorsk, the spiritual home of Russia, where one of the three surviving seminaries continues the hapless production of a dozen priests per year, like eye-dropping holy water into hell. The Bolshoi Ballet doing *Don Quixote*. Blini at the Metropole (in the restaurant reserved for clients who come forward with non-Russian currency: there are such restaurants everywhere, and PX-type stores, and they do to the Russian people what Jim Crow did to the Negroes), and then the midnight train to Leningrad. We

sat, Larry DuBois from *Time* magazine and I, in my little compart-
ment and offered Scotch whisky to William Jay Smith, America's
poet-in-residence at the Library of Congress, who had been invited
over to read his poems and to visit with Soviet poets; he kept
wondering where he could find Brodsky, who is in disrepute.
Everybody is vague about where Brodsky is, and Woody Demitz from
the Embassy, a young, experienced, Russian-speaking diplomat doing
werewolf-tending duty, could offer no help. . . .

Nina met us at the Intourist office and proved to be (except on the
one occasion when she was provoked ideologically) marvelously hospitable and obliging.

Yes, she confirmed, yes, this was the square where the Revolution
began. Over there—yes, stretching all the way down along the river—
is the Winter Palace, the formal residence of the czars during the two
centuries that St. Petersburg was the capital of Russia, up until the
Revolution. We will go through it, the parts that are open to tourists,
in just a few minutes—don't be impatient, she clucked. Over there,
on the river, is the gunboat, preserved as a national monument, which
fired the shot that triggered the Bolshevik takeover. You can see
the fortress where Lenin's brother was imprisoned, but you can't
quite see over to the fortress where he was hanged. Over there—we
cruised—is the great townhouse of Prince Yussupov, where he and
his friends murdered the monk Rasputin, just before New Year's Day
1917, throwing him finally (he was harder to kill than King Kong)
into the river, right in front of the house, and causing the shudder
which, some say, finally demoralized the royal family, who, a few
weeks later, lost their power.

The Winter Palace was never physically touched by Nazi hands,
because although the Nazis besieged Leningrad for five hundred days
they never penetrated the city's defenses: this was where Russian
civilian heroism ran the longest course, even as, at Stalingrad, military heroism saved the city—the same heroism, said Nina, the same
people. Do you realize, she asked, that this was a city of *three* million
people when the war began and I was a little girl, and when the war
was over, it was a city of less than *two* million people? The Nazis, failing to get into the city, satisfied themselves by wrecking everything

outside it—the whole complex of summer palaces of the czars, for instance—and then shelling Leningrad, doing great damage to the Winter Palace. Most of the treasures of the palace had been packed up and sent away to the Urals before the Germans came, but some of them were found, and many of those were damaged.

We walked into the palace, and the experience was breathtaking. I mean, there isn't in the West anything on the scale of the Winter Palace. Versailles is a Petit Trianon. The rooms, many of them reconstructed, are quite literally perfect, the taste unblemished, the conspicuous exception being the fabulous throne room, where a chauvinist's lackey replaced the throne itself with a postwar map showing in mosaic the territorial reaches of contemporary Russia. The jewels, a collection of czarist baubles, outmatch in vulgarity and in beauty anything else of the sort anywhere, and suggest the emotional reason for the conflicting drabness of the Bolshevik costume; indeed, for the drabness of Soviet art—the diabetic imperative. The architecture of the Winter Palace, and of the summer palaces, is mostly Italian in provenance. The czars no more thought to insist on Russian architectural or decorative pre-eminence than, say, we would think to insist on American pre-eminence in camera lenses. The scale of the thing—ridiculous and sublime—reflects the expanses of Russia, the lateral terrestrial infinity, the vertical complement of which was expressed in the Middle Ages by the height of the holy spires of the great cathedrals of France and Germany, which could not go higher only because of the dumb limits of contemporary science, which already were strained to exuberant lengths. But in building sideways there is no restriction, which is why the Winter Palace simply goes on and on and on. Although I did not take measurements, I warrant you could walk from one end of the White House to the other ten times before going the length of the Winter Palace; before reaching, if you started at the other end, the auditorium where, on the night that it was stormed, Georges Enesco from Rumania, young, talented, glamorous, gave his scheduled violin recital before a severely diminished house of aristocrats, who reseated themselves about him less, one supposes in reading about it, because they sought the gemütlichkeit which was otherwise unavailable in so large an auditorium, than because they thought, noblesse oblige, to console the artist against any suspicion that the plebeian irregularities outdoors in any way suggested a straitened appreciation of his art.

We told Nina how sad it was that we had so little time, but she did not repine; she is used to givens in any situation, whether it is the scarcity of food during the Nazi siege she survived, or the ebb and flow of tourist traffic, which could leave her overworked for weeks or underworked for months. She was at one point sent to Indonesia for two years, where she dutifully learned Indonesian, having kissed her husband good-bye as stoically as a whaler on Nantucket two centuries ago. We drove to the summer palaces, an hour's drive, and she led us to Catherine's palace, once again endlessly magnificent, only a dozen rooms restored, but exquisitely. I asked if I might visit Tsarskoe Selo, just down the road, because it was there that the last czar and his czarina made their home. She resisted, but she did not make a point of it. But when the car stopped outside the garden, she did not get out, a gentle act of symbolic resistance. So Larry and I got out, and roamed through the yard-high grass, towards the great columns through which, when Woodrow Wilson was President of the United States, the czar and czarina and their four girls and little hemophiliac son strolled, going from the garden into the house.

When the czar arrived at Tsarskoe Selo from the German front, after the storming of the Winter Palace, he had abdicated his throne en route. But in the next few days, walking through the columns into the garden, he could not suppress the habit of raising his hand to return the salute of what had been his imperial guard, which had surrounded the garden with adamant loyalty over the stormy years. That guard was gone, replaced by carefully selected revolutionary soldiers who would as soon have saluted the czar as taken an oath against vodka. The head of the detachment insisted that the very large garden should for reasons of security be ruled off-limits, except for the two or three acres nearest the house. Nicholas, seeking exercise, decided to bicycle around the remaining pathways; whereupon the guards, it is recorded, entertained themselves by poking sticks into his bicycle wheels, causing him suddenly to catapult over onto the ground, whence he would lift himself, silently, deliberately, unreproachfully;

remount the bicycle, unminding of the taunters, who for half such an aggression thirty days earlier would have been knouted and hanged; and head back towards his family, so as not to interrupt, by any melodramatic defiance, the grisly end that awaited them all, sixteen months later, in the cellar in Ekaterinburg, where they would be shot down on orders from Moscow, already beginning to practice the trade in which Moscow would become so proficient, ordering the executions of royal families, dissident ideologues, small landowners, prisoners of war, hundreds, thousands, millions.

I thought, as I walked through the grass towards the gutted palace, that it is all no more difficult than understanding the men who toppled the czar's bicycle, an act, under those circumstances, as exhausting of the resources of human cruelty as would be the signing of the order to eliminate a million kulaks in order to prove a large ideological point. At the veranda a soldier appeared, his dress as shabby as the palace he guarded, to say that we had already wandered too far. No matter, there isn't anything left there to see, because these apartments where the Romanovs lived, so intimately, so devotedly, have not been restored, and they do not lie on the Intourist route. I wondered why the government doesn't raze Tsarskoe Selo, but the commissars have always shown that certain caution that many iconoclasts show: thus, in Leningrad, they convert the Kazan Cathedral, where the czars prayed, into a Museum of Atheism and Religion; but they do not tear it down, whether for reasons of husbandry, or because they prefer the desecration of a cathedral as high-class revolutionary piquancy. I think there is a third reason, which is that the Russians, even the Communist Russians, cannot practice wholehearted Orwellianism; i.e., they cannot induce themselves to *destroy* that which they disapprove of (unless it is a human being).

The next day, the last day, Nina took us to the Kazan Cathedral to survey the Museum of Atheism and Religion, which is as impartially devoted to atheism and to religion as the Museum of Natural History is devoted to natural and supernatural history. Among the exhibits, all of them calculated to document Lenin's point that religion was an instrument of repression, was a chestful of implements of torture, labeled by the exhibitors as having been commonly used during the Inquisition. When I asked, kitchen debate–wise, whether they had been borrowed from the Lubyanka Collection, Nina was most firmly displeased with me, and I was not able to jolly her out of that displeasure; so I acknowledged the tastelessness of my remark, and, of course, it was in a way the remark of a bully. One does not make light of the doctrine of transubstantiation with an altar boy.

But as we drove back to the hotel, we were friends again, and I asked if she would like me to send her any books when I got back to New York. Well, she said, yes, she would, though she doubted that I would remember to send them. "They always say they will, but they never do." I asked her what books she wanted, and she did not hesitate. She wanted *Peyton Place, Hotel, Valley of the Dolls,* and *The Carpetbaggers.* I promised her that I would send them, and Larry interposed jocularly to ask Nina whether she would like to have my own then-current book, *The Governor Listeth,* and Nina said bravely that she did not know that I wrote books, but that she would certainly like to have my book, and she only hoped that it was not as biased as Harrison Salisbury's about the siege of Leningrad. I assured her that it was ten times as biased, and she smiled, and we pulled into the hotel. Her handshake was purely professional. I hoped to find a trace there of the tingle that distinguishes from the purely perfunctory experience, but I must admit that I did not. Whether, after she has read *Valley of the Dolls, Peyton Place,* and *The Carpetbaggers,* she will acquire that sensitization which our Eselin types preach of, which might have permitted us to embrace across the Iron Curtain, I cannot say; I would say only this, that I do not know what other books one could honorably recommend in the circumstances: what would you and I read, or want to read, if we were born and brought up in Leningrad? Solzhenitsyn's *Cancer Ward* sells there, on the black market, for eighty rubles, which is one-third Nina's monthly pay: but there are other reasons against reading Solzhenitsyn in Russia, even if it were known that one could do so with absolute safety. Nina does not want to be troubled; and I would not want to trouble her, not unless the prospects of success were assured. "We waited for years for the American Army," a Polish intellectual told me a few days later (in

Poland, by contrast with Russia, they all sound like Lenny Bruce), commenting on the recent visit of our astronauts. "And when it came, there were just three of them."

JOHN KERRY'S AMERICA

A Commencement Address at the United States Military Academy; West Point, N.Y., June 8, 1971

The morale in the armed services was low, reflecting the impasse and progressive demoralization in Vietnam and especially the trial of Lieutenant William Calley for the massacre at Mylai. A drastic charge, flamboyantly made by decorated veteran John Kerry (later a United States senator from Massachusetts), had been rapturously received by American opinion makers. Kerry ascribed to our soldiers in Vietnam uncivilized, barbarous practices. I devoted my talk to asking about Mr. Kerry's charges and reflecting on their implications.

A GREAT DEAL has been written lately on the spirit of progressivism at West Point. I note that a generation ago, cadets were not permitted to read a newspaper, whereas today, each cadet room receives a daily copy of the *New York Times*. I know now what it means to be nostalgic for the good old days.

I read ten days ago the full text of the quite remarkable address delivered by John Kerry before the Senate Committee on Foreign Relations. It was an address, I am told, that paralyzed the committee by its eloquence and made Mr. Kerry—a veteran of the war in Vietnam, a pedigreed Bostonian, a graduate of Yale University—an instant hero.

After reading it I put it aside, deeply troubled as I was by the haunting resonance of its peroration, which so moved the audience. The words he spoke were these:

"[We are determined] to undertake one last mission, to search out and destroy the last vestige of this barbaric war, to pacify our hearts, to conquer the hate and fear that have driven this country these last ten years and more, so that when, thirty years from now, our brothers go down the street without a leg, without an arm, or a face, and small boys ask why, we will be able to say 'Vietnam!' and not mean a desert, not a filthy obscene memory, but the place where America finally turned and where soldiers like us helped it in the turning."

"*Where America finally turned.*" We need to wonder: Where America finally turned from what?

Mr. Kerry, in introducing himself to the Senate Foreign Relations Committee, made it plain that he was there to speak not only for himself but for what he called "a very much larger group of veterans in this country." He then proceeded to describe the America he knows, the America from which he enjoined us all to turn.

In Southeast Asia, he said, he saw "not isolated incidents but crimes committed on a day-to-day basis, *with the full awareness of officers at all levels of command.*"

A grave charge, but the sensitive listener will instantly assume that Mr. Kerry is using the word "crime" loosely, as in, "He was criminally thoughtless in not writing home more often to his mother." But Mr. Kerry quickly interdicted that line of retreat. He went on to enumerate precisely such crimes as are being committed "on a day-to-day basis, with the full awareness of officers at all levels of command." He gave tales of torture, of rape, of Americans who "randomly shot at civilians, razed villages in a fashion reminiscent of Genghis Khan, shot cattle and dogs for fun, poisoned food stocks, and generally ravaged the countryside of South Vietnam in addition to the normal ravages of war."

Mr. Kerry informed Congress that what threatens the United States is "not Reds, and not redcoats," but "the crimes" we are committing. He tells us that we have "created a monster, a monster in the form of millions of men who have been taught to deal and to trade in violence, and who have returned with a sense of anger."

Most specifically he singles out for criticism a sentence uttered by Mr. Agnew here at West Point a year ago: "Some glamorize the criminal misfits of society while our best men die in Asian rice paddies to preserve the freedom which most of those misfits abuse." Mr. Kerry insists that the so-called misfits are the true heroes, inasmuch as it was they who "were standing up for us in a way that nobody else in this country dared to." As for the men in Vietnam, he adds, "we cannot consider ourselves America's 'best men' when we are ashamed of and hated for what we were called on to do in Southeast Asia."

And indeed, if American soldiers have been called upon to rape and to torture and to exterminate noncombatants, it is obvious that they should be ashamed, less obvious why they have not expressed that shame more widely on returning to the United States.

Are there extenuating circumstances? Is there a reason for our being in Vietnam?

"To attempt to justify the loss of one American life in Vietnam, Cambodia, or Laos by linking such loss to the preservation of freedom . . . is . . . the height of criminal hypocrisy, and it is that kind of hypocrisy which we feel has torn this country apart." It is, then, we reason retrospectively, not alone an act of hypocrisy that caused the Joint Chiefs of Staff and the heads of the civilian departments engaged in strategic calculations to make the recommendations they made over the past ten years, to three Presidents of the United States: it was not merely hypocrisy, but criminal hypocrisy. The nature of that hypocrisy? "All," Mr. Kerry sums up, "that we were told about the mystical war against Communism."

The indictment is complete.

It is the indictment of an ignorant young man who is willing to condemn in words that would have been appropriately used in Nuremberg the governing class of America: the legislators, the generals, the statesmen. And, reaching beyond them, the people, who named the governors to their positions of responsibility and ratified their decisions in several elections.

The point I want to raise is this: If America is everything that John Kerry says it is, what is it appropriate for us to do? The wells of regeneration are infinitely deep, but the stain described by John Kerry goes too deep to be bleached out by conventional remorse or resolution: better the destruction of America if, to see ourselves truly, we need to look into the mirror John Kerry holds up for us. If we are a nation of sadists, of kid-killers and torturers, of hypocrites and criminals, let us be done with it, and pray that a great flood or fire will destroy us, leaving John Kerry and maybe Mrs. Benjamin Spock to take the place of Lot, in reseeding a new order.

Gentlemen, how many times, in the days ahead, you will need to ask yourselves the most searching question of all, the counterpart of the priest's most agonizing doubt: Is there a God? Yours will be: *Is America worth it?*

John Kerry's assault on this country did not rise full-blown in his mind, like Venus from the Cypriot Sea. It is the crystallization of an assault upon America which has been fostered over the years by an intellectual class given over to self-doubt and self-hatred, driven by a cultural disgust with the uses to which so many people put their freedom. The assault on the military, the many and subtle vibrations of which you feel as keenly as James Baldwin knows the inflections of racism, is an assault on the proposition that what we have, in America, is truly worth defending. The military is to be loved or despised according as it defends that which is beloved or perpetuates that which is despised. The root question has not risen to such a level of respectability as to work itself into the platform of a national political party, but it lurks in the rhetoric of the John Kerrys, such that a blind man, running his fingers over the features of the public discourse, can discern the meaning of it:

Is America worth it?

That is what they are saying to you. And that is what so many Americans reacted to in the case of Lieutenant Calley. Mistakenly, they interpreted the conviction of Calley as yet another effort to discredit the military. And though they will not say it in as many words, they know that if there is no military, it will quickly follow that there will be no America, of the kind that they know, that we know: the America that listens so patiently to its John Kerrys; the America that shouldered the burden of preserving oases of freedom after the great curtain came down with that Bolshevik subtlety that finally expressed itself in a wall, to block citizens of the socialist utopia from leaving, en route even to John Kerry's America; the America that all but sank under the general obloquy, in order to stand by, in Southeast Asia, a commitment it had soberly made, to the cause of Containment. I shall listen patiently, decades hence, to those who argue that our commitment in Vietnam and our attempt to redeem it were tragically misconceived. I shall not listen to those who say that it was less than the highest tribute to national motivation, to collective idealism, and to international rectitude. I say this with confidence because I have never met an American who takes pleasure from the Vietnam War or who desires to exploit the Vietnamese.

So during those moments when doubt will assail you, moments that will come as surely as the temptations of the flesh, I hope you will pause. I know, I know, at the most hectic moments of one's life it isn't easy—indeed, the argument can be made that neither is it seemly— to withdraw from the front line in order to consider the general situation philosophically. But what I hope you will consider, during these moments of doubt, is the essential professional point: Without organized force, and the threat of the use of it under certain circumstances, there is no freedom, anywhere. Without freedom, there is no true humanity. If America is the monster of John Kerry, burn your commissions tomorrow morning and take others, which will not bind you in the depraved conspiracy you have heard described. If it is otherwise, remember: the freedom John Kerry enjoys and the freedom I enjoy are, quite simply, the result of your dedication. Do you wonder that I accepted the opportunity to salute you?

THE WEST BERLIN OF CHINA

An Address to a Conference Sponsored by the American-Asian Educational Exchange; the Hotel Commodore, New York, October 29, 1971

Four days before this long-planned conference took place, the United Nations expelled Taiwan and gave its seat to Mainland China. The resentment was widespread. President Nixon dissociated himself from the act, which many thought followed from his acceptance of the invitation to visit Peking the succeeding February. The expulsion intensified skepticism about the usefulness of the United Nations in the Cold War. In my address I make a recommendation for reforming U.S. participation in the UN.

W E MEET IN circumstances most of us regard as bitterly sad. We all became accustomed to the reality of Mainland China, which is that the men who won control of China after the Second World War had embarked on a revolutionary course which was totalist in its ambitions: to remake man, no less. The usual methods by which accountants measure the cost of social enterprises seem somehow inadequate. The learned debate among the necrologists is over the question whether ten or fifteen or fifty million human beings have lost their lives in the course of giving flesh to the thoughts of Mao Tse-tung. The ghastliness of it all has been on such a scale as to cause us to become almost clinical in our consideration of it, like the harried doctor who wanders through the streets of a city in the final throes of a deadly plague. We felt we could maintain our balance only by indulging a little counterrevolutionary vision of our own, namely, that the government of Chiang Kai-shek would recover the Mainland: even as, coming across the story of Anne Frank, the occasional reader experiences that sense of personal indignation which brings him to feel that by rushing personally to her aid he might, somehow, save the legions destined to die in the extermination centers.

Well, Chiang did not recover the Mainland, the government of

Mao Tse-tung did not fall, and the West did not have the stomach to make it fall; and soon it became the fashion to allege that we were ignoring the largest country in the world by our failure to extend to it diplomatic recognition.

Mr. Nixon's decision to accelerate the trend towards recognition was no doubt motivated by his conviction that the people of China cannot, A.D. 1971, reasonably hope to overthrow their oppressors. It is here and there argued that Mr. Nixon's decision to go to Peking did not in fact midwife the expulsion of the representatives of Taiwan from the United Nations and the admission of the representatives of Mainland China.

But the experience of this week leaves us with the burden of meditating on two or three things. The first is the United Nations. The second is our attitude towards it. The third is our relationship with the deposed government.

The general elation over at the United Nations was most graphically expressed when, after the United States was defeated on the important procedural point, the delegate of Tanzania stepped forward to the podium and danced a jig. The elation had little to do with the substantive point; it doesn't really matter that much to the delegate of Tanzania, who has to share the General Assembly with one hundred thirty other nations; whether one of those one hundred thirty is or isn't Formosa. The jig expressed that special delight one feels on beating a giant. It was the first time that the United States, premier economic and until very recently premier military force in the world, had gone down to inglorious defeat: and it was on a resolution sponsored by Albania, a little, reclusive country composed primarily of rocks and serfs, with here and there a slavemaster, a country whose principal export is Maoism. And, of course, the backdrop was perfect: the skyline of New York, metropolitan hearth of the giant who was felled by a coalition led by Albania, in an assembly which tallied the vote of Byelorussia as equal to France's and England's, and weighed the principles of the United Nations Charter, well, not at all.

Actually, it has been quite a while since it became apparent that the United Nations had no clothes. Its high-water mark was the

Korean War, when we dressed up our soldiers as agents of the United Nations and went along with the act. But soon after that, very soon after that, we were confronting—in connection with events in Poland, in Hungary, in Tibet, on the Sino-Indian border—the military and moral powerlessness of the UN, and shrewd international specialists, like Professor Hans Morgenthau, were warning that it is important to remember that "the United Nations is a procedure, not a policy." It was inevitable that the UN should become primarily an instrument of embarrassment: in the most recent instance, the embarrassment of the United States, through the manipulation of Taiwan. It makes a difference when we are singled out for humiliation. The UN's condemnation of Israel a few years ago made no difference at all to Israel because Israel is profoundly convinced of the correctness of its policies. The condemnation of China as an aggressor made absolutely no difference to China because China, like Russia—like Herbert Marcuse—insists that such condemnations are expressions of bourgeois morality: indeed, China is likelier to collect condemnations, as proof of its effectiveness, than be embarrassed by them.

But this is not true of the United States of America. We care very deeply when we see manifest injustices committed, primarily in order to embarrass us, by an international body of which we are a founder, which we serve as principal underwriter, and in which we are an active participant. The answer is to revise the nature of our participation in the United Nations. The French danced a jig on taking Moscow in 1812, but there was nothing there.

Back in 1945, critically situated Americans dreamed of an evolving world federation, the inevitable result of nuclear politics. Into its composition the architects injected strains of prudence and reality, as also strains of idealism and egalitarianism. Thus the Security Council would guard the essential interests of the essential powers. The General Assembly would have authority in matters of great consequence, but mostly in areas in which it was given explicit scope by the Security Council—areas where the moral force of the international body needed harnessing in order to advance its stated objectives, which are the objectives of the Eagle Scouts.

A few years after the UN's inception we discovered, through the experience of prolonged Soviet intransigence, that the Security Council was all but immobilized by the veto. It was then that we moved (successfully) to give more authority to the General Assembly, which emerged in the decade of the 1950s as the primary focus of attention. During the same decade, and continuing in the next decade, membership in the General Assembly multiplied with the end of colonialism in the non-Soviet world. And a feeling of collegiality grew among the nations of the so-called Third World. These nations dominate, numerically, the United Nations. And they are grown accustomed to a moral-sociological rubric which is altogether infectious, causing, for instance, the American delegate, Mr. Francis Plimpton, to proclaim proudly a few years ago that colonialism was dead—to say this in a chamber in which thirteen nations metronomically do the bidding of a single state, the alternative being to lie down to receive its tanks and infantry; a chamber in which the meaning of the word "racism" consolidates as an unfriendly act by any white man against any nonwhite man; a chamber in which democracy is something the absence of which is deplorable only in Spain, Portugal, Greece, Taiwan, and South Vietnam.

Even so, the United Nations has its uses, and the United States would be mistaken recklessly to withdraw from it. But in weighing our relations with it, we should bear it in mind that we are (and let us always be) a square country, which believes in the rules of the game. It has not occurred to us, since Adams defeated Jefferson in the election of 1796, to do other than accept the verdict of the voting majority. The General Assembly of the United Nations, as we have just now seen, has the raw power to admit to membership the de facto governors of Mainland China and to expel from membership the de facto governors of Taiwan. In virtue of our having participated in that vote we recognize that we have become involved in a process that has caused a great injustice, and one that is, moreover, intolerable in the light of our continuing strategic commitments.

I call on the President of the United States to instruct his ambassador to the United Nations to cease, beginning immediately, to vote in the General Assembly. He should argue there, yes; listen, yes; plead, explain, cajole, threaten, conciliate, yes; vote, never. Because to participate in the vote, given the American ethos, is psychologically to involve ourselves in an outcome which we cannot—as the world's major power concerned with ethical considerations—agree to. If the UN wishes to expel from membership all nations that resist domination by those nations the UN at that moment desires not to offend, why let it do so: but let it not understand itself as engaged in writing the moral law, or in making pronouncements which have presumptive weight in the chancelleries of the world: or, most particularly, in this chancellery. By a word, the President of the United States could effect the great reconciliation between the theoretical and the actual. If he does not give that word, he will have lost an opportunity for penetrating leadership.

Meanwhile we must cherish Taiwan, which is the West Berlin of China. It was to that island that a tired, bedraggled, dispirited group of refugees, under the leadership of a man already old but of flinty spirit, fled from a shipwrecked nation, and addressed themselves to the enterprise of bringing order and a measure of freedom to fifteen million people. We in America helped them. Nowhere was our help more productive. In twenty years, they contrived a standard of living second only, in Asia, to Japan's. They did this while nourishing the culture of their ancestors, adapting it, stressing those qualities in it of patience and fortitude, of emphasis on the spirit, which have given Taiwan that special presence which will survive Chiang Kai-shek.

That small country is abloom with promise. We are bound to it by a treaty which the gates of the United Nations shall not prevail against. It is a far cry from becoming the capital province of all of China. But Taiwan is the repository of the hopes and dreams of those Chinese in whose breast lingers the seed of resistance to the furies of Maoism.

And so while Mainland China struggles in its endless ordeal against human nature, the little island of Taiwan must grow and prosper. The people of Taiwan may feel lonely today, and isolated. But they should know that they are the more conspicuous for their loneliness and their isolation, and that in the years and decades to come their separated brothers on the Mainland will look all the more wistfully to Taiwan's government in consideration of what it has done for its people, and permitted to its people; and all the more puzzledly to that august derelict in New York City that took pleasure, that grey autumn day in 1971, from encouraging the slavemasters, and humiliating the little band of brave and faithful men who for twenty years, as members in good standing of the United Nations, sustained the vision of a better life for the people of China; and who now, rejected by the United Nations, will continue to sustain that vision— all the more proudly, all the more hopefully, all the more grandly.

Affection, Guidance, and Peanut Brittle

Remarks (excerpted) to the Annual Luncheon of the Red Cross Association; Vancouver, British Columbia, April 8, 1972

I excerpt from this talk only its introduction, a highly personal testimonial that I would not want to pass over, whatever the criteria.

I DO NOT pretend that I am here only to register my enthusiasm for the Red Cross. I could after all have done that, accepting to be sure certain risks about its arrival, via Western Union. I am here also to celebrate my enthusiasm for Mrs. Taylor, and to register publicly my docility as her son-in-law. If you are inclined to wince at my mention of matters so personal, permit me to remind you that my devotion to my mother-in-law, far from being irrelevant to your annual meeting, contributes substantially to its solvency. [A reference to my having waived my speaker's fee.]

Accordingly, I expect you to listen with great patience to any reminiscence I impose on you respecting Babe Taylor. I am, after all, forty-six years old, and this is the first time I have had an opportunity to speak about her without the risk that she will immediately contradict me, change the subject of my discourse in midsentence, observe that the chair on which I am tilting is an irreplaceable antique, close the bar, or turn off the electricity.

Babe Taylor has of course served the Red Cross for more years than I have served her. For all that she has accomplished prodigies as a civic servant, she has been first and foremost a wife, a mother, and a mother-in-law. She is a pillar of reliability not only in community relations but also in family relations, where her authority is absolute, except when her sense of humor is provoked—and inasmuch as her sense of humor is more easily touched off than Bob Hope's, her family usually manages to navigate around her sense of order and rectitude by the simple expedient of making her laugh.

I know of only one occasion when this failed. Her late husband, the formidable Austin C. Taylor, was a taciturn man, particularly respecting his business affairs, concerning which his family notoriously knew nothing. On one occasion, many years ago, Babe came home bursting with organizational pride, and launched at lunchtime into an extended account of her prowess in her capacity as chairman of the Vancouver Ladies Society in shepherding the society away from, let us call it, the Brighton Hotel, where for years it had had its headquarters at considerable profit to the Brighton Hotel, on over to, let us call it, the Piccadilly Hotel. Babe bubbled on about how she had finally won the fight, and had just that morning signed a ten-year lease in behalf of the ladies club with the Piccadilly Hotel. Austin Taylor had been stirring his coffee wordlessly throughout the extended account. At this point he spoke up. "You know something, Baby?"—as he called her. "You own the Piccadilly Hotel."

It is recorded that she did not speak to him for two weeks, and did so then only after forcing him to sell the hotel, preferably at a loss.

Babe Taylor is a running welfare department of her own, providing to her friends and to her family an inexhaustible supply of affection, guidance, encouragement, loyalty, shelter, and peanut brittle. I know that those of you who know her personally will not take offense at my exceeding my authority in proposing a toast to her, gratefully and affectionately, from her friends and family.

ON PRESERVING THE TOKENS OF HOPE AND TRUTH

Remarks at a Testimonial Dinner for Henry Regnery; the Racquet Club, Chicago, April 12, 1972

Henry Regnery was a publisher who brought out books by conservatives (his son is an official of the successor company, Regnery Publishing). I had just returned from visiting China as one of the journalists who accompanied Richard Nixon, and the experience was fresh in the memory.

WHEN I LEARNED that I would be preceded by Russell Kirk and David Collier and Jack Kilpatrick and Vic Milione and Stan Evans and Eliseo Vivas, I wondered why Louis Dehmlow hadn't, while he was at it, arranged to produce Ezra Pound. To present me at the end of this list of speakers is, to say the least, dramatically insecure. Kirk, Kilpatrick, Vivas, and Buckley. It was Abraham Flexner who remarked that "For God, for Country, and for Yale" was surely the greatest anticlimax in the English language. But I am here, as we all are, to register our solidarity with a man who has been important to all of us in one way or another, indeed to some of us in a combination of ways: as a friend, a publisher, a mentor—in my own case all three. I have not only read books he suggested I read, but even written books he suggested I write: and this requires a very special relationship.

It is a night for reminiscences, and I think it is accurate to say that I have known Henry longer than any of the other speakers here tonight, having met him even before Russell Kirk did. I am especially happy about the fecundity of his noble house, inasmuch as I remember, during the very dark days just after *God and Man at Yale* appeared, that Henry was wondering whether any writer would ever again consent to write for a publishing house which had midwived such an outrage. It is characteristic of Henry that when he reached this slough of despondency, he didn't do what most of us incline to do—call out for help, or reassurance, from our friends. I still have the letter from him, advising me that he had devoted the night before— after seeing the first rash of reviews—to rereading the book. He concluded that he had been correct to publish it and, so far as I know, never gave another thought to his decision to launch the book, not even when the University of Chicago took the occasion to affirm academic freedom by discontinuing its Great Books contract with the Henry Regnery Company.

It is hard to recall, in the light of later experiences, how much fun it used to be to publish a book. When I came to Chicago to meet with Henry and discuss such matters as jacket design, it was automatically assumed that I would stay at his big house in Hinsdale, where over the course of several years I, and subsequently my wife and I, spent so many evenings. I think I should pause, in deference to historical accuracy, to record that there was a certain risk at that time in spending the night with the Regnerys. To begin with, it was during the years of their martial Quakerism—if Professor Vivas will permit the oxymoron. Translated, that meant: No booze. This posed a quite awesome prospect for a young author only a few months away from Fraternity Row at Yale University. But providence has a way of stringing out its little lifesavers—and sure enough it transpired that across the street from Henry, in another big house, lived a most informal and exuberant gentleman, an artist named Kenneth, who had befriended Henry and, by the expansiveness of his temperament, Henry's friends, known and unknown, ex officio. So that at approximately six o'clock in the afternoon, Kenneth would throw open his shutters and, at the top of his lungs, cry out, "If Henry has any guests staying with him, thee-all can come over for a drink." That disposed of that problem.

The other problem was that Henry's guests sometimes tended to sleep later than Henry's four children. Depending on my mood, I give different answers to the question I am sometimes asked: When did you stop publishing with the Henry Regnery Company? When I feel provocative, I say: Sometime after I stopped sleeping with the wife of the company's president. In due course I chivalrously divulge that Susan was then six years old, and she and her two brothers and her little sister would all four of them come to bed with me at about six o'clock in the morning and giggle with apprehension when they heard the footsteps of their mother coming to relieve the beleaguered guest. I would do my sleepy best to entertain them, but they were thoroughly spoiled. Because the bed in question was often occupied by Roy Campbell, and he would begin instantly, on being boarded by the children, to improvise great tales of giants and giant-killers; and it was not long before they would find themselves under the covers with Russell Kirk, who would tell his tales of ghosts, in accents baroque and mysterious. I could not hope to keep them so much excited by tales of Keynesianism at Yale.

They were as I say very happy days, in which book publishing was something of a personal partnership between publisher and author. I remember hustling for *McCarthy and His Enemies*—a speech in Milwaukee, driving up in Henry's car with Regnery officials Bill Strube and Kevin Corrigan, Henry at the wheel, the trunk loaded with books, which we hawked shamelessly after the speech was concluded. I think we sold seventy-five books that night, and when, long after midnight, we finally reached Hinsdale, exhausted, it was with grins on our faces, as if we had drilled a gusher.

Henry has spoken, in a published piece, about the "dismal" 1960s, which is how he refers to the decade that introduced Camelot, the Playboy Philosophy, and Mario Savio. Usually when one refers to an unhappy decade it is in order to highlight the happy contrast with the succeeding decade. But concerning the 1970s, Henry Regnery is not at all optimistic, not at all. "The threat of extinction," he surmises, "is now much greater than it was then: those bent on destroying civilization are better organized, and the defenses are weaker." He tells us that there won't be—I use his language—any "money or glory" in it, but, he says, "we have inherited a great and noble tradition, and it is worth fighting for."

On that proposition we are all, I assume, agreed—at least, all those of us who paid $25 to attend this dinner. On the other hand, it is obvious that by no means everyone is agreed that this is so. It was ten years ago that I heard the most succinct statement on this point, by a fashionable young literary iconoclast, who put it this way:

Once upon a time, it was worth dying—for two reasons. The first was that heroism was rewarded in another world. The second was that heroism was rewarded by the memory of man. However—he said—now that we know from the scientific evidence that there is in fact no other world, no Christian heaven, and now that we have invented weapons which are capable of destroying all mankind and therefore all human memory, what reason is left to run the risk of death in war?

This is a blunt way of saying it, and by no means suited for mass consumption. After all, the average man is not absolutely convinced that H. G. Wells was that much more on top of history than, say, Christopher Dawson; or that George Bernard Shaw had the better of the argument with G. K. Chesterton or C. S. Lewis.

The accent is quite clearly discernible. The sharp edges of the arguments nowadays stress not so much the nuclear war that would abolish mankind, as the senselessness of war; indeed, derivatively, the senselessness of a convincing defense system. Why the Pentagon? What would be the point of it?

It used to be, finding oneself in such a corner, that one had merely to reach into one's quiver and pull out the arrow that had "Freedom" written on it. Touch it down on the skeptic, and he would waste away, like the witch come into contact with water.

You will have noticed that this does not work anymore. Freedom is increasingly a subjective condition, in the assessment of the thought leaders. Professor Ross Terrill, writing the two most influential articles that have appeared in our time on the subject of Red China, is to be distinguished from the famous apologists for Stalin's Russia, who made their way by simply denying the crimes imputed to Stalin.

Terrill denies nothing. Although he does not in fact dwell on the atrocities—the mass executions, the terrorism, that kind of thing—he does not disguise the conditions of life in China today. After informing us that there is no freedom to practice religion there, nor to vote, nor to express oneself freely, nor to read books or periodicals one desires to read, nor to change one's job, nor to travel to another city or another country, he says ingenuously, "People ask me, Is China free?" He answers them, incredibly, with great difficulty. Depends what you mean by freedom, he says. Freedom is always defined with reference to the limitations of the group, and whereas the operative group in the West is the individual, or the corporation, or the labor union, in China it happens to be the whole state.

And he illustrates: Consider the writer Kuo Mojo. In the 1930s he wrote books for a mere four or five or at most eight thousand people, and now he is required by the state to write books that will appeal to twenty, thirty, or fifty million people. "Is that wrong?" the young professor asks. Then there is the scientist whose affinity was for abstract science but who was recently directed to concentrate exclusively on pest control. "Is that wrong?" Terrill asks, anaphorically: as we begin to understand the lethal quality of the ideological egalitarianism that rushes in after practical diplomacy, such that Richard Nixon, who went to China to establish a dialogue with Mao Tse-tung, ends by likening Mao's revolution to America's revolution—ends by saying that we will have a "long march" together. And there is Nixon seated next to Madame Mao Tse-tung, watching a ballet which has become agitprop, a violation of art as well as of taste; it was as if we had invited the presidents of the black African republics to the White House to show them a ballet on the theme of Little Black Sambo. And Mr. Nixon, returning to the United States, proclaims the great enthusiasm the Chinese people feel for their government. Indeed. The Chinese government has many ways of generating enthusiasm, and no doubt Mr. Nixon is professionally fascinated by them, even as Henry Regnery would be fascinated by methods of teaching authors how to write books that sell not five thousand but fifty million copies.

We see then the movement of Western opinion: What, really, is so bad about Red China? Their ways are not our ways, to be sure, but is it seriously proposed that we should be prepared to die if necessary in order to avoid living by their word, rather than by our own—which is in any case corrupt, racist, and decadent?

Henry is right, when he generalizes that it will be hard to teach people to oppose the effronteries of the modern world. Henry published a book called *In Defense of Freedom*, by Frank Meyer, who would have been here tonight except that he died two weeks ago. Even in the early 1960s, Meyer's metaphysical defense of objective freedom was—somehow—just a little bit embarrassing, and even to the finest of people, the finest of friends, the most ardent of counterrevolutionaries.

"If the Republican Party does not find a way to appeal to the mass of the people," Whittaker Chambers wrote me after the election of 1958, "it will find itself voted into singularity. It will become, then, something like the little shop you see every now and then in the crowded parts of great cities, in which no business is done, or expected. You enter it and find an old man in the rear, fingering, for his own pleasure, oddments of cloth (weave and design circa 1850), caring not at all if he sells any. As your eyes become accustomed to the gaslight, you are only faintly surprised to discover that the old man is Frank Meyer."

Those oddments of cloth, by a familiarity with which a few men know to hesitate not at all when someone asks the question: Is it wrong for the state to tell the writer what to write? Is it wrong for the state to tell the scientist what to study? Those few do not hesitate for a moment to say: *Yes, it is wrong. It was always wrong, is now wrong, and will forever be wrong.* The old man with the oddments of cloth is fingering some of the truths that Henry Regnery has endeavored over the years to propagate: yes, in books, some of them, that sold only five or eight thousand copies; some that sold even less. But what more can a man do, than give himself to making available a book to the man who hungers for it? In Russia it costs what for many is a month's wages to buy a novel of Solzhenitsyn in the black market. And there are old men—and old women, and young men, and young women—who in the far reaches of that vast country transcribe by hand, from Radio Liberty, which they risk prison by listening to, the new novel of Solzhenitsyn, word after word, sentence after sentence, a process that takes months to complete: resulting not in thousands of copies, but in dozens or perhaps a few hundred: the oddments of cloth, circa the golden age of civilization, viewed synoptically. It is worth *everything* to preserve those oddments, to make them available to those who are graced with a thirst for them: or—nothing is worth anything at all. Henry Regnery was never confused on this point. As long as people are free to remember, there will be those who will give thanks to those who thought, as Henry has done, with loving care to preserve the tokens of hope and truth.

WITHOUT MARX OR JESUS?

Remarks (excerpted) to the Annual Meeting of the American Society of Newspaper Editors; the Empire Room of the Shoreham Hotel, Washington, D.C., April 19, 1972

The other participants in this panel discussion were Jean-François Revel, the French analyst and philosopher; Professor John Kenneth Galbraith, the economist; and David Rockefeller, chairman of the board of the Chase Manhattan Bank. The theme of the morning was "American Values on Trial: The System and the Search for Individuality." I spoke with some emphasis on the compatibility of individualism and capitalism.

I AM HAPPY to be with you once again, and of course always happy to serve in the truth squad that providence has deputized to follow Professor Galbraith to the corners of the earth. Mr. Revel has, as his reputation led us to believe he would do, spoken provocatively. There is reason to believe that Mr. Rockefeller will return the argument with interest, at prime rate plus at least 1 percent.

Mr. Galbraith is, as you all know, pretty well committed to the notion that capitalism is an abstraction, that—as he once formally put it—the free marketplace is a snare and a delusion. Thus far he has resisted drawing metaphysical implications from the argument that in the world of economics the individual counts for nothing—and for this we must be grateful. It is quite enough, in a lifetime, to convulse a single academic discipline. I know men and women who lie awake at night fearing that John Kenneth Galbraith will take an interest in philosophy, which would no doubt bring on disturbances as great as any that have occurred since Thales first undertook to restate the problem of understanding man and his universe.

Mr. Revel has written intriguingly about a future without Marx or Jesus. I elect to believe that he was being, as I say, provocative. I quite understand a future without Marx, but it has always seemed to me that if our future is indeed to be without Jesus, the decision will be His, not ours; and that in any event, Jesus is not bound even by the deliberations of the American Society of Newspaper Editors. Not that He should disdain them—Jesus desires a good press, and there are those of us who believe Him entitled to it. There are others who, notwithstanding that they have neglected to dwell on Jesus at all, or on the movement He launched—which movement some believe will prevail even against the gates of hell, let alone Karl Marx—hesitate intuitively to think of Jesus as fiction, though to be sure He is quite widely treated as such in the press. I have no doubt that the great revival will occur when Jack Anderson [the gossip columnist] reveals that, on the third day, Christ arose. Meanwhile the phrase "Neither Marx nor Jesus," if Mr. Revel will permit me to say so, I put aside gently as a rhetorical maneuver, attention-getting in design. I think I would read with presumptive interest any essay entitled "Neither Buckley nor Aristotle"—and nod sagely my approval for any reviewer who insisted that the reader must take the proposition whole: all, or nothing at all.

Our host has directed our attention to a single passage from Mr. Revel's book on which he asks us to dwell. Mr. Revel wrote that there is an "increasing rejection of a society motivated by profit, domi-nated exclusively by economic considerations, ruled by the spirit of competition, and subjected to the mutual aggressiveness of its mem-bers." And he added, "indeed, beneath every revolutionary idea we find a conviction that man has become the tool of his tools and that he must once more become an end and a value in himself."

Concerning these sentiments, a few observations:

(1) I do not know of any society that is dominated exclusively by economic considerations. Certainly our own is not; else we'd be a lot more straightforward in some of our enterprises. I speak not only about corporate America but also about individual Americans. Certainly *profit* had nothing to do with Mr. Galbraith's and my

appearance before you this morning, as your treasurer will confirm.

I think what we have in mind, rather, is the continuing disposition of some people to *ascribe* an economic motivation to every human transaction. This temptation, as we all know, antedated Karl Marx; indeed, it was penetrated as false before Karl Marx wrote his celebrated work. But like the behaviorist determinism of B. F. Skinner, economic determinism is no less fashionable for having been repeatedly discredited, theoretically and empirically. It was only a year ago that an organization of militant ladies who call themselves Another Mother for Peace bombarded the Congress of the United States with four hundred thousand signatures of Americans who protested the Vietnam War after being advised by Another Mother that the war was actually being fought in behalf of American oil interests. The report had circulated that U.S. oil companies were poised to take four hundred million barrels of oil out of the Indo-Chinese shelf beginning on the day that South Vietnam won its victory. What proved wrong with the story, a congressional committee patiently discovered, is that (a) four hundred million barrels of oil per day is a lot of oil; in fact it is ten times as much oil as is taken daily out of the entire world's oilfields combined; (b) U.S. companies own no concessions off Indo-China; and (c) no oil has yet been discovered off Indo-China. But that correction and others like it will not significantly diminish the number of pilgrims who will continue to believe that the principal motive of the United States in Southeast Asia is economic. And in New York City today, as no doubt in other major cities, a documentary on Richard Nixon is being shown called *Millhouse,* in which the director-producer dramatically flashes on the screen the "credit lines" for the Vietnam War: *fifty major American companies.* This, I am sure Mr. Revel will agree, is Marxist boob bait, on the intellectual level of suggesting that United States Rubber was responsible for sending Dr. Schweitzer to West Africa to found his hospital; after all, a year did not go by that Dr. Schweitzer failed to order rubber tubes.

(2) Surely once we have freed ourselves from formal Marxism, we grapple with the more significant point, which is cultural: sug-

gested by Mr. Revel's notion that there is growing among us a rejection of a society "motivated by profit" and "subjected to the mutual aggressiveness of its members."

I am constrained to comment that what occupies our attention is in fact an increasing rejection of society, *period*. During the most vociferous period in the late 1960s there were riots in Paris and Madrid, Chicago and Berlin, New Delhi and Mexico City; on and on they came, their coordinates unpredictable, such that the taxonomists finally threw up their calipers in dismay after attempting to correlate the dissatisfaction with private enterprise, or the Vietnam War, or clitoral orgasm, or racism—which are the comprehensive concerns of our age. If I may say so, the despair did not greatly surprise social observers whose Richter scales are less easily disturbed than Mr. Revel's. Christopher Dawson and David Riesman, a historian and a sociologist, have both been aware of the phenomenon of *anomie*—the great fault in human nature, which, like the geophysical faults that cause elemental disturbances beneath the surface of the earth, causes deracinated man to shudder with fright and loneliness and despair.

But since men are active, and above all talkative, they are disposed, even as they exercise their freedom, implicitly to deplore it, to talk disdainfully even about those human institutions which are arranged to give them, as individuals, the greatest scope. It is unfashionable—I am tempted to say unprofitable—to adduce in defense of economic freedom the utilitarian argument which led Dr. Johnson to remark that man is seldom so innocently engaged as when in pursuit of profit; but I pause nevertheless to pay that argument historical deference, and to announce my disposition to defend it should Mr. Galbraith deal too disdainfully with it.

I am more shaken by Mr. Revel's implied suggestion that the free marketplace introduces "mutual aggressiveness." Surely that is the climactic semantical effrontery: the notion that it is an act of aggression to lay before the individual a choice, whether of canned soups or of economic textbooks. By that token it is an act of aggression to write another song, or paint another canvas, or set down another verse, and so muscle into territory already spoken for.

We come then (3) to the complaint that underlies the epiphe-nomenal complaints, which melt away on contact with orderly thought. It is a philosophical complaint, not an economic one: namely, that man has "become the tool of his tools," ceasing to be "an end and a value in himself." There is absolutely no doubting that that is the direction towards which we are headed, and that there is a correlation between our advances towards individual anonymity and our ad-vances towards the kind of statism beloved of such as my friend John Kenneth Galbraith.

The complaint is the direct reflection of the diminution of the individual as the center of civilized concern. The causes of that diminution are many and complicated, and we may end up agreeing with Professor Oakeshott's haunting historical insight: that we are individuals *manqués*, that the burden of freedom proved to be too great.

Meanwhile the assault on the individual is continuingly success-ful. It is partly the result of fatigue, partly the result of sheer fright. Our defenses are grown very weak, both as individuals and as a nation. . . .

Mr. Revel's search for a revolution that will restore meaning to man is up against the most prominent revolutions of this century, whose extirpative passion is to eliminate man. I submit to the critics of the marketplace that if they are concerned about the restoration of the individual, they should begin by focusing on him; begin by pene-trating the anfracuosities by which we are somehow persuaded that we serve the individual by moving against the major institutions in which the individual has what freedom of movement the architects of the modern world have left him; begin by turning again to that reli-gion which tells us, in the words of Ecclesiastes, that "God has made men upright"—but which quickly adds, as if anticipating such mun-dane mutilations as Mr. Galbraith's price controls, "but they have sought out many inventions."

The whole subject is strangely, quietly saddening. As we meet here in Washington to deplore the excesses of the marketplace, in Russia the people go to the black market and pay eighty rubles, a month's wages, for a novel by Solzhenitsyn. And there in Russia, whose rulers denounced the marketplace fifty years ago with a blaze of trumpets and a rain of bullets aimed righteously at the temples of four teenaged girls and a hemophiliac boy in a cellar at Ekaterinburg, the books of Solzhenitsyn accumulate, even as, here, the introspective disillusion with the institutions of freedom perversely accumulates; for an understanding of which paradox we find no help in Marx, but considerable help in Jesus, whose servant Paul observed that "though our outward man perish, yet the inward man is renewed, day by day."

THE "LEFTWARDMOST VIABLE CANDIDATE"

The Opening Statement in a Debate with John Kenneth Galbraith on the Question, "Should Richard Nixon or George McGovern Be Elected?"; the New York Public Library, New York, October 26, 1972

It was a flashy affair, five hundred guests convened for a black-tie dinner under a large tent behind the New York Public Library. Humorist Art Buchwald was the master of ceremonies and launched the engagement on a rollicking start with his comment on the deposed Senator Eagleton, dropped by candidate McGovern as his running mate when it was disclosed that he had had psychological problems. "The question before the house," Mr. Buchwald roared out, taking a welcomed shot at Spiro Agnew, "is whether the nation is better off with a vice president who has been treated for mental illness or with one who hasn't." The combatants were given twelve minutes for their opening statements.

I T WAS WAY back in February that Mr. Elliott invited me by cablegram to defend, on this occasion, the Republican incumbent against Mr. Galbraith's advocacy of the Democratic challenger, whoever he might be. It happened that Mr. Galbraith reposed at that moment a local telephone call away, in Gstaad, where during the winter he pursues his study of skiing and economics. His skiing instructors are occasionally cheered by the news that Mr. Galbraith also has difficulties in mastering his other line of activity. I started to say his sedentary activity, but I am not sure that that would success-fully distinguish it from his activity as a skier.

Anyway, Mr. Galbraith told me that he too had received a cable from Mr. Elliott and had agreed to contribute his services on this occasion; at which point there was a pause. I thought, for the fun of it, to come flat-out at the most promiscuous end of what was then a technical possibility. "What will you do," I asked, "if it turns out that you will have committed yourself to appearing before so distin-guished an audience of New York liberals charged with the responsi-bility of advocating Senator Henry Jackson for president?" Henry Mencken, on being asked what he would say if, after his death, he found himself confronted with the angels and the saints, replied, "I guess I would say, 'Well, gentlemen, I was apparently mistaken.'" I don't think Professor Galbraith ever taxed himself to the point of wondering what he would say at such a level of contingency. He replied instead with characteristic confidence that he could serenely predict that he would not be subjected to any such embarrassment; and of course he was right. The embarrassment to which he is now subjected is of quite another nature.

There is no constitutional reason why Professor Galbraith can-not correctly predict what will happen in the short term, the long term having been dismissed by Lord Keynes as the point at which Professor Galbraith answers to the angels and the saints. I recall that in the spring of 1968, after the Tet offensive, Mr. Galbraith pre-dicted that the government of President Thieu would not last out six weeks. Well, you can't win 'em all.

Mr. Galbraith then divulged to me that he has a personal rule as regards Democratic contenders. The rule is that he will back the "leftwardmost" (I use his word) of the "viable" (again, I use his word) candidates. What isn't clear, not even from the closest reading of his work, is whether by the qualifier "viable" he means having a fighting chance to win the election; or whether he means personally tolerable to Professor Galbraith. The latter, to be sure, springs to the mind of those who have studied Mr. Galbraith's propensities. On the other hand, what if it had been not George McGovern but Leon Trotsky who defeated Hubert Humphrey in the California primary, pleading perhaps superior experience on how to deal with the Kremlin? One is entitled to wonder whether the Galbraith formula would have locked him into drawing, here tonight, on his deep reserves of eloquence and ingenuity and cunning to sell us on the virtues of voting for Trotsky. If you are out for ideological highs, you may as well use the purest stuff.

The New York Public Library is manned by a worldly force, rather like the confessors at St. Peter's. But their cosmopolitanism sometimes runs ahead of their professionalism. Vladimir Nabokov told me that a few years ago he came here to this library after receiving a letter advising him that for all his vaunted originality, in fact a novel had been published in the 1880s entitled *Lolita*. Nabokov came here and discovered that the title did indeed exist—right here in the card file. So he scratched the call number down and presented it at the desk. The clerk looked at the slip of paper, then at Nabokov. He leaned over and said in an avuncular whisper, "That's not the *Lolita you're* looking for, buster."

It is instructive to bear in mind that George McGovern, to the extent that he does not, in late October 1972, fully satisfy his supporters on the American Left, tends to fail them for reasons that some of his admirers, though by no means all, find forgivable only because George McGovern would not be a viable candidate if he adopted the formal theoretical positions of Leon Trotsky. For the most part, to be sure, the backers of George McGovern back him as a pragmatist, whose utterances are nicely tuned to left-utopianism and left-hobgoblinization: who, to be sure, has suffered the ignominy of the rites of passage of any Democratic candidate, which stipulate that he, e.g., worshipfully visit the LBJ Ranch, there to proclaim that that visit is "one of the most treasured moments of my life"; and then go to Chicago, there to praise a mayor who, a few years ago, recommended to the police that they simply shoot all looters.

Well, on the eve of the Miami Convention, Mr. Galbraith wrote for the *Saturday Review* an exuberant essay predicting that George McGovern would win the national election triumphantly. Mr. Galbraith's reasoning, way back during the elation of last July, was that the American people had a very simple choice before them: to vote for the candidate of the Rich People, or for the candidate of the Poor People (language that Leon Trotsky would have approved of). But three months later, the polls perplexingly suggest that, at this moment a week before the election, approximately twice as many Americans will vote for the candidate of the Rich People. Does that mean, accepting Mr. Galbraith's rigorous formula, that there are twice as many rich people as poor people in America?

But it is unkind to press such particulars. True, he wrote in *The Affluent Society* that by the end of the 1960s we would have primarily the problem of what to do with our affluence. Now he tends to write mostly about things like endemic poverty, and unemployment, and inflation, the elimination of which is supposed to be the object of the science to which he devotes himself, with what effects the people, poor and not poor, are entitled to wonder. But the polls then go on to tell us very strange things. They tell us that rich people on the whole, though not by any means all of them, will vote against McGovern. But the polls also tell us that middle-income people intend, on the whole, to vote against McGovern. And then—get this!—working-class people, on the whole, intend to vote against McGovern. And then—this is really getting to be too much—half the faculty in the American academy intend to vote against McGovern. And, finally, half the young people. So that George McGovern is not even certain at this point that he will get the votes of Bob & Carol &Ted & Alice.

What on earth is going on? you want to know—and so do I. We can hope that this evening will help to guarantee that in the months ahead we will be able to come to the New York Public Library and find here, in its generous and nondiscriminatory archives, the resources wherein to find out: Why? Why is the candidate of the majority party, running against a president with the smallest personal constituency since James Buchanan's, going down to such an inglorious defeat? Will the problem prove to be that pestiferous cultural lag which separates Mr. Galbraith from the people he labors so elegantly to serve? Will the facts, finally collated, say that it was the personal failure of the candidate that made the difference? Will the sympathetic clerk, sensing the anxiety of the young researcher, lean over and reassure him: "This isn't the McGovern you were looking for"?

Is THIS THE way to approach the question, before such a gathering, in the twelve minutes we have been allotted? It is I think the preferable way. It would be somehow callous, and certainly tedious, to reiterate the progressive modifications of George McGovern on his domestic score, whose contrapuntal complexity has reached such a point now that not even Leonard Bernstein could harmoniously conduct it. It would also be depressing to chronicle his adventitious discoveries: of Jerusalem, for instance. Imagine discovering Jerusalem only under the triangulating guidance of the three kings, Gallup, Harris, and Yankelovich. There is a sad witlessness in the tergiversations of George McGovern, whether on income redistribution, or on bases in Thailand, or on Thomas Eagleton, or on defense policy, or on Mayor Daley, or on the Mideast. Ronald Reagan, for instance, said it so much better two years ago when he recommended that we send to Israel at the end of every week exactly as many Phantom jets as the Egyptians claimed to have shot down during that week.

We are reduced, in defense of Mr. McGovern, to the most spectacular sophisms in modern journalistic history, the editorials of the *New York Times*, which proclaim clangorously the necessity of voting for George McGovern in protest—I ask you to believe me that I am quoting from last Sunday's editorial page—in protest against, for instance, the "budget deficits that have soared out of control" under Mr. Nixon. Therefore vote for the man whose projected budget would increase the deficit by—to use the least alarming estimate—$65 billion.

Or take yesterday's effort by the *Times* to reveal that George Mc-Govern, who twenty-five years ago deplored the Truman Doctrine and who today deplores NATO, is the *true* internationalist. I have described *New York Times* editorials as Eleanor Roosevelt rewritten by Cotton Mather, but I have to confess I do not know what I would do without them—they are as perversely cheering as the misanthropy of Scrooge, who, let's face it, ceased to be very interesting when he became wise and humane, like me, and Mr. Nixon. Besides, if you are looking for rainbows, you need only draw a line from the antecedent *New York Times* editorial on over to the historical development. I liked the editorial during the last general election that said about the beleaguered incumbent [Senator Charles Goodell] that his was "the voice of the public official determined to keep freedom from being assassinated by the ruthless nightriders of the political Right." Well, the nightriders had their way and elected to office—the saintly junior senator from New York. If my brother's sweet disposition is the stuff of which the *New York Times*'s nightmares are regularly made, we can all take heart.

And let those of you who reason that four more years of Nixon is an intolerable prospect remind yourselves that, without Nixon, you would not get four more years of Buchwald on Nixon. That's what *I* would call intolerable.

THE TERRIBLE SADNESS
OF SPIRO AGNEW

An Address to the New York Conservative Party's Annual Dinner; New York,
October 15, 1973

---

*Five days before the dinner, Vice President Agnew had resigned his office.
The shock was great to the party faithful, whose guest of honor he had
been a year earlier. There was a fleeting temptation, encouraged by emis-
saries of Mr. Agnew, to think him victimized. The challenge, I undertook
to say, was to distinguish the advocate from the causes he advocated.
Before the next year's Conservative Party dinner, Richard Nixon would
have resigned his office.*

I SOMETIMES HAVE the feeling that for me the balance of the year
is nothing more than an interruption of the continuing speech I
deliver to the Conservative Party. Worse, I sometimes feel that
that is the way many of you must look upon it. I have no doubt that
some of you have whispered to yourselves, "God, I wish Buckley
would take a bribe. We need a new face." I would not blame you,
though I hope you would blame me.

A year ago our guest of honor was Spiro Agnew. I gather, from
listening to the president's speech the other night, that Mr. Agnew's
name will not again cross presidential lips. This is what Mr. Nixon
must mean when he deplores what he calls our "obsession" with the
past.

One wishes that his instinct—to treat Spiro Agnew as an unper-
son—were an act of chivalry. One fears it is something other than
that. My own feeling is that it is an unkindness to Mr. Agnew to proceed as if he had never existed. I say this intending to make a human
point, and a social point as well. Charles Van Doren was permitted a
dozen years ago to slip into oblivion; many centuries have gone by
since it was prescribed that guilty men be exposed at regular intervals
for public castigation. But there was much to learn from the episode

involving Charles Van Doren, and there is much to learn from the tragic career of Spiro Agnew.

We go to such lengths in identifying positions with people that we find it hard to detach those people from those positions when we would like to do so. So comprehensively did Agnew emerge on the political scene as the incarnation of law, order, probity, and inflexible ethics that, now that he has fallen, we are made to feel that the case for law, order, probity, and inflexible ethics has somehow fallen too: that ethics is itself subject to bribe and delinquency. This tendency to anthropomorphize our ideals is an American habit that can get us, indeed has just now gotten us, into deep trouble.

The conservative community was outraged when, following the conviction of Alger Hiss twenty years ago, Dean Acheson said that he would not turn his back on Alger Hiss. It was felt then that Acheson was saying not merely that he would stand by an old friend, even one who had lied and lied and lied and who had worked for a foreign dictator and who had attempted (indeed still does) to bring down an innocent man in order to save his own skin; Acheson was saying not merely that he would stand by that man, but that—in effect—he doubted the processes of justice that had found that man guilty. That was why we were outraged.

And we have a right to be outraged against those who—for old times' sake, and in veneration of their ideals as so trenchantly defended by Vice President Agnew—will say now: I'm standing behind Agnew; Agnew was framed. Mr. Agnew, reaching for self-justification, is no more plausible than Alger Hiss. He lost his plausibility after looking the ladies of California in the eye and telling them that he would not resign under any circumstances, only to do so a fortnight later, pleading guilty to one felony and acquiescing in the publication of a dossier of data about his activities which, if it is indeed a tissue of lies, forces us to believe it possible that the Justice Department and the FBI and the judges conspired together to frame Alger Hiss. I do not see that it is a part of our creed to suggest that no one who affirms our creed could ever succumb to temptation. Rather our political creed is substantially built upon the need to advertise the lures of temptation:

government, we believe, is presumptively guilty of self-enhancement at the expense of the people's liberty.

The definition of a crime is often capricious, and can be a reflection of idiosyncratic cultural traditions. It is, for instance, perfectly okay to promise to make someone a judge when you come to power, but it is wrong for money to change hands. What you cannot tolerate, in politics, is precisely what is required in law: a consideration. Mr. Agnew knew all this, and it really would not affect one's judgment of what he did if he could prove that, while governor, he had selected among all the bidders and awarded the contract to paint the ceiling of the Sistine Chapel to Michelangelo. He looked us all in the eye and said he had done nothing wrong, was being persecuted by the Justice Department, and would not resign: and we believed him. I think it right that we should have believed him. But I think it wrong that, because we have over several years now treated Mr. Agnew and the ideas he is associated with as inseparable, we should, in order to salvage those ideas, attempt to salvage Mr. Agnew. The temptation is, really, to salvage our own pride. To say, as so many said to themselves about Alger Hiss, *The man I trust is therefore trustworthy.*

It is the highest tribute to Mr. Agnew to take his ideals so seriously as to apply them to Mr. Agnew himself. To say that the guilty should be removed from power, however great the sacrifice to those of us who are bereft; that we are mature enough to make moral decisions and abide by the consequences; that we are so gravely committed to high standards of behavior that we are willing to renounce those who stray from those high standards even if they are our friends and our heroes.

It is a terrible irony that at the moment in history when liberalism is sputtering in confusion, empty of resources, we should be plagued as we are by weak and devious men. The terrible sadness of Spiro Agnew's existence touches everything we do today: our manifestoes, our analysis, our hymns, and our laughter. Through our participation in this adversity we must seek strength, such strength as we derive from knowing that Mr. Agnew was profoundly right about many of the causes of our decline; that though he proved to be a physician who could not heal himself, in his words, as uttered over four years, there were the rocks of truth, and to these truths, however dazed and saddened, we rededicate ourselves, without hesitation, with faith, with hope, and with charity.

THE HIGH COST OF MR. NIXON'S DECEPTIONS

An Address (excerpted) to the New York Conservative Party's Annual Dinner; the New York Hilton, New York, October 18, 1974

Another appearance at the annual dinner, over which hung the cloud of President Nixon's resignation. There was lingering resentment among many there, enthusiastic supporters of Senator James Buckley's call to Nixon, in March, urging him to resign from office. On what Senator Buckley did and why, I ponder in this talk. He would be defeated for re-election two years later, yielding his seat to Daniel Patrick Moynihan.

I APPEAR BEFORE you once again, surrounded by men and women I admire, and the dutiful servant of our irreplaceable chairman, Daniel Mahoney, who spends his time equally worrying about affairs of state and, in his capacity as my attorney, my own affairs. I sometimes feel he would be better off if I were a world problem rather than a personal problem. After all, we can dispose of world problems in a single evening, advising the world what to do, failing which it must take the consequences. . . .

We are engaged, ladies and gentlemen, in a fitful search for candor in America. Candor and honesty and directness are certainly among the virtues conservatives approve of. But I must confess that the attraction of these virtues to the loudest proponents of them tends to be discriminatory. I have not heard a swell of candor coming up from the ranks of Democratic congressmen admitting that the inflation we suffer from is substantially the result of the overspending for which Congress and Congress alone is responsible.

I have not heard Ramsey Clark say that the only reason he is a hawk in the Middle East is that he cannot otherwise commend himself to the Jewish voters of New York City.

I have not heard Jacob Javits pause in his search for candor long enough to explain that the candid reason he wandered about the lot on Watergate was that he, candidly, didn't know which way the voters would come down.

Candor, of course, can be painful. And sometimes candor isn't diplomatically possible. But the *lack* of candor has cost the conservative movement a great deal in the last few years. It was only a year ago that Spiro Agnew resigned, and we came to know that *his* lack of candor, in professing his innocence, deepened the shock—and the gravity—of the little peculation he had committed.

In the past year we have gone through a terrible ordeal, one that divided conservatives—divided them for very good reasons. There were those who simply assumed that Richard Nixon was being candid with us when he insisted that he had not known of, let alone participated in, the cover-up of Watergate. Others—some of them relying on instinct, some of them naturally suspicious—felt that Mr. Nixon was *not* being entirely candid. Indeed it turned out that he was not. *His* lack of candor is going to cost the American people a great deal: it will result almost certainly in a Democratic Congress, probably a veto-proof Congress, which will lurch the country leftward, precisely in the opposite direction from the one the American people expressed themselves as desiring in their vote in 1972. It is of course an irrational act, to punish one's conservative congressman or senator or governor for the grave deceptions of Richard Nixon. But who ever said that democratic justice is orderly?

I do not wish to pronounce tonight on the future of the country, or to supply a few more dots on that infinitely expansive pointillist canvas that I see as the conservative vision, concerning which you have so patiently permitted me, so often, to dilate. I close simply by saying that in the dark days of doubt and worry and frustration of last winter and spring, when the country was very nearly paralyzed by Watergate and its implications, I experienced—from a very great distance away, because it happened that I was in Africa at the time—something of the personal pain my brother felt, on being roundly denounced by so many of his supporters for suggesting a course of action which, if it had been followed, would have spared the Republic the forthcoming disequilibrium in Congress, and would have spared Richard Nixon the ignominy of the awful, licentious poring over his private conversations. During the days that immediately followed Senator Buckley's reasoned, compassionate, and prescient call on Mr. Nixon to step down for the good of his country, he was accused by many conservatives of treason and worse. I knew that in due course he would be justified, and that many of his critics would—as they have done—return to his side. But for a while, there was nothing that would alleviate the hurt.

But I remember something happening to me which I did not chart at the time. What it was, and what it signified, I came to know only when I recognized what I had blurted out over the telephone. I was at a motel in the Midwest, near where I would be lecturing, and late in the afternoon the telephone rang, and I heard the words I hear so often. The voice said, "Is this *the* Mr. Buckley?"

"No," I said. "That's my brother."

On Serving in the United Nations

Testimony before the Senate Committee on Foreign Relations;
the Capitol Building, Washington, D.C., May 14, 1975

I had served as a public delegate to the United Nations' Twenty-Eighth General Assembly, from mid-September to mid-December 1973, and was asked to testify to the Foreign Relations Committee on the subject of human rights and the United Nations. I was asked to speak for ten minutes and thought to devote my time to disclosing two confidential memo-

randa I had written to my superiors. I then appended a fantasy that, I judged, would illuminate the problems of a U.S. representative serving on the Human Rights Committee of the United Nations.

(Footnote: In the fantasy I single out Jamil Baroody, the Saudi ambassador, a nonstop critic of Israel and much else.)

A COMMUNICATION FROM your committee, signed by the chairman, advises me in language most civil, but tilting rather towards sternness than permissiveness, that I am to address you for ten minutes in a prepared statement.

Last night I gave some thought as to how I might best serve your purposes under these circumstances. Needless to say, I should be happy to answer any questions you subsequently put to me. But to compress an analysis of the impact of détente on the policy of the United States concerning the United Nations is taxing, and requires a most stringent economy of language. I have decided therefore to give you a pastiche. In order to introduce it I require only a sentence or two.

The preliminary data are that I was appointed a public member of the United States Delegation to the Twenty-Eighth General Assembly during the summer of 1973, in which, it is recorded, President Nixon made other, perhaps even graver, mistakes.

I was induced to accept this appointment by being advised that I would represent the United States in the so-called Third Committee—the Human Rights Committee.

I move without further ado in medias res. There I am, at my first meeting of the Third Committee. I go back to my office and address a memorandum to the U.S. ambassador, copy to the secretary of state. I excerpt from that memorandum:

"The policy of détente with the Soviet Union and with China governs the activity of the State Department, and the State Department obviously will move in ways consistent with that policy.

"United States participation in the United Nations is in part a direct expression of United States foreign policy; in part it is an expression of the United States' contribution to strategic ideals of peace, justice, and freedom. It is not, in my opinion, inconsistent for the United States to express itself cordially to the representatives of the Soviet Union in Washington and in Moscow while at the same time representatives of the United States, in public debates on strategic questions having to do with human rights, maintain a dogged position seeking to reaffirm the ideals of the United Nations.

". . . The purpose of the extrapolitical agencies of the UN is ultimately diplomatic. When the Committee talks about the necessity for freedom of information, it votes for improved communications, which in turn lead to the encouragement of democratic and libertarian impulses. When the Committee talks about the right of emigration, or the right to practice one's religion, it argues for pressures on totalitarian entities which lure them towards the open society, which is the most reliable friend of stability and equilibrium. . . .

"Accordingly, unless I am instructed to do otherwise, I plan, as the U.S. member in the Committee on Human Rights, to feel free to discuss human rights even if the inference can be drawn from what I say that I also believe in human rights within the Soviet Union. . . ."

I concluded the memorandum with vows to a most tactful performance of my duties as I saw them, and was advised most tactfully the next day by the U.S. ambassador, for whom I have the highest regard, that any such approach would in fact stand in the way of the tactical demands of détente.

A SECOND ACT (I choose arbitrarily from a number that would serve).

I was, as public delegate, instructed to deliver a short speech on how the United Nations might appropriately celebrate the twenty-fifth anniversary of the passage of the Universal Declaration of Human Rights. I wrote, attempting to conform to the State Department's cabled instructions, a few paragraphs, the relevant ones of which I quote:

"Mr. Chairman, on the occasion of the twenty-fifth anniversary of the promulgation of the Universal Declaration of Human Rights, what is there to say this side of the cant which I hope to spare you? I plead inexperience in the art of saying nothing with much wind, and surely if we find, on meditating the thirty Articles in the Declaration, that there ought to be thirty-one, we should consider recommending an article that declares that all men were born free of the weight of political rhetoric but everywhere man is, in respect of this freedom, in chains.

"My government desires to make one or two observations, some of them concrete, some ceremonial.

"The Human Rights document is the pre-eminent catalogue of human rights in the world today. . . .

"The Declaration has been useful to several countries that have sought to devise bills of rights of their own. By consulting the UN Declaration of Human Rights, they can at least count those rights they have left out.

"My government desires to call attention, on the twenty-fifth anniversary of the Declaration, to a few of the enumerated rights which are conspicuously transgressed upon." I proceeded to enumerate these, as suggested in the telegram from the State Department. And I concluded:

"Now, Mr. Chairman, the world is divided not between those who say they do not believe in torture and those who say that they do believe in torture. Rather it is divided between those who practice torture and those who do not practice torture. Indeed, the world is divided not between those who say they believe in human rights and those who say they do not believe in human rights but between those who grant human beings human rights and those who do not grant human beings human rights. So that this organization is committed, for instance, to the proposition that there is a right to leave one's country. And yet we have not heard more profuse compliments paid to the Declaration of Human Rights than by some who maintain huge fortifications calculated to prevent the exercise of that right.

"The United Nations was not designated as a military juggernaut at the service of the Human Rights Committee to ensure that signatories practice those rights they praise. But, Mr. Chairman, surely it would mark the solemnity of the occasion if, on the twenty-fifth anniversary of the Declaration next December 10, those nations that systematically deny the human rights associated with the United

Nations Declaration should gracefully absent themselves from this chamber for one day?"

I was advised, most gracefully and warmly, that my short analysis, its great philosophical merits to the contrary notwithstanding, was inconsistent with détente: and, accordingly, pleading the urgency of business elsewhere, I arranged for an aide to read a speech recalling in copious detail the exalted oratory that had celebrated the promulgation of the United Nations Declaration twenty-five years ago.

MR. CHAIRMAN, the time having elapsed, I close with a paragraph. A fantasy from a journal I wrote at the end of my term as a public member. I take the liberty of reminding you that I am at your disposal to draw out the implications of this statement. I wrote:

"Wednesday. In the session following the day of the formal closing, a bulletin came in, and the place was in pandemonium. It appears that the military attached to the UN to give technical advice on world disarmament have staged a successful coup and have taken over the General Assembly, the Security Council, and the Secretariat. In due course the UN colonels will issue their instructions, but already it is disclosed that the Soviet Union will not be permitted to talk about disarming without disarming; the Chinese may not speak about human rights without granting human rights; the Arabs will not be permitted to speak about the plight of the less developed countries without forswearing the cartelization of their oil; the Africans may not talk about racism until after subduing the leaders of Uganda, the Central African Republic, and Burundi, for a starter; and, just to prove that the colonels are not above a bill of attainder, Jamil Baroody may not speak at all, on any subject, for ninety days—after which he will be put on probation, and permitted to increase the length of his speeches by one minute per month, until he reaches the maximum of ten minutes, except that at the first mention of Zionist responsibility for World War I, he has to start all over again. The delegates from Eastern Europe must wear red uniforms when they appear on the floor and, before rising to speak, must seek explicit and public permission from the delegate of the Soviet Union. A scientific tabulation will be made, under the colonels' supervision, of the compliance of individual countries with the provisions of the Universal Declaration of Human Rights, and each country's delegate will be required to wear on his lapel his nation's ranking on that scale, which will range from one hundred to zero. Any country with a ranking of less than seventy-five will not be permitted to speak on the subject of human rights."

Mr. Chairman: Please forgive the unorthodox testimony. I hope you will see the purpose in my electing to address you in this form. Thank you.

No Dogs in China

A Lecture (excerpted) to the National War College; Washington, D.C., May 22, 1975

I lectured a half dozen times to the National War College. The audience is select—Army, Navy, and Air Force field officers marked for special treatment, and members of the State Department and the CIA in corresponding stages of upward mobility. The amphitheater's sound system is superb, the introduction by one of the three resident ambassador-hosts extravagant, the attention acute. I include the fairly extensive introductory material in this talk, welcomed by an audience geared to heavy analysis. And I reduce the talk itself to a renewed offensive on the matter of Maoist China and human rights, using Professor Galbraith as my (favorite) pin cushion.

O N BEHALF OF *National Review*, I congratulate you on retrieving the *Mayagüez*.

I have always been made to feel very much at home here, except when being boycotted, and I appreciate the total liberty of expression which is encouraged in your speakers.

This is a highly polemical nation, living through a highly polemical period. I was reminded of this the day before yesterday when the telephone rang at seven o'clock in the morning at my suite in Eau Claire, Wisconsin. The telephone operator told me the district attorney wanted to talk to me. I did a quick examination of conscience and said, "Well, put him on." He turned out to have been a classmate of mine at Yale, a jocular and terribly energetic Democrat. He said that when word came to him that I was occupying this suite at the Howard Johnson motel, he thought it only appropriate to tell me that it was in that identical suite that, three years before, [cartoonist] Al Capp had allegedly attempted to rape a co-ed student. And what was I doing in town?

That's pretty early in the morning for that kind of thing.

I did remember that he had been chairman of Wisconsinites for Lyndon Johnson in 1964 and told him that, under the circumstances, I thought it an act of brinkmanship to make any reference to Republican rapacity. Besides, I told him, I had a fresh security clearance from the FBI as a result of my having served as a delegate to the United Nations.

I recalled that on the occasion of my appointment, in the summer of 1973, the FBI called the usual people, including my colleague William Rusher, who groaned and said, "Oh, not again! We went through this during the USIA days!"

"I know," said the agent, "but it is my duty to ask whether Mr. Buckley might have done anything since 1969 to embarrass the Nixon administration."

"No," said Mr. Rusher, "but the Nixon administration has done a great deal to embarrass Mr. Buckley."

On those occasions, as Ambassador Leonhart knows, and a lot of you, I am sure, also know, you get, after you have been confirmed by the Senate, a huge scroll. It is done in exquisite White House boilerplate, beginning with the name of the president. Then it has four blank spots: one of them for your name, the second for the office to which you have been appointed, the third for the length of the appointment, and the fourth introduced with the printed words "in recognition of." In my case that last blank was filled in with "his intelligence and integrity."

I was very pleased that Mr. Nixon knew about my intelligence and integrity, but I found myself wondering, after a while, what was the inventory of characterizations from which those two had been specially selected. The lawyers have a phrase: *Numero unius est exclusio alterius*; that is to say, you draw attention to that which you don't name by that which you do name.

I found myself in Saigon a couple of months later talking, in the course of duty, with Mr. Bunker, who was suddenly called out of the room. My eyes floated around the furniture, and I saw his scroll and rushed over to see what was in *his* blank space: "In recognition of: his intelligence, integrity, and prudence."

I didn't get very much done in the United Nations except write an imprudent book about it. As a matter of fact, for a while I didn't think I would be permitted to give any speeches at all, most of those I suggested being inconsistent with the spirit of the time. But some machine there detected that I had run for mayor in 1965, and so I was asked to give the speech on New York City's UN Day, an annual luncheon devoted to instructing foreign delegates on New York's civic practices. So I spoke my few paragraphs, and then, in the question period, a gentleman got up and said, "Mr. Buckley, what is your opinion of the $3.5 billion transportation bond?"

I said, "To tell you the truth, I have no opinion of it because I vote in Connecticut and, under the circumstances, I have spared myself the travail of looking into the merits and demerits of that particular proposal."

Whereupon the lady who is the New York City commissioner to the United Nations—and the hostess of the luncheon—rose and said, "You see, Mr. Ambassador, in America we vote where we sleep, not where we work."

I said, "That's not *exactly* true, because if I voted where I slept, I'd vote in the United Nations."

I have been made aware that you are focusing your attention on a reassessment of national-security policies. I propose to speak, if I may, on the theme of American values—more specifically, on one American value, integral, I think, to human freedom. I am—as you are, of course—aware that the national security is vehemently defended around the world, even by military hierarchies committed to an unthinking defense of a totalitarian society. The instinctive protectiveness of the military and even of the civil institutions towards an incumbent government tends, I think, to stem from a fusion of instincts—patriotism and loyalty and fear and vanity and xenophobia. The advantage of the totalitarian state is very great. You can go miles and miles in the People's Republic of China without running into Jane Fonda. The free society needs to depend heavily for its national security on the bond of its citizens' affection. If it is strong, no effort is too great to provide for the national security. If it is weak or factious, the requirements of the national security blur in the alienated perceptions of a citizenry disgusted with itself, unconvinced of the value of that which the national security is there to guard.

It is, accordingly, my judgment that the source of attrition of the national security during the past decade is less military rebuffs or diplomatic ineptitude than the erosion of a simple but dogged pride in the axioms of human freedom.

Last January I participated in a forum, along with Mr. John Kenneth Galbraith and Mr. Jean-François Revel, to discuss the virtues and vices of America. . . .

Mr. Galbraith, whose most recent book had been reviewed only a few weeks earlier in the *New York Times*, proclaimed himself—accurately, I think—a socialist. No doubt he wrote so enthusiastically about the People's Republic of China in that book in part because he found Mao's China liberated from the "affliction" of the free marketplace. Mind you, he acknowledges in his book the authoritarian character of the regime, but he quickly puts a gloss on it. "Dissidence," he writes (that is how he describes the behavior of Chinese who want to read books of their own choosing, or who want to change their jobs or practice their religion or leave the country), "is brought firmly into line in China, and, one suspects, with great politeness. It is," he says, "a firmly authoritarian society in which those in charge smile and say 'please.'"

In Mr. Galbraith's book, Mao Tse-tung emerges as a sort of Rector of Justin. But let us focus narrowly on the economic arrangements in China. Authoritarianism can indeed work marvels, at least in the short term, as Mr. Galbraith, ever the wistful former head of the Office of Price Administration during the Second World War, discerns. Listen. "In any other country," Mr. Galbraith observes, "the difference between urban and rural incomes would set in motion a large movement of people to the cities, and in China it once did. This is not now happening. The reason is straightforward. The Chinese are assigned jobs and remain where they are assigned."

And then Professor Galbraith, perhaps America's leading cultural critic of the free market, gets quite specific. After all, he was in China as an economist, indeed as president of the American Economic Association. He was traveling there with the two previous presidents of that association. And so, in one chapter, the great economist strips for action, becomes all professional, like Charles Darwin whipping out a magnifying glass. "While the higher authority decides what prices ought to be," writes Professor Galbraith about the workings of the municipal marketplace in Peking, "such authority is intelligently susceptible to suggestions as to when abundance requires reduction and scarcity an increase. The keeper of the apple stall whom I consulted informally told me that, of course, apples are reduced in price as the autumn advances and the supply becomes more abundant." Leaping lizards! Reduce the price of apples when they are abundant, increase the price of apples when they are scarce! Score one more thought for Chairman Mao!

Granted, "higher authority" (that is the term, as you know, that they use in China) isn't always finely tuned to the vagaries of supply and demand. There are such things as harvest yields, fluctuating tastes, and reallocations of still higher authority. And when the highest authority himself makes wrong decisions—well, Mr. Galbraith quotes his traveling companion Professor Tobin (himself a former head of the American Economic Association and economics adviser to George McGovern) as observing that there are no dogs or cats in China. The reason, Mr. Galbraith explains, is "presumably economic. If food has been scarce and rationed, affection for a participating pet must diminish. This seems especially probable," he concludes, "if the pet is itself edible."

Let me tell you something, Professor Galbraith, and Professors

Revel and Tobin, and anyone else who wants to hear it. The reason for eating one's pet dog isn't economic, it is biological. It is the assertion of primal biological needs over affection, and it is to such biological compulsions that the Chinese were recently driven by higher authority. And when higher authority, assuming the mantle of the marketplace, makes miscalculations so serious that not even great politeness serves to bring dissidents into line, why then the muzzle of the gun becomes the only relevant article in the marketplace. And the supply of guns in China never fluctuates with the seasons. . . .

THE COURAGE OF FRIEDRICH HAYEK

An Address to the Annual Meeting of the Mont Pelerin Society; Hillsdale College, Hillsdale, Mich., August 26, 1975

The Mont Pelerin Society, described in the text here, asks for, and receives, serious commentary oriented to the free market and its implications. The center of attention on this occasion was Professor Friedrich Hayek. I undertook to examine relevant contemporary phenomena, including an insouciance towards intellectual/political deceptions, the amorality of prominent capitalists, and the ultimate philosophical weaknesses of liberalism.

NOT HAVING PREVIOUSLY addressed the Mont Pelerin Society, I indulge myself with a few introductory words of homage, admonition, and reassurance. I have of course been aware of the work of the society almost since its inception and have eagerly read many of the papers delivered before you over the years, great transfusions of genuine liberal thought and analysis into the anemic Western bloodstream.

I remember with great amusement one mark of the increasing consternation brought on by your endeavors. It was a reference to this society by John Kenneth Galbraith a dozen years ago, in that tone of insouciant paternalism which makes him at once so attractive, and so outrageous. He wrote, if I remember accurately, that shortly after the war, "the small remaining band of free-market economists met on an Alpine peak to form a society which, however, soon foundered over a division within its ranks on the question whether the British navy should be owned by the government, or leased from the private sector." I knew then that the Mont Pelerin Society was beginning to get in the way of Professor Galbraith's co-opting of all the noble minds and gentle hearts of the academic and professional worlds for his march down the road to equality in serfdom, and I rejoiced greatly.

By way of warning, I am obliged to say that I could not hope to clarify any of the weighty technical issues on which so many of you have lavished so much invaluable time. I am simply incapable of contributing weight to the scales on which your millimeasurements are calibrated.

And so, by way of reassurance, I intend carefully to steer a course outside the territorial waters of the professional scholars, whose achievements, as I say, I so greatly admire, and whose jurisdictions I should never presume to poach upon.

As we look back on the excitement caused by the publication of Mr. Hayek's *Road to Serfdom*, we wonder how it could have happened. It is a tribute to him, and to his small book, that we should be able to say this. The principal theses of the book are by now so very well known, even if they are not by any means universally accepted, that they appear almost self-evident. Mr. Hayek has always taken scrupulous care to give credit, if it is faintly plausible to do so, to others who articulated ideas before he did; indeed one almost has the feeling, on reading the footnotes to his *Constitution of Liberty*, that the book is a collection of after-dinner toasts to great philosophers, political thinkers, and economists from Thales to Ludwig von Mises. But Hayek cannot shrug off the credit for having brought much of it together: the integrated perception of the relation between law and justice and liberty. And, in an age swooning with passion for a centralized direction of social happiness and economic plenitude, it is a

"There were eighteen hundred of us [in 1946]—triple the normal enrollment—because one of Yale's contributions to the war effort had been to make a comprehensive promise to matriculate, once the war was over, every single student it had accepted during the war" (p. 354). An enterprising student went around the first week of the semester offering to photograph the incoming freshmen; my roommates and I accepted.

"A half dozen times a year [in the 1950s], *National Review* sponsored public meetings at Hunter College—lively affairs, this one a debate with James Wechsler on the proposition: Resolved, That liberalism should be repudiated" (p. 20).

"I had accepted the Conservative Party's nomination to run for mayor of New York City [in 1965]. I got 13 percent of the vote. The preceding Conservative Party candidate had scored 2 percent. Five years later, James L. Buckley, my brother, would be elected to the Senate on the Conservative ticket" (p. 88).

Bernard Gotfryd

"The thing about [my brother] Jim is: he is out of this world. If Jim were a witness to an accident in which an automobile driven by his very best friend collided with an automobile driven by Eldridge Cleaver, and Jim saw that Cleaver had the green light, the testimony would be very direct on the matter, and Jim's good friend would—somehow—bear no resentment at all against Jim" (p. 164).

"It is hard to recall, in the light of later experiences, how much fun it used to be to publish a book. I think I should pause, in deference to historical accuracy, to record that there was a certain risk at that time in spending the night with [Henry and Eleanor] Regnery" (p. 192).

"His skiing instructors are occasionally cheered by the news that [John Kenneth] Galbraith also has difficulties in mastering his other line of activity. I started to say his sedentary activity, but I am not sure that that would successfully distinguish it from his activity as a skier" (p. 203). Here, I meet my friend and favorite adversary on neutral ground—the top of the Eggli, overlooking Gstaad, Switzerland.

Slim Aarons/Getty Archives

"I found myself in Saigon a couple of months later talking, in the course of duty, with [Ellsworth] Bunker, who was suddenly called out of the room. I saw his scroll [announcing one's appointment to public service] and rushed over to see what was in *his* blank space: 'In recognition of: his intelligence, integrity, and prudence'" (p. 220).

"Fifteen years ago I was interviewed by *Playboy* magazine [and] was asked the question, Had I, in middle age, discovered any novel sensual sensation? 'My novel sensual sensation,' I told *Playboy*, 'is to have the President of the United States take notes while you are speaking to him.'" (p. 321).

"Teddy [White] described with feverish anticipation the forthcoming trip to China of President Nixon. I responded that, prompted by his enthusiasm, I too would apply to the White House. Teddy paused, his eyebrows furrowed. He stared over at me brandishing contingent fear and loathing. 'Buckley,' he said, 'if you are on that plane and I am not, I will never talk to you again!' We were not only both on that press plane, but seated together" (pp. 416–417). Recorded here is the visit to the Great Wall.

"Although Allard Lowenstein was at home with collectivist formulations, one had the impression that he might be late in aborting a third world war because of his absorption with the problems of one sophomore" (pp. 261–262). At right, *Firing Line* producer Warren Steibel.

"I said to Monsignor Clark after our celebration of the thirtieth anniversary of *National Review* that I did not remember ever hearing a more inspiriting benediction than the one he gave that night" (p. 379). From left to right, Eugene Clark, Priscilla Buckley, Ronald Reagan, Clare Boothe Luce.

"When I look at [Henry Kissinger], I am not seeing Caesar, or Metternich, or the greatest secretary of state in American history. In the most turbulent and possibly apocalyptic stage in history, one clings to such a serenity as I have found in the friendship of Henry Kissinger" (p. 254).

"This is a dramatic evening. We will hear from the gentleman who put together the hydrogen bomb in behalf of the West, and the gentleman who put together the hydrogen bomb in behalf of the East and who, to say the least, has mixed feelings about it all" (pp. 332–333). This photograph records the first meeting of Dr. Andrei Sakharov and Dr. Edward Teller, a half hour before the Shelby Cullom Davis award dinner.

"The very last [letter to me from] the White House, [Ronald Reagan] began, "Dear Mr. Ambassador: Congratulations! The Soviets are moving out of Afghanistan. I knew you could do it if I only left you there long enough, and you did it without leaving Kabul for a minute" (p. 463).

"We have come, Mr. Chairman, to the end of your two-year-long inquiry into the roots of American order. We comfort ourselves that right reason will prevail, that our heritage will survive" (pp. 476–477). Heritage Foundation president Ed Feulner (right) had invited my son, Christopher Buckley, to introduce me (p. 464), and my sister Priscilla Buckley to present me the Foundation's Clare Boothe Luce Award.

"'I see it as one of the greatest ironies of this ironical time,' writes Malcolm Muggeridge, 'that the Christian message renouncing the world should be withdrawn for consideration just when it is most desperately needed to save men's reason, if not their souls'" (p. 116). Muggeridge meets His Holiness John Paul II as my wife, Pat, looks on. David Niven and I stay discreetly out of the picture.

"Another issue of *National Review* has gone to bed; and you acknowledge—the thought has ever so slowly distilled in your mind—that the time comes for us all to go to bed, and I judge that mine has come" (p. 364). Leaving *NR*'s thirty-fifth anniversary dinner with my son, Christopher, and his wife, Lucy.

squirt of ice water, presaged by the quotation he selected as epigraph to his book, the wry observation of David Hume that "it is seldom that liberty of any kind is lost all at once." Rather, Hayek explained, it is lost gradually; and it is lost by assigning vague, extralawful mandates to men of political authority who take on tasks which they could not be expected to perform without absorbing all the knowledge, values, preferences, and passions of all their fellow men; and this no political authority—indeed, no animate or inanimate body—can do. Accordingly, the political authority has no alternative but to usurp. The necessary result of that usurpation is the corresponding loss in the freedom of the body politic. Over a period of time, that kind of movement must lead us down the road to serfdom, into that amnesiac void towards which, Orwell intuited, evil men were for evil purposes expressly bent on taking us; which void Professor Oakeshott sees us headed towards under the impulse of our own indisposition to bear the heavy responsibilities of freedom.

Hayek brought to his thesis the great prestige of an economist unblemished by the tattoo of ideology. Indeed, during the 1930s his reputation was almost exclusively technical, and we are informed that historians will in due course remark that the great technical debate of that decade was between Hayek and Keynes. One can only hope that by the time they get around to saying this, they will get around to saying that Hayek won. But here I am venturing into economic theory, having promised not to do so.

One can leave it at this, that the Nobel Prize committee took pains to honor Professor Hayek's technical contributions to economic science, alongside Gunnar Myrdal's contributions to something or another. One is reminded of a sentence from Hayek's essay "The Intellectuals and Socialism": "It is especially significant for our problem that every scholar can probably name several instances from his field of men who have undeservedly achieved a popular reputation as great scientists solely because they hold what the intellectuals regard as 'progressive' political views; but I have yet to come across a single instance where such a scientific pseudo-reputation has been bestowed for political reasons on a scholar of more conservative leanings."

HAYEK BROUGHT THEN a great prestige and a dazzling capacity for synthesis to propositions which were widely thought, by the academic community in particular, to constitute nothing much weightier than the ululations of a propertied class suddenly bereft of power in virtue of its incompetence to handle a great depression and its forfeited authority over public opinion. To hear such propositions uttered by businessmen at conventions of the National Association of Manufacturers and quoted in *Reader's Digest* was one thing. To hear them uttered by a quiet, profound academician, and reprinted in *Reader's Digest*, was something else. The counterattack was vigorous. In some cases highly personal and vindictive, in other cases grand and supercilious. Before long Hayek was writing that the "hot socialism" against which he had polemicized in *The Road to Serfdom* was doctrinally dead, but that its "conceptions" had penetrated so deeply into the public consciousness that it mattered not very much that the theology of socialism was discredited, any more than it appears to matter greatly that, if we take Solzhenitsyn's word for it—and I will, today, tomorrow, and always—one cannot find in all of Moscow an orthodox Marxist. The *forms* of socialism are quite sufficient to do the deadly work.

The intellectuals, many of them all along uneasy about the chimerical vanities of utopian socialism, are no less inimical to the kind of society they understand to be the necessary consequence of a free-market economy. The passion for freedom that catapulted us two hundred years ago into national independence and into the most exciting attempt in history at the incorporation of human freedom into a federal constitution has been vitiated. A circumspect libertarian vocabulary has been constructed the purpose of which is to demonstrate that freedom is in fact enhanced, rather than diminished, when we assign to the government substantial control over our lives. Irving Kristol has said that the stunning paradox is that, even as the intellectual fight against socialism is triumphant, the forces of socialism triumph; they manage to do this by arguing that socialism isn't really about economic efficiency and, correlatively, by disdaining freedom insofar as it attaches in any way to property or commerce.

We are several times disadvantaged in the struggle. For one thing, the arguments of the collectivists are more obviously appealing. For another, "it seems to be true," as Hayek wistfully put it in his essay on the subject, "that it is on the whole the more active, intelligent, and original men among the intellectuals who most frequently incline towards socialism, while its opponents are often of an inferior caliber." And, finally, you can spot, slouching about in the grander statements of socialist purpose, inflections of an eschatological character; which, in the nature of things, traditional liberalism quite properly lacks. Yet even if we eschew a redemptive creed we should, Hayek says, "offer a new liberal program which appeals to the imagination." In fact, he goes further, as we shall see.

I ELECT TO touch on three observations of Mr. Hayek's, taking the liberty of treating his essay on the intellectuals as something of an afterword to *The Road to Serfdom*. To this end I advance three propositions.

(1) *The freedom to deceive is overindulged.*

In one of her excellent essays, Simone Weil remarked that Etienne Gilson's account of the history of ancient Greece was factually incorrect in respect of the life of the helots, and that in a just and well-ordered world his book would be suppressed and he would himself be subject to a civil lawsuit, the plaintiff being the Truth.

Now this position is something of a caricature, but it is crankily instructive in an age where freedom of expression has brought virtual immunity for those who deceive. Foremost among those who do so as a class are, of course, the politicians. But in a society in which there is also freedom to criticize, the politicians would not get away with it except for the indulgence of the only class of citizens professionally trained to spot untruth and shoot it, bang bang, right down to earth.

I do not seek to codify this proposition by giving it constitutional lineaments or even by proclaiming a Hillsdale Manifesto. But I do propose that we meditate, far more extensively and seriously than we have done since the publication of *The Road to Serfdom*, on the civil consequences of the extraordinary immunity of the advocates of the superstitions of Communism, of socialism, of redistributionism, of inflation, of dirigisme, at the bar of critical opinion. It has been remarked that Professor Hayek's public manners are exemplary. Nowhere does he give way to spite; nowhere—quite the contrary— does he suggest that there are ulterior motives in those who, piping us down the road to serfdom, make the music of abundance and justice and joy. It is perhaps the most frequently summoned jape at the expense of representative democracy: the story of the earnest legisla- tor who sought to lighten the load of the schoolchildren of Indiana by introducing a law that would trim the value of pi from 3.1416 to the more manageable figure of 3. The response was instantaneous. It did not come alone from men and women professionally capable of han- dling calculus. The hilarity came alike from the mathematicians and their fellow travelers, whose derisory laughter is even now renewed with each retelling of the famous episode, but who remain deaf to economic solecisms.

I am here for only a few hours, returning this afternoon to the nerve center of the cultural world, which groans under the weight of the greatest density of intellectuals this side of Socrates' academy. Yet I have not heard it asserted by any New Yorker, save the isolated immigrants from Mont Pelerin, that no respectable canon of redis- tributive justice recognizes the duty of residents of Detroit, or West Virginia, or Key West—or even Palo Alto—to subsidize the cost of rapid transit in New York City. Much there is that we do not know; but some things we do know. And self-respect requires that we stim- ulate the social and academic sanction against that which is mislead- ing, let alone preposterous. But Ralph Nader, the only social hero of our time, is obsessed by how many cornflakes are missing from the package sold at the grocery store, while undisturbed by how many middles are undistributed in the speech of a typical politician of the Left.

The social success of freedom requires something of an extra- ideological devotion to analytical rigor and to the integrity of lan- guage. Hayek quotes Dorothy Fosdick in a state of what one can only describe as despair, upon reading John Dewey on the meaning of freedom: "The stage . . . is fully set," she writes, "for . . . [the identification of liberty with some other principle, such as equality] only when the definitions of liberty and of equality have been so juggled that both refer to approximately the same condition of activity. An extreme example of such sleight of hand is provided by John Dewey when he says: 'If freedom is combined with a reasonable amount of equality, and security is taken to mean cultural and moral security and also material safety, I do not think that security is compatible with anything but freedom.' After redefining two concepts so that they mean approximately the same condition of activity," Miss Fosdick sighs, Dewey "assures us that the two are compatible."

As the intellectual case against socialism becomes, by experience and analysis, firmer, the threat of socialism becomes, paradoxically, greater; and I find myself wondering whether the soupy indulgence shown by right-minded intellectuals does not emerge as an act less of intellectual charity than of moral despair and epistemological pessimism.

My next proposition (2) is that *The intellectual inferiority of the defenders of capitalism is less critical a factor in contemporary circumstances than the moral inferiority of capitalists.*

Hayek has complained about the "inferior caliber" of those intellectuals who incline in favor of the free market, by comparison with those who defend socialism. He is right, though less so by far than when he wrote those dismaying words, before the great intellectual offensive of the past twenty years, for which he is so substantially responsible. Professor Galbraith, giving an interview recently to a London journalist, said that he was forced to admit that, whereas fifteen years ago he and his colleagues were pretty well convinced that there were no serious problems left unanswered in economics, he now recognizes how much there is left to discover.

If there is so much left for you to discover, a fortiori we can imagine how much there is left for Professor Galbraith to discover. One wishes, discreetly, that, as one experiences one's ignorance, pari passu one would lower one's voice. But to be apodictic is of course a necessary part of Professor Galbraith's style. I was recently with him in Switzerland attempting, at lunch, to find a common blank in our calendars, in order to schedule a network exchange in New York for which we had contracted. I proposed to him the first week in April, but he replied, studying his engagement book, that that would not do: in the first week in April he would be lecturing at the University of Moscow. "Oh?" I said. "What do you have left to teach them?" So long as Mr. Galbraith continues to teach economics to the Soviet Union, we will have a market for our excess grain. His contribution to the Ever Normal Granary.

For all his tergiversations, Mr. Galbraith has never wavered on one inclination and that is his contempt for American capitalists—I speak, here and below, of the class, not of individuals. I fear that in this matter uniquely he is correct. He chronicles not only the cupidity but also the parasitic habits of so many of them, the predatory character of their belief in the marketplace. I hope to be understood as saying something more interesting than that greed is the root of many evils, a bipartisan conclusion about human nature. Although Adam Smith did not use the word to describe the instinct of industrial man to improve his lot, he was sardonically aware of the factor of inordinate self-interest, and of the sublimated variations one could play on it. "I see," he wrote in his journal, "that the Pennsylvania Quakers have freed their slaves. We may deduce that they were few in number."

Recently, addressing the AFL-CIO in Washington, Solzhenitsyn proclaimed the natural alliance of the American worker and the Russian worker. But, he added, there is "another alliance: the alliance between our Communist leaders and your capitalists." He went on to discuss a recent exhibit in the Soviet Union of U.S. anti-criminal technology that engrossed the Russians, who instantly put in orders for the lot, cash on the barrelhead. The problem being, Solzhenitsyn pointed out, that we were selling our scientific paraphernalia not to the law-abiding for use against criminals, but to criminals for use against the law-abiding: rather like inventing the guillotine for the purpose of slaughtering cattle, and then selling it to Robespierre in full knowledge of the uses to which he intended to put it.

"This is something which is almost incomprehensible to the human mind," Solzhenitsyn said: "that burning greed for profit which goes beyond all reason, all self-control, all conscience—only to get money." Solzhenitsyn cannot be expected to be familiar with the nuances by which a successfully ordered free-market economy finally puts a limit on the uses of greed. We can hardly blame him if he sees, with that laser purity of his moral vision, only the silhouettes: American businessmen, like their great-grandfathers trading in the slave market, anxious to turn a profit by trafficking with the present generation of slavemasters.

But that greed, which outraged such resonant critics of the free market as Veblen and Tawney, is less I think a mutation of capitalism, let alone an organic development of it, than a culturally conditioned indifference to principle, a stubborn moral nescience. I speak of a class of self-conscious men atrophied by two generations of contempt from academicians and moralists, men who react by exhibiting a cultivated ignorance of the quality and direction of political-economic instruction in the colleges to which they send their sons and daughters for impacted indoctrination in the evils of the society they are sustained by. Of a class that permitted Ludwig von Mises and even Hayek to live in an economic insecurity very nearly paralyzing. Of a class that sustains, indeed causes to flourish through gaudy advertising, the popular journals that combine, in resolutely fixed ratio, licentious assaults on the venerable, delicately nurtured restraints on rampant biological appetites, and fundamentalist condemnations of American institutions and ideals. The American capitalist whose image reifies in the mind of the young is not even the smug, canny, willful power broker of Upton Sinclair. He is the inarticulate, self-conscious, bumbling mechanic of the private sector, struck dumb by the least cliché of socialism, fleeing into the protective arms of government at the least hint of commercial difficulty, delighting secretly in the convenient power of the labor union to negotiate for an entire industry, uniformly successful only in his escapist ambition to grow duller and duller as the years go by, eyes left, beseeching popular favor. Poor Miss Rand sought to give him a massive dose of testosterone, to make him the virile and irresistible leader of a triumphant

meritocratic revolt against asphyxiative government; but soon it transpired, even as Russell Kirk predicted, that her novels were being
read not because of their jackbooted individualism, but because of the
fornicating bits.

The entrepreneurial class can change its image only by taking
lusty joy from its achievement. I shall not soon forget the scene, symbolic of the triumph of demagogic terror over productive enterprise:
Senator Henry Jackson, sitting high in his committee chair, addressing the twelve top officials of the oil and gas industry, publicly chas-
tising them on their obscene profits. How bracing it would have been
if, as one man, they had risen to their feet early in the tirade and
walked out, leaving the senator lecturing only to the television cameras which of course he was primarily addressing. Cecil B. De Mille
gave up a million-dollar contract because he refused to pay the sum
of one dollar to a labor union with a closed shop. Cecil B. De Mille is
dead, and all the mighty work of Hayek and Mises and Friedman has
not bred his replacement.

My final proposition is (3) that *The opposition to socialism must remain
primarily negative, and can take strength from being so.*

Professor Hayek, in the passage already quoted about the need for
new liberal programs that appeal to the imagination, goes on. "We
must," he says, "make the building of a free society once more an
intellectual adventure, a deed of courage. What we lack is a liberal
Utopia, a program which seems neither a mere defense of things as
they are nor a diluted kind of socialism, but a truly liberal radicalism
which does not spare the susceptibilities of the mighty."

Mr. Hayek is so very correct in so much of what he says that one
hesitates to cavil, and does so only under the libertine dispensation of
this permissive organization.

Of *course* we need imagination: so does B. B. D. & O. in selling hot
dogs or shampoo.

Certainly we need courage, a quality of Evel Knievel [the dare-
devil motorcyclist who jumped over canyons and such] as of Thomas
More, with however a world's discrimination between their use of it,

though I do not need to be reminded that Knievel has survived, and More did not.

The need for a liberal radicalism is manifest, and no single person living has contributed more than Hayek to an intimation of what such radicalism might bring us by, for instance, a separation of the legislature into two bodies, the one authorized only to pass laws of the kind associated with the rule of law; laws generic, impartial, intelligible; the structural beams around which the folkways of society weave like ivy, susceptible to training, direction, fancy, caprice even.

What we do *not* need is anything that suggests that human freedom is going to lead us to Utopia. For one thing, it isn't going to happen; and therefore any conceits on the matter are quickly seen as ideological vanity.

Mr. Hayek is so cautious a craftsman as to cause even someone intoxicated by his summons to intellectual adventure to wonder whether his call for Utopia might have been caused by the mischievous working of atmospheric pressure on his numinous pen. My knowledge of his work is limited to his nontechnical writings and flawed by my porous memory, but I cannot remember any other call by him to the pursuit of Utopia or even Utopia's poor relation, eudaemonia, though I am buoyant enough to believe that if we were to follow Hayek's prescriptions, we would come, if not to eudaemonia, at least to something not far removed from that happiness which results from the governance of reason.

Hayek quotes, approvingly, Michael Polanyi as saying, "The conceptions by the light of which men will judge our own ideas in a thousand years—or perhaps even in fifty years—are beyond our guess. If a library of the year 3000 came into our hands today, we could not understand its contents. How should we consciously determine a future which is, by its very nature, beyond our comprehension? Such presumption reveals only the narrowness of an outlook uninformed by humility."

Hayek himself says, "It would be an error to believe that, to achieve a higher civilization, we have merely to put into effect the ideas now guiding us. If we are to advance, we must leave room for a continuous revision of our present conceptions and ideals which will be necessitated by further experience." I find it perplexing to combine this high relativism with any notion, however nuanced, of Utopia.

Mr. Hayek gave an example of his intellectual courage when, in his great book on liberty, he girded his loins, made out his will, kissed his wife good-bye, and came out against the progressive income tax. That was audacious and exhilarating; and indeed if ever his counsel on the matter were accepted, I have no doubt whatever that the tuning fork of justice would resonate with the bells of joy in the morning. But we would not have achieved Utopia. We would be left without even a sense of how the liberated taxpayer would spend his repatriated surplus; I know of nothing in libertarian literature that is instructive on the point. There is a great and brooding literature that is instructive, but it is a literature that speaks with a humility that goes far, far beyond the historicistic humility of Michael Polanyi. It reminds us that heaven is not for this but for another world, and that final satisfactions are taken from adventures in faith, hope, and charity unrelated to the marketplace. In that other world, I do not hesitate to predict, Friedrich von Hayek will be garlanded and praised for his contributions to a social philosophy that reflects the dignity of metaphysical man. If I should happen to make it there, I shall gladly join as a minor member of the chorus, confident that that final act of utopianization will bring my voice into total harmony with those of the legions who praise his name.

THE PROTRACTED STRUGGLE AGAINST CANCER

Introductory Remarks (excerpted) at the American Cancer Society Dinner; the Americana Hotel, New York, June 2, 1977

Levities, on a serious subject, at the request of Governor Nelson Rockefeller.

T HANK YOU, Mr. Coleman. Introductions of that nature are always welcome. Although, like cigarettes, they should be served with the notice: Do Not Inhale.

We are here tonight to celebrate the memory of Alfred P. Sloan Jr. and to give two awards in his name. Alfred Sloan was a singular man, combining talents distinctly, if not exclusively, American. He was a producer, a scientist, and a philosopher. He was always attracted by problems that lesser men were prepared to think of as insoluble. In the world of mechanics and production he succeeded triumphantly, and General Motors is his monument. In medical research he took on the most tenacious, the ugliest, at once the most protracted and the most definitive killer of human life. I cannot believe there is anyone in this room who would not prefer to die quickly on a battlefield, even fighting a war that was the result of Democratic ineptitude, rather than die slowly of cancer. Even since the death of Alfred Sloan some ten years ago, the odds have begun, slowly, grudgingly, but exhilaratingly, to change. Because of his work, his determination, his philanthropy, because of the efforts of those fired by the same resolution, progress is made every day. Like the struggle for world peace, this one may prove asymptotic: always there will be cancer, one supposes; but, one hopes, with fewer and fewer victims, as, painfully, with determination, coordinating the generous impulses of society and the skills of our scientists, we grope our way up out of the darkness. The Sloan-Kettering Institute for Cancer Research will, I am confident, one day be hailed as having been responsible for more lives saved than cars were produced by General Motors under the direction of the man who founded the one organization, while heading the other.

I am instructed at this point to introduce to you the guests who are seated on the dais. I am furthermore instructed to instruct you please to contain any impulse to enthusiasm as I read out their names. This is not a political contest, notwithstanding the presence here of Governor Rockefeller. We are anxious both to expedite the evening, and to avoid invidious comparisons between the applause achieved at the mention of the name Alpha and that achieved at the mention of Omega. Furthermore I shall not introduce—the rhetoricians call this *paralepsis*—the wonderful woman sitting, appropriately, at my left, Mrs. Robert Kennedy. The guests of honor you may in due course cheer as wildly as you like. They deserve it.

SEATED NEXT TO Dr. Rauscher is the executive vice president of the American Cancer Society's New York City division, Mr. William F. Ward. Mr. Ward thinks of *everything*. He even managed to deliver to my office this morning the entire script of everything I would say here tonight, which included a physical description of *my own wife*. Never having attempted to script a venture in the administration of cancer research, I have taken the liberty of writing my own lines, while thanking Mr. Ward, as I know all of you would want to thank him, for his exemplary discharge of the extraordinary load he shoulders, for his thoughtfulness, and for his wonderful good humor.

TO QUOTE NOW exactly from the notes that were given me, I would read the sentence, "The *next* lovely lady is my wife, Patricia." The problem with that sentence is that it requires us to think of Mr. Ellmore Patterson as a lovely lady; and whatever else we think about him, it strains the imagination to think of him as that. My wife is a member of the board of directors of the Society of the Sloan-Kettering Memorial Cancer Center. On Mondays, Wednesdays, and Fridays, she advises me that she is certain she has cancer. I tend, even so, to look forward to Mondays, Wednesdays, and Fridays, because they are different from Tuesdays and Thursdays, when she advises me that I am the carcinogenic agent.

But I agree with Mr. Ward, she *is* a lovely lady.

FOR SOME REASON, on seeing that I would be introducing Governor Rockefeller, my mind traveled back twelve years, to an episode when I was running for mayor—an unrequited proposal to the voters of New York City. On that occasion I was informed by a reporter, moments before my scheduled luncheon address to the Overseas Press Club, that at *his* lunch at the other end of Manhattan John Lindsay had just uttered a witticism at my expense. "Buckley is such a bastard," Lindsay had told his audience, "I sometimes wish he *would* be elected mayor of New York."

I replied with a story impossibly labored, yet splendidly rococo, which I had come across years before in the autobiography of G. K. Chesterton. It appears that at Chesterton's preparatory school, St. Peter's, the headmaster maintained the tradition of delivering a eulogy upon any departing member of the school staff. On this occasion the boys were duly assembled to hear him remark the virtues of a mathematics teacher who was leaving to join the staff at St. Paul's. Chesterton and his fellow students, having endured a dozen such tributes at the hands of an orator whose ponderousness was an institutional byword, settled down to daydream or to doodle. Fifteen minutes into his somnolence Chesterton sat up, having been elbowed by his deskmate, and indeed the entire assembly was astir. *The headmaster had uttered a witticism!* He had said triumphantly that the boys had witnessed the very act of "robbing Peter to pay Paul."

That night, Chesterton and his roommate composed an extended fantasy, based on the assumption that the headmaster had devoted the sum of his life's wit to plotting a career that would make possible that afternoon's climax. He had studied to become a teacher; had pursued the headmastership of St. Peter's; had hired a young mathematics instructor, but only after arranging with St. Paul's that he should in due course be hired away: and thus had contrived his destiny and others' to make possible his witticism. Thus had I served John Lindsay in 1965.

I wonder now, wildly, whether Alfred P. Sloan Jr. did not arrange his career so as to found an institute which would cause the American Cancer Society to sponsor a biennial event which one day would lock the former governor of New York State and vice president of the United States in a position from which he could not retreat from a lecture by me on political philosophy. But as my personal sacrifice to the American Cancer Society, I eschew the opportunity to lecture Governor Rockefeller on the virtues of political conservatism and, instead, salute him as a friend and a devoted public servant.

A Salutary Impatience

A Commencement Address at the Ethel Walker School; Simsbury, Conn., June 5, 1977

A talk to a prominent girls' boarding school, with a personal introduction: on my previous visit there, I had crash-landed in my airplane.

I FIRST LAID eyes on the Ethel Walker School in 1940. At age fourteen I was awed by it. The girls struck me as sophisticated, blasé even; the faculty as formidable; the administration as unapproachable.

During those war years Ethel Walker was, by today's standards, a grimly disciplined institution, evoking, even then, another time, another age. I always thought that its most provocative tie with history was in its music teacher, whose name now escapes me. Madame X was grand, portly, talented, patient; at eighty-five she could accompany her star pupils, substituting for an entire orchestra. This woman, I learned, had as a girl studied under Clara Schumann. Mrs. Robert Schumann! When Ludwig van Beethoven died, Robert Schumann was older than I was when I first visited Ethel Walker. Viewed thus, Ethel Walker had as a member of its faculty the student of a contemporary of the later Beethoven, who himself was born six years before the Declaration of Independence.

My last view of your campus, before today's, was ignominious. It was in 1950 that my best friend at Yale became engaged to my sister Patricia, and I thought it seemly to bring him around to introduce him to my beloved younger sister Maureen, the mother of a member of the present graduating class. Accordingly, I wrote to Maureen such a letter as the Great Gatsby might have written while a senior at Yale. I asked her casually to send me a map of the lawn here at the school, so that, on the following Thursday, I might arrive with her prospective brother-in-law in my little airplane. I remember the apprehension with which I approached those tall trees over there, but taking advantage of the innocence of my companion, I successfully feigned great confidence, and managed to drop abruptly over the treetops, landing at seventy miles per hour, and triumphantly looking over at him as we slowed down; at which point we abruptly found ourselves looking deep into a ditch. At the Ethel Walker School they offer no classes in cartography, and Maureen had neglected to include in her sketch a ditch that ran—perhaps it still does—right across the lawn, hidden from airplanes; placed there, I wondered later, to guard against a surprise invasion by the Luftwaffe? Unhappily, our landing was anything but surreptitious. Maureen had, for the scheduled landing, aroused the entire school, which found itself extricating us physically from the wrecked airplane. The headmistress greeted us with that marvelous Ethel Walker savoir faire, as though we had strolled in through the park just in time for croquet and tea, which she obligingly served to us, and to Maureen and her roommates. Maureen, taking her cue from me, maintained a most solemn expression as we discussed such matters as the Marshall Plan, the organization of NATO, the decolonialization of India, and anything else that didn't touch on aviation. This we brought off with some aplomb until an assistant to the headmistress arrived with one-half of our propeller and asked if it was of any further use to us.

I am honored that you should have invited me to appear at Ethel Walker under more dignified circumstances. It is probably the case that, since 1940, I have had here, every year, at least one sister or niece; and so I have continued to be conscious of the Ethel Walker School, and admiring of its traditions.

I am not, however, an expert in them, and will affect no knowledge of their evolution, either in a direction I approve of, or in a direction I disapprove of. I have often been made unhappy as a captive of a visiting speaker, but never more so than by those who lecture me concerning something of which I have a direct knowledge, and they only an indirect knowledge. I feel confident only in saying this about the school which in a matter of minutes you will be able to call your alma mater: there is none better that I know of. All of you, in the years to come, will experience happiness and unhappiness, satisfaction and restlessness, torment and serenity. You will, by the standards of civilization, be better off in virtue of your experience here.

It would be irresponsible of me not to take the opportunity to share with you a fragment or two of my renowned political wisdom. But let me do so sparingly, as my personal contribution to the felicity of the hour.

Even at secondary school, you are introduced to grave doubts about our society, about its premises and its performance. At college, these doubts will be most studiously cultivated; most licentiously cultivated, in some instances. You would need to be dumb to the point of disqualification to study at Ethel Walker to believe that our society is satisfactory, let alone perfect. But you would be ungrateful to the point of dumbness if you failed to recognize the strengths of our society.

Quite matter-of-factly, the scholarly deputy prime minister of South Korea last week reminded a reporter from *Time* magazine that there is not a single developing country in the world governed by Western-style democracy. That statement is much more nearly true than false. The same reporter, in the Philippines, heard from the wife of the dictator of *that* country that the United States cannot expect other countries to follow exactly in our own political traditions: and she is more nearly right than wrong, neglecting only to say that our political traditions are universally to be preferred over those that vest in a single man total power over public law. The strongman who rules Singapore wisely advises us not to apply our own standards in judging other countries; rather, judge them by the direction they are traveling in, in their regard for the individual. Implicit in his statement is the recognition that the United States, along with only a handful of other countries, has institutionalized continence, sufficiently to permit the exercise of political freedom. "I have a great admiration for the American Constitution," the Spanish philosopher Pedro Saenz Rodríguez said from exile in Lisbon a dozen years ago. "But if I wanted the American Constitution to prevail in Spain, I would import not the Constitution, but Americans."

But such traditions as we have that permit self-government and the exercise of other freedoms are challenged every day by natural and other forces. There is, to begin with, attrition. That which we take for granted has a way of atrophying: and one day you look up at it, and it is moribund—like the tradition against obscene language in mixed company. Then there is the organized hostility of forces external and internal. The former covet, for reasons ideological and material, the great capital deposits of a free society, and organize whole armies and navies and air forces with the primary purpose of acquiring control over them. Internally, there are always those who—whether out of despair over present imperfections, or impatience with the notion that man should be free rather than follow the instructions of the leader-ideologue—seek to erode these traditions. Ten years ago these forces were in effective control of not a few of our colleges and universities, reminding us that where there is a repository of learning, there is not necessarily a repository of wisdom.

Dissatisfaction, in many of its forms, is an engine of social and personal advancement. Those who were dissatisfied with the institution of slavery eventually overcame it. Those who were dissatisfied with drudgery devised machines that eased the physical overhead of life. Those dissatisfied with the arbitrary ravages of pestilence continue to develop medicine. It is remarked that impatience is the vice of the intellectual, and it is rightly suggested that impatience can be taken to hubristic lengths leading to ideology; but, on the other hand, impatience can be the lubricant of progress.

The formula, surely, is a certain impatience, side by side with standards, seasoned with an informed understanding of the rhythms of progress. The evangelist who will not be satisfied except to end poverty and discrimination on a five-year plan will not be satisfied; and is unlikely to mitigate poverty or discrimination. It is neither fatalism nor moral sloth to moderate the rhetoric of idealism: it is a statement about the morphology of man. Man is a creature not—as their rhetoric would sometimes lead us to believe—of the Democratic Party, but of a divine plan, whose mysteries we will never fully understand, but which vouchsafes us some moments of pleasure and of tranquil gratitude; such moments as, on this day, in this place, reflecting on your achievements, on the beneficences of your parents and friends, on the labors of your faculty, you are entitled to experience. I am happy to share the moment with you.

Cold Water on the Spirit of Liberty

A Commencement Address at Notre Dame University; South Bend, Ind., May 21, 1978

The previous year's commencement speaker, President Carter, had inveighed against what he termed an "inordinate fear of Communism." In doing so, in the view of conservative analysts, he was ignoring the critical challenges of the Communist powers, most pointedly, at that moment, in Cambodia and, as ever, in China.

As a commencement address, mine was not successful: it is unwise to introduce melancholy at occasions organically exuberant. I even had a protest or two from parents of graduating seniors. But the message was a rallying cry, and was read by the politician who would be Mr. Carter's successor.

TODAY IS A happy event, a witness to your achievement. You began your learning a long while ago. You will continue to learn after you have left Notre Dame. Before today you became aware of the keennesses of the human experience. After today your perceptions will continue to sharpen, and, even while enjoying bread, wine, love, poetry, the air we breathe, and the seasons' changes, gradually you will begin to understand why it is that so many men grow weary. "History hit us with a freight train," Whittaker Chambers wrote me, one month before he died. "We," he continued, "—my general breed—tried to put ourselves together again. But at a price—weariness."

Why inflict that weariness on you? As a gentle, not to say penitential, demurral from the words uttered from this lectern one year ago, when the speaker said to your graduating predecessors, as if the great struggle had been won, that "we have found our way back to our own principles and values, and we have regained our lost confidence." Where is the evidence? Earlier in his address the speaker had said that, "being confident of our own future, we are now free of that inordinate fear of Communism which led us to embrace any dictator who joined us in our fear." If we are so confident of our own future, why does he tell us [in this week's press conference] that life and death await the results of our SALT negotiations? The president went on to say that "for too many years we have been willing to adopt the flawed principles and tactics of our adversaries, sometimes abandoning our values for theirs. We fought fire with fire, never thinking that fire is better fought with water. This approach failed, with Vietnam the best example of its intellectual and moral poverty."

Herewith a few observations:

(1) In August of 1973 Lord Home, opening the great conference on European security at Helsinki, spoke these words to the assembly: "If your conference is essentially about people and about trust, then it is essential that we should do something to remove the barriers which inhibit the movement of people, the exchange of information and ideas." Elaborating on these sentiments one month later before the General Assembly of the United Nations, Lord Home said: "I trust that the Communist countries will be able to prove that they are for the basic freedom of people everywhere."

Two years later the Helsinki Accords were promulgated.

Last week Yuri Orlov, a Soviet citizen who had undertaken to monitor Soviet compliance with those accords—which the Soviet government had initiated and then signed—was sentenced to seven years of hard labor, to be followed by five years of exile in Siberia. He was not allowed independent counsel, was not permitted to question his accusers, was held incommunicado for the thirteen months preceding his conviction. He was tried in a courtroom in which the words of Lord Home were mocked, and from which the press, charged with expediting the "exchange of information" of which Lord Home had sung at Helsinki, was matter-of-factly excluded. To be sure, the family were present. On Thursday, leaving the courtroom, the wife of Yuri Orlov was stripped naked by three female Soviet officials in the presence of three male Soviet officials, and searched. Perhaps she was suspected of carrying the text of the Helsinki Accords in her underpants. May we suppose that Yuri Orlov's fear of Communism has not proved to be inordinate?

(2) A week ago Saturday, the *New York Times* published an extensive dispatch collating information, gathered from numerous observers, on doings in Cambodia. In Cambodia in recent months there have been aggravated shortages. Of the usual things—food, fuel, shelter, medicine—to be sure. But most pressing, it appears, has been the shortage of ammunition with which to kill Cambodian civilians. Accordingly, on orders of the government headed by Pol Pot, the Cambodian militia has shown great economic ingenuity. Tens of thousands of men and women suspected of having been related in some way—perhaps they had gone to school together, or grown up in the same hamlet—to men who had resisted the Khmer Rouge have been clubbed to death while standing, arms tied behind their backs, in ditches they had thoughtfully dug to receive their imminent remains. The young children of these men and women, we are informed, are bounced about playfully on the bayonets of the soldiers until they are dead, or almost dead, upon which they are tossed into the common ditches. Pol Pot does not devote the whole of his time to overseeing this enterprise in population control. He is otherwise engaged—for instance, as guest of honor recently in Peking at a banquet tendered by the rulers of the People's Republic of China, who,

now that we have got over our inordinate fear of Communism and our corollary addiction to dictators, we are finally ready to embrace. Who, contemplating the Cambodian hell alongside official optimism, can get by without feeling the cold wind of weariness?

(3) In the period since the class of 1977 was informed that we are now "confident of our own future"—so that we were enabled to eschew the use of fire against fire, our ideals restored by the pledge to use only water—we have diluted the Voice of America. It no longer fires the libertarian spirits of the Yuri Orlovs, dousing them instead, in the spirit of détente, with cold, cold water. We have watered the little Cuban garden in Africa [the military presence in Angola], and now its blooms decorate much of the continent. In Europe, by way of expressing our confidence, we have risen above the vulgar attractions of enhanced radiation technology [through President Carter's veto of the neutron bomb]. And we have given concrete form to our contempt for anti-Communist dictators by embracing the democratic leaders of Poland, Rumania, and Yugoslavia, and hailing our purposes in common.

In the groves of quiet thought we tell ourselves—quietly—that we care about all this. Care about poor Orlov, about the new holocaust in Cambodia, about the creeping hegemony of Communist thought and techniques in both hemispheres. But ours is a fugitive solicitude, damped by the prevailing rhetoric, which is one part evangelistic, one part pharisaic, one part anaesthetic. Our foreign policy is bad enough. The rhetoric of our foreign policy is, if not the efficient cause of, then the sufficient reason for the three-martini lunch [whose tax exemption was rescinded by President Carter].

LADIES AND GENTLEMEN, I can give you on this feast day—like Our Lady's juggler—only that little I have to offer. It is, at this juncture in history, the settled view that we have traveled further—much further—than ever we intended to go when we began our retreat from the Wilsonian ideal. Two hundred years ago we proclaimed the universality of those truths we hold about the nature of man. One hundred fifty years ago President John Quincy Adams cooled a burgeoning national idealism with the astringent observation that though the American people are friends of liberty everywhere, they are custodians only of their own. The most explicit modern expression of Wilsonianism was quite recently uttered—during your infancy—by John F. Kennedy, at his inauguration, when he cried out to the world that we Americans will "pay any price, bear any burden, meet any hardship, support any friend, oppose any foe to assure the survival and the success of liberty."

This was an objective commitment by a chief executive. Surely he acknowledged the awful weight of that commitment?

On the contrary. "In the long history of the world," he continued, "only a few generations have been granted the role of defending freedom in its hour of maximum danger. I do not shrink from this responsibility—I welcome it." Well then, instead of going forward burdened down by a great weight, our mission transports us. Will our idealism prove contagious? There was no hesitation on the morning of January 20, 1961: "The energy, the faith, the devotion which we bring to this endeavor will light our country and all who serve it—and the glow from that fire can truly light the world."

Looking back, it is as if the glow from that fire had been routinely blacked out by the Department of Energy. Granted, it is everywhere agreed nowadays that our Marines cannot be made available to axe down anti-democratic growths in the halls of Montezuma. But neither are our short-wave facilities available to transmit the record of noncompliance with the Helsinki Accords. In our retreat, there were those who thought to modify our idealism by suggesting practical alternatives. Senator J. William Fulbright, during the most despondent period of the Vietnam War, articulated a useful distinction when he said that the American government has no proper quarrel with any country in the world, no matter how obnoxious its doctrines, so long as that country does not seek to export them. Under the Fulbright mandate, we are charged to contain Cuba, while ignoring Haiti. Contain Cuba where?

Our immobility, our incoherence, is more merely than the consequence of strategic indecisiveness and rhetorical confusion. What happened, during the Johnson-Nixon years, was a great seizure of self-disgust which fused handily with the newfound exigencies of our foreign policy. Even as a generation earlier we had looked tolerantly on "Uncle Joe," the grand engineer of Gulag for whom President Truman publicly professed a certain fondness, this time we discovered, far more profoundly, the great society of Mao Tse-tung, concerning whose material achievements there may be differences of opinion, but concerning one achievement, none at all. Under Mao the Chinese achieved the total suppression of every liberty catalogued in our own Bill of Rights: none to practice one's religion, to speak out, to read, to educate oneself, to travel, to own land or a home, to be tried by due process. But our wise men traveled there, poets, priests, and piccolo players, returning with expressions of undiluted praise: Richard Nixon, John Kenneth Galbraith, Seymour Topping, Harrison Salisbury, Barbara Tuchman, Shirley MacLaine. My favorite of the lot is James Reston, who perfectly expressed the veneration of the new by means of the rejection of the old. He wrote, "I am a Scotch Calvinist. I believe in the redemption of the human spirit and the improvement of man. Maybe it's because I believe that, or I want to believe it, that I was struck by the tremendous effort [in the China of Mao Tse-tung] to bring out what is best in men, what makes them good, what makes them cooperate with one another and be considerate and not beastly to one another." Those words were written in 1971, even before the Cultural Revolution could be said to have ended.

So that our retreat has been not only from the practical evangelism of Wilson, but also from a metaphorical commitment to Wilsonianism, as witness the reluctance of President Carter to speak about human rights where they are most systematically suppressed—in China. Slowly, disillusionment comes, and for those who have charged so often up the mountain only to come down again, weariness is experienced. The fire that John Kennedy shouted out would illuminate the whole world flickers here at home. Not only shall we withdraw our troops from Southeast Asia, we shall look the other way as the societies we abandon get down to the business of transforming men according to the vision of James Reston and the Bishop of

Cuernavaca, who proposed the canonization of Chou En-lai. On odd days, the State Department or the White House will issue demurrals, often self-described as "strong protests." But mostly our talk is an endless extension of the homily with which Lord Home launched the Helsinki conference.

This, I think, is the demon that made Whittaker Chambers weary, this dialectic helplessness: you see what ought to be done, you shrink from the exertions required to do it, and you compensate by elevating your rhetoric, whose inevitable hollowness subverts the very ideals that animated you. This experience, Sisyphean in our time, brought Chambers to predict that weariness would almost certainly strike out at his more sensitive countrymen.

But in your case, not yet; not nearly yet. It isn't only that you are young, and properly hopeful. Your education has been touched by those intimations of purpose, divine and irreversible, that make hope natural and despair sinful. "And I heard a great voice from the throne saying, 'Behold, the dwelling of God is with men, and He will dwell with them, and they shall be His people, and God Himself will be with them; He will wipe away every tear from their eyes . . .'" Whatever the reasons for objective concern, the imperative continues.

In the final paragraph of the final letter I received from Whittaker Chambers—after he confessed his weariness, from which, before the month was out, he would be reprieved by his death—was a sharp reproach, which I pass along to those of you who flirt with melancholy. "Something quite different which struck me," he wrote "—what seems to have been your desolation by [Malraux's novel] *Man's Fate*. But Hemmelrich goes back (supreme tenderness) to close the door left too hastily open on the bodies of his murdered wife and son. Tchen, about to throw himself and [the] bomb under the automobile, believes that Pei (spared to life because Tchen acts alone) will be able to write more meaningfully by reason of Tchen's act. Kyo takes the cyanide with the sense that the concept of man's dignity enjoins control over his own death. Katow, surrendering even that ultimate, divides his cyanide with those less able to bear man's fate; and walks towards the locomotive [into whose furnace he will, by his execution-ers, be dropped alive] through a hall of bodies from which comes something like an unutterable sob—the strangled cry. It may also be phrased: 'And the morning stars sang together for joy.' It may also be phrased: '*Il faut supposer Katow heureux*' [as Camus had written, "Il faut supposer Sisyphe heureux"]. For each age," Chambers concluded, "finds its own language for an eternal meaning."

You will contribute to the formulation of your own idiom for our times. Make room in it—for the love of God—for the love of God; for the love of our fragile and embattled and wonderful country; and for the love of this university, which has cared so deeply for you.

THE RECKLESS GENEROSITY
OF JOHN CHAMBERLAIN

Remarks at a Testimonial Dinner; the Metropolitan Club, New York, November 9, 1978

A testimonial to a writer, editor, and critic so singularly beloved by all who had ever worked with him or for him as to elicit warm, near torrid, tributes from across the political spectrum, from Clare Boothe Luce to John Kenneth Galbraith.

IT IS SATISFYING beyond any expectations to which I ever thought myself entitled to close a program of tributes to John Chamberlain, whose reckless generosity changed the course of my life if not, alas, the course of American history or even the history of Yale University. I noticed even as a twenty-three-year-old at Yale that John had an extraordinary facility for making you feel that every service performed by him for you was really a kindness initiated by you. I think he thanked me, even, for the privilege of writing an introduction to a book that got him very nearly ostracized in an academic community that preached the virtues of an open mind, on the tacit understanding that it should remain closed.

Not only has John expressed, in his own inarticulate way, his appreciation to me for all the favors he has done me over the years, he has expressed his affection for every institution in the United States that has ignored, disparaged, or underrated him. When he told me, after writing the introduction to my book, that the *Yale Review*— to which he had contributed over the course of a generation, beginning back when William Lyon Phelps said about the young John Chamberlain, daily book reviewer for the *New York Times*, that he was the outstanding literary critic of his generation—when he told me that the *Yale Review* had from that moment on declined to commission any further essays or criticism from him, his smile, his almost noiseless chuckle, was more nearly a gesture of appreciation than of remonstrance. What was he appreciating? If it had been an artist of another temperament—an Alexander Pope, let us say—he'd have been celebrating the validation of one of his misanthropic theses, namely that the intolerance of the reigning intellectual order required at the very least that men in responsible editorial positions greet dissent with what John called the Averted Gaze. What John was appreciating, however, was the ironies that, insofar as they illuminated men's little vanities, made a man just that much more endearing.

Of course, there were exceptions. In a much abused line, E. M. Forster is quoted as saying that if the choice is to betray one's country or one's friends, one must not hesitate to betray one's country. Much abused, I say, because it is not easy, in modern circumstances, to betray one's country without betraying one's friends along with it. Of John's friends, the most conspicuous of those from Yale is Thomas Bergin, his classmate, a man with as piercing an intellect as John's but whose total mastery of the language and poetry and politics of the fourteenth century unhappily left him with no political intelligence to apply to the problems of present-day America. Tom Bergin is, perhaps by not so extraordinary a coincidence, not unlike John in the gentleness of his nature, though he cultivates a brusqueness that intimidated several generations of students. He always knew that whatever direction John was taking, he was guided by a rigorous intellect, at the service of surely the most generous heart anyone in this room has ever known.

We aren't here to pleasure the muses most of us serve, or to conduct a Festschrift detailing the contributions John Chamberlain has made to right thinking. Once upon a time John Chamberlain was a socialist. I have a feeling that if he had remained one, I'd be here as willingly tonight as I otherwise am, the difference being merely that in the one circumstance I could celebrate only the man, whereas in the second I can rejoice also at his contributions to our understanding of the problems our beloved country is beset by. It is appropriate, under the circumstances, to contemplate gratefully the tribute from John Kenneth Galbraith, who has done more to disrupt the free society than anyone else this side of Pol Pot, but who, when invited to pay tribute to John Chamberlain, wrote so gracefully, acknowledging in effect that there is still an unrestricted free market among men seeking out their own company, and that in that free market Ken Galbraith moves towards John Chamberlain: attesting to his "personal character," his "general goodness," his "literary competence"; to whom he sends, quite simply, his "love."

Clare Boothe Luce writes me, "Tell John I too had my seventy-fifth birthday this year and that age has its compensations, such as— oh damn, I forget for the moment what they are. But I wish I could be with you to hear the wonderful true things you will all say about John. Please add to the birthday toasts a toast from me to what I have loved best about him for forty years: his wise, rare boyish smile, so sweet with certainties."

There is little to add—except this, a little detail, that I have never before mentioned. It was in the early years of *National Review*, and there had been a division among the editors, one of them announcing his intention of withdrawing from the common enterprise. A meeting was set up, and John came to it, as one of the founding fathers, and as the oldest friend of all the relevant parties. His mere presence in the room prevented acrimony from dominating the scene, but soon it was apparent that the differences excluded a continuing collegiality. Two hours later I found myself at Grand Central station, en route to Stamford, and ran into John, en route to New Haven. He brought up the subject; and then, ever so briefly, he wept: because this pain, between friends, he could not disguise. The stoic gaiety with which he could greet world wars and *New York Times* editorials deserted him.

It was only a little while later that I received a letter from Whittaker Chambers, who once said of John Chamberlain that he was the nearest thing to unalloyed goodness that Chambers had ever known—a letter in which Chambers wrote that reading a particular passage by Arthur Koestler had brought him to tears. "American men," he commented, "who weep in droves in movie houses, over the woes of lovestruck shopgirls, hold that weeping in men is unmanly. I have found most men in whom there was depth of experience, or capacity for compassion, singularly apt to tears. How can it be otherwise? One looks and sees: and it would be a kind of impotence to be incapable of, or to grudge, the comment of tears, even while you struggle against it. I am immune," he closed, "to soap opera. But I cannot listen for any length of time to the speaking voice of Kirsten Flagstad, for example, without being done in by that magnificence of tone that seems to speak from the center of sorrow, even from the center of the earth." That apparently mundane episode, the rupture of a relationship, had evoked tears, and I knew then, and have known ever since, that what draws us to John Chamberlain is: the magnificence of his tone, that speaks to us from the center of feeling.

A PARTY FOR HENRY KISSINGER

Remarks on a Fifty-Sixth Birthday; New York, May 26, 1979

A gathering of forty friends at dinner at the apartment of the former secretary of state, on the eve of the publication of his first book of memoirs, White House Years. *The not entirely jocular reference to Solzhenitsyn bounced off Dr. Kissinger's advice to President Ford not to meet with him in Washington at a delicate moment in Soviet-U.S. relations.*

A COUPLE OF years ago, participating in a roast at my expense, Henry Kissinger took the occasion to say that we had three things in common. Both of us, he explained, have Irish wives; both of us have difficulty in committing sentences that are less than a paragraph long; and both of us speak in foreign accents. Before the evening was concluded, I had a chance to retaliate. It happened that the incoming chairman of the Young Americans for Freedom, who sponsored the event, was a young man surnamed Buckley. One speaker had argued that there were too many people named Buckley in the conservative movement and suggested that I change my own name to William F. Solzhenitsyn. I said I would be happy to do so, but how thereafter would I get through on the telephone to Henry Kissinger?

Henry should have added the point in common that both of us have imperious wives. Nancy, inviting me to this joyful celebration, ordained that I should—I quote her words exactly—"say something nice about Henry." Obviously she believes I am unprincipled. But I note that she took the precaution of prescheduling comments by one of the wittiest and most elegant representatives of the English-speaking world [Peter Glenville], who has done justice to Henry. Unlike the client who, when advised by his lawyer that the court had done justice, ordered the lawyer to appeal immediately, I have heard nothing to which I would take exception: Henry is a figure who poses credibly, and not unwillingly, for apotheosis.

Interestingly enough, I owe my twenty-five-year-old friendship with our guest of honor to Senator Joseph McCarthy. It was in 1954 that I received a letter, followed by a visit, from the editor of a distinguished academic quarterly who said he was searching for a literate explanation of the rationale of McCarthyism. I wrote the article, which he never published; from which, I am certain, Arthur Schlesinger will rejoice to conclude yet again that no literate explanation of McCarthyism is construable, no matter how profound the resources of the sophist. I observed Henry in action on two or three occasions when I participated in his famous Harvard summer seminars, Henry having sensed an obligation to his foreign students to exhibit to them the most exotic specimens in the American political zoo.

What happened during those years is something I make bold to say—notwithstanding the shock value of the word, used in such urbane company—what developed was: a friendship.

There is no other way to put it, and no other way that I would choose to put it. One reads about our guest of honor all the time, in all the journals; words written by admirers, and by critics. On and on they go. They analyze this statement of his, that nuance; they praise or blame him for this policy or that; they assign to him responsibility for this crisis or that démarche. It is comforting to believe that history will sort it all out. Henry's forthcoming book will, of course, not begin to end the historical controversies, though, mark my words, that book will itself prove to be a historical event.

What I have come to know over the years is one truth no one can challenge: the petrology of our association. I say about Henry simply this: He is my friend. Our friendship is entirely unaffected by any disagreements we have; unaffected by what I write about his policies, his opinions, his techniques, what he does to the world I live in: with all of which I am frequently in agreement—which does not matter to me nor, I expect, to him. He is, as Peter has said—as all of us know—an extraordinary public figure, and I hardly dissociate myself from that chorus which gathers to praise famous men.

I say that, but when I look at him, I am not seeing Caesar, or Metternich, or the greatest secretary of state in American history. A sister of mine, keeping our father company in his last sickness, took an afternoon job with the local radio station in the little town in South Carolina where we lived, writing advertising copy for local enterprises that bought radio time. One day she was approached by an elderly black gentleman of great dignity who presided over a funeral parlor, whose services he wished to advertise. My sister asked him what exactly he would like her to say, and he replied, "It doesn't matter, Miss Buckley. Just so it's serene." In the turbulent career of a man of many parts, in the most turbulent and possibly apocalyptic stage in history, one clings to such a serenity as I—and you, I know—have found in the friendship of Henry Kissinger.

WHAT AMERICANISM SEEKS TO BE

Remarks (excerpted) on Accepting an Americanism Award at the Young
Republicans' National Convention; the Hyatt House, Orlando, Fla., June 23, 1979

---

*A useful format, in accepting an award given by members of the same
fraternity: light material up front, and a high-octane paragraph or two
in closing.*

T HE PLEASURE OF your company is very great. I spent a part
of this afternoon on television with Rick Abell, Lynn Ward,
and David Barron, discussing the achievements of this convention. Reflecting, after we were through, on what they had said, I
was reminded of the answer President Eisenhower, in the last month
of his term, gave to the reporter who asked him what had been the
achievements of his vice president, Mr. Nixon. "If you give me a
week, I'll think of them," Ike said thoughtfully.

Ike didn't mean to be sarcastic; he simply slipped on a banana
peel, like Carter at Vienna. John L. Lewis, the crusty labor leader, was
something else again. At the 1938 annual convention of the CIO,
which he had founded and headed, the various subdivisions of the
union repaired to distant hotel suites to consider their special interests. After nine hours, Lewis dispatched a communiqué to the Ethical
Practices Committee, which read, "Have you discovered any ethical
practices yet?"

John L. Lewis was being ironic; and so, of course, was I. Your
achievements will, I trust, be measured concretely eighteen months
from now. . . .

Believe me, even if I know nothing about politics as an instrument
of self-service, I am happier than any of you can suspect to receive an
Americanism Award, and therein lies a tale.

Years ago, I edited a book on the House Committee on Un-
American Activities. That book, called *The Committee and Its Critics*,
received mostly withering reviews, most memorably from Professor
Henry Steele Commager, who summed up his grievances in the *New*

York Times: "How—after all—can anyone say what Americanism is?" I was quite despondent for a while until I had a telephone call from Professor Sidney Hook. He said to me, "Why don't you write a letter to the *New York Times* and ask how is it that, if Henry Steele Commager tells you that no one can say what Americanism is, Henry Steele Commager wrote a book which he called *The American Dream?*"

I thought that particularly witty, especially coming from an old socialist like Sidney Hook; and I have never forgotten the point he made with such oblique acuity. Two weeks ago I was on a television panel with Father Robert Drinan, congressman from Massachusetts, along with Lou Harris, Elliott Richardson, and Herman Kahn, the chairman of which panel was a prominent member of the American Civil Liberties Union. Father Drinan described his tactics upon entering Congress. "I applied," he said, "for a seat in the House Committee on Un-American Activities, because I intended, once I got in, to move for the abolition of the committee. And"—he winked benignly at his audience—"I succeeded."

The chairman asked if I had any questions. "Yes," I said. "I'd like to ask Father Drinan whether he also succeeded in abolishing un-American activities?"

His reply, in a spirit of charity, I shall treat as confessionally privileged.

So you see, in doing me this great honor, you give me the opportunity to identify myself once again, athwart that most corrosive cynicism, with the position that our country and its ideals survive in a sense which is both definable and normative. I.e., it is intellectually possible to say, with historical authority, that this ideal and that ideal are American; and to say that, whatever the circumstantial problems of maintaining those ideals, they are, and will continue to be, normative. George Bush [the guest of honor at the convention], who combines a sense of realism with a sense of the meaning of America, spent much time in the bowels of the most finished totalitarian society in the world, the People's Republic of China. About China, Edward Luttwak once wrote that you can make this distinction, when contrasting it with the Soviet Union. In the Soviet Union there is an infinitely long list of that which one is forbidden to do. In China, it works the other way. One may do *nothing*—except those things which one is explicitly permitted to do. The list, in other words, begins exactly the other way around.

The Constitution of the United States, and in particular the Bill of Rights, is essentially a list of prohibitions: but it is a list of things that the *government* cannot do to the *people*. What a huge distinction: a majestic distinction. It grew out of a long, empirical journey, the eternal spark of which, of course, traces to Bethlehem, to that star that magnified man beyond any power of the emperors and gold seekers and legions of soldiers and slaves: a star that implanted in each one of us that essence that separates us from the beasts, and tells us that we were made in the image of God and were meant to be free. America cannot presume to offer itself up, in a frenzy of moral vanity, as the secular reflection of the Incarnation. But Americans can say, as Lincoln did, that our country was founded on a proposition: that government of the people, by the people, and for the people is of the nature of Americanism. That our ideals are proudly ours. If I have contributed to the maintenance of those ideals, then I am happy and proud that you should say so. If I haven't, then accept my word that any failure of mine is a failure of will and intelligence, and no reflection on the ideals of America or on your charity in thinking of me in the same august breath.

THE EIGHTIES

His Rhythms Were Not Of This World

Remarks at the Memorial Service for Allard Lowenstein; Central Synagogue, New York, March 18, 1980

The circumstances were tragic. Allard Lowenstein, the brilliant young liberal activist, a former teacher, journalist, and congressman, was killed by a deranged former student. Three days later at a crowded memorial service in New York City, the speakers expressed their grief. Senators Kennedy and Moynihan were among the mourners. Jackie Kennedy was there with her son and daughter. I was the conservative dissenter, a friend for fifteen years. The next day, the New York Times *gave the service front-page treatment.*

POSSIBLY MY OWN experience with him was unique, in that we conservatives did not generally endorse his political prescriptions. So that we were, presumptively, opponents of Al Lowenstein, in those chambers in which we spend, and misspend, so much of our lives. It was his genius that so many of those he touched—typically arriving a half hour late—discovered intuitively the underlying communion. He was in our time *the* original activist, such was his impatience with the sluggishness of justice. His habits were appropriately disarrayed. He was late to breakfast, to his appointments; late in announcing his sequential availability for public service. He was punctual only in registering (though often under age) for any army that conceived itself bound to righteousness.

How did he live such a life, so hectic with public concern, while preoccupying himself so fully with individual human beings? Their torments, never mind their singularity, he adopted as his own, with the passion that some give only to the universal. Eleanor Roosevelt, James Burnham once mused, looked on all the world as her personal slum project. Although Allard Lowenstein was at home with collectivist formulations, one had the impression that he might be late in aborting a third world war because of his absorption with the problems of one sophomore. Oh, they followed him everywhere; because they experienced in him, as we all did, the essence of an entirely personal dedication. Of all the partisans I have known, from the furthest steppes of the spectrum, his was the most undistracted concern, not for humanity—though he was conversant with big-think idiom—but for human beings.

Those of us who dealt with him, often in those narrow passages constrained by time clocks and fire laws and deadlines, think back ruefully on the happy blend of purpose and carelessness with which he arranged his career. A poet might be tempted to say, "If only the Lord had granted us that Allard should have arrived late at his own assassination!"

But all his life he was felled by mysteries, dominant among them that his rhythms were not of this world. His days, foreshortened, lived out the secular dissonances. "Behold, Thou hast made my days as it were a span long: and mine age is even as nothing in respect of Thee; and verily every man living is altogether vanity." The psalmist spoke of Al, on Friday last: "I became dumb, and opened not my mouth; for it was Thy doing." To those not yet dumb, the psalmist also spoke, saying, "The Lord is close to the brokenhearted; and those who are crushed in spirit, He saves." Who was it who said that Nature abhors a vacuum? Let Nature then fill this vacuum. That is the challenge which, bereft, the friends of Allard Lowenstein hurl up to Nature and to Nature's God, prayerfully, demandingly, because today, Lord, our loneliness is great.

THE RUDOLPH VALENTINO
OF THE MARKETPLACE

Remarks at a Heritage Foundation Gala Dinner; the Sheraton Washington
Hotel, Washington, D.C., May 14, 1980

A conservative jamboree, celebrating a large gift to the Heritage Foundation from Shelby Cullom Davis, former ambassador to Switzerland. The speakers' hour was shared with Professor Milton Friedman. Lincoln was invoked, as also God.

I T IS A pleasure to be recognized by Ambassador Davis, but having said as much I should reveal to you that he is capable of recognizing anybody. The first time I met him was at the ambassadorial residence in Berne, where he gave a testimonial dinner for Sir Arnold Lunn, the philosopher, historian, mountaineer, evangelist, and wit. There were twenty-four guests there, all of them (myself, Lunn, and two others excluded) ambassadors. They came from India, South Korea, Nepal, Ceylon, Australia, Uruguay, Chile, Pakistan, Japan, Great Britain, Ireland, the Seychelles, Jamaica, and New York. In the single greatest display of diplomatic virtuosity I have ever seen, Ambassador Davis, without a note in his hand, went around the table mentioning each figure, perfectly rendering the unpronounceable names and recalling something from each one's past that related in some way to the interests of Arnold Lunn. Ambassador Davis, as you know, received a doctoral degree from the University of Geneva, where he majored in glossolalia.

It is always a pleasure to run into Milton Friedman. As a general rule, we meet only to ski together at Alta, where he gives me transfusions of libertarianism; and on the best-seller list, where he likes to flaunt his rank, and obviously has achieved tenure.

However, I was recently present in a quasi-official capacity to introduce Milton Friedman at a party in Erie, Pennsylvania, to celebrate the conclusion of his important television series, *Free to Choose*. To introduce Milton Friedman in the five minutes I was given was a venture in reductionism even I haven't accumulated the effrontery to attempt. "Anything," Professor Ernest van den Haag once wrote in *National Review*, "can be said economically, but the question is: How much is lost? For instance, how much was lost when Immanuel Kant described marriage as the 'mutual monopolization of the genitalia'?"

Have you noticed that certain ideals, which for so long survived only in the catacombs, are right up there? In Milton's case, as remarked, *leading* the nonfiction best-seller list? I mean, just to take the free market from fiction to nonfiction was itself something of an accomplishment. The press is grudgingly required to recognize Milton's new career as the Rudolph Valentino of the Marketplace.

Permit me to venture the thought that providence smiles on Milton's enterprise, and on the Heritage Foundation. It strains the memory to recall when last American businesses conspired together to support an enterprise that supported American business. There are men coming out of the woodwork of corporate America today who could play parts in *Atlas Shrugged*. Especially tonight we are all indebted to the Samuel Roberts Noble Foundation; to Joe Coors and the Adolph Coors Company; and to Bill Simon—always, to Bill Simon.

As for Milton, I have entertained the thought that the only truly relevant challenge for modern technology would be to develop a currency which literally shrinks in proportion with inflation. Every bill in our wallet, at the end of this year, would be 85 percent the size of the bill at the beginning of the year. And then, at the center of every bill, there would be a very small portrait of: Milton Friedman. And suddenly we would recognize, with that graphic force that only visual recognition gives us, that what is left of economic sanity centers on: Milton Friedman. And that if his ideas go, so too will go the very last hope we have for the survival of a whole lot of things of which our currency is only the symbol.

When I was through at Erie and Milton came to the microphone, I embraced him. He winced. "What," I said to him, "does the King of Sweden have that I don't have?"

Really, there are few situations when laughter is out of place, though those few, as Hilaire Belloc reminded us, are august. Impiety is no laughing matter in the slaughterhouses of the body and spirit which are the single abundance in the modern ideological state. The Heritage Foundation is felicitously named. It is, after all, a part of our heritage to grow up admonished to count our blessings. This we have tended to do, if at all, without giving these blessings much thought, even as some of us find ourselves saying our prayers with insufficient thought to their meaning.

It simply does not occur to most Americans that it is an absolutely dazzling historical datum that all of you in this room tonight came here because—you elected to come. You elected to come without giving any thought whatever to political implications. You consulted exclusively your own discretion in making that decision. And anyone here is free to rise and leave the room. Who on earth would stop you? When, at the ballet in Peking, I decided to exercise my freedom to choose not to see the concluding act—a freedom President Nixon didn't have, since he was seated between Chou En-lai and Madame Mao Tse-tung, who nowadays constitutes 25 percent of the Gang of Four—when I rose during the intermission and headed out towards the street, I was stopped: told that I was not free to leave. I was permitted to go only after Higher Authority, as they call it in China, was summoned, and I explained that I was sick to my stomach. That of course was not literally the case, although no more apt metaphor for my frame of mind could have been selected. In his memoirs, Henry Kissinger talks of that ballet as "the most stupefyingly boring three hours I have ever spent. I forget the end of the plot, but I think the girl fell in love with the tractor and lived happily ever after."

Just pause to consider the situation. I was not to be permitted to leave the ballet, go out into the street, and return to my hotel. Last week I spent too long in the lounge at Carnegie Hall, coming back into the chamber just as Sir Georg Solti raised his baton. The usher stopped me: I was required to stand in the back of the hall throughout Mussorgsky's *Pictures at an Exhibition*. I find myself pondering the symbols. In China, the instinct was to require you to remain in the collective unit. In America, the instinct was to protect the collectivity from your intrusion—to grant it what it came to hear, the Chicago Symphony uninterrupted by the distractions of latecomers.

One afternoon in the 1930s, G. K. Chesterton found himself, to his astonishment and irritation, absentmindedly without reading material on a train ride. And so he elected to empty his pockets and to reflect on what he found there. The experience gave birth to a memorable essay decocting from those simple articles his whole style of life, his habits, the society he lived in; indeed, Western civilization. So can we reconstruct what is our heritage by looking freshly at such simple phenomena, inexplicable to most of the wretched of this world, as the little freedoms to choose: to stay in this hall, or leave it. To return to our abode instantly, or slowly. To go to sleep right away, or to read first. Read what? Read whatever we wish to read. To eat or drink before sleeping. Eat or drink what? Eat or drink what we wish, subject only to the licenses of nature.

During the war it became a cliché that you do not find atheists in foxholes. There are, of course, exceptions. I think Sidney Hook would rather die in a foxhole than be wafted to heavenly rest by St. Christopher. And there are no doubt Americans who yearn to be governed, who take satisfaction from depersonalization, but most of them fancy the totalitarian life only in the imagination. How many Americans are struggling to breach the straits of Florida in order to live in Cuba? As many as there are West Germans struggling to scale the Wall in order to live in the East. What we do have in America is not a few people, but tens of millions, who are well acquainted with the dictum that we should count our blessings, but who don't actually perform the exercise. They simply do not imagine circumstances substantially altered. They take for granted that when they elect to return to their homes, no one will stand in their way. No one will have taken their quarters from them. No one will deny them any right to appeal to civil authority for help; or bar them access to their family or friends; or move them from the city to the country, or from the country to the city; or force them to undertake certain tasks when other work is available, and preferable.

Yet this is how a numerical majority of human beings today live out their lives. And the distinctive perversion of the century is that those who govern this legion are unsatisfied to preside merely over the misery of their own people. They lust after authority over the freedoms we here in this room exercise. Why is it so? Solzhenitsyn has told us. It is so because one free man, anywhere, is a threat. The monolith can stand no termite. Moscow was not big enough to accommodate Sakharov. Russia was not big enough to accommodate Solzhenitsyn.

What we inherit is not necessarily what we pass on. There are terrible, entropic forces in between, and these we resist successfully, or we do not, in which event we head toward that frozen chaos which Solzhenitsyn has memorialized.

Abraham Lincoln told a biographer that his worst fear for America was that the revolutionary experience would dilute as the country grew older. His parents remembered the revolution as a part of their own experience. His own generation, he said, remembered it as a vivid part of the experience of their parents. But what of future generations, to whom the struggle of the Founding Fathers would become an abstract reminiscence, of no greater personal concern than the struggles of the ancient Romans, or of the medieval Englishmen, for their liberties?

The failure to invigorate our attachment to freedom brings a brittleness, a structural weakness which history takes grisly opportunities to exploit. Is there, then, a graver task, or a more jubilant one, than to labor to preserve the heritage? That is the object of Ed Feulner and his associates. We are unlucky in many things in our time, but among our blessings is the quality of those, so many of them here tonight, who have risen to defend our heritage. It is they whom we gather here to celebrate. Their industry, learning, wit, generosity: their passion for our country and its ideals.

With which affirmation, I advise you that you are now *really* free to leave and go home.

THE GREATNESS OF JAMES BURNHAM

Remarks at *National Review*'s Twenty-Fifth Anniversary Dinner; the Plaza Hotel, New York, December 5, 1980

There was jubilation (Ronald Reagan had been elected president) and disappointment (Ronald Reagan was not physically present). And there was sadness. The towering James Burnham had suffered a stroke that incapacitated him from writing. But he was there. We never knew whether he fully understood the tribute paid to him.

THIS IS A joyous occasion, and there are too many people to whom I and my colleagues feel gratitude to make it safe to name names, though in due course I shall make a single exception to The Rule. I elect tonight to abjure solemnity. It is barred from the proceedings. I reiterate Stan Evans's sentiments with respect to our missing guest, the president-elect. A few weeks ago I advised him that I had received the periodic form from *Who's Who* asking whether there were any changes I wished to make in my forthcoming entry. I asked the president-elect whether he would acquiesce in my contemplated change from "Profession: editor and writer" to "Profession: ventriloquist." He laughed. But he laughed longer than I would have done, and this persuaded me that, as a ventriloquist, I was a failure.

But I am not a total failure tonight: because I have been made to feel like an extension of the Equal Employment Opportunity Commission. When it transpired that the president-elect could not be with us, I received a telegram: "DEAR BILL: SORRY ABOUT THE PRESIDENT-ELECT. COULD I SUBSTITUTE? I'M ABOUT THE SAME AGE, WAS ONCE IN A TRADE UNION, HAVE PAST A.D.A. CONNECTIONS, AND, UNLIKE GOVERNOR REAGAN, I WILL ASSOCIATE WITH PRACTICALLY ANYBODY. ALL THE BEST. JOHN KENNETH GALBRAITH."

We would welcome Professor Galbraith to our ranks. *National Review*, like the White House, makes way for late vocations.

I note that I said to Miss Carmody of the *New York Times*, rather weightily, that the role of *National Review* in the months ahead would be to attempt to measure the distance between the paradigm and the actualization of policy. (Grandfather, what big words you use!) It is part of the conservative philosophy to be grateful that no single person will ever achieve sufficient power to transcribe into public policy all the prescriptions of his own voice. Our journal, although it is primarily a vehicle for thought and analysis understood as conservative, is many other things, none of them conflicting. We seek to illuminate and to entertain, to criticize and to heighten the sensibilities. Inevitably, the observance of criteria as otherworldly as the injunction against coveting one's neighbor's goods means that success must be both partial and tentative. Mr. Reagan departs now from his sometime role as tablet keeper, to take up the role of executor of policies that, as so often remarked, share certain elements with the sausage, namely, that familiarity with the processes by which they are made would kill the appetite for either.

Still, there is pleasure in even a little progress, even among those of us taught, at our mother's knee, not to seek to immanentize the eschaton.

The spirit is keener in America today than it was five weeks ago, and on this point I doubt that there is widespread disagreement. This is not because there is an abatement in the power of those who seek to destroy liberty, or an evanescence of such forces as bring lending institutions to ask for 18 percent interest on their money. We are revived by the enfranchisement of a fresh set of governors, with fresh recognitions of ancient vices and temptations. Ronald Reagan writes me, "After all, I've been reading *National Review* for twenty-five years"; and five years ago, in this hall, he said, "I want to express to *National Review* my appreciation for a fund of great knowledge that I've acquired." I take girlish pleasure, on behalf of the editors and writers at *National Review*, in that statement. Even while feeling the same embarrassment experienced by President Lincoln when, in a receiving line, a lady thrust into his hands a huge bouquet of flowers, leaving him physically paralyzed. His handling of the situation was exemplary.

"Are these really mine?" he asked.

The lady giggled with pleasure, and said, "Yes."

"In that case," said Mr. Lincoln, returning the flowers to his guest, "I wish to present them to you." With all gratitude to Governor Reagan, we make him a gift of that fund of great knowledge he has acquired by reading *National Review*.

I said that there was an exception to the rule that cautions me against acknowledgments. James Burnham, who is here tonight, withdrew from active participation in the affairs of *National Review* only a year ago, having suffered a stroke. Beyond any question, he has been the dominant intellectual influence in the development of this journal. He brought to it—speaking of a fund of knowledge—widely advertised qualities as a scholar, strategist, and veteran of the Cold War. He had been a practicing philosopher, an editor, and the author of seminal works on the nature of the current crisis. Other qualities he brought to the magazine are almost certainly the primary reason for its survival. He had, to begin with, a (totally self-effacing) sense of corporate identification with it. He devoted, over a period of twenty-three years, more time and thought to more problems, major and minor, than would seem possible for an editor resident in Kent, Connecticut, who came to New York only two days every week.

But every aspect of the magazine interested him. Its typography—just for instance. He cared always for what he would only call "tone." He believed in sentiment but not in sentimentality. At the regular editorial meetings, which by tradition we began by listening to his recommended list of issues we should address that week, his comments were always made calmly, with the analytical poise that is the trademark of the professional philosopher. Notwithstanding the gentleness of his manner, he brought great passion to his work: not ungovernable passion, because Jim doesn't believe that passion should be ungovernable. But his commentary, during such crises as are merely suggested by mentioning Budapest, Suez, Berlin, the Bay of Pigs, Vietnam, was sustained by the workings of a great mind and the beating of a great heart.

Although he once told me that twenty years of teaching was enough—he was twenty years a professor of philosophy at New York

University before going to Washington to serve as a policy consultant—his instincts remained pedagogical. Probably fifty writers have in the past twenty-five years had editorial experience in the offices of *National Review*. I don't think any of my colleagues would question that the figure for whom they had the greatest respect, and to whom they felt the greatest sense of gratitude, was James Burnham, who was never too busy to give the reasons for thinking as he did, or too harassed to interrupt his own work to help others with theirs. His generosity was egregiously exploited by one person, whose only excuse, now, is that at least he has documented his gratitude by penning these words.

Words. Many of us in this room live off them, if not by them. They are useful, dangerous, salvific. "If any man offend not in word," St. James tells us, "the same is a perfect man, and able also to bridle the whole body. Behold, we put bits in the horses' mouths, that they may obey us; and we turn about their whole body. Behold also the ships, which though they be so great, and are driven of fierce winds, yet are they turned about with a very small helm, whithersoever the governor listeth. Even so the tongue is a little member, and boasteth great things. Behold, how great a matter a little fire kindleth!"

I join you in saluting *National Review*.

HALFWAY BETWEEN SERVILITY AND HOSTILITY

A Commencement Address (excerpted) at William and Mary College;
Williamsburg, Va., May 17, 1981

The primary message communicated is reproduced later in a different context. Retained here are observations ad hoc, such stuff as catches the interest of straying students.

A COUPLE OF weeks ago I was talking with the Prince of Wales. Earlier that day he had received the hospitality of this institution, which he characterized as quite wonderful. I suggested to him that the geographical location of William and Mary symbolized perfectly the appropriate relationship between the American people and British royalty. Williamsburg, after all, is equidistant from Jamestown, the point at which the British elected to establish a North American empire, and Yorktown, the point at which the North American empire made conclusively clear to the British that they had gone too far.

So history suggested that the proper relationship between America and Great Britain is halfway between servility and hostility. Besides, William and Mary's charter should have warned his royal highness that he would be well treated. Your charter speaks of founding a college "to the end that the Church of Virginia may be furnished with a seminary of ministers of the gospel and that the youth may be piously educated in good letters and manners." We all realize that any attempt to teach virtue has got, in this imperfect world, to be asymptotic. And by no means is this always the fault of the students. Professor Edmund Morgan, in whose company I am honored to find myself, recorded in his classic *Virginians at Home* the remarks of a shrewd observer during the last decades of the colonial period, namely, that he had known "the professors [of William and Mary] to play all night at cards in public houses in the city and often seen them drunk in the streets."

But Williamsburg was to go through a great deal, particularly during the Revolutionary War and immediately after it. Bishop Asbury, the great circuit rider, noted in his journal on December 11, 1782, "I rode to Williamsburg, formerly the seat of government, but now removed to Richmond. Thus the worldly glory is departed from it. As to divine glory, it never had any. The place has suffered and is suffering: the palace, the barracks, and some good dwelling houses burned. The capitol is no great building and is going to ruin. The exterior of the college not splendid; and but few students. The bedlam house is desolate, but whether none are insane or all equally mad, it might perhaps be difficult to tell."

All institutions have high and low points. So is it with commencement speakers. What should our posture be? Surely also somewhere between servility and hostility. What rule should govern our attitude toward honorary degrees? A pragmatic one, surely. Nicely expressed by Professor John Kenneth Galbraith, who told me that his policy with respect to honorary degrees was to have one more than Arthur Schlesinger.

My policy in commencement addresses is straightforward, namely, not to let words come from my mouth which I would be embarrassed to utter before my colleagues at *National Review*, who are my chosen colleagues. Because to do otherwise would be to beguile and cheat the student body, which it would be infamous to do on the day you complete your formal education and matriculate into extra-academic life.

It is also important, I think, to acknowledge that there is no law which says that commencement speakers are any better—or any worse—that they utter nobler, or less noble, thoughts than student speakers. I remember about ten years ago serving as commencement speaker at Gettysburg College. The student speaker who preceded me arrived at the lectern with two differently pitched saxophones strapped around his neck. He spoke about the complicated inter-relationships among truth, justice, peace, beauty, and love. Each time he completed one of his dozen formulations, he would put one or the other saxophone to his lips, emitting a single note which he understood to be the musical equivalent of the harmonious interrelationship he had verbally constructed. His exegesis lasted forty minutes. That evening, short on cosmic material, I wrote a newspaper column describing the tortured afternoon. Three days later I received an indignant letter from the president of the graduating class advising me that in *his* opinion my *own* address had been no great shakes. Allowing me to make the obvious reply, namely, that I was hardly surprised, since after all Gettysburg owed its reputation substantially to its historical underestimation of great orations.

I note from the *William and Mary Quarterly* a dispatch published in August of 1798 as follows: "Our noble president was burned in effigy in Williamsburg on the fourth of July by the students of William and Mary College." The president in question was of course John Adams. It was he who promulgated the Alien and Sedition Acts. But the purposes of those laws fade in the memory, as witness that—again I quote from the *Quarterly*—a hundred years later, in answer to an examination question on the subject, a student wrote: "The Federalists passed the alien and sedation act to quiet Republican opposition." Meditating on this, it occurs to me that since the Alien and Sedition Acts had been passed precisely to suppress Republican criticism of the government under President Adams, the student had in fact got to the root of the matter.

But it is hard to penetrate the thinking of the student at William and Mary who late in the nineteenth century, when asked to give the name of an early American farm invention, wrote, "On a Virginia wheat field in 1830, Cyrus McCormick demonstrated his automatic raper, which automatically threw fifty thousand men out of work." At any rate, if you proceed to burn me in effigy after I am done, you will demonstrate that John Adams and I have yet one *more* thing in common. . . .

EARL WARREN AND THE
MEANING OF THE CONSTITUTION

A Commencement Address (excerpted) at New York Law School;
New York, June 7, 1981

I did not learn until arriving that there would be two commencement speakers—the other, Mr. William Casey, serving now as director of the CIA in the administration of Ronald Reagan. Here, excerpted, is only my introduction.

ERHAPS MORE EVEN than you, *I* have ruminated on the question why I was asked to address you in this final encumbrance standing between you and the degree you have labored so mightily to earn. I suspect that one of those computers we are always reading about divulged that I am the principal consumer of lawyers in the United States, and that your amiable dean thought therefore to give you a flesh-and-bones taste of the kind of person you will be serving, or harassing, according as you put your skills to the service of noble or ignoble ends.

To be sure, some nonlawyers have a certain feel for the Constitution of the United States. I remember an incident—it was about ten years ago. I was seated next to a friend at the great outdoor refectory of the Bohemian Grove. Opposite me, talking with the man next to *him,* was the Chief Justice of the United States, Mr. Earl Warren. Suddenly his companion keeled over. Intuitively, my friend and I busied ourselves in pointless but animated conversation, because when that sort of thing happens at summer encampments, the causes of it tend to be overindulgence, and one tends to avoid staring at other people's embarrassments. But in short order a doctor came, and then another, and then a third. And in a few minutes it transpired that the gentleman was quite dead.

This threw the fifteen hundred members of the camp into a fit of melancholy, not alone from the sense of fraternal loss, but because it occurred to many that such bucolic excesses as had caused one of us to go might easily have caused others of us to go. But the next morning the identity and habits of the deceased became known, and lo, it developed that he was fifty years old, a Mormon who had never smoked or drunk in his life, and a man who exercised regularly; so that conversation turned to what might have been the cause of his extraordinary collapse.

At noon, at the Grove, there is traditionally a public talk by the lakeside, and I found myself seated on the grass next to a figure whose features I dimly recognized but could not identify. After the speech concluded, he turned to me and said, "Bill, I'm Potter Stewart. I'm a friend of your brother Jim." We exchanged pleasantries, and inevitably the subject turned to the mysterious cause of the death of our fellow Bohemian. I told the associate justice that I had a personal thesis as to what happened. He politely asked what it was, and I replied that I was convinced that what had happened was that the chief justice was attempting to explain to his victim the meaning of the Constitution of the United States, bringing on the seizure. To my horror, Mr. Stewart turned and shouted to a dignified Scandinavian figure standing by a redwood tree, "Earl! Earl! Come on over. I want you to hear something!" I instructed my attorneys, for a year or two afterwards, not to apply for certiorari before the Supreme Court in any of my pending cases. . . .

SING A SONG OF PRAISE TO FAILURE

A Commencement Address at the Cornell University Graduate School of
Business and Public Administration; Ithaca, N.Y., June 13, 1981

---

*The auspices begged for something other than a commencement address
one would give to undergraduates: a dose of economic analysis, especially relevant a few months after the inauguration of President Reagan.*

I HAVE BEEN asked to talk about the debate going on in
Washington over the startling new approach to economic policy.
One week ago I spent an hour on television with my old friend
John Kenneth Galbraith. The nature of the economic revolution going
on these days is best measured by my informing you that Professor
Galbraith spent most of the hour talking about the dangers of infla-
tion. If Ronald Reagan accomplishes nothing more, he will go down
in history as having catalyzed a fear of inflation in John Kenneth
Galbraith, Edward Kennedy, and Tip O'Neill.

Permit me to proceed by setting forth a few propositions that bear
on business and management, which I will then examine.

My first proposition is that *Economic policy suffers disproportion-
ately from the ease with which anyone can say anything.* So long as the
subject is economics, a national audience tends to show a docility
nearly total. I cite as an example former president Jimmy Carter.

Every time we began to feel a little sympathy for President Carter,
as during the Billy affair, he reached out and massively retaliated.
There are any number of recallable episodes from last year's campaign, but it is as convenient as any to refer to his appearance before
the Urban League in August, at which he spoke words and gave out
figures such that, had he concluded his speech by planting a three-
cornered hat on his head and declaring himself the descendant of
Napoleon, he could not have left sober analysts more astonished.

The president began—perhaps you will remember—by announcing that he would soon reveal his "economic renewal program."
As we all know, he proceeded in due course to do this. The details

of that program, for reasons totally understandable, eluded the memory even before the election had washed them down the drain pipe of history. But with regard to that prospective agenda, the president told the Urban League, and I quote him in all his copiousness, that "millions and millions and millions of people" would come "back to work . . . in new jobs, exciting jobs, stimulating jobs." He left this member of his audience convinced that millions upon millions of unemployed Americans would soon be hired as assistants to Walter Cronkite.

It was a coincidence, but the very day the president spoke, the *Boston Globe* carried a notice deep in its Help Wanted section. The juxtaposition must have been plotted by a divine and mischievous poet. The classified ad had been placed by the Comprehensive Educational Training Administration (CETA, they call it)—the principal job-creating agency of the Carter administration. I beg you to listen to it and warn you that although it is short, it requires intense concentration. Here it is: "28 Brockton CETA Program. Temporary staff position. Economic development linkage coordinator. Grade 9, Step I, $19,780 per year. Job Summary: Facilitates the accessing by the private employer to the community of the various economic-development assistance programs available to them in the consortium service areas and disseminates information to private employers so that they may more fully utilize CETA funded programs." In a spirit of fairness one must award Mr. Carter full credit for sponsoring the proliferation of such job opportunities and, in a spirit of fairness, one should acknowledge that President Reagan has advocated the elimination of this agency.

But President Carter arrived at the Urban League not only with carrots for the unemployed, but with thunderbolts to hurl at Mr. Reagan, who had announced his support for a tax cut and for increased military expenditures. Here is what President Carter told his audience: Reagan's proposal consists of "rebates for the rich." It is "sugar-coated poison." "This proposal—put it this way"—I am quoting his extemporized remarks exactly—"if moderate increases are made in the defense budget, if the Social Security program is just protected, not improved, and the budget is balanced, every other agency and department and program in the federal government would have to be eliminated 100 percent."

We have all now seen Mr. Reagan's budget, which indeed calls for increased military expenditures and for tax cuts. It anticipates a diminishing budget deficit. But even if his tax relief yielded zero "flowback"—the term you professionals appear to have settled upon to describe the supplementary tax revenues that would logically come in from gratefully liberated suppliers—the federal government would be left with a surplus of $298 billion with which, among other things, to secure the services of more economic development linkage coordinators for Brockton, Massachusetts. I do not myself believe that a 10 percent across-the-board tax cut is the soundest way to proceed, favoring prescriptions you will perceive as a great deal more radical. But the proposition here put forward concerning Mr. Carter's surrealism is merely for the sake of alerting us to only one of any number of available examples of economic illiteracy that attract no attention whatever.

The Democratic Convention, you will remember, sought the immediate expenditure of $12 billion for the sake of "creating" eight hundred thousand jobs. No orator, during that prolonged session, made mention of a datum strikingly relevant, namely, that during the preceding eighteen months, twice eight hundred thousand jobholders had *lost* their jobs—notwithstanding that, under President Carter, we had run a cumulative deficit not of $12 billion, but of $166 billion. The figures would appear to suggest that any implied correlation between deficit spending and full employment is uneasy, to say the least.

The unemployment figures, and the myriad causes of a situation that brings tragedy to some families, lead me to state with some caution my next proposition, which is that *Public policy must tolerate, and indeed anticipate, economic failure.*

I desire, perversely, to sing a song of praise to failure; as well as, of course, to success; and to urge that we reappraise the dialectical voltage generated by these two polarities.

I begin with a reminiscence. The time was April 1960. The place, West Virginia. The actors, Senators Hubert H. Humphrey and John

F. Kennedy, contending in a primary for the nomination for President of the United States.

I was struck by a pictorial account of the contest that appeared in *Life* magazine. One picture stands out in the memory. It was of John Kennedy talking to a middle-aged workingman in the company of his visibly dispirited wife and six children. The caption told us that Coal Miner John Garth was forty-seven years old, that he had begun mining coal at age seventeen, that in the thirty ensuing years he had been employed a total of only fifteen years, and that at this point he had been out of work for three years. The demand for coal from that part of West Virginia, at the price for which it could be extracted, we were left to conclude, was insufficient to give Mr. Garth steady work. The caption went on to say that Candidate Kennedy promised John Garth that if elected he would call on Congress to pass a Distressed Areas Act, the purpose of which would be to identify those parts of the United States where unemployment was chronic, in order to send money regularly to permit inhabitants to remain there. Mr. Kennedy was faithful to his promise: about a year later, the Distressed Areas Act was put into being, and the government of the United States found itself saying to Mr. Garth, in effect, "You may now not-mine coal for a living." The philosophy that prompted the government to assure John Garth that he might continue to live where he lived, semi-employed, has now, twenty years later, delivered one and a half billion dollars to Chrysler, so that one hundred seventy-five thousand people can continue to make unsold cars for a living. In between, the government paid out three billion dollars to prevent the bankruptcy of New York City.

It is important, in passing, to acknowledge that the emotional satisfactions from helping an individual coal miner, from helping the tenth largest corporation in America, and from helping the largest municipality in America are as pleasant as the benevolent expression on the face of John F. Kennedy in West Virginia. It had been over thirty years since Calvin Coolidge shrewdly observed that "When men are out of work, unemployment results." By the same token, when dollars come in from government, it is not necessary that as many dollars should come in from consumers. That discovery has proved, in instance after instance, the key to much political advancement, but it may yet prove to be the catalyst of national impoverishment. "The difference between the politician and the economist," Peter Jay has written, "is that the politician asks, 'What do you want?' while the economist asks, 'What do you want most?'" John Garth and Chrysler both want economic security. Both, it is safe to say, want economic progress. Which do they want more?

The proposition before the house is that it is essential that there be a high rate of failures, because without them there will not be a tolerable rate of successes. The absence of success causes the spirit to atrophy and societies to become moribund. The pathological fear of failure breeds a devotion to the techniques and practices of the present and the past. On this point there is a perplexing complacency among many American conservatives, who sometimes appear to be telling themselves that although the enterprising spirit is welcome, under no circumstances should society risk the dismantling of an established corporate giant.

Three years ago there was some excitement in the entrepreneurial community at what the majority of the House Ways and Means Committee had resolved to do. Under the pressure of cogent arguments from small businessmen, the committee had resolved to roll back the capital-gains tax from the high level to which it had been taken under the Nixon administration. President Carter reacted as if he had just seen all Ten Commandments violated at high noon in the Rose Garden. In his disapproval he was joined not merely by the usual voices (the publishers of the *New York Times* and the *Washington Post*, whose distrust of growth other than of their own companies is obsessive) but also by the Business Roundtable. Representing executives of one hundred ninety major corporations, the Roundtable preferred a reduction in the corporate tax and an increase in the corporate investment tax credit—both of them highly desirable measures, to be sure, but designed rather to fortify existing businesses than to encourage new ones.

Congress looked at the facts. After the 1969 tax laws were enacted, new stock issues by smaller firms had plummeted, from several hundred per year, to four in 1976. So the reform bill was passed. The situation has improved, though it is significant that Japan and Germany, our two most vigorous competitors, have no capital-gains tax whatever, and it is disappointing that President Reagan did not include a recommendation to do away with the tax. Still, new stock issues have been floated, to launch new businesses that seek to keep America young, and vibrant, and resilient. Every year, as you know, three hundred thousand new businesses are launched, two-thirds of them fated to die within five years. The median income of these businessmen is less than that of a New York City sanitation worker. But it is they who make the jobs, who hire the John Garths away from unproductive semi-employment, who look to the future, who challenge the metaphor of the closed frontier or the exhausted planet.

It is never possible with absolute assurance to predict success based on assessable factors. Existing demand, existing fields of choice almost always conspire to suggest a contraction of possibilities. George Gilder perfectly sketches the society dominated by the fear of failure, the fear of risk. It is characterized, he says, by "an absorption with the status quo, a fear of competition, an exhausting preoccupation with contingency." The most penetrating evaluation of the role of the *spirit* of enterprise was done, ironically, by John Maynard Keynes. "Enterprise," he wrote, "only pretends to itself to be mainly actuated by the statements in its own prospectus, however candid and sincere. Only a little more than an expedition to the South Pole is [the typical corporate prospectus] based on an exact calculation of benefits to come. Thus if the animal spirits are dimmed, and the spontaneous optimism falters, leaving us to depend on nothing but a mathematical expectation, enterprise will falter and die."

What then? Why, then, we turn—increasingly—to government, as John Garth and Chrysler and New York City did. But here we run into a problem of a different order—which brings me to my third proposition, namely, *The government is organically unsuited to effect economic progress.*

Last July, in the *New York Times*, the historian Barbara Tuchman was quoted: "A problem that strikes one in the study of history, regardless of period, is why man makes a poorer performance of government than of almost any other activity." A newly published study by Charles Morris is called *The Cost of Good Intentions: New York City and the Liberal Experiment 1960–1975,* a period which, I note in passing, includes the year in which I offered myself to the city's voters as their mayor and mercifully was rejected. Mr. Morris characterizes the ordeal of a city, beset by good intentions, which endeavored to underwrite virtually the entire burden of life. "The inability [of the city] to perform," the author comments, "cuts right across the most routine business. The city couldn't issue birth certificates on time, pay overtime when it was due, maintain its automotive fleets, deliver asphalt to men filling potholes, submit claims for federal and state aid programs, supply diaper pins to obstetric wards, or hire key staff. If employees were late or participated in job [slowdowns] the payroll system couldn't dock them; when they were hired [often] they weren't paid; and when they retired they would as likely keep on being paid."

But why do such data continue to surprise us? Once again, George Gilder offers a masterly analysis of the problem of fusing government and industry: "As the experience of the U.S. railroad industry, the Post Office Department, [and] New York City public services all attest, access to the U.S. Treasury [begins] by crippling management in negotiation with unions. The resulting contracts consistently exceed productivity gains and thus erode the assets of any company until, at last, it fails and must seek the support of government. A federal fund to subsidize failing companies [thus becomes] a self-fulfilling prophecy of company failure."

The creeping alliance between big business and big government has been identified by such enemies of big business as Professor Galbraith. It is time that that creeping alliance be identified by such friends of big business as Henry Ford and David Rockefeller.

I move, then, from the propositions that risk is healthy and that government intervention is unhealthy, to the proposition that *Success must be meaningful.*

It is a striking paradox that the same voices that seem to cry out to shield John Garth are otherwise bent on universalizing risk—by causing not only great industries to be increasingly subservient to government, but also the whole of the citizenry. This of course is accomplished by the simple contrivance of taking money from those who, whether by enduring risk and making sacrifices or by reaping good fortune, accumulate it—and then benevolently doling it out in such measures as are deemed appropriate by a few hundred legislators through whose hands six hundred fifty billion dollars pass in a single year, none of which dollars accumulated as a result of any of their own exertions.

During the 1960s it became fashionable to quote the social couplet that it is the job of government to "comfort the afflicted and afflict the comfortable." The little jingle had going for it even then as little as most ventures in reductionism do. But today we are required to give thought to its implied imperatives, and I think it seemly to begin by asking, "*Why* should we afflict the comfortable?"

The great paradox, as I say, is that this passion to afflict the comfortable tends to issue from the mouths of the same social theorists who talk to us about the desirability of *making* people comfortable. Let us take a hypothetical case, which however describes the predicament of millions of Americans: Henry Garcia works his way through school, apprentices in a hardware store, borrows the money to start his own store, works sixty hours a week, marries, raises four children, at age sixty-seven sells his business and buys a condominium in Florida expecting to be comfortable for the rest of his life. It beggars the imagination just why we should be anxious to afflict this comfortable man: though that exactly is what we have been doing, by taxing unearned income at 50 percent beginning at $32,000, the rate rising rapidly to 70 percent at $106,000—while industriously engaged in diminishing the value of his principal through inflation.

And so to my penultimate proposition, namely, that *The healthiest tax reform is one that would grant instant relief to those paying taxes in the highest brackets.* A healthy tax reform is here defined in purely Benthamite terms, namely, relief designed to help the most people, at the least cost.

The principal objection to the progressive feature of the income tax is of course philosophical. But the empirical arguments against it are also formidable. Senator Kennedy at Madison Square Garden [during the 1980 Democratic National Convention] made much sport of a statement attributed to Mr. Reagan, namely, that the progressive income tax originated with Karl Marx, whereas, said Mr. Kennedy, in fact it originated with Teddy Roosevelt.

In fact it originated with neither, although its formal promulgation as an instrument of redistribution was first done in the Communist Manifesto of Marx and Engels. It had been proposed on the eve of the French Revolution, but when the idea was brought to the liberal Turgot, his comment was that the author of the idea, not the proposal, should be executed.

Leaving to one side the philosophical question, the incandescent fact of the matter, which fact no politician running for president dares to acknowledge, is that the higher rates of taxation are glaringly unproductive. If one were to confiscate the whole of the remaining income of those who pay a tax of more than 50 percent on the top dollar, one would raise enough money to pay the cost of the federal government for six days. Professor Milton Friedman has recommended that the top rate be reduced to 25 percent. Were that to be done, the ostensible diminution in income taxes would amount to 13 percent of present revenues. But Professor Friedman flatly asserts that government revenues would actually rise. "No one," he points out plausibly, "would pay 30 or 40 or 50 cents on the dollar [maneuvering] for tax [relief], as many of us now do, in order to avoid a tax of 25 cents." The increase in revenues, he predicts, would be an immediate rather than a strategic return, which to be sure would also come from the uncorseting of American economic energy.

Unhappily, the dialogue goes forward in what one might call convention-hall rhetoric, as when Vice President Walter Mondale denounced Mr. Reagan's tax-cut plan—never mind that it would return to the taxpayer less than he stands to lose from inflation—as "the most regressive tax proposal in history": which is very bad history, since progressive taxation was not introduced until 1913. Mr. Mondale spoke of it as "tax cuts for the wealthy, trickle-down for the rest of Americans. If you're earning $200,000 a year, you save enough to buy a new Mercedes. But if you're a teacher, you save enough to buy a hubcap." One notes, in passing, that Mr. Mondale prudently chose as his symbol of ostentatious luxury a Mercedes rather than a

Cadillac. It apparently occurred to his speechwriter in the nick of time that one-half of the people who make Cadillacs are currently unemployed.

The rich-fixation phenomenon, relatively new to America, is a flagrant import from class-conscious Great Britain. It isn't that the socialists desire, really, to *own* the steel companies: it is that they desire that the people who own the steel companies should cease to own them. Thirty million Americans are paying taxes of 25 percent or more on the top dollar, arriving at that exposure after earning $12,900. The conclusion is inescapable that the men and women who dominate political fashion in America would rather that these people should be taxed at over 25 percent, indeed up to 70 percent, than that the benefit of their industry should bring sustenance to the poor, stability to the dollar, the revitalization of industry, and security to, among others, the affluent. We are, I think, paying an exorbitant price for the masochistic pleasure of harassing the rich, here defined as those whose pre-tax earnings exceed $12,900. In Great Britain some years ago, the writer Anthony Burgess simply gave up, leaving the country. Those who have read his work are unlikely to conclude that he was motivated by crass materialistic idolatry. He felt it an indignity to live in a country that does not need his paltry surplus but declines to let him have it. Something is wrong with any society a sensitive luminary of which feels, along with others, that, Procrustes having taken his measurement, he is found guilty of being too tall; and so he tiptoes out of the country, lest he rouse the Walter Mondales from their egalitarian reveries.

My final proposal I advance with some trepidation, because it will strike many of you as a cliché. And, in any case, it is not a part of the professional portfolio of those who set out to write about business and the economy. My proposition is that, *In America, we should count our blessings.*

Our political differences may be great; in our tactics we are divided; in our understanding we are deficient. But we can, I hope, at least unite in affirming that, whatever the verdict that an inscrutable, so often unforgiving, always jealous History will finally speak on the great question asked by Abraham Lincoln on the battlefield at Gettysburg, *we* know; we know that man was born to be free. To the end that he should remain so, we dedicate ourselves.

HOW LEO CHERNE SPENT CHRISTMAS

Introductory Remarks at the Annual Luncheon of the Sales Executives Club of New York; the Grand Ballroom of the Waldorf-Astoria, New York, January 8, 1982

At a luncheon speech every January, beginning in 1939, Leo Cherne addressed a crowded banquet hall and undertook to predict the events, economic and political, of the year forthcoming. He was so audacious as to begin his talk each year by reciting the previous year's predictions, an undertaking that would have embarrassed Erasmus. Cherne was the president of the Research Institute of America but served also as executive head of the International Rescue Committee.

THE DAY BEFORE yesterday, Leo Cherne's secretary called mine, and the message was transmitted. It said, "Tell Mr. Buckley that if he wants to say anything—well, you know— a little rough about Mr. Cherne, that's okay, because Mr. Cherne will say something—well, you know—a little rough about Mr. Buckley." Such oblique communion between speakers may well attract the attention of the Securities and Exchange Commission, and why not? since everything else has.

Now what should I do to justify Leo's speaking roughly about me? Let me see.

Once, many years ago, Leo Cherne told an audience that he did not agree with me on everything. I replied that I admired such professions of modesty.

Twenty-five years ago we debated on the subject of Senator McCarthy and I greatly irritated Mr. Cherne, and perhaps he has not forgotten my discovery of the two hundred five card-carrying Communists working for the Research Institute of America.

Two years ago he predicted to this gathering that the Republicans would nominate Mr. Bush or Mr. Ford, but he did concede that Mr. Reagan was increasingly perceived as a moderate. During that period I was predicting that Mr. Reagan was likely to be nominated to the extent that he succeeded in rejecting the image of himself as a moderate.

But what is there, really, to quarrel about with such a man as Leo Cherne? In the first place, as I mentioned when introducing him eight years ago, it is not at all safe to quarrel with him. I thought it would be amusing to test the boast that Lloyd's of London would insure anything, by asking my insurance agent to quote me the odds against prevailing over Mr. Cherne in an argument, and the answer came back: "Five to one, unless it's Buckley, in which case four to one." Those are long odds, and such instincts as I have for survival caution me against taking them.

I give up. I cannot get rougher on Leo Cherne. My heart isn't in it.

Accordingly, in deference to the anxiety I know you all have to learn what is going to happen in 1982, I abbreviate my introduction.

To say what will happen is, we all know, very different from saying what we wish would happen. Last Christmas, as so often is the case, Leo Cherne was not at home with Phyllis, his superb wife, companion, and critic. As one might have predicted, he was abroad, helping political refugees, this time in Vienna, where he interviewed everyone he could who might throw light on the awful fate of the thousands who had escaped Poland, only less dire than that of those who remained. He found in Vienna, as he had found there after the Soviet brutalities of 1956 and 1968, a heavy concentration of the wretched of this world, whose plight, for so many years, Leo Cherne as head of the International Rescue Committee has sought to mitigate. I have seen a cable he sent four days after Christmas, and take the liberty of quoting the final paragraph.

"For thousands who fled Poland, the International Rescue Committee must provide emergency assistance, especially to help professionals, teachers, scientists, students, engineers, writers who are a vital resource for Poland's future. Apart from emergency aid, many refugees have family members in the West, the largest number in the United States. Other countries, especially Canada, Australia, Scandinavia, are also offering resettlement opportunities. Our IRC teams will assist all who turn to us for resettlement, working with government officials to facilitate the effort. More U.S. admissions will be needed, and many thousands remaining in Europe urgently need assistance."

Followed by his appeal: yes, for funds. What else can we do?

Leo Cherne may be embarrassed at the injunction that he look back on his life and take the satisfaction that he is due. But I am not embarrassed to issue that injunction, nor you, I expect, to overhear it. He is the full human being, covetous of the music of this world, however expressed: in literature, in sculpture, in song. He is the modern man in the best sense, who has learned technology and its uses but who has shown himself above all to be a member of the human race and a partisan of those members of that race who reject the invitation to submit to oppression. As much as anyone I know—and this quite apart from the astonishing gall he shows in coming here forty-three years in a row to tell us, forgodssake, what is going to happen during the next year—as much as anyone I know, he is entitled to the sound of that comprehensive benediction: "Well done, thou good and faithful servant."

10 DOWNING STREET: THE GIRLS CLUB OF BRITAIN

Introductory Remarks at the Annual Dinner of the Girls Club of New York;
the Grand Ballroom of the Waldorf-Astoria, New York, June 8, 1982

---

*For several years I introduced the speakers at the Girls Club's annual
money-raising dinner. The guest of honor this time was John Shad, the
chairman of the Securities and Exchange Commission, with which I had
had a professional quarrel a few years earlier. A good time was had by all.*

E VEN THOUGH WE are in the presence here tonight of the chairman of the Securities and Exchange Commission, you are supposed to enjoy yourselves. Our hosts have planned a program with strict concern for consumer protection. That is to say, no oratory is scheduled, and the only burdensome part of the evening will be the struggle to say something kind about a head of the SEC.

We are here to recognize one of the city's philanthropies which, in growing from a cottage industry to a conglomerate, can give its sponsors not only the sense of satisfaction you are entitled to feel for the work you have made possible, but also an occasion to do a little celebrating. This banquet is a ball; your hosts desire that you should eat, drink, dance, and be merry. And to the extent we speakers can make this possible by being relatively inconspicuous, we will oblige.

The only significant social affair competing for attention tonight is a dinner at 10 Downing Street, a British division of the Girls Club of America, featuring tonight Margaret Thatcher, Nancy Reagan, and Queen Elizabeth, three high achievers who owe everything they are to their early experience with our girls clubs. If our satellite communication system doesn't fail us, we'll be hearing later this evening from these ladies, congratulating you and wishing you every success. Meanwhile, please proceed.

YOUR PROGRAM LISTS only the outlines of the career of John Shad. Others will specify his contributions to the Girls Club of New York. Let me say only that Jack Shad has not only contributed to the Girls Club's capital fund, he has given it advice. And not once has the Girls Club been hauled up before the SEC, with accusations that its directors are unfamiliar with the Girls Club's 10-K.

People who know Shad wonder at his capacity for hard work. The rumor has plagued the SEC that its chairman is actually in *favor* of American business enterprise. Indeed, one anonymous observer has said about him darkly that he views the SEC as being like "the Agriculture Department, whose job is to promote the interests of the farmers." Mr. Shad has moved into an organization whose most conspicuous figure moved, after a long siege, to the CIA. Churchill is credited with the remark about Emanuel Shinwell, when *he* moved from minister of coal to minister of war, that even as under his old ministry there had been no coal, England might hope that under his new ministry there would be no war. One can hope that Mr. Shad's predecessor in the enforcement division will not rule that our spy satellites are defrauding Russian investors in the destruction of America.

But Jack Shad has the requisite energy to execute *any* program. During his senior year in high school in Los Angeles he worked during hours off in the daytime as a hod carrier on a construction project, in the evening as a soda jerk, and on weekends as a lifeguard. At the University of Southern California he worked from midnight until eight making airplane parts. At the Harvard Business School he ran a laundry and dry-cleaning operation. When he decided that he ought to be a lawyer, he induced Mrs. Shad to enroll with him in New York University Law School, a cozy arrangement because that way Mrs. Shad could takes notes at those classes Mr. Shad couldn't attend because he was busy making a financial giant out of E. F. Hutton. They both got their degrees.

John Shad's appreciation of girls is—well, total, however chaste. It is recorded that he once gave a charity ball, part of the entertainment being a competitive sketching of the female figure. To the consternation of some of the guests, the model arrived absent-mindedly without the leotard she was supposed to appear in, and proceeded to pose. Mr. Shad on that occasion reinforced his reputation as a profound advocate of full disclosure.

John Shad is a proud American, proud of America's institutions, of the opportunities here for those who will take them. His philanthropic activity, energized by his singular ability and devotion to his work, has meant a great deal to the friends and patrons of the Girls Club of New York.

MORAL DISTINCTIONS
AND MODERN WARFARE

The Inaugural DuBois Lecture at Mount St. Mary's College; Emmitsburg, Md., May 6, 1983

This is a full-blown address questioning distinctions widely accepted dealing with fit and unfit objects of attack in defensive war. During this period the Catholic bishops were especially active in challenging, and even renouncing, the use of nuclear weapons and were making distinctions I thought unsafe. There were many prelates sitting in the front row at this inaugural lecture, and applause from them was formalistic. The introduction, self-denigrating, is raw bait for critics.

I AM HONORED to be associated with your one-hundred-seventy-fifth anniversary and of course honored to have been asked to inaugurate the DuBois Lecture series. I should reveal to you that I received a most intimidating letter from your president, Dr. Wickenheiser, in which he suggested that my remarks here today might serve as a model for future speakers. I am normally reluctant to contradict college presidents. But it is not only unlikely that I shall serve up a precedent, it is also undesirable. I have always assumed that I had things to say that were worth listening to; to claim otherwise, given the life I lead, would be to engage in imposture on a very grand scale. But I have incurable stylistic and intellectual mannerisms I wouldn't want others to imitate, assuming the inconceivable, namely, that anyone would be tempted to do so. I am attracted to varieties of anomalous thought which, expressed by more prudent men, would be taken as contumacious. I wish that all the world were of my opinion about most things, but it makes me nervous to be set up as a paradigm of anything at all. So then with some formality, speaking mutatis mutandis ex cathedra, I hereby liberate all successor speakers in this august series from any obligation, explicit or implicit, (a) to sound like me, (b) to behave like me, (c) to reason like me. To be sure, the residual problem of those speakers who avail themselves of all these licenses is how to make their way into the Heavenly Kingdom.

I am going to devote my time today to setting forth a few propositions, some of which I tender asseveratively, others—well, inquisitively.

The first of these is, *How does one go about defining, in the vocabulary of full-scale war, an "innocent party"?*

You will correctly have supposed that I am vexed by the thinking that undergirded the conclusions arrived at by the bishops at their plenary session in Chicago. Much time had been given to the attempt to translate into public policy the protectiveness Christian thought is expected to extend to innocent parties in a hostile confrontation.

A simple statement of the obvious distinction is given by imagining an escaped murderer who disposes of a hostage. It is clearly immoral to proceed against the murderer without any care taken for the survival of the hostage.

We tend, though only by slighting analytical precision, to graduate the isolation of the innocent bystander to situations in which it is not easy to hold fast to the progenitive distinctions. Consider, for instance, the distinction—especially pressed since the Second World War and the advent of nuclear weaponry—between "counterforce" and "countervalue" weapons.

By counterforce we mean weapons aimed at aggressively postured military installations. In the imagination of moral man it is accepted that those who garrison such concentrations are, in wartime, fit objects of our retaliatory, defensive, or pre-emptive war machines.

Now it is one thing to comprehend that in order to prevent a rifle from continuing its fire it may be necessary to aim a bullet at the man whose finger is pulling the trigger. That is instrumental knowledge. If the man firing that rifle is a social outlaw—a criminal, a murderer— one can with moral confidence return his fire.

Moving one step further, members of an armed force may not themselves be, in any clear sense of the word, "aggressors." And yet if they serve in the armed forces of an aggressive political regime, we are entitled to think of them as aggressive *agents*.

We are left with by far the most difficult distinction to contend with. Let's take it on:

Dmitri and Valerian are twin brothers. Both are interested in the arts, particularly in ballet. They turn eighteen and Valerian fails his physical—he has a disqualifying heart murmur. Dmitri, however, is drafted, and in due course finds himself attached to a missile silo. Valerian, meanwhile, goes to the ballet at night, but during the day he works at a factory that manufactures missiles. Dmitri, standing by the controls of his SS-20, is doing what he is told to do. Valerian, stand- ing by the assembly line pouring whatever it is you pour into missiles to enable them to destroy Paris and Detroit, is doing what *he* is told to do. If missile factories fall under roughly the same category as mis- sile launchers, then it is morally acceptable to include Valerian's fac- tory as a counterforce target.

But the organic porosity of that factory tends to overwhelm the search for logical moral boundaries. You see, Valerian and Dmitri's cousin Nikita works out there in the Urals, mining the special metals required to manufacture those mortal missiles. In fact just last year he got a medal, along with his co-workers, in acknowledgment of the national dependence of the Union of Soviet Socialist Republics on his work.

I do not need to draw it out that this exercise can as easily be done to demonstrate the dependence of the frontline soldier on the farmer who grows the wheat without which Nikita the miner could not con- tinue to forward to Valerian the missile maker the metals necessary to forward to Dmitri the finished missiles that aim at Paris and Detroit.

It may be that the next war, if there is to be another war, God forbid, will be over so to speak after a single volley, rendering subsequent support from the farmer to Nikita, from Nikita to Valerian, and from Valerian to Dmitri a routine logistical problem, transacted without the urgency of warmaking. But of course that might not happen. The missile silo might be needed again. And if the war goes forward with tactical weapons, then all the farmers and all the Nikitas and all the Valerians will be working day and night, causing the moralists to chew their nails over the question: Are these, indeed, innocent parties?

WELL, THEN, IF the mutual interdependence of the warmaking world is such that you cannot successfully distinguish between the soldier who fires the rifle and—at the other, and ostensibly pacific, end of the spectrum—the farmer who feeds that soldier, is it easier to distinguish between counterforce and countervalue by inquiring into motives? The soldier knows that he is engaged in an act designed to kill people. The farmer has no such direct knowledge. He does not know whether the wheat he is harvesting will reanimate the soldier who mans the nuclear-missile silo, or the ballerina who that night will find the strength to leap to record heights in her solo in *Don Quixote*.

But does this observation liberate us? Can we assume that Dmitri's experience in basic training transmogrified him so that now he has become by nature an aggressor, sharply to be distinguished from Valerian, by nature a balletomane? The trouble with this is that (a) it isn't so, and (b) we know it isn't so.

During the last few months of my military career as a second lieutenant in the infantry I was in charge of what they call a Casual Department—about one thousand transients who arrived at Fort Sam Houston in San Antonio, Texas, in order to be discharged, but were for various reasons not yet fully qualified for a discharge. About half of them had venereal diseases, the other half, pending court-martial charges; so they had to while away their time, substantially at my direction, awaiting their formal return to civilian status. About the lot of them the single generalization could safely be made that these were Americans who yearned to return to civilian life—to abandon careers in which the use of guns was intrinsic. Fifteen million Americans served during the Second World War. It is not the finding of any sociologist I know of that these men evolved as a lumpen-aggressive body which, on reintegration into the civilian community, coarsened it, bringing on a deterioration in the prevailing gentility.

Do we have any reason for supposing that it is different in the Soviet Union? That there is a temperamental difference between Sergeant Dmitri and Factory Worker Valerian, such that we feel justified in prescribing the destruction of the one and the survival of the other? Who ever said that Dmitri was happy doing what he is told to do? Who ever demonstrated that he harbored ill feeling toward the French in Paris, or the Americans in Detroit? When he vacations with his twin brother, is there visible any aggressiveness in the soldier, distinguishable from that in the mechanic? No. The differences between them are rather a formal convenience for foreign moralists than a reality.

If moral retribution were ruthlessly pursued, surely we would enter into the vocabulary of war the term "counterauthority." Because it is those who instruct Dmitri to fire his weapons at Paris and Detroit against whom we have the truly legitimate claim. Except for them—and we are speaking of a half dozen men associated with the Kremlin—Dmitri's silo might as well hold soybeans as intercontinental ballistic missiles. Theirs are the true fingers on the trigger of war. But although they do not always escape punishment—especially since the Nuremberg and Tokyo trials—more often than not they do. Hitler died by his own hand, not ours. The Kaiser, leaving fifteen million dead, lived out a long life in Holland. And corresponding chiefs of state mostly wrote memoirs.

One difficulty with a counterauthority strategy is that just as authority has the power to begin a war, so it has, one must assume, the power to end it. And in the absence of authority, we do not know what are the contingent instructions left with Dmitri. If he picks up the telephone and nobody answers, is he supposed to fire off his missile, or let it dawdle there pending the resurrection of Comrade Andropov? So that while there is no apparent moral case against a counterauthority strategy, there is a prudential case against it.

From all of which I emerge doubting the relevance of moral ped-agogy based on traditional distinctions by which we have sought to discriminate, for a relatively short period in history (remember that during the Middle Ages the siege of whole towns was the convention; and in the Old Testament, entire regions were made to suffer for the sins of the few), between combatants and noncombatants.

I ask, then: Does the proposition that it is no longer possible morally to distinguish between the military and the civilian popula-tions in any way help us to advance our strategic thinking along moral lines? I think it does; but, in between, it becomes necessary to linger over a second proposition.

It is that *The most important endeavor of man is to seek to distinguish between right and wrong.* Hardly a new proposition; but one which, in my own judgment, we tend to view, these days, without a secure sense of what it is we value more, what less. Our apparent attachments would certainly have confused, among others, your founder, Father John DuBois.

And this leads to the proposition that *The love of life is a holy, sanctified impulse, while the veneration of life is idolatry.*

The meaning of this is hardly perplexing to a Christian audience. It may well be that the future will judge the commotions of the 1960s, which revolved about Vietnam, and the ongoing mini-commotion of the 1980s, which revolves around the question whether young men should register for the draft simply because Congress tells them that that is what they should do, as an incipient struggle between free men and democratically elected governments over the exact locus of power over the individual's life. For generations, Western tradition has accepted the convention that soldiers, whether volunteers or con-scripts, go where they are told to go. If they die, they may have died in order to make a morally transcendent point that will resonate through the ages for as long as we admire heroism—so are the men remembered who fought the Battle of Britain. Or they may have died among the six hundred in the Light Brigade, proving nothing more than that officers can exercise command over life and death even if they are quite stupid.

Now during the protests of the 1960s, there crept into view

something called selective conscientious objection. Father John Courtney Murray, shortly before his death, acknowledged that the idea was less than entirely frivolous. That is to say, a young man cannot automatically be condemned as having acted frivolously if he sets out to weigh the demands of loyalty to his country's government against the cogency of the military objective he is being conscripted to risk his life for. What Father Murray did not conclude—perhaps because it cannot be schematically concluded—is whether the challenge posed to democratic authority by the very idea of selective conscientious objection is lethal. We don't know. We don't know because the moment has never come to America when at once its life was blatantly threatened and it found itself short of men willing to serve, whether as volunteers or as conscripts.

But the impact of the scientific developments that have absorbed the moral energies of our bishops and of the American clerisy in general prompts questions more basic than the question of selective conscientious objection. By "basic" I mean touching on assumptions so axiomatic for the Christian that life for centuries has proceeded on their tacit acceptance, so that suddenly to question them is on the socially disruptive order of suddenly asking the boy whose teeth are parted to break into a hamburger, "By the way, Johnny, do you really think it moral to kill an animal?"

Many people today are beginning, as I see it, to blur the distinction between loving life and venerating it. To love life is wholesome. To venerate it is, surely, to violate the Second Commandment, which permits the veneration only of God. To venerate life is to attach to it first importance. Surely if we were all to do that, any talk of war, just or unjust, prudent or imprudent, limited or unlimited, provoked or unprovoked, would be an exercise in moral atavism.

If we love life, then we are forced to ask, *Why* do we love it? To answer merely by giving biological explanations—for instance, that sensual pleasures ensue on breathing when suffocation threatens, on eating when one is hungry, resting when one is weary, defecating when the bowels are full—is morally uncivilized. That is to say, it is to give answers that are incomplete, for those who understand man as more merely than a biological composition.

We cherish life mostly because it permits us to love and to be loved. And we cherish it in a dimension wholly other than that in which we obtain pleasure by satisfying biological appetites. We love life because there is a range of experience given to us that regularly pleases, sometimes excites, occasionally elates. I have mentioned, preeminently, the joys of loving and being loved. And there are the delights captured by poetry and music. But all these are overwhelmed by God. And so it is at this point that I intrude the distinction between love and veneration. We venerate Him, we love one another. It is my suspicion that the evolution of the idea of selective conscientious objection is in fact leading not so much in the direction of a discriminating love of life—against which a blind patriotism is defensibly measured—as in the direction of a veneration of life such that all other considerations are as quickly subordinated as a computer nowadays reorders all derivative calculations, once you have altered the value of the prime figure.

I think that that is the direction, mistakenly, in which many of our moralists are headed. They begin by making false distinctions, such as those between combatant and noncombatant members of an aggressive community. Then they find themselves speaking about prudent and imprudent uses of deterrent weapons, and finally we have the sense—or at least some of us do—that what is going on is a creeping philosophical reconciliation with that definition of life that does not stop short—ask Bukovsky, ask Medvedev, ask Solzhenitsyn, ask Shcharansky—of transforming life, the life we properly love, into mere biological life. And when, the challenge having confronted us, we choose mere biological life over the *risk* of death in pursuit of Christian life, we come perilously close to worshiping false gods.

Or so it would appear to me.

It is most awfully strange for a man approaching senior citizenship, born to Catholic parents who loved God, each other, and their ten children with joy, with curiosity, with respect, to find myself, after three-quarters of a lifetime in the faith, almost everywhere assaulted by arguments emanating alike from agnostics, Christian laymen, and churchmen of all faiths, that seem to pay in most cases literally no attention whatever to Christian teaching, which speaks of the end of the world quite fatalistically; or, where attention is given to apocalypse, it is done with the kind of mythological detachment that characterizes quaint literary references to Eve and the serpent, or Jonah and the whale.

I am hardly here to celebrate the one-hundred-seventy-fifth anniversary of Mount St. Mary's for the purpose of suggesting that your two-hundredth anniversary may be postlapsarian in a new sense of the word. But I am here—and this is my final proposition—to say that *No biblical paradox can be more relevant today than Christ's which said that His Kingdom is not of this world.* As a child, I simply interpreted this as meaning that Christ had a different address from my own, and perhaps could be reached only by airmail. As a young man, I interpreted this as an injunction to care about Christlike things rather than about things of this world; but in due course I smelled Manichaeism in this, which a natural hedonism helped me to overcome.

As an older man, though no doubt one who has yet to reach full maturity, I understand Christ to have told us that although His Kingdom was not of this world, it is a Kingdom He will one day share, leaving it to us, inhabiting our own city, to be counseled by the lessons He taught us and inspired by the example He set of His love for us. It can never be suspected of the man who died on the Cross that He venerated the life which, to be sure, He loved.

DOES THIS REDUCE to strategic formulae? Only negatively. Yes, I would resist any philosophical usurpation that sought to put biological life on the throne. No, I do not deduce from this any concrete arrangements for facing the most awful threat of this century, animated by a fetid materialism. How blessed we are that the Bolsheviks so specifically reject God! How unbearable it would be if they committed their workaday horrors under the putative guidance of the Cross!

But I would deduce this much, namely that any stratagems we follow ostensibly in pursuit of morality, when what we are really pursuing is false idols, do not become a country as blessed as our own has been. How much America, and Americans, do suffer; but we suffer mostly as human beings living in natural conditions. How can we deny the horrors of the human condition when as recently as two days ago four children were killed in California by a stochastic typhoon?

But how much range has been given to us, given to you at Mount St. Mary's, finding yourselves a few steps from a library where you can read what you wish, a few miles from bus stations and railroad stations and airports where you are free to travel as far as your savings will take you. A few miles from political offices to which you have a constitutional right of access. And a few steps from a chapel in which you can pause to venerate that which alone is venerable.

DEMOCRACY AND THE PURSUIT OF HAPPINESS

A Commencement Address at Johns Hopkins University; Baltimore, Md., May 27, 1984

A pleasantry or two, and then an invitation to look at Vietnam and ask whether there was unmitigated satisfaction to be got from our withdrawal there a decade earlier. On to the deteriorating standards of modern political discourse, with an invitation to found a Democratic Anti-Defamation League.

I AM HAPPY to be here on a happy occasion—an occasion the memory of which I cannot add to, or subtract from. I have concluded, after years of experience, that the only generality one can make with a high degree of confidence about commencement addresses is that no one is likely to remember what you said, unless you promulgate a Marshall Plan, or disclose that America has suffered from an inordinate fear of Communism. Those of us not in a position to launch a thousand ships from a lectern have got to come to terms with the evanescence of our speeches. You will perhaps have picked up, in your reading, occasional references to "commencement-day prose." They are not intended to compliment the orotundity of style associated with valedictory exercises. So let us at least strive to avoid that.

I had a memorable experience a dozen years ago when at Charlottesville to deliver the commencement address at the University of Virginia the next day. The tradition there is that a different speaker will deliver the baccalaureate address the afternoon before. To this end, the president had got the services of the profusely gifted architect-philosopher Buckminster Fuller, who would arrive on the scene at any moment now.

After lunch, the president approached me to ask whether I knew Mr. Fuller. I replied that I did not, but that a good friend of mine, Professor Hugh Kenner of Johns Hopkins, was among Fuller's intellectual biographers.

And so he took me into his confidence. "I just learned," he said, "that Mr. Fuller has the habit of speaking on at quite undisciplined length, and the baccalaureate program is a long one, during which student awards are given out. How can we get it through to Mr. Fuller that we are quite serious in asking him to speak for only twenty minutes?"

I volunteered to call Professor Kenner, who said: It is extremely easy. It requires merely this, that you interpret any of Mr. Fuller's cadences—they come regularly, every five minutes or so—as the termination of his speech. Tell the president to select the cadence that falls nearest to his twenty minutes, and prearrange a signal with the school band. The band should strike up a lively chorus of "For He's a Jolly Good Fellow," or whatever; whereupon everyone on the dais should rise and applaud the speaker. The students will proceed to do the same thing, and Buckminster Fuller will think that everyone simply assumed that he had finished. He will smile benignly, nod his head in his characteristic way, and sit down.

It went exactly as predicted. But I was left with the fantasy of the Endless Commencement Address: the voice that will be talking about wars and population control and conservation when there are only ashes out there, or angels, and maybe two louseworts.

From time to time, when I am invited to speak at a commencement, someone objects to the invitation's having been extended to me in the first place. I remember in 1969, just after the invasion of Cambodia, being informed by an anonymous student at the University of Syracuse that a group of students intended to mount a protest in the middle of my speech. In anticipation of that possibility I began by telling the assembly that, after reading the papers that morning, I was apprehensive about the chances of concluding the ceremony without interruption. The *New York Times* reported that at Brown University the day before, when Henry Kissinger began his speech, one-third of the senior class stood and turned their backs on him.

That report, I confessed, discouraged me, given that Henry Kissinger was associated only with the invasion of Cambodia, while I had been publicly advocating the invasion of North Vietnam. It all reminded me of the little boy seated in the front row on the first day of school who was asked by his teacher, occupied with composing the class roll, what his name was.

"Stinky," he replied, and persisted when asked two more times by the patient teacher.

Finally provoked, she wrote out a note, handed it to the little boy, and told him to go home and give it to his mother. He picked up his books disconsolately and trudged back towards the door at the end of the classroom. He was almost out of the room when he suddenly stopped. Leaning over to a classmate, he said, "Come on, Shithead. You don't stand a chance." But it all went well for me at Syracuse.

So then, to slip into the hortatory mode: What would this conservative like to see the generation that begins its postgraduate career in 1984 do for this country, for the world, and for yourselves?

Well, I would be very pleased if, in your pursuit of happiness, you happened on it. It is very unlikely that you will do so conclusively. One does not discover happiness in the same way that Columbus discovered America. Can any advice be helpful as you go along? Only, I think, advice that suggests on the one hand reduced expectations, on the other hand more exalted expectations. To expect romances—with your country, your profession, your family even—to be uninterrupted by doubts, temptations to disloyalty, and disappointments is unrealistic. And unhappiness intensifies as its uninterrupted opposite is anticipated.

On the other hand, there is the persistent tendency to think of one's adult career as the wayward narrative of the journey of a single person who is nothing more than a concatenation of chemical substances whose flight on earth is no more meaningful than the flight of the sparrow. Reflection brings many of us to discern more in life: a grander design, in which what you do matters, not merely to yourself and to your family and fellow citizens, but also to the Maker of us all, whose will be done, which will's august findings will be revealed to my generation soon, to yours much later but no less inevitably; a rendezvous with the sublime, at which time our conduct on earth will be supremely relevant.

Having pursued personal happiness, what might engage those idealistic faculties that have been aroused by your reading, and by our intensifying knowledge that we live in a single world, in which we are intimately involved with one another? Fifteen years ago, on college campuses, there was feverish political activity, most of it designed to disparage the venture we were then engaged in in Vietnam. I was much struck, during those years, by the glide pattern of our retreat from the Wilsonianism reaffirmed by John F. Kennedy in his celebrated Inaugural Address, a commitment to lend all our strength to the spread of freedom abroad. By the late 1960s, we were heading towards a geopolitical, cultural, and moral isolationism. Our retreat from Southeast Asia was much more than a military retreat. If it had been only that, one could with some equanimity have simply concluded that our commitments had outreached our strengths.

But what happened, no doubt in part prompted by consciences hungry for self-justification, was that in order to feel better about our retreat, we nurtured the idea that we had no reliable criteria by which to proclaim our superiority—no grounds, presumably, for judging the work of Thomas Jefferson and Woodrow Wilson to be more elevated than that of Mao Tse-tung and Ho Chi Minh. So that when our men came back from the wars, it was to a miasma of American self-doubt, which has by no means dissipated. It is one thing to be isolationist in the sense that Switzerland is isolationist: isolationist, yet utterly confident of its own well-lodged claims to being a civilized society. It is something else to be isolationist on the grounds that we cannot say, with confidence, that we are advanced in basic ways over cultures that are, yes, less civilized.

People shrink at such sounds, dismissing them as chauvinist. But the opposite of chauvinism, in this case, isn't humility, it is nescience. If we cannot hold up the Bill of Rights over against the Communist Manifesto and declare the one a benchmark of civilization, the other of modern atavism, then learning is really of little use, and you may forget everything you got here at Johns Hopkins that is extrautilitarian in character.

In Vietnam, on the thirtieth anniversary of the victory of General Giap at Dienbienphu, life goes on and is described by Ginetta Sagan of Amnesty International, once a prisoner of the Nazis, later an opponent of American participation in the Vietnam War, now a chronicler aghast at what has happened in Vietnam. Her summary was compressed in one paragraph that appeared in the *Wall Street Journal*: "The situation [in Vietnam today] includes the familiar signposts of Communist repression. Religious worship is persecuted and churches have become warehouses. Private shops have mostly been confiscated, with ethnic Chinese shopkeepers the favorite victims. Several hundred thousand Vietnamese have spent time in the 're-education camps,' and as many as eighty thousand people remain there. The lucky prisoners dig latrines or plant crops. The unlucky clear minefields. Prisoners eat a few vegetables and a bowl of rice or two a day. Anyone who rebels against this regime is quickly punished. Prisoners' arms and legs are bound into contorted positions before they are tossed into metal boxes to bake in the tropical sun. One former prisoner was thrown into an abandoned water well for five days because he sang 'Silent Night' on Christmas Eve. The re-educated . . . are dispatched to New Economic Zones, which are hardscrabble areas where growing even enough food to survive is difficult. Hoang Hue Quynh, a former Communist Party member, now in France, said,

'Today, if Hanoi allowed the people to freely leave the country, even lampposts would apply.'"

I take this moment, even if anxious to avoid the ponderous, simply to gesture, to those who suffer, that there are such as Miss Sagan, who see them, and who cry out loud to express fraternal grief. And to record my own conviction that if there is such a thing as a corporate challenge to American idealism, we cannot accept a better one than to stand fast against the juggernaut of which Vietnam is only one national victim.

A third and final injunction is that you mind your democratic manners. Surveying the primary campaign in New York, James Reston of the *New York Times* wrote, "The Democratic performance was not only a disgrace, but an insult to the voters, and, even worse, an embarrassment to the democratic process." One candidate, in the summary of *Time* magazine, promised a group of Jewish voters more than any Israeli running for public office would dream of doing, including a promise never publicly to criticize the government of Israel. Senator Hart stopped short that day only of submitting to public circumcision, assuming that that was not already done in 1936, if ever it has been established whether Gary Hart was alive in 1936 [he had given conflicting dates of birth]. Senator Mondale associates himself with a domestic-production law that Smoot & Hawley would have balked at. And Jesse Jackson, who used to identify himself with the cause of racial equality, tells us now that he is first and foremost a black, only incidentally an American, thus repudiating entirely the dream of color-blindness celebrated by Martin Luther King.

Professor James MacGregor Burns has written a new book in which he deplores the creeping apathy of American voters, only 40 percent of whom turned out in 1980, down from 60 percent in 1952. One explanation not explored by Professor Burns is that a contempt is generating for the behavior of democracy's practitioners. We are told of the great achievements in the past one hundred years of our schools and colleges, and indeed more Americans by far receive higher education than citizens of any other country; yet during that one hundred years, we traveled from the Lincoln-Douglas debates to the Nixon-Kennedy debates. In our passion for maximizing the franchise, we have tacitly encouraged a level of polemical discourse appropriate rather to a fourteen-year-old voter than to an eighteen-year-old voter. Mayor Jimmy Walker of New York, who during the 1920s distributed without hesitation the favors of Tammany Hall to his friends and cronies, was thought finally to have gone too far when he appointed a renowned mediocrity as judge of the juvenile court in Brooklyn. When accosted with this effrontery, Mayor Walker commented, "The appointment of Judge Hylan means the children can now be tried by their peer." The way we are moving, in the public intercourse, voting might appropriately be restricted to juveniles.

I think we need a Democratic Anti-Defamation League, and I urge you to found an institute to that end, so that even as Johns Hopkins gave graduate work distinction, so will it be said that Johns Hopkins returned distinction to political democracy. The institute would monitor, and hand down grades to, men and women responsible for political utterances—whether delivered over radio or television or before a live audience, or written in books or on billboards. I would like to see your Democratic Anti-Defamation League defend the honor of democracy by attacking those who abuse that venerable convention of self-government by public travesties of orderly thought. How fine if we succeeded in convincing American voters that the index to the political health of the nation was not the density of the vote, but the thoughtfulness of it! Voting is a civic sacrament, which should not be exercised carelessly.

Do you solemnly swear that you will tell the truth, the whole truth, and nothing but the truth, so help you God? is the ritual by which, on the witness stand, we are introduced to gravity. How would the Republic fare if, before voting, one disciplined oneself to ask the question, *Do you solemnly swear to vote for the welfare of the Republic, the whole welfare of the Republic, and nothing but the welfare of the Republic, so help you God?*

I have perhaps overexposed myself in encouraging the formation of a tribunal that hands down judgments on polemical speech.

But, having enjoined you to monitor even my own expressions, I have nothing left to say, save to wish you Godspeed.

THE GENESIS OF BLACKFORD OAKES

A Lecture at the University of Arizona; Tucson, Ariz., October 2, 1984

The invitation to describe the origins of Blackford Oakes, the protagonist of my spy novels, moved me to reminiscence of the publisher's bait, description of the thinking behind the characterization of Oakes, and opinion on the nature of the challenge in modern espionage. I focus on the question of what is distinctive about "the distinctively American male."

I HAVE FREQUENTLY been asked, but did not until recently undertake to answer, what was the genesis of Blackford Oakes, the protagonist of my novels. Critics are divided on the question whether these novels are political. There is a sense in which they are that, though not obtrusively so. Carlyle was correct when he said that politics is the preoccupation of the quarter-educated. But politics is an affliction of this century, in which there is more and more power concentrated in fewer and fewer hands, so that it becomes more and more difficult to keep politics outside in the cold, where one would like it to be; either there, or in the poorhouse, or both.

The historical genesis of Blackford Oakes, to be sure, was nonpolitical.

It was November of 1974 and I had been invited to lunch by a genial editor at Doubleday, my friend Sam Vaughan. He had with him two colleagues, and we enjoyed a vinous lunch with discursive conversation, in the course of which I expressed admiration for a suspense novel I had just finished reading, called *The Day of the Jackal.*

"Why don't you," Sam said, smiling, "write a novel?"

"Why don't you," I replied with that improvisatory wit for which I am renowned, "play a trumpet concerto?" Everyone laughed, sort of; the subject changed; and the next morning on my desk I found a signed contract for a novel.

So I would write a novel. Or attempt to do so.

I arrived in Switzerland for my annual book-writing session with only a single idea in mind. And that idea was to commit literary iconoclasm. I would write a book in which the good guys and the bad guys were actually distinguishable from one another. I took a deep breath and further resolved that the good guys would be—the Americans.

I had recently seen a movie called *Three Days of the Condor.* Perhaps you will remember that Robert Redford, a CIA agent of Restless Intelligence, working in a CIA front in New York City called the American Literary Historical Society, goes out one day to buy a hamburger and comes back to the CIA brownstone to find all nine of his colleagues quite dead. Murdered. By pistols firing ice pellets. In due course we discover that Mr. Big, who ordered the killing, is very high up in government. Indeed, by the law of compound interest, if the movie had lasted another half hour one would have been satisfied only on discovering that the evil spirit behind the killing of Robert Redford's CIA colleagues was the President of the United States or, to be really dramatic and reach all the way up, maybe even Ralph Nader.

Thus the movie went, deep in suspense. It transpired that Mr. Big had made the decision to eliminate all those nice people at the American Literary Historical Society because they were about to stumble onto a contingent CIA operation—by following a lead turned up by Robert Redford's Restless Intelligence.

So finally, in a dramatic sidewalk confrontation, Mr. Jr.-Big—on instructions from Mr. Big—explains to Redford that the unfortunate killings were really all to do with high patriotism, that they were a necessary safeguard against the discovery of a top-secret plan to protect America against a shortage of oil. Stressing the overwhelming importance of Redford's keeping his knowledge to himself, he now invites Redford to come back into the Agency and simply accept the imperatives of life as an intelligence agent in the modern world.

But Redford, taking off his glasses, says, "No, *never.* This very day, I have told everything to . . ." The camera slithers up to a marquee above the two men, and you see the logo of . . . the *New York Times.* The director of *Three Days of the Condor* neglected only to emblazon on it, "Daniel Ellsberg Slept Here."

Mr. Jr.-Big reacts like the witch come into contact with water. He snarls and shivers and slinks away, muttering half desperately,

"Maybe they won't print it!" But Redford has by now seeded the audience with his Restless Intelligence, and we all know that the *New York Times will* print it, and thus we shall all be free.

The film's production notes state, "Over a year ago, Stanley Schneider, Robert Redford, Sidney Pollack, and Dino De Laurentiis decided to create a film that would reflect the climate of America in the aftermath of the Watergate crisis." "The climate of America" is a pretty broad term. They really meant "the climate of America as seen by Jane Fonda, the Institute for Policy Studies, and maybe Jesse Jackson." One recalls Will Rogers returning from the Soviet Union, where he had witnessed a communal bath.

"Did you see all of Russia?" a reporter asked.

"No," Rogers said, weighing his answer carefully. "But I saw all of *parts* of Russia."

Schneider-Redford-Pollack-De Laurentiis had shown us the climate in all of *parts* of America. It was very cold out there.

AND SO I thought to attempt to write a book in which it would never be left in doubt that the CIA is, when all is said and done, not persuasively compared to the KGB. Whatever its failures, the CIA seeks to advance the honorable alternative in the great struggle for the world.

The novelistic urge of the great ideological egalitarians who write books with such titles as *The Ugly American* has been to invest their protagonist in the CIA—or his counterpart in the British MI-5— with appropriately disfiguring personal characteristics. So that the American (or British) spy had become, typically, a paunchy, alcoholic cuckold; moreover, an agent who, late at night when well along in booze, ruminates to the effect that, after all, who really is to judge whether the United States is all that much better than the Soviet Union? The KGB and the CIA, when all is said and done, really engage in the same kind of thing, and what they do defines them, not why they do it, right?

When, having no pre-set idea of where I was going, I sat down in Switzerland to write that first novel, it suddenly occurred to me that it would need a protagonist. The alternative of trying to persuade Doubleday that I might create a new art form and write a novel featuring *nobody* struck me as unprofitable; and so by the end of the day I had created: Blackford Oakes.

A year later, the editor of *Vogue* magazine wrote to me to say that many reviewers had denominated Blackford Oakes as "quintessentially" American. She invited me to explain "the American look." I rejected the invitation, because I reject the very notion of quintessentiality as here applied. You cannot have the quintessential American for the very same reason you cannot have the quintessential apple pie, or the quintessential anything else that is composed of various ingredients. In all composites there has got to be an arrangement of attributes, and no such arrangement can project one quality to the point of distorting others.

So, Blackford Oakes is not the quintessential American, but I fancy he is *distinctively* American, and the first feature of the distinctively American male is, I think, spontaneity—a kind of freshness born of curiosity and enterprise and native wit.

Would you believe that three days after meeting her, Blackford Oakes was in bed with the Queen of England? (Not, I hasten to elucidate, the incumbent queen. Blackford Oakes, as the distinctive American, is a young man of discretion, who sleeps only with fictitious queens, thereby avoiding international incidents.) There is something distinctively, wonderfully American, it struck me, about bedding down a British queen: a kind of arrant but lovable presumption. But always on the understanding that it is done decorously, and that there is no aftertaste of the gigolo in the encounter. In that novel, Queen Caroline was the seducer, Blackford the seduced.

I remember—even now, eight years later—my trepidation when my novel came out in London. The first questioner at the television conference there was, no less, the editor of *The Economist*, Andrew Knight, and he asked me, I thought, a question quite un-English in its lack of circumspection: "Mr. Buckley, would you like to sleep with the queen?"

Now such a question poses quite awful responsibilities. Just to begin with, I am a married man. And then, there being a most conspicuous incumbent queen, one could hardly wrinkle up one's nose as if the question evoked the vision of an evening with Queen Victoria on her Diamond Jubilee. The American with taste has to guard against any lack of gallantry, so that the first order of business becomes the assertion of an emancipating perspective which leads Queen Elizabeth II gently out of the room, lest she be embarrassed. This was accomplished by saying, just a little sleepily, as Blackford Oakes would have done, "Which queen?" And then quickly, before the interrogator could drag his incumbent monarch back into the smoker, "Judging from historical experience, I would need to consult my lawyer before risking an affair with just *any* British queen." The American male must be tactful, and tact consists mostly in changing the subject without its appearing that you have done so as a rebuke.

Blackford Oakes appears on the scene in my first novel at age twenty-three; so I stuck him at Yale, which gave me the advantage of being able to write about a familiar few acres, and, I suppose, Blackford emerged with a few characteristics associated with Yale men.

Like what? Principally, I think, self-confidence; a certain worldliness that is neither bookish nor in any sense of the word antiintellectual. Blackford Oakes is an engineer by training, the kind of engineer who learns how to build bridges, and his nonroyal girlfriend is doing her doctoral dissertation on Jane Austen. *She* is not expected to dwell on her specialty in conversation, let alone show any curiosity about how to build bridges. The American look wears quite offhandedly its special proficiencies: if one is a lawyer, one does not go about sounding like Oliver Wendell Holmes, any more than Charles Lindbergh went about sounding like Charles Lindbergh—although Blackford quite rightly shows a qualified, if not extensive, curiosity about Jane Austen, and probably has read (actually, reread: one never *reads* Jane Austen, one only *rereads* her) *Pride and Prejudice*.

Blackford Oakes is physically handsome. Here I took something of a chance. I decided not to make him routinely good-looking, but startlingly so. I don't mean startling in the sense that, let us say, Elizabeth Taylor is startlingly beautiful. It is hard to imagine a male counterpart for what we understand as pulchritude. An extremely handsome man is not the *equivalent* of an extremely beautiful woman, he is her *complement,* and that is very important to bear in mind in probing the American look—which is not, for example, the same thing as the Italian look. When Schopenhauer exclaimed that a sixteen-year-old girl is the "smash triumph of nature," he was making a cosmic statement that could only have been made about the female sex. So that when I decided that Blackford Oakes should be startlingly handsome, it was required that he be that in a distinctively American way, and what does that mean? Well it doesn't mean you look like Mickey Rooney, obviously. But it doesn't mean you have to look like Tyrone Power, either. I think the startlingly handsome American male is made so not by the regularity of his features, however necessary that regularity may be, but by the special quality of his expression. It has to be for this reason that, flipping past the male models exhibited in the advertising sections of the local newspaper or of *Esquire* magazine, one never finds oneself pausing to think: That man is startlingly handsome. But such an impression *is* taken away, from time to time, from a personal encounter, or from a candid photograph. Because the American look, for the Startlingly Handsome Man, requires: animation, tempered by a certain shyness; a reserve.

I thought of Billy Budd. I have long since forgotten just how Melville actually described him, but Melville communicated that Billy Budd was startlingly handsome. But looks aside, his distinctiveness was not that of Blackford Oakes. Billy Budd is practically an eponym for innocence; purity. Oakes, though far removed from jadedness, is worldly. And then, and then . . .

Billy Budd, alas, is humorless. Correction: not *alas.* "Do not go about as a demagogue, urging a triangle to break out of the prison of its three sides," G. K. Chesterton warned us, "because if you succeed, its life will come to a lamentable end." Give Billy Budd a sense of humor and he shatters in front of you into thousands of little pieces. Blackford Oakes doesn't go about like Wilfrid Sheed's protagonist in *Transatlantic Blues,* or John Gregory Dunne's in *True Confessions,* being hilariously mordant. The American look here is a leavened sarcasm. But careful, now: Escalate sarcasm and you break through the clouds into the ice cold of nihilism, and that is my last word on the American look. The American must *believe*. However discreetly or understatedly. Blackford Oakes believes. He tends to divulge his beliefs in a kind of slouchy, oblique way. But at the margin he is, well—an American, with Christian American predilections; and he knows that, like the clothes he wears so casually, the ideals, and even most of the practices, of his country fit him.

I remember reading with delight a review of that first novel, published in the *Kansas City Star*, written by a professor of English from the University of Missouri, I think it was. I had never heard of the gentleman, but he made it quite clear that he had spent a considerable part of his adult life abominating me and my works and my opinions. He was manifestly distressed at not quite disliking my first novel. He salved his conscience by concluding, "The hero of *Saving the Queen*, Mr. Blackford Oakes, is tall, handsome, witty, agreeable, compassionate, and likable, from which at least we can take comfort from knowing that the book is not autobiographical."

WHAT IS ATTEMPTED, in the tales of Blackford Oakes, is to make the point, so difficult for the Western mind to comprehend, that counterintelligence and espionage, conducted under Western auspices, are not exercises in conventional political geometry. They are a moral art.

Consider one hypothetical dilemma. I give you a question and ask that you wrestle with it, confining yourself, if you can, within the maxims of the conventional morality.

Question: *Is it wrong to effect the execution of a chief of state with whom you are not at war?*

Answer: Yes, it is wrong.

Is it wrong to countenance a destructive event of such magnitude as conceivably to trigger a world war?

Yes, it is wrong.

What then do you call it when it appears to rational men that the second injunction cannot be observed save by defying the first?

Scene: Uganda. Colonel Idi Amin has got possession of a nuclear bomb and plans at midnight to dispatch a low-flying plane to drop that bomb on Jerusalem. A CIA agent communicates to Washington that Idi Amin will lie in the cross-hairs of his rifle at the airport before the bomber is dispatched. Should he squeeze the trigger?

There are those, and Blackford Oakes is one of them, who would answer that morally wrenching question by saying two things: (1) As to the particular question, yes: authorize the agent to shoot, in order to abort the destruction of Jerusalem, and all that might then follow. But (2) do not require as a condition of this decision that rules should subsequently be written that attempt to make lapidary statutory distinctions. It is not possible to write such judgments into law, any more than to specify to the artist the exact arrangement of circumstances that call for a daub of Prussian blue, or to the composer the exact rules that admit the striking of an A augmented seventh chord.

Blackford Oakes lives in an age when what matters most is the survival of basic distinctions. These distinctions tell us that, notwithstanding that America faces grievous problems, even so, we are sharply to be distinguished from those awful political cultures in the Soviet Union and the People's Republic of China, in which human beings are treated as mere aggregations of random biological circumstance, to be dealt with according as said human phenomena further, or hinder, the surrealistic visions of totalitarian superpowers that acknowledge no role whatever for morality in the formulation of public policy. And any failure by beneficiaries of the Free World to recognize what it is that we have here, over against what it is that they would impose upon us, amounts to moral and intellectual nihilism: far more incriminating of our culture than any transgression against eristic scruples of the kind that preoccupy so many of our moralists concerning the protocols that properly bind the CIA.

Blackford Oakes has weaknesses spiritual and corporal. But a basic assumption guides him. It is that the survival of everything we cherish depends on the survival of the culture of liberty; and that this hangs on our willingness to defend this extraordinary country of ours, so awfully mixed up, so much of the time; so schizophrenic in its understanding of itself and its purposes; so crazily indulgent of its legion of wildly ungovernable miscreants—to defend it at all costs. With it all, this idealistic republic is the finest bloom of nationhood in all recorded time, and save only that God may decide that the land of the free and the home of the brave has outrun its license on history, we Americans must contend, struggle, and if necessary fight for America's survival.

WALTZING AT WEST 44TH STREET

Remarks on the Launching of *US-44;* the U.S. Merchant Marine Academy, Kings Point, N.Y., May 24, 1985

As an old salt I was asked to give the dedication at the launching of the New York Yacht Club's challenger for the America's Cup, aiming to compete with Australia two years later in Perth. The goal: to win back the Cup, lost in 1983 for the first time since the race's inception in 1851. It was a brilliant spring day, high noon, high festivity, high hopes.

ABOUT FIFTEEN YEARS AGO I attended with my wife a state dinner at the White House—in fact, for us, the first. I was not intimidated by the presence of our host, the President of the United States, whom I had met here and there when he was engaged in climbing the grimier rungs that led to that high office. But the prospect of being presented to him by the chief of protocol was positively unnerving. Getting dressed a half hour earlier, across the street at the Hay–Adams, I said to my wife, "You do realize that the chief of protocol is Bus Mosbacher, who won the America's Cup."

To which she replied, "You evidently don't realize that you have told me that five times in the last five days."

It was with great awe that I took the hand of Bus Mosbacher, staring at him as I suppose I'd have stared at Christopher Columbus, or Galileo. You see, in those days I used to do ocean racing quite regularly, and hard though we tried, we never managed, somehow, to come in with the winners. I remember, after my fifth Bermuda race, being asked by a reporter what was my ambition and replying disconsolately, "My ambition is to beat at least one boat." And indeed, the sum-

mer before, arriving at three o'clock in the morning at the finish line
in Halifax, in a race from Marblehead, I saw a ray of light coming
from a sailboat ten yards behind us. The light lingered over our stern,
descrying the name of our vessel, and then traveled up the mainsail to
check our racing number. Then I heard the unmistakable voice of F.
Lee Bailey say, "My God. Even Buckley beat us." I learned years later
that he sold his boat the following week.

I managed, in the receiving line, to shake the awesome hand that
had guided the tiller that in 1962 had defeated the Australian challenger; and then to greet the president; and then to greet the guest of
honor, who by ironic masterstroke was the prime minister of
Australia, Mr. John Gorton. I remember thinking that surely
President Nixon should have presented the prime minister to Mr.
Mosbacher, rather than the other way around. So you have some idea
of the awe I feel for the company I am keeping today.

I have heard many gibes about the high cost of asserting what is
obviously the providential right of the New York Yacht Club, with the
distinguished assistance of the United States Merchant Marine
Academy, to claim the America's Cup, but of course one hears that
kind of thing all the time. It was, I think, thirty years ago that I became a member of the New York Yacht Club, and my sponsor, pointing to the cup, said to me, "You know, more money has been spent
attempting to win that cup than was spent on the Spanish Armada."
Well no, I hadn't known this, nor did I know what was the anticipated reply to such an observation.

I remember groaning, at Cape Canaveral in July of 1969, when
one of those awful people who write editorials said that for the cost of
Apollo 11, which was going up the following day to land on the moon,
we could build four thousand eighty-two lower-middle-income
dwelling units.

But one cannot parse life's enterprises in any common coin. If
Vladimir Horowitz had exercised his fingers on a sewing machine
instead of on a keyboard, stroke for stroke, he might have stitched a
blanket that would keep eighty-two thousand Eskimos plus Mary
McGrory warm on a cold winter's night. The sailing sport is an

appanage of a class of enthusiasts who are aristocratically concerned with excellence at sea. For them—for you—no sacrifice is implausible, whether measured in savings invested in the architecture and engineering of a vessel, or in hours spent cultivating the intellectual and physical skills necessary to overcome marginally the resistance to speed at sea, the margin in question distinguishing you from the boat that, two years hence, you will have left behind. I think it's a sign of great spiritual health that even as some men risk their lives to ascend a mountain peak, others devote a part of their lives and the produce of a part of their lives to designing and manning the fastest vessel of its size in the world. In John Kolius you know you have someone appropriately fanatical to pursue your designs. In Sparkman & Stephens you have the services of Stradivarius. And in Bus Mosbacher you have the shadow of the man who reminds us that he wasn't in command when we lost the Cup, which we shall now retrieve, after the expeditionary force leaves here to travel to Perth in Australia.

We will get the Cup back, but we will do this without severing diplomatic bonds with that young, robust, alluring country whose prime minister our sometime chief of protocol took such splendid care of back in 1969.

It happened that seated next to me at the White House banquet was a young Australian diplomat on the staff of the prime minister who served as his speechwriter. This he confided to me after a few bottles of wine, White House protocol having neglected only to remember to make draft beer available to that evening's guests. And so, when Prime Minister Gorton began a robust and affectionate speech about U.S.-Australian relations, his speechwriter's face was caught in contortions of bliss, as he heard pronounced, one after another, the words he had written. And towards the end of the toast he dug his elbow quietly into my side and whispered, "Listen! Listen! Listen now . . ." Whereupon the prime minister, reaching for his glass to conclude his toast, declaimed to his distinguished audience, "Continue as you are, my American friends, friends of liberty, and friends of progress, and we"—my Australian speechwriter closed his eyes now in anticipation of the rhetorical coda, "we will go a-waltzing, Matilda, with you."

Well now, the sentiment was lovely; the cultural embrace between the two peoples, enduring.

But on one point, there remains the need for a little clarification.

The America's Cup belongs back here. Not only back here in America, but back here inside that glass case, in that nice little understated room four, five steps down from the landing on 44th Street, because without it we are very lonely. Indeed, I myself have pledged that until we have it back, I shan't waltz at all, let alone with kangaroos.

One day in February of 1987, at about four in the afternoon, in the waters off Perth, the Australians will know what it was that Cinderella experienced. It is a pity that Australia's reintroduction to realism must come at the hands of, among others, the man who served as chief of protocol when the Australian prime minister was with us: but you see, the protocols of the America's Cup are that it belongs in America, so that we are here engaged in nothing less, and nothing more, than a venture in repatriation. Here's to *US-44*. May she bring us back what we have come to regard as an American birthright, so that my wife and I can waltz again, under the Milky Way, when all is right once more on 44th Street in Manhattan.

THE BLOOD OF OUR FATHERS
RAN STRONG

Remarks (excerpted) at *National Review's* Thirtieth Anniversary Dinner;
the Plaza Hotel, New York, December 5, 1985

---

*I had been asked by the White House to make every effort to guard
against too long an evening, given that President Reagan was there as
guest of honor. I wrote a brief speech, talking on dark subjects but letting
in light.*

XPRESSIONS OF GRATITUDE can be most awfully trying to the
ear of an audience, generally captive. But the act of gratitude
nowadays is probably more often neglected than overdone. We
published recently, in *National Review*, an essay on patriotism, in
which the author made the same point rather more ornately than
Edmund Burke did when he observed that a country, in order to be
loved, must be lovely. Professor Thomas Pangle concluded that there
is plenty in our Constitution that justifies love of country; and,
indeed, if the life we live here is not significantly different from the
life they live over there, then George Kennan & Company are correct
that we oughtn't to keep nuclear weapons in our deterrent inventory.

A year before *National Review* was founded, I spent an evening
with Whittaker Chambers, and he asked me, half provocatively, half
seriously, what exactly it was that my prospective journal would seek
to save. I trotted out a few platitudes, of the sort one might expect
from a twenty-eight-year-old fogy, about the virtues of a free society.
He wrestled with me by obtruding the dark historicism for which he
had become renowned. *Don't you see?* he said. *The West is doomed, so
that any effort to save it is correspondingly doomed to failure.* I drop this
ink stain on the bridal whiteness of this fleeted evening only to
acknowledge soberly that we are still a long way from establishing, for
sure, that Whittaker Chambers was wrong. But that night, challenged
by his pessimism, I said to him that if it were so that providence had
rung up our license on liberty, stamping it as expired, the Republic

deserved a journal that would argue the historical and moral case that we *ought* to have survived: that, weighing the alternative, the culture of liberty *deserves* to survive. So that even if the worst were to happen, the journal in which I hoped he would collaborate might serve, so to speak, as the diaries of Anne Frank had served, as absolute, dispositive proof that *she* should have survived, in place of her tormentors—who ultimately perished. In due course that argument prevailed, and Chambers joined the staff.

To do what, exactly? The current issue of *National Review* discusses of course the summit conference, the war in Afghanistan, Sandinista involvement in Colombia; but speaks, also, of the attrition of order and discipline in so many of our public schools, of the constitutional improvisations of Mr. Rostenkowski, of the shortcomings of the movies *Eleni* and *Macaroni*, of the imperatives of common courtesy, of the relevance of Malthus, of prayer and the unthinkable, of the underrated legacy of Herman Kahn. The connections between some of these subjects and the principal concerns of *National Review* are greatly attenuated. Attenuated, yes, but not nonexistent: because freedom anticipates, and contingently welcomes and profits from, what happens following the calisthenics of the free mind, always supposing that that freedom does not lead the mind to question the very value of freedom, or the authority of civil and moral virtues so to designate themselves. There are enough practitioners in this room to know that a journal concerned at once to discharge a mission and to serve its readers needs to be comprehensively concerned with the flora and fauna of cultural and political life. We have done this in *National Review*, and because we have done this, you are here—our tactical allies, most of you; our strategic allies, all of you. . . .

Mr. President, fifteen years ago I was interviewed by *Playboy* magazine. Towards the end of the very long session I was asked the question, Had I, in middle age, discovered any novel sensual sensation? I replied that, as a matter of fact, a few months earlier I had traveled to Saigon and, on returning, had been summoned by President Nixon to the Oval Office to report my impressions. "My novel sensual sensation," I told *Playboy*, "is to have the President of the United States take notes while you are speaking to him."

You need take no notes tonight, Mr. President. What at *National Review* we labor to keep fresh, alive, deep, you are intuitively drawn to. As an individual you incarnate American ideals at many levels. As the final responsible authority, in any hour of great challenge, we depend on you. I was nineteen years old when the bomb went off over Hiroshima, and last week I turned sixty. During the interval I have lived a free man in a free and sovereign country, and this only because we have husbanded a nuclear deterrent, and made clear our disposition to use it if necessary. I pray that my son, when he is sixty, and your son, when he is sixty, and the sons and daughters of our guests tonight will live in a world from which the great ugliness that has scarred our century has passed. Enjoying their freedoms, they will be grateful that, at the threatened nightfall, the blood of their fathers ran strong.

THE DISTINGUISHED MR. BUCKLEY

Remarks Introducing Christopher Buckley at the East Side Conservative Club;
New York, June 24, 1986

A little paternal haiku.

I AM VERY HAPPY to be here again in the company of the most distinguished conservative club in the United States, unless there's a more distinguished one I haven't heard of, which is unthinkable. Which reminds me of an episode recounted to me by my late mentor, Professor Willmoore Kendall. A humble priest, calculating that the mortgage on his church would be paid off at the end of the month, called on his rather pompous bishop to ask whether he would speak at the mortgage-burning ceremony. The bishop replied, with a heavy sigh of self-pity, that he would come, provided the priest could not manage to find somebody "less distinguished" to come instead. The priest searched high and low, but finally was forced to redeem the bishop's pledge, and His Grace reluctantly appeared. In introducing him to the parish, the priest apologetically stuttered out the story and then said, "And so, ladies and gentlemen, having looked high and low and failed to find *anyone* less distinguished, I present to you our bishop."

The Lord specializes in humbling the proud. As a father, last spring I was ecstatic to learn that, on the following Sunday, my son would visit with me on the best-seller list of the *New York Times Book Review,* where I keep a little apartment in which I reside for a few weeks every year.

The following week, looking down at the best-seller list, I saw my son's name: but my own was no longer there. I had been ousted. By my own flesh and blood. I knew how King Lear felt. I marched over to Dan Mahoney and said, You know that will I made out a few years ago? Well, I want to make it over. Every time you see the name Christopher Buckley, substitute Serph Maltese [Dan Mahoney's successor as chairman of the New York State Conservative Party].

But then I thought: The Lord can be wonderfully playful. I have no doubt what happened. The guardian angel of the *New York Times* was neglecting his duties one afternoon, and he picked up a copy of [my son's novel] *The White House Mess.* He roared with laughter— uncontrollable laughter—and he pushed the button on his desk and said: "Put the author of *The White House Mess* on the *New York Times* best-seller list."

An intimidated voice came back: "But, sir, there is *already* a Buckley on the list."

The guardian angel said: "Remove *that* Buckley. The one I'm talking about is more distinguished."

Well, this time—just this one time—the guardian angel of the *New York Times* did the right thing. You will get a specimen of *The White House Mess* from my distinguished son, Christopher, here introduced by his proud father.

On Her Way to the Cross

A Eulogy for Clare Boothe Luce; St. Patrick's Cathedral, New York,
October 13, 1987

She had asked that I and her stepson, Henry Luce III, be her eulogists.
The memorial Mass was celebrated by Cardinal O'Connor.

I FIRST LAID EYES on her in 1948. She was speaking to the
Republican Convention, and she said of Henry Wallace, who was
running for president on the Progressive ticket, that he was "Joe
Stalin's Mortimer Snerd." They all rocked with laughter.

I saw her next at her quarters on Fifth Avenue. She had telephoned and asked if I could come by to discuss the worsening crisis
under President Diem in South Vietnam. I was there at four, and she
opened the door with paintbrushes in one hand. I told her by all
means to finish what she was doing before we got down to the problems of Southeast Asia, and so she led me happily to her atelier. But
instead of herself painting, she undertook to teach me, there and
then, how to use acrylics, launching me on a mute inglorious career.

Two months later there came in the mail at my office a big manuscript pulsating with scorn and indignation over the treatment of
President Diem by Washington, with special focus on Diem's sister-
in-law, Madame Nhu. She called it "The Lady's Not for Burning." I
put the article on the cover of the next issue of *National Review* and
had a startled call from the press editor of *Newsweek*. He wished to
know how it came about that . . . Clare Boothe Luce . . . was writing
for . . . *National Review*. I told him solemnly (I could manage a hidden smile, since we were speaking on the telephone): *Tous les beaux
esprits se rencontrent*—roughly translated, Beautiful spirits seek each
other out. The following day, President Diem and his brother, the
Dragon Lady's husband, were murdered. The only happy result of
that Byzantine mess, for me, was that I was never again out of touch
with Clare Boothe Luce, for whom, months ago, my wife and I

scheduled a dinner—at her request—to be held here, in New York, on September 29, which turned out to be ten days before she died.

I have thought a lot about her in the past few days. The last time we stayed with her in Honolulu we were met at the airport by her gardener, Tom. There were twelve of us for dinner. We were seated in her lanai, being served cocktails, while Tom was quietly lighting the outdoor gas lamps. Suddenly he fell. In minutes the ambulance arrived. Surrounded by Clare's anxious, silent guests, Tom was given artificial respiration. Clare gripped my hand and whispered to me, "Tom is going to die." There was dumb grief in her voice; and absolute finality. Two hours later, the hospital confirmed that Tom was dead. Clare said good night to her guests, and departed to keep the widow company.

Clare knew when an act was done. In so many respects, she was always a woman resigned.

I think back on her career. . . . Look, you are a young, beautiful woman. Pearl Harbor was only yesterday, and you have spent several months poking about disconsolate Allied fronts in Asia and the Mideast. You have written a long analysis, cruelly objective about Allied disorder. It would be infinitely embarrassing to the Allies and correspondingly useful to the Axis powers. On the last leg of your journey, a sharp-eyed British customs officer in Trinidad insists on examining your papers. His eyes pass over your journal; he reads in it, snaps it shut, and calls in British security, which packs you off under house arrest. What do you do?

Well, if you are Clare Luce, you get in touch with the American consulate. The American consulate, sizing up the situation, gets a message through to your husband, Henry Luce. Mr. Luce calls General Donovan, the head of U.S. intelligence. General Donovan arranges to appoint you *retroactively* an intelligence official of the United States government. The British have to agree to let you fly to New York, and there they turn your report over to the British ambassador. He is so shaken by it that he instantly advises Winston Churchill of its contents. Churchill pauses from the war effort to cable you his regards, and meanwhile you have been asked by the Joint

Chiefs of Staff to brief them on your analyses, which, suitably bowd-lerized, appear in successive issues of *Life* magazine and are a jour-nalistic sensation.

Thus passeth a week in the life of the deceased.

The excitement and the glamor, the distinctions and the awards, a range of successes unequaled by any other American woman. But ten years later Clare was writing not about tanks and planes, but about the saints. She began coquettishly by quoting Ambrose Bierce, who had defined a saint as a "dead sinner, revised and edited."

But quickly Clare Luce's tone of voice altered. She wrote that perspectives are very much changed now. "Augustine," she wrote, "came into a pagan world turning to Christianity, as we have come into a Christian world turning towards paganism."

St. Augustine fascinated her. She wrote that "he explored his interior suffering with the same passionate zeal with which he had explored exterior pleasures, and he quailed to the depths of his being at the [projected] cost of reforming himself. 'These petty toys of toys, these vanities of vanities, my long-time fascinations, still held me. They plucked at the garment of my flesh, and murmured caressing-ly: Dost thou cast us off? From this moment on shall this delight or that be no more lawful for thee forever? Dost thou think that thou canst live without these things?' And Augustine, haunted by truth, hounded by love, harried by grace, 'had nothing at all to answer but those dull and dreary words: Anon, Anon; or Presently; or Leave me alone but a little while. . . .'"

Clare Luce knew that it was truly miserable to fail to enjoy some of life's pleasures. When asked which priest she wished to confess to, on entering the Catholic Church, she had said, "Just bring me some-one who has seen the rise and fall of empires." Some years later, told by someone how utterly admirable were the characters in her play, *The Women*, she replied in writing, "The women who inspired this play deserved to be smacked across the head with a meat axe, and that, I flatter myself, is exactly what I smacked them with. They are vulgar and dirty-minded and alien to grace, and I would not, if I could, which I hasten to say I cannot, cross their obscenities with a wit which is foreign to them or gild their futilities with the glamor which by birth and breeding and performance they do not possess." So much for the beautiful people.

"Stooping a dozen times a day quietly"—Clare was writing now about another saint, Thérèse of Lisieux—"she picked up and carried the splinters of the Cross that strewed her path as they strew ours. And when she had gathered them all up, she had the material of a cross of no inconsiderable weight. The 'little way of the Cross' is not the 'way of a little cross.'"

One of Clare's biographers, a friend since childhood, wrote ten years ago about a trip with her, visiting first The Citadel in Charleston, and then Mepkin, which used to be the Luces' Southern retreat. "Here," Wilfrid Sheed wrote, "the welcome is very effusive, in the manner of priests in old movies . . . and it looks for an uneasy moment as if they are buttering up the patron.

"But Trappists are tricky. Being released from almost perpetual silence by guests, the talk bubbles out gratefully like fizz from a bottle. As this subsides, they turn out to be quite urbane and judicious talkers. . . . They seem genuinely to love Clare, [and] she considers them her last family. I have never seen her more relaxed."

"After her daughter's death," Sheed continued, "Clare could no longer bear to go to Mepkin for pleasure, and [giving it away to a religious order] was an ingenious way of keeping it and letting it go at the same time. The expansionist abbot of Gethsemani, Kentucky, was only too happy to take it, and I dimly remember the Luces' ironic discussion of this back in 1949 while the deal was being completed. They were onto the abbot's game but did not think less of a priest for being a shrewd businessman. And what better way to retire the place that young Ann Brokaw had loved more than any other in the world?

"Clare immediately moved both her daughter's and her mother's remains to Mepkin, where they now share adjoining graves. And then, to everybody's surprise, it turned out, sometime later, that Presbyterian Harry had decided to join them, and he was buried in the middle, after a nervous ecumenical service. The cost-conscious abbot of the moment suggested a double tombstone with Clare's name on it too—cutting off, as she noted, all possibilities of future husbands or new religions"—at this point she must have given off that wonderful, wry nasal laugh.

LAST WEDNESDAY, in Washington, Clare's doctor confided to the White House that Clare would not live out the week, and suggested that no doubt she would be pleased by a telephone call. The president called that night. Her attendant announced to her who it was on the telephone. Clare Luce shook her head. You see, she would not speak to anyone she could not entertain, and she could no longer do this. The call was diplomatically turned aside. The performer knew she had given her last performance, but at least she had never failed.

And then last Sunday, her tombstone at Mepkin no longer sat over an empty grave. She is there with Harry. Over the graves is "a shady tree sculpted above the names, and to either side, her mother, Ann Clare, and her daughter, Ann Clare, in a grove of oak and cypress and Spanish moss running down to the Cooper River."

When Wilfrid Sheed wrote those lines, ten years ago, he quoted Abbot Anthony telling him quietly as they walked away, "She's taking it pretty well this year. She's usually very disturbed by this."

Clare Luce, now at Mepkin finally, is no longer disturbed. It is only we who are disturbed, Hank Luce above all, and her friends; sad, so sad without her, yet happy for her, embarked finally, after stooping so many times to pick up so many splinters, on her way to the Cross.

OUT OF OPPRESSION, A POLITICAL POET

Remarks (excerpted) Introducing Vladimir Bukovsky at the Ethics and Public
Policy Center's Shelby Cullom Davis Award Dinner; Washington, D.C.,
November 17, 1987

---

*A tribute to a heroic Soviet dissenter and a reflection on the diplomatic
consternation caused by his meeting at the White House with President
Carter ten years earlier.*

I AM EXPECTED, as master of ceremonies, to dilate at this point for
a moment or two on the motto of the Ethics and Public Policy
Center, which is "Values Have Consequences."

I don't think anyone doubts that this is so, but it is also possible
that, without giving the matter sufficient thought, we have subscribed
to institutional arrangements that tend to dilute, rather than to
enhance, the potency of the values we seek to promote.

My wife and I live, during February and March, in Switzerland,
and for several years we were regularly visited by the United States
representative to the Commission on Human Rights, which convenes
in Geneva for several weeks during January and February.

The first U.S. commissioner to visit us in Rougemont was Allard
Lowenstein. The day he arrived he was breathless with enthusiasm.
Granted, that does not isolate any day in the life of my late beloved
friend, as he was always breathless with enthusiasm.

But on this day, in March 1977, he reported that he had given a
speech in Geneva in which he mentioned the Soviet Union as a regular malefactor in the field of human rights.

Having served as a public member in the General Assembly of
the United Nations, I knew what risks he ran in criticizing the Soviet
Union. It wasn't that he might be mugged by a Soviet representative—no, the likely mugger would be the State Department bureaucracy. It had been accepted years earlier that criticism of the Soviet
Union, delivered at an international forum, was probably unproductive, and certainly in bad taste.

Allard told me that he had submitted his speech to his immediate superior, Ambassador Andrew Young, timing the transmission cunningly so as to be certain that his old friend would see the speech only after it had been delivered.

The whole matter of Lowenstein's rogue behavior in Geneva was taken to the State Department, where Secretary Vance stared at the transcript—whether speechless or not, my sources have not revealed to me. But the matter actually went to the White House, and a summit conference considered the question.

"What happened?" I asked Al, breathless now myself.

"Well," Lowenstein said, "they said okay, okay this *one* time—you see, I managed a denunciation of South Africa and of Chile in the same speech. But then they said—now Bill, what I am telling you now is absolutely confidential, you understand?"

I told him I did understand, and until tonight I have never mentioned what he went on to say.

"There is one absolute prohibition. It was relayed to me. Under no circumstances am I to mention the name of Vladimir Bukovsky."

We recall that in the first blushes of his presidency, well before he discovered the nobility of the leaders of Poland and Rumania, President Carter had met with Bukovsky in the White House, and those legions in the world we especially care about were wild with joy. The contrast with President Ford's refusal to greet Solzhenitsyn was widely remarked.

But what was not anticipated was the hysterical indignation of Official Moscow. At about that time, President Carter had sent over an enticing basket of disarmament proposals, which Brezhnev returned to Washington before even, so to speak, they had passed through Soviet customs. It was widely suggested that this setback in the campaign for "peace with honor" was a retaliation against Mr. Carter's meeting with Mr. Bukovsky.

That, so soon afterwards, our representative on the Human Rights Commission should be forbidden to mention the name of one of the bravest men alive, a noble survivor of Soviet sadism, suggests that our concern for human rights and our institutional obligations proceed without reciprocating gears. It is perhaps true that the President of the United States cannot on Monday morning convene with the head of the Soviet Union, seeking an arrangement of common interests, and on Monday afternoon meet with the press to describe the evil empire of his guest. But we need to probe the axioms of postwar diplomacy. We have for the most part treated the Soviet leader as, so to speak, the leader of the Blue Team, with whom we are engaging in fraternal international exercises. Inevitably we sacrifice the architectural integrity of our position. It boils down to this, and it is nowhere more appropriate to say it than under the auspices of the Ethics and Public Policy Center: Our values are civilized, theirs uncivilized. That our values are widely neglected in practice does not affect the point. We honor the Word, and seek to live by it. They dishonor the Word, and scorn the very concept of it.

Even so, they manage to nurture aberrations, among them a princely figure whom we are gathered tonight to honor. Even as grinding adversity could produce Dr. Johnson, so grinding oppression can produce a political poet. I am honored to be a part of any ceremony of which Vladimir Bukovsky is the principal.

The Massive Eminence
Of Dr. Sakharov

Remarks (excerpted) Introducing Andrei Sakharov at the Ethics and Public
Policy Center's Shelby Cullom Davis Award Dinner; the Washington Hilton,
Washington, D.C., November 16, 1988

---

*A brief levity, and then the momentous event, an introduction of Andrei
Sakharov, in the same room with Edward Teller, whom he met for the
first time a half hour before the dinner. Spooky background: Sakharov,
on his return from internal exile in Gorki, denounced the anti-missile program (SDI) of President Reagan. Informed elements in Washington
surmised that Sakharov did not know the extent to which his own countrymen were engaged in attempting such technology. The covert mission
was to hand over to him, translated into the Russian language, documents
that would apprise him of events in his own homeland. The design: that
he should reconsider his public discouragement of our pursuit of a technology that, we hoped, would diminish the threat of those weapons he
(along with Dr. Teller) had helped to devise.*

*It is not known whether the information slipped to him in the course
of the evening influenced his policy recommendations. Within a year of
this event—on November 9, 1989—the Berlin Wall came down; five
weeks after that, Sakharov died.*

I HAVE VERY happy memories of my two previous evenings at your
dinner: to be sure, evenings not without engaging and interesting
flukes. It was here on November 17, 1986, that President Reagan
whispered to me during the initial proceedings that his only complaint against his staff was that they tended to over-
protect him. The next day, the Iran-Contra scandal broke. And then
there was the night when one of our guests was Paul Nitze, whom
Charlton Heston persisted in addressing as Mr. Nietzsche, causing
Mr. Nitze little by little, as I observed him, to wonder whether arms
control was worth all that trouble.

This is a dramatic evening. We will hear from the gentleman who
put together the hydrogen bomb in behalf of the West, and the

gentleman who put together the hydrogen bomb in behalf of the East and who, to say the least, has mixed feelings about it all. That he is here this evening with us and is free to return to the Soviet Union is a tribute to the indomitability of his spirit, and perhaps also to the creeping realization by at least one leader of the Soviet Union that it is no longer as easy, when dealing with obtrusive Russian saints, as simply to shoot them.

No doubt tonight we will learn a great deal about what has become the principal problem among nations, namely how to keep Dr. Teller's bombs from landing on Moscow, always assuming the inconceivable, namely that they should be dispatched on such a mission; and how to keep Dr. Sakharov's bombs from landing on Washington, to assume something just a little bit less inconceivable.

Well, we wish Dr. Sakharov everything in the world he wants, but we don't propose to give him as a souvenir from America, to take back to Moscow, a lapsed resolution to proceed with our SDI. . . .

WE ARE GREATLY honored tonight by the presence with us of Andrei Sakharov. The totalitarian century has created many heroes, but few are destined to live forever in the memory. Obviously Dr. Sakharov's initial distinction was his intellectual endowments, which made him one of the leading creative scientists in the world.

I have mentioned what everybody knows, namely his role in the evolution of nuclear physics in the Soviet Union. More important by far than his scientific abilities was his great spirit, that massive eminence that permitted him, an almost inconceivable twenty years ago, to challenge the totalitarian premises of Soviet society.

His wasn't merely one blast, followed by a return to scientific isolation. Month after month he challenged Soviet leaders to grant freedom and introduce democratic values. At about the same time, he was (a) awarded the Nobel Peace Prize, and (b) sent off to live in internal exile in the Soviet industrial city of Gorki, a metropolis forbidden to foreign visitors and, one gathers from a description of its delights, a city that should be forbidden to the proletariat.

He was there for five years, in sickness and in health, with his devoted family, in only attenuated touch with the rest of the world, the object of routine harassment and torment. Mr. Gorbachev brought him back to Moscow, and there Dr. Sakharov continues the struggle.

Ladies and gentlemen, one of the most courageous men in the world, our esteemed guest Dr. Andrei Sakharov.

Towards a Recovery of Gratitude

Remarks (excerpted) at the Intercollegiate Studies Institute's Thirty-Fifth Anniversary Dinner; the Mayflower Hotel, Washington, D.C., November 29, 1988

At a seminar on the topic "Sources of Renewal: The Permanent Things and the Recovery of Man," a reminiscence about the founding of the Intercollegiate Studies Institute (originally named the Intercollegiate Society of Individualists) and an invocation of the need for gratitude.

F RANK CHODOROV PUBLISHED, about forty years ago, a pamphlet called *A Fifty-Year Plan*. He calculated that at least a half century would be needed to displace the dominant shibboleths of socialism. That pamphlet was greeted so enthusiastically that he set out to organize a society to further its aims. Organizing anything was alien to the vaguely anarchic spirit of Frank Chodorov, and so he told me one day that I would be the president of the Intercollegiate Society of Individualists. It was my habit in those days to do anything Frank asked, and so for a while I was president of ISI. Then one day I got a note from him, a note that sticks easily to the memory. It said, "Dear Bill: You're fired. I've decided a Jew will do better as president of ISI, so I have appointed myself. Love, Frank."

He reigned for a very little while before he fell ill and became dispirited: but, with help from providence, he gave the organization a fresh president. Not Jewish, to be sure, which may be why ISI is always broke. But so are we all always broke, with the possible exception of Ed Feulner, who renounced the vows of poverty some years ago. In any case, Victor [Milione] set out, in his quiet way, to be of service to a half century's young men and women. He didn't make it through the fifty years, which is why the resourceful, witty, learned, and imperious Bob Reilly is here. The idea is that by the year 2003, Frank Chodorov's Fifty-Year Plan will have been consummated. . . .

In reflecting on the theme of recovery, I thought to point to the recovery of a faculty conspicuous for its torpor.

It is of course true that there is much to be discouraged by. But it is true also that we have only to pick up this morning's newspaper— riots threatened and thwarted in Algeria, starvation in Ethiopia and the Sudan, a purge threatened in Yugoslavia, the prospect of military government in convulsed Armenia, a probable chemical-warfare plant in Libya, renewed activity by the Khmer Rouge in Cambodia, the eternal insecurity of life in Russia and in China—to know that, as the British poet wrote a hundred years ago, "Westward look, the land is bright." Almost surrealistically bright. Plagued, yes, by vicissitude; but, nevertheless, the Republic for which we stand, as schoolchildren in Massachusetts aren't supposed to say. My point is that we need to cultivate the faculty for gratitude.

When I was thirteen years old I was chaperoned here & there, along with two sisters of about the same age, around the environs of London. My music teacher, whom I loved and still do, was by my side when I went to the counter of a little souvenir shop in Stratford-upon-Avon and paid out three or four shillings for Shakespearean sundries I had picked out. The elderly lady behind the counter took my money, returned me some change, and then withdrew from the display case a tiny one-square-inch edition of *Romeo and Juliet* and, smiling, gave it to me. A gift. I took the sixpence she had just given me in change, and deposited it in her hand: a reciprocal gift. Once outside, I received a resonant rebuke from my teacher. I had done an offensive thing, she informed me. A gift is a gift, she said. I must learn to accept gifts. They are profaned by any attempt at automatic reciprocity.

Many years went by. Then, just last summer, I received one day on my trusty MCI mail a typed message from a friend who is also a computer specialist. He said that the retrieval system I had been yearning for, one which would permit me to locate individual book titles in my library via my computer, had been completed: he had worked on it in the interstices of his busy schedule for over a month. "It is yours," his message read on the screen, "as a belated Christmas present." Impulsively I tapped out and flashed back that I insisted he send me a bill for professional services. One minute later, my mind traveled back and I was again a little boy at a souvenir store in Stratford, embarrassing a kindly woman who had made an act of generosity. There and then I shed the grown-up equivalent of a thirteen-year-old's tears at my awkwardness.

But, as I reflect on it, there is a distinction. The gift repaid in roughly equivalent tender is corrupted. It ceases to be a gift, and the philanthropic impulse is traduced. The unrequited gift is, in Burke's phrase, one of the unbought graces of life.

Moreover, a country—a civilization—that gives us such gifts as we dispose of cannot be repaid in kind. There is no way in which we can give to the United States a present of a bill of rights in exchange for its having given us the Bill of Rights.

Our offense, however—the near universal offense, remarked by Ortega y Gasset as the fingerprint of the masses in revolt—is that of the Westerner, rich or poor, learned or ignorant, who accepts without any thought the patrimony we all enjoy, those of us who live in the Free World. We are left with the numbing, benumbing thought that we owe nothing to Plato and Aristotle, nothing to the prophets who wrote the Bible, nothing to the generations who fought for freedoms activated in the Bill of Rights. We are basket cases of ingratitude, so many of us. We cannot hope to repay in kind what Socrates gave us, but to live without any sense of obligation to those who made possible lives as tolerable as ours, within the frame of the human predicament God imposed on us—without any sense of gratitude to our parents, who suffered to raise us; to our teachers, who labored to teach us; to the scientists, who prolonged the lives of our children when disease struck them down—is spiritually atrophying.

We cannot repay in kind the gift of the Beatitudes, with their eternal, searing meaning—*Blessed are the poor in spirit, for theirs is the kingdom of heaven.* But our ongoing failure to recognize that we owe a huge debt that can be requited only by gratitude—defined here as appreciation, however rendered, of the best that we have, and a determined effort to protect and cherish it—our failure here marks us as the masses in revolt; in revolt against our benefactors, our civilization, against God Himself.

To fail to experience gratitude when walking through the corridors of the Metropolitan Museum, when listening to the music of Bach or Beethoven, when exercising our freedom to speak or, as happened to us three weeks ago, to give, or withhold, our assent, is to fail to recognize how much we have received from the great wellsprings of human talent and concern that gave us Shakespeare, Abraham Lincoln, Mark Twain, our parents, our friends, and, yes, the old lady in Stratford. We need a rebirth of gratitude for those who have cared for us, living and, mostly, dead. The high moments of our way of life are their gifts to us. We must remember them in our thoughts and in our prayers; and in our deeds.

A HERO OF THE REAGAN REVOLUTION
Introductory Remarks (excerpted) at a Dinner Honoring Jack Kemp;
Washington, D.C., December 1, 1988

A packed house, one thousand fans. On the dais: President Reagan, President-elect Bush, speakers Jeane Kirkpatrick, Lew Lehrman, and Caspar Weinberger. A highlight of the evening: President Reagan, escorted by his security retinue, leaves after his speech, reaching the exit door thirty yards from the podium. "Hey, Mr. President!" Kemp calls out. Reagan turns. Kemp shoots a football at him at dazzling speed. Reagan reaches out with one hand, catches it. The crowd goes berserk.

MR. PRESIDENT, Mr. PRESIDENT-ELECT, we are here to celebrate. It is a happy circumstance that the White House has given us one of those Cape Canaveral countdown schedules that frighten away such pauses as analyze but do not necessarily refresh.

. . . There is the further complication that we are here to celebrate the retirement of Jack Kemp from the Congress of the United States, which is on the order of celebrating the retirement of Niagara Falls from Niagara.

No one, with the possible exception of Arthur Schlesinger, can doubt that Ronald Reagan will leave Washington having effected a historical transformation in thought not only economic in nature, but also ethical. And no one questions that our guest of honor, Jack Kemp, was to Reaganomics what Eli Whitney was to mass production. The president will take many trophies back to Los Angeles in January. None should be pre-eminent over the Kemp-Roth Bill, the original draft of which, one of these days at auction at Sotheby's, will make Picasso an also-ran.

Such has been the impact of the Kemp-Reagan revolution: the operative insight, economically, that high taxation is an exercise in national austerity, the equivalent of national economic masochism; but, more important, the creeping ethical recognition that steep discriminatory taxation raises philosophical problems that roil the conscience of men and women who believe in equal treatment under the law. Mr. Reagan has accomplished a great deal, but perhaps he will be remembered by our great-grandchildren for two reasons: the first that he presided over the counterrevolution against the creeping idea that the state has a pre-emptive right to the production of its citizens; and, second, that he is almost certainly the nicest man who ever occupied the White House.

But we must move on quickly, because if we do not meet our schedule, terrible things will happen. In our culture it is only professional football that is permitted to stop the clock.

THE PAGAN LOVE SONG
OF MURRAY KEMPTON

Remarks (excerpted) Introducing Murray Kempton at the 92nd Street YMHA;
New York, May 31, 1989

The circumstances were these: Columnist Murray Kempton was award-
ed a prize, the wrinkle of which was that he would share an evening
with anyone he designated, at the 92nd Street Y, locally renowned for
its evening programs. He tapped me, and I opened by quoting from an
article I had written about him thirty years earlier. It conveyed much of
his special magic.

T O DOCUMENT THAT Murray Kempton and your visitor write biodegradable prose, my entire brief opening statement is taken from an essay I published twenty-eight years ago on Murray Kempton. In it I examined the columns written by him the week before the deadline for my piece.

On Tuesday, twenty-eight years ago, Murray Kempton was angry
with the steel companies for refusing to meet the demands of the steel-
workers to receive one week's pay in exchange for twenty hours of work. I
analyzed his column and wrote:

What would happen, one wonders, if the Devil should take the scales from Kempton's eyes, and let him see the world of economics? I say the Devil, because the Lord would not do so fiendish a thing. What a terrible end! His muse would dry up, and the pagan love song to humankind which he has been trilling for so many years would get all hung up under the discipline of keys, and measures, and clefs. A calamity, in a word: because Kempton—though he does not realize that theory is as liberating in social science as dogma is in theology— nevertheless is as necessary to humane industrial organization as Sam Goldwyn is to idiomatic English. Linguistic solecisms remain sole- cisms, as do economic solecisms. But they have their uses, some of them wholly unpredictable. My guess is the Communists moved with whatever caution it can be said they did between 1953 and 1960 because they hadn't the least idea what President Eisenhower was talking about, and thought a little prudence might be in order.

Conclusion: Murray Kempton doesn't really understand economics.

On Wednesday, Murray Kempton wrote about the defeat of Carmine De Sapio. I commented:

One of the most satisfying things about Kempton is his impartial iconoclasm. I remember his writing when Roy Cohn was finally and ignominiously forced out of McCarthy's committee, "So help me God, I feel sorry for Roy Cohn"—which I am sure he did, as well he might have, having for months galloped miles ahead of the posse (never did so many supererogate upon so little!). It is as distasteful to use a machine gun to deliver the coup de grace as it is to have to wait for the fourth coda to terminate a Tchaikovsky symphony. [In 1960] Kempton didn't want to go to the Republican Convention in Chicago. "If I do," he told me, "I'll knock Nixon—it's like junk. But I *like* Nixon!" He feels sorry for mangled corpses; but it is also for artistic reasons that he feels the need to back away.

Today he goes after Robert Wagner again. Kempton, of course, immediately saw through the phoniness of the anti–De Sapio frenzy [of the summer and fall of 1960], of which Ed Koch was the beneficiary. Kempton passed the day of the execution with De Sapio, following him around everywhere, closely observing his manners, and reacting prodigally to his remarkable personal gentility. "I sometimes think," he wrote, "that if Carmine De Sapio were running against Lucifer he would consider it ungentlemanly to mention that little trouble in heaven." When it was finally clear that he had been overthrown by the ideological janissaries and the playboy reformers, there were still the conventional and highly poignant rituals to go through, after which De Sapio walked out from his deserted office after midnight, into the streets. "His visitor"—Kempton's wonderfully unobtrusive way of designating himself, in all his interviews—"left him and walked into the streets and noticed that there were no slums anymore, and no landlords, and the Age of Pericles had begun because we were rid of Carmine De Sapio. One had to walk carefully to avoid being stabbed by the lilies bursting in the pavements. I wish the reformers luck—with less Christian sincerity than Carmine De Sapio does. I will be a long time forgiving them this one."

Conclusion: Murray Kempton will help anybody when he is down.

His next column explained why it was that Kennedy had beaten Nixon in the election of the preceding November. He had got the information from going through Public Document 75459 from the Senate Committee on Commerce, labeled "The Joint Appearances of Senator John F. Kennedy and Vice President Richard M. Nixon and Other 1960 Campaign Presentations." Murray Kempton quoted from an exchange on the Jack Paar Show:

VICE PRESIDENT NIXON: Could I ask you one favor, Jack?

JACK PAAR: Yes sir; you can ask any favor you'd like.

VICE PRESIDENT NIXON: Could we have your autograph for our girls?

"That was September 11, 1960," Kempton noted, "and Nixon had packed [for the White House]. The Kennedys rallied two weeks later."

CHARLES COLLINGWOOD: Hello, Caroline.

CAROLINE: Hello.

MRS. KENNEDY: Can you say hello?

CAROLINE: Hello.

MRS. KENNEDY: Here, do you want to sit up in bed with me?

MR. COLLINGWOOD: Oh, isn't she a darling?

MRS. KENNEDY: Now, look at the three bears.

MR. COLLINGWOOD: What is the dolly's name?

MRS. KENNEDY: All right, what is the dolly's name?

CAROLINE: I didn't name her yet.

Kempton went on: "But the mystery of [Nixon's] collapse taunts us yet. It was a terribly close election and who can say what small mistake cost him it?

"There is this one clue:"

BILL HENRY, OF NBC: I am so fascinated with that little kitten. Does the kitten have a name?

JULIE NIXON: Yes, its name is Bitsy Blue Eyes.

"Maybe," Kempton concluded his column, "Caroline saved the package when she held off naming the doll."

Conclusion: Murray Kempton has a jeweler's eye for the ghastly signs of sycophancy.

The next day Kempton wrote about the Right. He is fascinated by the Right, especially the hard Right. Fulton Lewis Jr., Kempton observes, has become a security risk in some quarters of the hard Right because "as an honored speaker at the Human Events *Forum in Washington the other day . . . he abused the privileges of the rostrum to attack certain unidentified flying objects who confuse the issue by thinking that everybody is a Communist."*

Here Kempton is at his absolute, unbeatable worst. It has been said there is no theological question Billy Graham cannot vulgarize; so there is no issue touching the Communist problem that Murray Kempton cannot sentimentalize. The Communist enterprise, or at least that part of it that goes on in this country, is in his opinion *opéra bouffe* (*Così Fan Tutti Atomica*). I have never seen a pointed sentence by Murray Kempton on the subject of the Communist problem at home: the systematic refusal to face the systematically demanding question—a question which Sidney Hook has tried to face systematically in his book *Heresy, Yes—Conspiracy, No.* "The trouble with Kempton," Hook once said, "is he thinks with his stomach." (The trouble with Hook, your visitor admits, is he doesn't think often enough with his stomach.) But Hook is right here. I give you the locus classicus, Kempton's report on the election of the new president of the CPUSA. "It is impossible to look at Miss [Elizabeth Gurley] Flynn without collapsing into the molasses of the American dream. She is the aunt Dorothy longed to get back to from Oz. . . . If the old-fashioned virtues really had any impact on our culture, the disenchanted of our society would rush to this dear sister's bosom. . . . [She has] a face that would be irresistible on the label of an apple-pie mix."

Had enough? Well, I don't care. You will have more. "You could sum up the domestic history of a dozen years just by printing a picture of Elizabeth Gurley Flynn and putting under it the caption, 'From 1948 to 196– a great nation was afraid of this woman!' But what generation unborn could possibly be expected to believe that?"

There are other problems more likely to urge themselves on generations unborn. The incumbent young generation in Cuba will wonder less why some Cubans were afraid of Fidel Castro, than why other Cubans were not.

Kempton's glands are, alas, no substitute for a humorless appraisal of the role of the Communist parties of the Free World. He is foremost among those the burden of whose thought is that it is the grave responsibility of the Free World to ensure the serenity of those in our midst who would subvert our freedom. E. Flynn's face is, after all, no more pleasing than poor Kerensky's. One has the feeling that the poet Kempton, whose grasp of reality so often surpasses that of the humdrummers whom destiny has charged with the evolution of our destiny, is resigned to turning over the future to the poetically benighted; just so long as he can be around to write the requiem for our time. A fine requiem it would be. And your visitor, to the extent he is ever tempted, where such solemn issues are involved, would care greatly to read that requiem. But it would be easier reading if one knew that unborn generations would wake free, into free countries, unbewitched by such as Elizabeth Gurley Flynn, who worked for Lavrenti Beria, who is less than apple-pie mix.

I greet Murray Kempton with pleasure and admiration.

THE NINETIES

———◆◆◆———

DISMANTLING THE EVIL EMPIRE

An Address (excerpted) to a Conference Sponsored by Sun Bank;
Orlando, Fla., January 9, 1990

My first speech of the 1990s, reviewing the achievements of the Reagan years and breathlessly awaiting the evolution of perestroika *in the Soviet Union.*

O N TRAVERSING New Year's Eve and thinking back on the decade just past, I have come to the conclusion that the 1980s was a triumphant decade.

It was a decade that began with the election of Ronald Reagan and ended with a Soviet offer of aid to tranquilize Rumania after the execution of its Communist tyrant. Enough to make us all Whiggish in our reading of history—the eternal optimists. Yes, yes, of course, whenever there is good news, there is the need to remind ourselves that the human predicaments will always be with us. Couéism, so popular in the 1920s ("Every day, in every way, we are getting better and better"), leads to lying down to sleep when the Hitlers of this world, big and small, mobilize their strength. Let the historians hand down final judgments. I, for one, shall think of this as Mr. Reagan's decade. No era associated with a single successful leader— not Pericles', not Metternich's, not Victoria's—is fairly evaluated by dredging up surviving delinquencies, deeds left undone. The 1980s are most certainly the decade in which Communism ceased to be a creed, surviving only as a threat. And Ronald Reagan had more to do with this than any other statesman in the world.

Reagan is not Solzhenitsyn. It was Solzhenitsyn who emerged as the Homer of anti-Communism. After the publication of *Gulag*, the European intellectual class could no longer—believe. But *Gulag* notwithstanding, what was beginning to happen, thirty-five years after the end of the Second World War, was sheer accommodationism. We must not doubt the disposition of even civilized people simply to adjust to ugly realities. The Democratic Party leadership dropped its determination to oppose not merely the expansion of the Communist world, but its very being. With the death of Senator Scoop Jackson, steel went out of a great political party. And when the country turned to a new president, and only a few months into his term he pronounced the Soviet Union an "evil empire," the Western diplomatic firmament shook with indignation. How, just how, could a superpower under the leadership of someone who spoke such conclusive words handle the diplomatic challenge of co-existence with that empire? Two years before he left office, the year after the Communists had celebrated the twenty-fifth anniversary of the Berlin Wall, Ronald Reagan was in Berlin, and his words were, "Mr. Gorbachev, tear down this wall!" And then he made that speech in which he especially infuriated the Kremlin by insisting that its system had a rendezvous not with the classless society that was the vision of Marx and Lenin, but with the ash heap of history.

As he spoke, reality was creeping in on Eastern Europe. Before the decade was out we were choking over the wonderful paradoxes, of which the possibility of Soviet troops helping Rumania get rid of a Communist government was perhaps the most spectacular, though my own favorite is Radio Martí, an invention of Ronald Reagan bitterly opposed by American appeasers, broadcasting to Cuba digests of *Moscow News*, which had been banned by Fidel Castro as being too bourgeois.

The great heroes of the decade—Walesa, Solzhenitsyn, Sakharov—have earned their place in freedom's House of Lords; but the political leader was Ronald Reagan, who was trained as a movie actor. Only in America, one is tempted to say; except that Lech Walesa was trained as an electrician.

And I have come to a second conclusion at the beginning of a new decade, and it is that the time is exactly right to attempt to move the Soviet Union towards critical disarmament.

The question we hear most often asked is, "Do you hope Gorbachev will succeed?" The formulation that typically follows is, "Do you *think* Gorbachev will succeed?" And the answer to that question is: Gorbachev *cannot* succeed. He cannot succeed because he is seeking to fuse polarities. The problem of the Soviet Union resides in its primary ideological commitments. Mr. Gorbachev has time and again renewed his commitment to those commitments, jettisoning (for the time being? we do not know) only those that have to do with the historical mandate of Communism to conquer the world. When the question was asked as recently as two months ago whether *perestroika* would permit private property, the answer was, No, it would not. Would it permit leadership other than under the Communist Party, as especially protected by Article 6 of the Soviet Constitution? Again, no. It is time for us also to be emphatic. In answer to the question, Will *perestroika*, under the circumstances, work the economic reforms Mr. Gorbachev desires? we must say: No. You cannot square a circle.

WHAT IS IT we do *not* want to see in the Soviet Union? Clearly, what we don't want is an economically reconstituted Soviet Union braced to renew its seventy-year offensive against the Free World. The evidence is overwhelming that with the collapse of the Brezhnev Doctrine and the loss of Eastern Europe, finally the Marxist-Leninist afflatus that commanded the Soviet Union to spearhead, arm in arm with history, the drive against the Free World is intellectually and spiritually dead. But although we recognize the abundant signs of an exhausted historical imperative, we know also that there are theaters in the world in which activity goes forward of exactly the same character as went forward under the leadership of Stalin and Khrushchev and Brezhnev. That Mikhail Gorbachev has tacitly renounced his own pledge to Communize the world is meaningless to Cubans, Nicaraguans, Vietnamese, Ethiopians, Angolans who feel the iron of the Soviet boot.

While we cannot say that the Marxist tocsin is completely silenced, or even that the historical Russian compulsion to expand is dead, we do know one thing of salient importance. It is that the Soviet Union is in dire economic straits. Less than a year ago the deputy prime minister, Leonid Abalkin, who serves directly under Mr. Gorbachev, addressed a meeting of his fellow economists and declared flatly that the Soviet Union as currently constituted had eighteen months left to live; that if economic reforms had not by then taken hold, anything might happen. Specifically, Mr. Abalkin mentioned the possibility of a right-wing coup, by which is meant, in Soviet terminology, a Stalinist coup.

Professor Richard Pipes of Harvard, the distinguished historian, who has completed a monumental work on Russia, advanced to me last summer the interesting thesis that Gorbachev's apparent immunity rests only in part on his institutional pre-eminence. That immunity, Professor Pipes believes, rests largely on the recognition by all conceivable alternative rulers of the Soviet Union that were they to take power, they would end by being powerless themselves. The shortage of housing and food and medicine and basic materials is not something that can be corrected by any change in leadership or by any fresh dogmatic brew. There is only one thing that can save the Soviet Union economically, and that is: hard currency.

In 1988, the Soviet Union spent, in constant dollars, 3 percent more than it had ever spent before on its armament industry. We were told that it intended to reduce its defense expenditures by 10 percent in 1989. But, simultaneously, it was refitting its SS-18s, the most lethal weapon in military history, to make them more sophisticated. We know that today, even after the INF treaty [Intermediate-Range Nuclear Forces—the treaty signed after Reykjavik], the Soviets are more powerful as a nuclear nation than ever they were before, and also more powerful in conventional arms.

I would propose we make an offer: to purchase Soviet military equipment, nuclear and nonnuclear, for $100 billion per year for the next three years. A carefully tabulated catalogue should be compiled of Soviet military hardware that is redundant to a purely defensive conventional force and a deterrent nuclear force. The excess missiles and warheads and tanks would file out of Soviet ports on U.S. ships, which would, upon reaching the continental shelf, jettison their cargo at sea.

Three years of such activity would accomplish two goals. The first is an iron-lung prolongation of Soviet economic life pending the evolution of *perestroika* into the acceptance of private property and marketplace economics. The second is the destruction of that incremental inventory of Soviet weapons that endangers peace on earth.

The financing of the enterprise would be done by reducing our own military budget by $100 billion per year for three years, which under these special circumstances we could afford to do. Our cash, their guns. But any contract designed to effect this exchange must be conclusive in character. We need to establish that that element of the Soviet war machine that constitutes a potential threat to the world should be dismantled. Ream the barrels of those launchers and artillery pieces and grow flowers there, and visit them every week or two to clip the blossoms, which we can spray about our military cemeteries, rededicating ourselves to our determination not to fight again—unless necessary.

I don't deny that the proposal is complicated in detail—so is Star Wars—but it is correspondingly simple in conception. The outcry that the Soviet Union would never consent to such an arrangement leaves it for us to say only that the Soviet Union has never before been so hard pressed. Stalin, after all, brought himself, under pressure, to sign the Stalin-Hitler Pact. To all of which we need only add: If the Soviet Union refuses the exchange, we will have learned much that is useful for us to know; indeed, much that is vital for us to know about the still-evil empire. . . .

THE SIMON PERSONA

A Tribute to a Critic; the Union League Club, New York, May 23, 1990

A testimonial to a valued National Review *contributor; distinguished company in attendance.*

WE HAVE ALL heard tonight about the art of John Simon, even though we didn't strictly need to do so, since it is self-evident. But, really, that doesn't matter, does it? We have had a balsamic reiteration, done in different tongues, of what we know, are glad that we know, pity those who do not know, and are proud to be associated with. Back when Bill Sheed was reviewing movies for *Esquire*, he confided to me—I suppose I am at this point required to acknowledge that the confidence has run its life cycle—that he "reviewed movies in the same sense that pigeons review statues." One has the impression, reading Simon by the metric ton, that he also is thus engaged; but is it his fault that the demands of the consuming public outweigh the resources of our gifted artisans? In this respect, even the most orthodox of us at *National Review* would need to concede that the doctrine of supply-side has its limits. If one insisted on viewing every week a new play of the quality of Shakespeare's, the generative economic impulse would, unhappily, fail to effect the genetic transmutation. Anyway, even if supply-side worked in art as it does, say, in T-shirts, it isn't obvious that the pressures would be there to create one after another John Simon–flick. This is in part because the demand isn't truly there. There are some among us who don't always want to see the kind of movie that excites our guest of honor. There are some of us who, spotting at the end of a day's work, in the subway or in the limousine, a copy of *USA Today* and one of the *Christian Science Monitor,* will find ourselves electing the former. We need to understand, though, that such critics as we can be especially proud of do not sleep through the lazy hours of the day. They are on duty to tell us what we missed, as also to tell us what we didn't miss.

Our dealings with John Simon at *National Review* over ten years have been with one exception as perfect as one could have with a contributing editor. He is unfailing in the quality of his work and unfailing in the courtesy of his manner. We face from time to time the problem of the review that is seven hundred words too long, and so we have our mini-crises, which are climaxed by John calling to tell me, with just a hint of drama in his voice, that he desires to be a critic, not a reviewer. This is followed by an accommodationist gesture on *his* part, and an accommodationist gesture on *our* part; and before long, everybody is happy, and John Simon is consuming about as much space as he desires.

It is widely supposed, by people who tend to routine thought, that life in and about *National Review* is a life obsessed with politics. I doubt anyone could more confidently note that this is not the case than John Simon. I haven't the slightest idea what his own politics are, though I do hope he has learned as much from us as we have learned from him. He doesn't come into the office that frequently: no editors do anymore, in the age of fax and modem. But usually not more than a month goes by before one or more of us see him, in the office, or at a restaurant, or at my house. Those who meet him for the first time are struck by his gentility, as of course by his wit and erudition. There is something about him that is a dramatic betrayal of the persona one expects from the public reputation.

I close by recalling an intellectual approached by a journalist at a café in Madrid during the high days of Francisco Franco. The journalist leaned over and whispered, "What do you think of Franco?" The intellectual raised a finger and beckoned to the journalist to accompany him.

They walked silently through the maze of urban Madrid. Across grand avenues. Down the length of the huge park. To a canoe at the playground. The intellectual rowed silently to the center of the lake, raised his oar, and said: "I like him."

Well, I like John Simon. Whom I toast with pride and affection.

A DISTINCTIVE GENTILITY

Remarks at the Fortieth Reunion of the Yale Class of 1950; New Haven, Conn., June 1, 1990

Looking back, four decades later.

S OME OF US who wondered if we would ever be this old now wonder whether we were ever young.

Most of us are older today than Franklin Delano Roosevelt was when he died, five months before we arrived in New Haven.

Were we ever young?

Three weeks before matriculating at Yale I was in a little hotel bar in Edgartown with my future college roommate and two of my sisters after a day's sailing. I ordered a beer and was surprised when the waitress asked to see my driver's license. I was not quite twenty-one years old and so was told to settle for a Coke, or a 7-Up. I remember the great welling of resentment. Should I tell her that six months earlier I had been in charge of a detachment of one thousand men at Fort Sam Houston, Texas? I thought the indignity monstrous—but had the sense to keep my mouth shut. There wasn't a barmaid in Newport you could impress by reciting your war record. And anyway, it was all very good training for reaching Yale as a freshman.

There were eighteen hundred of us—triple the normal enrollment—because one of Yale's contributions to the war effort had been to make a comprehensive promise to matriculate, once the war was over, every single student it had accepted during the war from the graduating secondary-school classes. Never mind how many we would be: somehow Yale would find food, quarters, and teachers for us. It is a good thing the war did not go on to Peloponnesian length, given that even as it was, several hundred freshmen were forced to occupy Quonset huts built during the war for service use, and the rest of us to double up. The shortage of teachers in certain fields was so acute that in my freshman year I found myself being taught economics by a freshman in the Law School, and the following year I, along with two other undergraduates, was teaching Spanish.

There was an indistinct class structure, I remember: the war veterans and the nonveterans. Formally, the administration pursued egalitarian policies in dealing with us, with only the incidental perquisites (veterans got the Old Campus, not the Quonset huts). In fact, a little winking of the eye was done at mannerisms and outlawry Yale would not, I think, have indulged in a class made up of seventeen-year-olds. Frank Harman (RIP), a notorious physical slouch who had spent three sedentary years in the army learning how to speak Japanese, was told matter-of-factly at the compulsory physical exam at the Payne Whitney gymnasium that he should proceed, like the student ahead of him, to leap over a vaulting board. He turned to the athletic examiner and said simply, "You must be joking"—and walked quietly around the obstacle, on to the next station, deciding, for one test after another, whether he would submit to it or treat it as he treated the ash on his cigarette. He got away with it.

How do you handle freshmen back from Omaha Beach? I remember the tryouts for the freshman debating team. One of the applicants we'll call Henry Atterbury. He delivered a fiery oration. When the time came for the septuagenarian historian/debate coach to deliver his critiques he said quietly to Henry, "Mr. Atterbury. You really don't need to speak quite so . . . loudly." He got back from Atterbury: "I'm sorry about that, sir. I got into that habit having to shout to my men over the roar of tanks." Roaring Henry Atterbury (as we ever after referred to him), a college freshman, had been a captain in the artillery, and was living now with his *second* wife.

Henry was not easily governed. I won't forget his encounter with Dean De Vane at the beginning of our sophomore year. Henry returned to New Haven one week after the semester had begun, and one of the few regulations about which Yale was inflexible, you will remember, was that all students must be present on the first and the last day of classes. He was accordingly summoned to the office of that calm, courteous, scholarly Southerner, who asked why Mr. Atterbury had been late.

"Well, sir," said Roaring Henry, "I spent the summer studying the Middle Ages, and I became so engrossed in the subject I completely forgot about the Gregorian calendar change."

The response of Dean De Vane became legendary: "Ah, Mr. Atterbury. In that event, you would have arrived in New Haven a week early." Roaring Henry went into hiding for a while after that one.

My roommate Richie O'Neill (RIP) was not easily trifled with. He came early to a decision that he needed to do something to tame the fastidious dean of the Engineering School, who, an inflexible disciplinarian, required attendance at all classes by engineering majors unless at midterms—which were several months away—they achieved the honor roll. When Richie slept in one Monday he received on Tuesday a summons to the office of Dean Loomis Havemeyer. Richie was six feet two, had fought as a Marine in Okinawa, was all Irish, and had the smile of Clark Gable; every time Richie smiled I was prompted to count the silver.

"Why did you miss your class yesterday, Mr. O'Neill?"

"Diarrhea, sir," Richie smiled.

He was thereafter immune to summonses from that office.

I reflect on the extent to which lines were drawn between veterans of the war and apple-cheeked freshmen straight out of high school. At first the difference was marked primarily by dress: veterans were almost studiedly wedded to khaki pants. But after a month or so, the nonveterans followed the lead of their grizzled elders; and, really, it was not all that easy to stare into the face of an eighteen-year-old and a twenty-year-old and discern in the latter the distinctive scars of service in the military.

There was, before the days of the superdirectors of Hollywood, who learned exactly how to atrophy the young mien in order to document time served in Vietnam, no clear way to distinguish between the features of such as another of my roommates—he had taken part in the invasion of Iwo Jima, his closest friend dying at his side on the beach from machine-gun bullets—and such as me, who had spent twenty-four months in the infantry stateside, miserably uncomfortable months, but the bullets we needed to dodge as we crawled on our bellies under barbed wire were carefully aimed several feet above our rumps.

In part the lack of indistinction between us at college, veterans and nonveterans, grew out of the general knowledge that, overwhelmingly, those of us who had served were draftees, not volunteers. I suppose most of us, by the time we were old enough for the draft, several years into the war, would have enlisted: the Second World War, unlike its successors in Korea and Vietnam, was a relatively popular war, causing the patriotic juices to run. But the differences between the six hundred freshmen and the twelve hundred freshmen gradually dissolved, and maybe all that was finally detectable was a faint air of urgency. I was older when I entered Yale than my brother Jim was when he graduated from Yale.

If I measured it accurately—in 1947 we were introduced to a class of conventional nonveterans and could make comparisons—the veteran population in the class of 1950 wasn't an altogether wizening influence on campus activity. Perhaps we were noticeably in a hurry to get on—to get some learning, get married, get started in life. Money wasn't much of a worry—the GI Bill was paying our way, or substantially paying our way. There was carousing, if nothing on the scale of *Animal House*. Those of us who drank had learned two or three years earlier how to do so and when to stop doing so. Much of the time.

Eighteen hundred bright, individualistic men cultivated a lot of unusual pursuits. Fernando Valenti was practicing to become the world's leading harpsichordist. Claes Oldenburg was—I guess—dreaming of great ironwork constructions, worrying only whether museums would be large enough to house them. Jimmy Symington was wondering whether he would ever learn enough to become a Republican. I rounded up a few friends and jointly we bought an airplane, learned to fly, and did a little crash landing—for instance, one afternoon on the lawn of the Ethel Walker School. I was hauled out from the plane, along with my brother-in-law-to-be Brent Bozell, by three hundred girls in high hilarity at the ignominious end of the two fly-happy Yale men. Friendships were instantly struck up, sometimes under the oddest impulses. I sat for the first lecture in Physics 10 alongside another freshman, a young man of grave countenance. We were two of perhaps one hundred students in the room, and at the end of the lecture, which had been given by a retired naval captain, we turned to each other—strangers—and the extrasensory circuit was instantly completed: we burst into convulsive, almost hysterical laughter. We had a bond. Neither of us had understood a single word uttered by the instructor. We ended fast friends and co-patrons of a private tutor, who barely escorted us through the survivors' gate of Physics 10AB.

I think most of us, probably even including Henry Atterbury, were struck by something we had not, for some reason, anticipated: the awesome, breath-catching brilliance of some of our teachers. The basic course in philosophy, a survey course that began with Thales and ended with Whitehead, was taught by Robert Calhoun (RIP), a member of the faculty of the Divinity School. Remember? A tall, ruddy-faced man with crew-cut hair who wore a hearing aid. He spoke the kind of sentences John Stuart Mill wrote. Never a misplaced accent, qualifier, verb: sentence after sentence of preternatural beauty, formed as if in a magical compositors' shop, by golden artisans. Never pretentious, just plain beautiful. His learning so overwhelmed him that sometimes—and he was a man without affectation of any kind—sometimes as he traced a philosopher's thought schematically on the blackboard he would find himself lapsing into Greek, or perhaps Hebrew. When this happened there would be a quiet tittering in the classroom, but Professor Calhoun was deaf and didn't hear; so, after a while, we would just struggle to understand. He undertook, at the request of a few of us, to deliver a lecture at Dwight Hall bemoaning the Soviet coup in Czechoslovakia in 1948, and I can't believe that Demosthenes ever spoke more movingly. Yet Mr. Calhoun, at Yale, was just another professor in a department of philosophy star-studded with learning and brains.

Lewis Curtis, professor of European history, had a lecture course, and each of his lectures—they ran exactly forty-eight minutes—was a forensic tour de force. His description of the Battle of Jutland could have had a long run off Broadway. Pyrotechnics were deemed, at Yale in 1946, a little infra dig, so it wasn't thunder and lightning and morning lights that Lewis Curtis gave his class: rather, wit and polish. We could not believe it, and I still wonder at it, that anyone could deliver, three times a week, on schedule, discrete lectures sculpted so lovingly: they came out as Renaissance statues, buoyant yet lapidary. How do they do it? I think the wonder of scholarly profundity hit us as freshmen here, even if we were destined to wonder about the uses to which learning is so often put.

Another thing that struck us was something I came to think of as a genetic attribute of Yale, and this was a distinctive sense of gentility. We were addressed as adults and, for the most part, treated as adults: by men sharply to be distinguished from those noisy martinets we had experienced at boot camp. We had, however briefly, a vision of an entirely different order of social arrangements: a community of scholars. We would eventually learn, through experience and through reading, that no petty human vice is neglected in the academy, that fratricide does not stop at academic moats. But as students we were substantially shielded from such frictions because students are after all transient, and we were not competing with the faculty for anything. Perhaps our experience was in that sense denatured, but it is an ineffaceable part of the memory of four years at Yale: the very idea of institutional courtesy. We have never been quite the same after those four years. Perhaps not better in every way; but certainly we were now men who knew something about the scales of human achievement.

I THINK, IN these mellow circumstances, of the great centrifugal forces in modern life. I sat late one night last week in the garage-study of my home in Stamford, putting these words together. My wife and I have lived there for almost forty years. Even so, I reflected last Monday, I have only twice laid eyes on the neighbor north of my property, and have yet to meet my neighbor to the south, who has occupied *his* house for fifteen years. By temperament I am content with the doctrine that good fences make good neighbors; but good fences shouldn't evolve into barbed-wire barricades, though much of this is happening: the atomistic pull of high-tech living, in a high-tech age.

It was here at Yale, forty years ago, that a professor introduced me to a book by Anton Rossi, with its striking introduction that spoke of two Frenchmen, strangers at a sidewalk café, each one reading his newspaper and sipping his coffee in the late afternoon. Suddenly one raises his voice to the other: "Say, do you like Jews?"

"No," the other man replied.

"Well, do you like Catholics?"

"No."

"Do you like Americans?"

"No."

"Do you like Frenchmen?"

"No."

"Well, who *do* you like?"

The naysayer raised his head slightly. "I like my friends," he said, going back to his newspaper.

So do I. And most of my friends I met forty-odd years ago, met them within a radius of two hundred yards of where I am now standing. It occurs to me that forty years is a very long time. Less than forty years went by between the day Lincoln was shot and the day Victoria died. Just forty years *before* we graduated was the year the Chinese abolished slavery, the year Edward VII died, as also William James and Mark Twain. Friendships that last forty years are something. Monuments, I call them. There are few better grounds for celebration. So let's toast to the class of 1950, and to the college that brought us together.

TIME TO GO TO BED

Remarks at *National Review*'s Thirty-Fifth Anniversary Dinner; the Waldorf-Astoria, New York, October 5, 1990

I announce my retirement, speculate a bit, and let the audience in on what it's like putting an issue to bed.

I SUPPOSE THAT if there is a single occasion on which a professional will be indulged for speaking personally, it is when he retires. (If that isn't the case, then *National Review* will establish yet another precedent.) When my father first saw the offering circular with which in 1954 I traveled about the country attempting to induce American capitalists to invest in our prospective journal, he spotted only one sentence that disturbed him. I had written that I pledged to devote ten years of my life to *National Review*. My father, who was very . . . formal about personal commitments, told me he thought this exorbitant. "Ten years is simply too long," he said. "Suppose you decide you want to do something else with your life?"

Well, the warning became moot, because there never was anything else around seriously to tempt me. For the fun of it I divulge that in 1970 I was approached by a very small delegation of what one is trained to call "serious people" whose proposal was that I should run for governor of New York; I should expect to win the election, I was told, thus positioning myself to run for the presidency. I was nicely situated to say two things, the first that anyone who had run for mayor of New York City getting only 13 percent of the vote shouldn't be too confident about winning a general election. And I finally silenced my friends by adding that I didn't see how I could make the time to run for governor, given my obligations to *National Review*. My friends couldn't understand my priorities. But I was very content with them.

Oh yes, I won't cavil on that point. The magazine has been everything the speakers tonight have so kindly said it was—is. It is preposterous to suppose that this is so because of my chancellorship. How gifted do you need to be to publish Whittaker Chambers and Russell Kirk, James Burnham and Keith Mano? But, yes, the journal needed to function. Somehow the staff and the writers had to be paid—if an editorial note is reserved for me in the encyclopedias, it will appear under the heading "Alchemy." But the deficits were met, mostly, by our readers: by you. And, yes, we did as much as anybody with the exception of—Himself—to shepherd into the White House the man I am confident will emerge as the principal political figure of the second half of this century, and he will be cherished, in the nursery tales told in future generations, as the American president who showed the same innocent audacity as the little boy who insisted that the emperor wasn't wearing any clothes, back when he said, at a critical moment in history, that the Union of Soviet Socialist Republics was an evil empire. It is my judgment that those words acted as a kind of harmonic resolution to the three frantic volumes of Solzhenitsyn. *The Gulag Archipelago* told us everything we needed to know about the pathology of Soviet Communism. We were missing only the galvanizing summation; and we got it from President Reagan: and I think that the countdown for Communism began then.

Since you were so kind as to ask about my personal plans, I disclose that I intend to continue to be active on other fronts. Early this week I performed a harpsichord concerto with the North Carolina

Symphony and resolved—with the full acquiescence, I am certain, of the orchestra and the audience—that I will not devote my remaining years to performing on the keyboard. One month from today I will set out, with my companions, on a small sailboat from Lisbon, headed toward Barbados via Madeira, the Canaries, and Cape Verde, forty-four hundred miles of decompression at sea, the cradle of God; inevitably, a book will come out of this. But on reaching the Caribbean, unlike the Flying Dutchman, I will jump ship, to get on with other work. I have not scheduled the discontinuation of my column, or of *Firing Line,* or of public speaking, or of book writing. But these activities by their nature will terminate whenever the Reaper moves his supernatural, or for that matter democratic, hand, whereas *National Review,* I like to think, will be here, enlivening right reason, for as long as there is anything left in America to celebrate.

And of course, it will always crowd my own memory. One thousand fourteen issues of *National Review.* The hour is late, nearing five in the afternoon of press day, and the printer's messenger is already waiting, so we move into the conference room, the only room at *National Review* in which more than four people can fit, and Priscilla reads out the editorial lengths, and I mark them down on the paleolithic calculator I bought in Switzerland in 1955, and Linda checks to see that I have got the right count. We have twelve hundred fifty-nine lines of editorial copy but space for only seven hundred eighteen. We absolutely need to run something on the subject of Judge Souter's testimony, but I see we can't afford the seventy-eight-line editorial I processed earlier in the day. "Rick, would you shorten this?"

"To what?" he asks, as matter-of-factly as a tailor might ask what the new waistline is to be.

The copy is spread about the room, occupying every level surface, and you walk about, counterclockwise, turning face down any editorial that can wait a fortnight to appear, and subtracting on your little calculator its line count from the rogue total. We need to cut five hundred forty-one lines. First your eyes pass over the editorials and paragraphs that deal with domestic issues, Priscilla having grouped them together; then those that deal with foreign countries or foreign policy; then the offbeat material. You look down at the calculator, having made the complete circuit of the room, returning to where you began: it shows eight hundred fifty-four lines, and so you start the second counterclockwise circuit, the killer instinct necessarily aroused: you have *got* to cut another one hundred thirty-six lines. "Jeff, shrink this one by ten lines, okay?" At *National Review* the editors always answer "Okay" when a deadline looms.

So it is done, down to length. And then you ask yourself: Which paragraph is just right for the lead? The rule: It has to be funny, or at least piquant; directly or obliquely topical; engaging of the broader imagination. I remember one from years and years ago: "The attempted assassination of Sukarno last week had all the earmarks of a CIA operation. Everyone in the room was killed except Sukarno." And, during the days when we feuded almost full-time, "Gerald Johnson of *The New Republic* wonders what a football would think of football if a football could think. Very interesting, but not as interesting as, What would a *New Republic* reader think of *The New Republic* if a *New Republic* reader could think?" Last week there wasn't anything absolutely, obviously pre-eminent, but ever since it came up on the dumbwaiter at 2 P.M. from Tim Wheeler's fortnightly package, this one about colors had burrowed in the mind. Time is very short now. Okay, we'll lead with it. It reads:

"Iraq and the budget are as nothing compared to the firestorm following the retirement of maize, raw umber, lemon yellow, blue grey, violet blue, green blue, orange red, and orange and their replacement by vivid tangerine, wild strawberry, fuchsia, teal blue, cerulean, royal purple, jungle green, and dandelion, by the makers of Crayola crayons."

Nice, no? Orson Bean used to say that the most beautiful word combinations in the language were "Yucca Flats" and "Fernando Lamas"; though Whittaker Chambers, along with Gertrude Stein, preferred "Toasted Suzie is my ice cream."

And then you need the bottom eye-catcher, the end paragraph, traditionally very offbeat; usually nonpolitical, but not necessarily. You knew which would be the end paragraph the moment you laid eyes on it, early in the day—another by Tim, whose reserves of mischief are reliable—and now you find it and designate it as such. It reads:

"This week's invention is a sort of miniaturized zapper, battery-powered, to be inserted in the cervix for contraception and, the inventor hopes, prophylaxis. If you aren't shocked by this, you will be."

The editorials are now in order, and the line count is confirmed.

Another issue of *National Review* has gone to bed; and you acknowledge—the thought has ever so slowly distilled in your mind—that the time comes for us all to go to bed, and I judge that mine has come, and I leave owing to my staff, my colleagues—my successors—my friends, my muses, my God, an unrequitable debt for having given me so much, for so long. Good night, and thanks.

Taxation and the Rule of Law

An Address (excerpted) to the Swiss-American Chamber of Commerce; Geneva, March 5, 1991

While in Switzerland for my annual book-writing session, I gave my hosts the view of an American conservative on the economic accomplishments of Ronald Reagan and the wonders they have brought.

I AM HAPPY to be here with the Swiss-American Chamber of Commerce, even if, by speaking to you, I jeopardize a long record of spending time in Switzerland without exploitation. My first winter here was in 1932, in Grindelwald; my second, in 1933, in Gstaad. Since 1959 I have missed only two winters in this part of the world, and have got by giving only two speeches, the last one ten years ago. I reason that every time I speak, I may be encouraging the Swiss authorities, should I ever find myself applying for a resident's visa, to turn me down on the grounds that there are enough problems in Switzerland without importing alien avalanches. I don't pretend that

I am without credentials. My mother's great-great-grandparents left Switzerland in the 1830s to go to New Orleans, so that my pedigree is appealing, if not necessarily my policy recommendations.

I have always thought about Switzerland that it succeeds in breaking all the rules: the Confederation just seems to work, though I would hate to be the man charged to write a treatise on Switzerland and the Rule of Law. I amuse myself every year, at the first dinner party my wife and I attend, by asking the Swiss sitting next to me what is the name of the president of Switzerland. Inevitably she is greatly embarrassed, and whispers inquiringly to the person next to her. The question usually passes down through a half dozen people before some scholar comes up with the incumbent's name. I find this the true realization of the republican ideal: nobody can think of the name of the president, so essentially unimportant is he, in so well run a state. Once, riding up a mountain in a small gondola on a hot day in March, I carefully removed the crystal pane that held out the air. When I arrived at the top station the attendant saw what I had done and severely scolded me, after which he told me that the fine was 3 francs 75 centimes. That night I had a nightmare: I had assassinated the Swiss president! I stood in front of the sentencing judge, who gave me a most fearful dressing-down, then opened a wide ledger, looked under "Assassination, President," and said that would be 4,575 francs.

But I must stop the frolics and get on.

On the economic front, it is my contention that the so-called Reagan Revolution will not be consummated until opposition to discriminatory taxation becomes a part of the public philosophy.

The battle of last fall resulted in a massive restructuring which included the collapse of George Bush's lips. In prospect for the twelve months after the budget bill was a $100 billion budget saving. What actually happened was that spending increased by $100 billion.

That battle may prove to be only a preliminary skirmish. Mr. Bush has said that he proposes to stand by his recommendation to lower the capital-gains tax. Governor Mario Cuomo, lecturing at Gettysburg, recently designated the Republican Party as deserving to be called the "party of slavery." What we need, he said, is a government that would "take up the challenge of narrowing the gap between the haves and the have-nots in this society, of reuniting the two cities where Americans live today—one a rich and glittering city on the hill, the other full of pain and despair and lost potential, the new slavery." No less. The two men are likely to face each other in the next presidential election. The voters will need to decide which one of them errs.

A recent essay in *Time* magazine charged that only the rich have benefited from the Reagan Revolution. The Reagan Revolution began in 1983, after the recession brought on by the policies of the Federal Reserve Board in October 1980, and after the tax reduction of 1981 began to take effect.

Time failed to note that since then, the wealthiest 20 percent have increased the share of taxes that they pay—increased that share from 55.8 to 58.1, an increase of 4.1 percent. Meanwhile the poorest 20 percent were paying 1.9 percent of the taxes, and are now paying 1.6, a decrease of 16 percent.

Time failed to note that under Reagan, 4.3 million Americans were relieved of any income taxation.

Time failed to note that in the ten years before Reagan, we all, the poor included, were paying progressively higher taxes as we were lifted by inflation into higher rates of taxation. Reagan brought indexation.

Time failed to note that the income cited in the statistics does not take into account the cash value of Medicare, Medicaid, food stamps, public housing, and employer-provided nonwage benefits, such as health insurance.

Time failed to assign any relevance to the increase in the Social Security tax—which was not a Reagan measure—and *Time* listed the contribution of the employer to Social Security as a contribution by the employee.

Time failed to note that during the past ten years the number of families in America with only a single parent increased substantially, lowering family income among the poor. The rise in the rate of illegitimacy is not, really, a responsibility of Ronald Reagan.

Time failed to note that when the top tax rate was reduced from

70 percent to 50 percent, $11 billion more in taxes was collected from the top quintile. And failed to note that while federal revenues were reduced by a total of $33 billion per year under Ronald Reagan, GNP increased by between $80 and $120 billion per year.

But all these points, arithmetical in nature, seem somehow immaterial, up against the philosophical point. As I read the lament in *Time*'s essay my memory flashed back to September of 1986, when I spent an hour with Anibal Cavaco Silva at his offices in Lisbon. The prime minister of Portugal is young, urbane, vaguely intense in manner, in the style of the academic rather than the politician. He had just returned from an official visit to Washington. We talked about this & that, but his attention was elsewhere.

He blurted it out halfway through the hour. "Do you realize," he said, "that the tax bill signed into law yesterday in Washington means that when 1988 rolls along, your highest federal tax rate will be lower than our lowest marginal rate?" I didn't quite know what was the appropriate comment. I think I said something pleasant about Magellan. He pursued the point, as if engaging in a soliloquy. As a former academic himself, he is part of a culture trained to think of high incremental taxation as—well, as the civilized thing to do.

I reminisced that twenty years earlier, when touring in Denmark, our professional guide had taken us by the parliament and said proudly to my son and me, "Here in Denmark we have the highest tax rate in all Europe! It is 90 percent at the highest level. And next year we hope to lift that to 95 percent!" I didn't doubt that Portugal's prime minister would be giving much thought to the economic consequences of drastically lower marginal tax rates; but not this afternoon. This afternoon he was the dumbfounded graduate of an academic culture contemplating a conundrum. That a Republican president who two years earlier had captured the vote of forty-nine states should have won an overwhelming vote in a Democratic Congress in favor of so large a tax reduction was simply not the way democratic politics was supposed to work.

The tax policies of the past decade, beginning with the House Ways and Means Committee's decision to lower the top capital-gains tax from 49 to 28 percent, added up to a revolution in ethical thought, not merely in economic thought. It involved a renewed understanding that economic prosperity, brought on by success at any level, is a tonic not only for the economically successful, but for the society as a whole; and that those whose activity brings on a substantial rise in employment and in productivity ought not to be thought of as public enemies.

In due course (it takes two or three years before the data silt up) the Department of Commerce released figures quite astonishing to opponents of the lower tax rate. Tax revenues from Americans declaring a capital gain were not only higher than they had been at the confiscatory rate, they were very much higher. Already, returns from the lowered marginal rates on income establish that they lead to increased revenues for the federal government, and diminished taxation of the poor.

The whole idea of supply-side economics was being vindicated at an empirical level, and this caused great distress to the egalitarians. My friend John Kenneth Galbraith, who in calling himself a socialist makes one of the few noncontroversial statements of a talkative lifetime, spoke from deep in the bowels of the egalitarian ethos when he said that the lowered tax rates deeply disturbed an important ideal in America, namely, the satisfaction of the public in knowing that the affluent are being taxed—well, punitively. For much of this century, high taxation has been viewed as a fitting rebuke to entrepreneurial success or inherited good fortune. That ethical perception is no longer secure, for all that Congress gave it fresh life last November. The inquisitive practical intelligence asks a basic question: Doesn't it in fact help everyone in the long term if obstacles are removed to saving and to the accumulation of wealth? And then there is an intuitive moral concern: Can progressive taxation be reconciled with the rule of law? Here and there people dare to whisper among themselves, "Explain that to me again: A taxi driver who elects to work seventy hours per week should be taxed at a higher rate than a taxi driver who works forty hours per week? When did *that* happen?"

Any reform needs a period of consolidation, and the rise in the rates of taxation last fall suggested the extent to which genuine philosophical spadework still needs to be done. But any tax reform that heads us away from discriminatory practices adds a solid plank under the floor of representative government. Professor Hayek, in his seminal book *The Constitution of Liberty*, warned against the progressive income tax. The political history of this century emphasizes private property as the broadest brake on omnipotent government. Socialism operates, as Lord Percy of Newcastle wrote in his famous essay, only by "making property perpetually insecure." The flight of capital from the Third World is a reflection not so much of better opportunities elsewhere, as of political chaos at home and safer sanctuaries abroad. The Reagan Revolution appears to be spreading to other countries even as it recedes from our own—there are lower incremental tax rates in India, Canada, France, Japan, Sweden, and Australia. If at the turn of the century it is said that the momentum of socialism finally stopped, as dramatically as the Berlin Wall came down, it will be substantially on account of the restabilization of property. . . .

CAN EASTERN EUROPE BE SAVED?

An Address (excerpted) to the Annual Meeting of the Philadelphia Society; the Inn at Long Wharf, Boston, Mass., April 26, 1991

In the spring of 1991 the Soviet Union was coming apart. I recalled the prescriptions of Milton Friedman and recounted from recent personal experience the kind of problems visitors still had in Moscow, after four years of perestroika.

TOM WOLFE SAID at the thirty-fifth anniversary dinner of *National Review* that he saw nothing wrong in gloating from time to time. I'm not sure I'd use the same word, but what *is* exactly the right word to describe the pleasure one takes in empirical verification of postulates we have held? We are entitled to celebrate— a celebration is prescribed, indeed even scheduled, in the Lenten season. In our world it is always a Lenten season, in that there is nothing even the Philadelphia Society can do to root out either invincible ignorance or the wreckage that ensues from the writhings and thrashings of the iconoclastic imperative. But every now and again we have our Laetare Sundays, in which we rejoice, and there is much to rejoice over, even as we know that, when the clock strikes twelve, we'll need to redouble our efforts merely to maintain the ground we have achieved, it being a human temptation to take shortcuts in attempting to realize Utopia. And shortcuts are almost always attempted through the instrumentality of the state, which at once can organize armies of soldiers to fight for liberty, and armies of soldiers and policemen and bureaucrats to attenuate liberty, and to enslave.

Having slipped quite by accident into the use of martial language, I remind myself of when our Commodore, Don Lipsett, asked me in February to give a title for my speech. As many of you know, Don deploys prestidigitative techniques not equally mastered by any other human being on earth, with the exception of Mother Teresa, to prevail over your own inclinations, which in my case are to defer until the last minute the selection of the title and text of any talk. So insistent was he that I finally blurted out, over MCI Mail from Switzerland, "Call it, 'Reflections on War & Peace.'" Indeed that is how he has advertised my remarks to this, my favorite forum; and lo, what is on my mind is questions of war and peace.

I will proceed, as I am given to doing, by affirming a few propositions, the first being that, *While we rejoice over the end of the Cold War, it is unlikely that Adam Smith can save the East European states, let alone the Soviet Union.*

In *National Review* a year ago Milton Friedman told us that, in his (habitually unassailable) judgment, the newly liberated East European nations need to take drastically anti-statist steps in order to make substantial economic progress. What he says applies, a fortiori, to the Soviet Union.

Mr. Friedman believes that no state that has suffered from so protracted an experience with socialism can handle the problem of economic resuscitation while simultaneously taking on the welfare load routinely accepted by affluent Western democracies. If Mr. Friedman is correct, the alternatives faced by Poland, Bulgaria, Rumania, and Czechoslovakia—to say nothing of the Soviet Union—are of breathtaking political consequence. We may find ourselves dealing with people who have a vision of liberty and prosperity, and who, denied prosperity, will be attracted to false utopianism. Hermann Goering testified at Nuremberg that it was as simple as this: in 1933, Germany had *no* alternative but to move in the direction it did.

"The transition to freedom cannot be accomplished overnight," Professor Friedman writes. "The formerly totalitarian societies have developed institutions, public attitudes, and vested interests that are wholly antithetical to the rapid creation of the basic economic requisites for freedom and prosperity."

He lays down what he deems the absolute requirements of success. The most important is that "The bulk of wealth (including means of production) must be privately owned in the fullest sense." By this Mr. Friedman means that the owner of property must be free to dispose of it as he sees fit. There can be "no control over wages or prices, including foreign-exchange rates; no restrictions on imports or exports."

It follows (2) that private property must be secure; (3) that the constitutions of the fledgling democracies must acknowledge the responsibility of securing property by maintaining law and order, enforcing contracts, and establishing coherent and acceptable rules of commerce; and (4), moving into his specialty, that the upwardly mobile countries will need a relatively stable monetary system.

It is especially sobering to hear Mr. Friedman tell us that no *Western* society today possesses these requisites "in anything like full measure." This means that the new nations have to do much more than merely imitate the ways of the United States, let alone those of Sweden or France. The Soviet Union and its former satellites need to re-create the situation as it used to exist in the Western countries before they adopted what goes by the name of the Middle Way. "Only our attained wealth enables us to support such wasteful, overblown government sectors. Hong Kong is a far better model."

It is worth it to travel to the Soviet Union—as many of you have done, sometimes, to be sure, voyeuristically.

There is a lot of good news coming out of that part of the world, but pilgrims who travel there to see a land transformed by *perestroika* and *glasnost* should be warned that although free-market principles have been accepted by the government, they are very far from having been implemented. Anyone who doubts that there is a need for reform should spend a few days at an Intourist hotel in Moscow.

The economic idea of arbitrage—the process in which people buy a product where it is cheap and sell it where it is dear, until prices level out—has not even worked its wonders within the hotel we stayed in last summer, let alone in Greater Moscow, let alone in Great Russia. On the second floor of the hotel you can buy five ounces of caviar for twenty-nine dollars. On the first floor, the same can of caviar costs forty-four dollars. Outside, the five of you who are traveling together ask for a taxi to go to a museum. You are told that five passengers are too many for one taxi, that you will need two taxis, and to take you to where you are going will be five dollars per cab. You hesitate ever so briefly to digest alternatives—and the driver becomes an entrepreneur in the Russian style. Well, he tells us grandly, we are not to worry: he will make an exception, and take all five of us in his one cab—for ten dollars.

In your room there are problems. There is no air conditioning in the tiny living room, and to go to the bedroom requires that you turn on the light that illuminates the dark stairway. But you then need to turn off the light when it is time to sleep. But you cannot do that without descending the stairway: there is only the single switch. So, you climb back up in the dark.

You need to telephone a companion staying in another room. You call the operator. Her line is busy. It is busy for one hour. The call is very important, so you descend to Reception and ask the woman at the desk for Mr. Peter Samara's room number. This proves to be on the order of asking your grandmother to come up with the picture of her high-school graduation. The receptionist hauls up a lapful of yellow slips and begins to go over them one by one. At the end, she says, "He is not here."

"Yes he is here," you insist. "He has been here for two days."

"He is not here," she repeats.

At that moment, Peter shows up, you exchange intelligence, and you ask for his room number, which is 601, so that from now on you can dial him directly. The next morning you wish to call 601. You follow the hotel dialing instructions. To call 601, you must dial 203 20 97. Well, you can manage that. Does that mean that to call 602 you would dial 203 20 98? No: 203 50 40.

At 3:30 P.M., on your way out, you report to the concierge that your toilet is stopped up. You come in at 11 P.M. and note that it is still stopped up. At 9 A.M. it is still stopped up. It occurs to anyone scheduled to check out of the hotel that morning that there is an obvious way to leave the mark of his displeasure.

The airport in Moscow is an extension of hotel life. You arrive three hours before flight time, as you are told to do. You need to complete a form which reminds you of Professor Parkinson's book *Oneupmanship*, because you are not given room enough to supply the information Moscow desires, in its glasnostian fury, to get from you. (If you are carrying eighty-seven dollars, you are required to write not merely "$87," but "eighty-seven dollars," in approximately one half inch of space, on a form which no Russian in his right mind, which includes some Russians, is ever going to read.)

But, somehow, it is not as it was in previous visits. There is the smile—not universal, granted: Gorbachev hasn't, in a couple of years, made Moscow into Tahiti. His popularity, according to a recent poll, was about the equal of the popularity in the United States of Lyndon LaRouche. What exactly is the voice of the Russian people is not easy to determine. It would be presumptuous to infer from the popularity of Mr. Yeltsin that their voice is the same as the voice of those who, two hundred years ago, were instructed by the insights of Adam Smith.

Meanwhile we need to guard against one of the fruits of frustration and despair, which is aggression. Any Lithuanian will explain just what that is. The Soviet Union has the mightiest strategic force in the world. We do well to take primary stock of Soviet capabilities, rather than bank on Soviet intentions. These are pacific now, but until the Soviets trim their capabilities to harmonize with their intentions, the West must stand watch.

My ensuing proposition is that *The decline of the Soviet Union cannot be arrested by United States foreign policy.*

Late in December, the Soviet government instituted rationing in the city of Leningrad, for the first time since the Nazi invasion in 1941. That is a measure of current Soviet hardship. Nine months ago I was told in Moscow that the Russian harvest was overflowing, but that less than one-half of it would reach the markets, owing to the collapse of rail and road transportation.

It has been nearly two years since then–Prime Minister Ryzhkov, facing the Congress of People's Deputies, announced that in his judgment the Soviet Union had eighteen months left to live, "unless drastic alternative courses are taken." We know that drastic alternative courses have not been taken, and that we are indeed seeing the dissolution of the Soviet state.

Over the course of a year, I advocated extravagant purchases by the United States of Soviet military equipment aggressive in character and redundant in quantity. What the Soviets needed, I reasoned, was one hundred billion U.S. dollars a year for three years, until they could turn their country around; and what we needed, to secure the peace, was the end of the destructive potential of the Soviet state.

My reading of recent events persuades me that the Soviet Union cannot really use the money. Its problems are organic. I am reminded of the short story by Oscar Wilde. The young man with the disfigured face pays a large sum of money to a sculptor to make him a mask to hide his ugliness. This is done and the man with the mask grows into old age, although the world knows only the fine young face provided by the master sculptor. And the man with the mask devotes his life to ennobling work, spending his time and resources to relieve the misery of others. In old age he falls sick and his doctor diagnoses the need to remove the mask, does so, and to the astonishment of the anxious company discovers young and beautiful features: the old unsightly face has been transfigured by the nobility of the life the man led, and now the mask has become reality.

The Soviet economy can't work its way out of the cesspool it has lived in until it shrives its past, and this can't be done by a transfusion of foreign money. The Soviets need to go to work, building something other than concentration camps and military hardware. "How did you manage to develop such a beautiful green lawn?"

the American GI asked the British gardener outside Windsor Castle.

"Well, sir," he said, "first you plow the ground lightly, then you sprinkle the seed carefully, then you water it for seven hundred years." . . .

I close by saluting you all. It was almost thirty years ago that Ed Feulner and I each put up fifty dollars to incorporate the Philadelphia Society. I swear, I never got a bigger bang for a buck. Don Lipsett has been our Big Bertha. We owe him the kind of debt that only sincerely convinced free men can give, the debt of gratitude. He has been the organization's catalyst. I am sure you share with me the sense, as I have suggested, of being his creature. But we are docile servants, sharply contrasting with that dumb servitude our enemy the state organically desires to impose on us. I wish you a spirited weekend which I wish I could share with you, but that would mean sharing with you my wife, and this the Supreme Court has not yet demanded. Good night.

SINGULARLY HUMANE

Remarks Introducing Aileen Mehle, at a Banquet Celebrating Her Honorary Degree from Marymount College; New York, May 29, 1991

A valentine to a talented fellow journalist (better known as "Suzy" to readers of her society column), though an unsuccessful teacher of the speaker on matters of dress.

WHEN I THINK of all the rabid-tongued folks in the world who have been awarded doctorates of humane letters I sigh with satisfaction that one of these degrees is going to one of the most singularly humane writers on the public scene. I noticed this a very long time ago. It must be twenty years since I remarked to my wife that whoever it was who was writing under the name of Suzy had an extraordinary capacity to communicate all kinds of things under a blanket of benignity just faintly mischievous. Her genius is quite exactly that: she can communicate any thought in humane tender. Satan in *Paradise Lost,* intending to go out through the gates of Hell, stumbles across the gatekeeper and accosts him in the following language:

> *Whence and what art thou, execrable shape,*
> *That darest, though grim and terrible, advance*
> *Thy miscreated front athwart my way*
> *To yonder gates?*

Now Dr. Mehle wouldn't put it that way, would she? How *would* she put it, intending to communicate identical thoughts to a monster of Hell? Well, do you know?, I can't compose it as she would do, and I possess quite a few doctorates of humane letters. You see my point: her skills are singular, and Marymount should be proud to have recognized them. All the more so since Mrs. Mehle's profession is not philanthropy. She is not in a position to donate a new wing to Marymount. As we all know, colleges are built by degrees.

Her skills include an extraordinary technical command of the sartorial vocabulary. Years ago I was with her for ten days on a charter sailboat at a time when I had published five novels without succeeding in dressing my ladies in anything other than a white pleated skirt, or a long-sleeved cashmere sweater. Aileen, who has so generously reviewed my books, confessed she could no longer stand my illiterate, undernourished, Apollonian costuming, and undertook to teach me a few words. I remember practicing them while onboard. One night I wrote down in my notebook that Aileen wore "tulle dungarees with a voile blouse, positively streaming with scarlet ribands that rustle with the wind in the cockpit over dyed Chinese characters." The next night I brought off, "Beautiful Shirley was dressed in tapered white suede pants with a mauve shirt with pouch pockets studded with mother of pearl." The final night I was so carried away that I described my wife going up to the top of the mast to fix the wind vane. Pat, I wrote, "was wearing a hoop skirt of green chiffon, laced

with a gold trim that would have knocked out the Incas themselves—
but Pat Buckley didn't even seem to notice, though she wasn't in a
position to talk about it, what with that nasty big black wrench in her
mouth."

I love Aileen dearly, and we have spent many otherwise boring
evenings, made palatable by giggling together. We have among other
things in common that as children we were both brought up speaking
in Spanish. Accordingly, to compete with the Latin that will appear
on her lambskinned doctorate, I offer her this, written by a romantic
poet several hundred years ago, Juan Alarcón:

> *Si Dios me permitiera,*
> *O dulce anhelo,*
> *Engastar la bóveda del cielo*
> *Con dos astros más,*
> *Allí fijaría tus ojos,*
> *O Celia mía.*
>
> *Y por qué, me preguntas, insensata?*
> *Porque así dos deseos cumpliría.*
> *Arrancarte tus ojos por ingrata,*
> *Y hacer más claro y luminoso el día.*

That is a private message for our guest of honor, only the last
line of which I will render in English. It tells us, in the splendidly
illuminating language of Cervantes, that were her eyes fixed in the
heavenly sphere, they would make clearer and brighter the day. She
has made clearer and brighter one thousand nights of toil, in the vine-
yard she serves.

"If He Gives the Blessing . . ."

A Toast to Monsignor Eugene Clark; the Union League Club, New York,
May 30, 1991

---

*No matter how eloquent, learned, obliging, and inspiriting they may be,
priests, ministers, and rabbis are seldom feted. Some of us decided this
should not be so, whence the evening in honor of Monsignor Eugene
Clark, celebrating the fortieth anniversary of his ordination.*

I CAN ONLY add to what has been said that no one could plausibly
imagine the special burdens over the years that I have imposed on
our guest of honor. I remember calling him to say that I had had
a letter from the head of the Nazi Party of the United States, George
Lincoln Rockwell, who said to me that if I could prove that he was
spiritually disoriented, he would renounce his platform. I asked permission to direct him to Monsignor Clark, reckoning that the
Fuehrer would have a much better chance of total immersion at
Monsignor's hands than at my own. They met: and what happened
between them of course we will never know. But here was Christian
outreach if ever I saw it.

That was bad enough, but perhaps even worse was to come. On
her second flight from the Soviet Union I had had a telephone call
from Svetlana, the daughter of Josef Stalin, who, even on slight
acquaintance, I had concluded was absolutely the daughter of her
father. She told me that she was thinking of becoming a nun and that
she would like to have a little time with that "nice priest" I, or Jim
McFadden, had introduced her to on her first visit. I told her (she was
calling, incognito, from Wisconsin) that I would instantly relay her
message to the nice priest—I knew instantly who she was talking
about: I mean, how many nice priests are there? She had asked me to
send her some magazines so that she could catch up with the Free
World, and I absentmindedly included a copy of the last issue of
National Review. A few days later I received a fiery letter from her
on which was pasted an editorial paragraph from that issue. It read,

"Svetlana's second return to the United States is, we gather, more in the nature of expulsion than sanctuary. There are some things even the Soviet Union can't tolerate for very long, and this is evidently one of them." She told me she never wanted to hear from me again, nor from "my" priest. I never sensed a greater relief than when I gave this news to Monsignor Clark.

And then there was the call twenty years ago. Monsignor, I said, we have a great problem. Our wonderful friend Frank Meyer desires to join the Church, and he is going to die in a matter of days. I spent most of today with him, and as a devout libertarian he is having a problem with one phrase in the Apostles' Creed. He simply can't get himself to believe in the "communion" of saints—it sounds vaguely collectivist to him, and he cannot desert his libertarian principles. The next day Monsignor Clark was in Woodstock, New York, at Frank's bedside. A few hours later, Frank was received into the Church, and the following day he died.

As I recount these stories I suddenly understand why it is so extraordinarily difficult for me to reach Monsignor Clark on the telephone. No doubt I would enhance my prospects of getting through to him by declining to give my name. I suppose I could say that Svetlana was calling, and his devotion to his mission would bring him to the phone.

I said to Monsignor Clark after our celebration of the thirtieth anniversary of *National Review* that I did not remember ever hearing a more inspiriting benediction than the one he gave that night. And I hope that, on hearing it, you will agree with me. Yes, I am becoming at this point a producer, with a three-minute "presentation"—which, I should warn you, overtaxed my mechanical resources, which is why here and there it is interrupted by odd noises, sights, sounds, and "Drink Coca-Cola" ads.

What you will see first is a minute or so of tape of the gathering guests at that anniversary dinner five years ago. You will no doubt recognize some of them. Some of them may be you.

Then the president enters the room. He is taken to sit at the place of honor, Monsignor Clark's table.

What happened then took about an hour and a half, with

speeches from the editors and from George Will and Jack Kemp and toastmaster Charlton Heston, and finally the president. Skip all that. We go directly to the benediction by Monsignor Eugene Clark.*

After he is through praying for the triumph of freedom in the world, you will see for a half minute or so what happened then. That is why I thought to put on tonight's program the legend, "If He Gives the Blessing, the Bad Guys Don't Have a Chance."

I salute my devoted and holy friend.

*"*Lord, our gratitude is flawed. We ever ask for more. Thank You, Lord, we say, for thirty years; may we have thirty more. But You, Lord, know this completely. You allow us to thank You in prayer; but, to console us, You graciously allow us to thank You through delight in Your gifts.*

"David danced for joy. Joshua reveled in victory. The Book of Wisdom celebrates inspiration, and the Song of Songs, sensuous beauty—all saying thank You by loving the gift.

"Lord, we have these thirty years loved those at National Review *who led us through our desert and cheered us with their legend-making roundtable. They kept our minds and spirits high.*

"Lord, bless every one of them, those with us and those with You; prosper National Review *for another generation; bless Bill Buckley, our founder, and all those who have sustained him these thirty years. Give him and them grace, joy, and protection.*

"Bless especially our president, who knows how much he needs Your guidance and help, to fulfill the noble purposes of his splendid service to the nation.

"We pray this, secure and happy in Your providence. Amen."

WE WON. WHAT NOW?

A Lecture (excerpted) at Vanderbilt University; Nashville, Tenn., September 18, 1991

Twenty-one months after the fall of the Berlin Wall, the Soviet Union dissolved, and the Cold War came to an end.

M Y FIRST PROPOSITION is that *After engaging in the greatest ideological struggle in the history of the world, we won.*

I was nineteen years old at the time the Yalta conference was held. Soon after that came Potsdam, and the West lost

Eastern Europe to the Communists. The Cold War had begun. On the last day of August, just eighteen days ago, the Communist Party was banned in the Soviet Union. Coincidentally, I am sixty-five years old. I passed from teenage to senior citizenship, coinciding with the duration of the Cold War.

It was a very long haul. Richard Nixon, writing a year ago and perhaps anticipating the delirious events of the last ten days in August, was substantially correct when he said that the West didn't win the war, the Communists lost it. Still, that verdict has to be qualified to make room for major and minor players. Where, to drop perhaps the biggest name of them all, would we have been without Aleksandr Solzhenitsyn? He and a dozen other figures from the Soviet Union earned their places in Freedom's House of Lords. The crowds in Russia, descendants of the men and women who stormed the Winter Palace, placed themselves between the Soviet tanks and the White House that sheltered Boris Yeltsin, and pledged their lives, their fortunes, and their sacred honor to preserve the fetus of Russian constitutionalism. And they prevailed.

In the West there were, everywhere, steadfast friends of liberty, but by no means can it be said that they dominated the public policy of the West. That can be said of only one figure. It was Ronald Reagan, history is certain to confirm, who suddenly forced the leaders of Soviet Communism to look in the mirror, and what they beheld was their advanced emaciation. The Western superpower, thought to have been castrated by the defeat in Vietnam, was busy deploying theater nuclear weapons in Europe, shattering any prospect of Soviet ultimatums directed at Bonn, Paris, and London. Moreover, the leader of the bourgeois world was determined to launch a program which the technological genius of America would almost certainly have caused absolutely to frustrate a Soviet first strike, and therefore any political advantage from threatening such a strike. It was, moreover, the same leader who had resurrected the moral argument, so successfully neutered by a generation of ambiguists. He spoke of the Soviet Union as an *evil empire*! He said that history would consign Communism to the ash heap: transforming Lenin's own words as an ode to historical determinism!

Soon after that, the rot began to take over in the Soviet Union. The war in Afghanistan, never mind that 1.4 million resisters had been killed, was not ending. The economy was ceasing to move. A new Soviet leader attempted to revive the morale of a deadened culture with transfusions of freedom, and the results were magical, the whole thinking world within the Soviet Union suddenly intoxicated by the glasnostian license. Structural reforms were, if not permitted, at least debated. The long design to overcome Europe had been frustrated, and one after another the nations of Eastern Europe peeled off. The debated reforms at home brought on a crisis, and on the eve of the most important of these reforms—a reconstitution of the Union of Soviet Socialist Republics—the dissenters raised their mailed fist in a final show of defiance. Within forty-eight hours, the counter-counterrevolutionary mandarinate fell. We would learn that the eight leaders who had sought to stem the tide were, during most of those critical hours, drunk on vodka. They had for most of their lives been intoxicated by more lethal drugs. Before the end of the week, the Communist Party was legally suspended.

We won.

My next proposition is that *Our victory in the Cold War gives us grounds for great satisfaction, but satisfaction diluted by historical humility.*

The human tendency is to forget past suffering, especially if it was other people's suffering; most especially if you were conceivably responsible for it, as we were in major ways responsible for the suffering behind the Iron Curtain, beginning at Yalta and continuing through the failure over four decades of successive administrations to pursue liberationist measures.

Looking over the dead Wall, if there is contrition going on among the hundreds of thousands of Soviet agents, including Mr. Gorbachev, who imprisoned, tortured, and killed during the past forty-six years, their grief is stoically contained. The Jewish community will never let the world forget about the Holocaust. Understandably so. Every living German is aware of that holocaust, most of them unborn when it happened. By contrast, not one in five hundred Westerners could answer the question, How many Ukrainians were starved to death by Stalin from 1930 to 1933? Not one in one thousand would know that that figure is higher than the figure for all those killed during the Holocaust. One wonders how many Oliver Stones, so mindful of the suffering associated with Vietnam, will during the next ten years devote their splendid, indignant energies to dramatizing the fate of Eastern Europe during the forty-six years just past.

We can sleep better for knowing that our cousins have regained their freedom. But we can't bring back those who lost their lives, nor bring back lifetimes in freedom to those who spent theirs without it. Like the Jews who survived the Holocaust, we are left only with the moral mandate: It must not happen again, to the extent that we can prevent it. Which raises instantly such vexing questions as, Might we have prevented the slaughter among the Kurds? And derivatively—because the answer is of course, Yes, we could have prevented it—would it have been prudent to do so? Strategically sophisticated? Historically mature? Politically advisable? . . .

THE POLITICS OF THE COMMON MAN

An Address (excerpted) to the St. Vincent's Foundation; Jacksonville, Fla., September 22, 1992

The primary season had ended. I excerpt from a larger talk the opening sections that speak of the primaries, and the political survivors.

I HAVE THE habit of collecting, every few weeks, data that interest me, and formulating a few propositions, which I'd like to try out on you. I hope wistfully for agreement from some of you, though I am reconciled to residual differences. If that happens, it shouldn't worry either of us. I have experienced rejection before, and you have doubtless been wrong before.

My first proposition is that *In a political democracy, where the campaign season is protracted, we can expect that much attention will be given to the theatrical side of politics.* Those critics who ask that all campaigns reflect the tone of the Lincoln-Douglas debates are bound to be frustrated. Accordingly, we need to inquire into the nature of the theater being given us.

Consider, for instance, the charge recently leveled against Mr. Bush that he is an ersatz Texan. Texas columnist Molly Ivins puts it this way: "There are certain minimal standards for citizenship. Real Texans do not use the word 'summer' as a verb. Real Texans do not wear blue slacks with little green whales all over them. And real Texans never refer to trouble as 'deep doo-doo.'"

It's true that someone raised in Connecticut who went to schools in Massachusetts and New Haven doesn't sound entirely natural when attending a barbecue in Texas. But the answer to all of that surely is: So what? It is the distinctive stamp of America that people from every corner of the country can and do move to opposite corners, or perhaps stop and put down roots halfway; and whatever the residual cultural or linguistic incongruities, they become legitimate residents of their new state, as Michiganite Tom Dewey became a New Yorker, and Illinoisan Ronald Reagan a Californian.

Granted, one trouble with politics is that it is by nature so awfully sycophantic. Consider Mr. Bush's forays into New Hampshire in February. Now we have no reason to doubt that Mr. Bush is enraptured by the beauty of the state. Why? Because it is a very beautiful state. But he asked us to believe that it was the very spinal cord of his geographical attachment to his native land, lying as it does between Massachusetts, where he went to boarding school, and Maine, the site of his principal nonofficial residence. On top of that, everybody knew that he was "fixin' to begin" to say the same kind of thing about Texas when he campaigned there, and about other states when he went there. Senator Estes Kefauver, when he campaigned for the presidential nomination, often forgot in which state he was speaking: so that he would dumbfound an audience in Montana by giving them a dithyrambic tribute to Wisconsin, which he had left that morning.

It is truly a disease, scrambling for votes. Take Pete du Pont, formerly the governor of Delaware. I have spent a fair amount of time with Governor du Pont in the last couple of years and he is a man of total directness. I swear when talking to him you are convinced that he has just finished consuming a month's supply of truth serum. But when I asked him a while ago how many nights he spent in the state of Iowa when running for president in 1988 he answered, "One hundred three." I gasped and said, How could you stand it? He actually looked me straight in the eyes and said he loved it. One's skepticism has nothing to do with the pleasantness of life in Iowa. But one is entitled to wonder whether anybody can really enjoy one hundred three nights in different motel rooms in any state of the Union.

It gets worse. President Bush has lately tried to give the impression that he is up on country music and rock lyrics—that, for instance, he is familiar with the Nitty Gritty Dirt Band (which he calls the "Nitty Ditty Nitty Gritty Great Bird Band").

George Bush happens to be a superior human being, attractive, generous, loyal, animated, warm. But politics tends to pass by anything that is understated, encouraging a kind of flamboyance corresponding to the politician's idea of what is truly ingratiating. The result is the distractions of synthetic endearments, exacerbated by the compulsion to substitute, for one's own natural diction, the vernacular of the region. Could it be that Bill Clinton is, actually, a private man of modest attainment?

I discovered last spring in Boston that young people are in high merriment over Governor Clinton and marijuana. Their attitude, after the wisecracks are done with, is: Well, what can you expect from a politician? To which the answer ought to be: More.

There are two aspects to the confessions of Governor Clinton that arrest the attention. The first is his statement that "I have never broken the laws of my country"; the second, that when he smoked marijuana he did not "inhale."

Concerning the first, there are all kinds of things wrong with it. In the first place, smoking marijuana is against the laws of Great Britain. So that he would appear to be saying that it's okay to break other people's laws, so long as you don't break your own. That is a distinction that might be honored in abstruse discussions of the reach of positive law. I speak as someone twice impaled by these little distinctions. Years ago, when asked by Johnny Carson, I blurted it out that, yes, I had once smoked marijuana but I had done so at sea, where there is no jurisdiction that governs the use of drugs. This led subsequently to the question: How did the marijuana get onto your boat? To which I gave the obvious answer: Parthenogenesis.

And, of course, anyone who has worked for the CIA as a covert agent has to change the subject if ever he is asked whether he has broken the laws of other countries.

Still, on that point alone, Bill Clinton reveals an ambivalent attitude towards lawbreaking. Besides which it is simply unconvincing to proceed as if civic-mindedness correlates exactly with lawful behavior. Anyone who has exceeded the speed limit has broken the law. Anyone who has left a five-dollar bill with a bookie has broken the law. Anyone who has quaffed down one more beer after the legal closing hour has broken the law. Anybody in Connecticut who practiced birth control before *Griswold* was breaking the law, and anyone who fornicates in a dozen-odd states breaks the law, to say nothing of sodomizing in some other states. This is hardly counsel to treat laws indifferently: it is merely a sociological observation. The claim that one has never broken any of one's country's laws is (a) incredible and (b) unnecessary.

And we get to the matter of inhaling, which is what most tickles the young. The reason for this is obvious: if one is going to experiment with marijuana, one is going to inhale. In fact, one pauses to speculate over a definitional point: Can you say that you have smoked marijuana if you *haven't* inhaled? Can you say that a marriage has been consummated if the bride is still a virgin? That's one for the graduate of the Yale Law School to answer, and it would be good to hear Bill on the subject. Really, it would have been so much cleaner if he had said, "Yes, I tried marijuana once. My impression is that most people my age did. It didn't happen to do anything for me, and I'm glad when I read that the incidence of marijuana use is decreasing." If he had said that, I doubt that he'd have lost a single vote, except among the gag writers in Las Vegas, who'd have been left without a whole repertory about inhaling that is a patrimony of the Clinton campaign.

The theater of modern politics appears to demand that someone running for President of the United States be a superior human being who on no account is permitted to display superiority. Mrs. Robert Taft was accosted on the first day of her husband's campaign for re-election to the Senate in 1950, a race in which Mr. Conservative was the object of much organized vituperation, particularly at the hands of the labor unions. She was asked at a huge assembly of women, "Mrs. Taft, is your husband a common man?"

She looked up, visibly put off. "Oh no," she said. "He is not that at all. He was first in his class at Yale, and first in his class at Harvard Law School. I think it would be wrong to elect a common man as a representative of the people of Ohio." The faces of the professionals around her turned ashen white after her first words. They were astonished at the standing ovation she received. . . .

"BETTER REDWOODS THAN DEADWOODS"

Remarks on Receiving an Award from the National Institute of Social Sciences; the Colony Club, New York, December 2, 1992

Fun and games on receiving an award in the company of Arthur Schlesinger Jr. (See the introduction to my debate with Murray Kempton, April 16, 1963, for a fuller account of the long-ago feud with Professor Schlesinger.)

YOU WILL NOT be surprised to hear me say that I am honored to receive, and gratefully accept, the award you have been so reckless as to give me. My first book, published over forty years ago, had some unfriendly things to say about the spiritual vector of the social sciences in America. I will spend very little time reflecting on whether the social sciences have become more agreeable to me, or whether I have become more agreeable to the social sciences;

and no time at all reflecting on which of the two explanations is the more desirable.

Wonders never cease! The last time that Professor Schlesinger and I appeared jointly was in 1967, or perhaps 1968, when we materialized at the PBS studio, having been asked to comment on President Lyndon Johnson's State of the Union message. It was a year in which President Johnson recommitted himself to fighting in Vietnam until that sad republic fought off the invaders. In order to assuage the dissenters in his party, he felt it necessary to conjoin, to that plank in his foreign policy, myriad planks in his domestic policy calculated to appease every appetite in his constituency. It was about fifty minutes after his speech began that he pledged to do everything he could to, and I quote the president, "save the red trees." At this point Arthur Schlesinger—who was only barely on speaking terms with me because I had once sneakily lifted a sarcastic tribute he had paid at a public debate to my skills as a wit and rhetorician and pasted that tribute all over the cover of my next book—turned to me and said, "Better redwoods than deadwoods."

I was startled by this explosion of witty impudence. I turned to him and said, solemnly, "Arthur, that is *very* funny." He looked at me, with that academic forbearance he uses on students who recognize the obvious, and offered me a jigger of whisky, which was the least he could do, given that we had still twenty more minutes of Lyndon Johnson to listen to.

Well, so it goes: the National Institute of Social Sciences has discovered common gold in Roy Goodman, Richard Stark, Arthur Schlesinger, and me, which reminds us of the high eclectic calling of the social sciences, among whose current responsibilities is explaining to the American public how it is that the Constitution prohibits a crucifix from being exposed in a public place while protecting a public agency's right to grant money to an artist for the purpose of installing a crucifix in a bottle of his own urine.

Well, the social sciences have problems, but tonight these are suspended as the recipients of your kindnesses acknowledge the honor we have been paid by an agency constituted by the Congress of the United States. It can't help occurring to some of us that the much-berated Congress, whose prestige is so very low these days, may be showing some of its crafty intelligence. Isn't it possible to guess that tonight, from sea to shining sea, ours may be the *only* organization deferring to the Congress of the United States? I do hope Arthur will conform to the inherent discipline of the evening. A generation ago Joe McCarthy used to give out the impression that Congress was red, and the term-limitation people nowadays give out the impression that Congress is, or should be, dead; and I am sure that from it all Arthur would say, "Better a red Congress than a dead Congress," on which proposition, I fear, I would need to continue a lifetime's disagreement with my talented and honorable friend.

With repeated thanks to you all, I bid you goodnight.

THE ARCHITECTURAL SPLENDOR OF BARRY GOLDWATER

Introductory Remarks at a Goldwater Institute Conference; Phoenix, Ariz., May 1, 1994

Margaret Thatcher was the guest of honor that evening.

I T WOULD BE fine if an evening in which we pay tribute to two great figures were entirely nonpartisan, but then if that were so, I'd be speaking about different people; their salt would have lost its savor, and so would we lose much of the pleasure that lies ahead of us.

We should admit it—up front, as they say—that certain declarations by Senator Goldwater have rattled some of his friends. But that is the way life goes, say I, who have declared in favor of decriminalizing drugs. Senator Goldwater was born with an inclination to keep his listeners on their toes. This is not to suggest that he has provoked everything that has been said about him.

Back then, the Reverend Martin Luther King Jr. observed

judiciously, "We see dangerous signs of Hitlerism in the Goldwater campaign." American Jewish Congress President Joachim Prinz warned, "A Jewish vote for Goldwater is a vote for Jewish suicide." And George Meany, head of the AFL-CIO, saw, in Senator Goldwater's nomination, power falling into "the hands of union-hating extremists [and] racial bigots." How lucky we are to have survived Goldwaterism!

But gradually the skies cleared, and now he is the object of nostalgic curiosity, and even of a certain self-reproachful awe. When someone about whom you warned so direly turns out to be as dangerous as your local druggist, as destructive as a summer shower, the conscience is pricked. And so it was not surprising when, a couple of years ago, *60 Minutes* did a segment on Barry Goldwater that bordered, by the standards of that draconian program, on the reverential.

I remember the fascination we all felt during his famous campaign of 1964. Our standard-bearer was disdainful of any inducements to bloc voting. Sometimes he even gave the impression that his design was to alienate bloc voters. He had no such thing in mind. He was simply engaged in acts of full disclosure of the architectural splendor of his views, at once simple in basic design, and artful in ornamentation. Campaigning in St. Petersburg, Florida, a center for senior citizens, he deplored the excesses of the Social Security program. Then he chose Knoxville, Tennessee, to wonder out loud whether the TVA—Tennessee's greatest shrine—was really a very good idea. Then on to Appalachia, where he deplored the Depressed Areas program.

For me, the crowning memory of the campaign was a tiny item at the end of a long anecdotal piece that appeared the day after the election in the *New York Times*. I have saved it, and you can still read the yellow, crinkled newsprint. It says:

"A neighbor asked, 'Who did you vote for, Lillian?' The question was put in Concord, New Hampshire, yesterday to a 72-year-old woman, who replied that she had voted for Lyndon Johnson.

"'What do you mean?' her neighbor asked. 'You've voted solid Republican for fifty years!'

"The neighbor explained that she was 'afraid' to vote for Senator Goldwater.

"'Why?'

"'Because he will take away my TV.'

"'No, no, no,' her friend reassured her. 'Senator Goldwater is opposed to the TVA, not TV.'

"'I know, I know,' her neighbor replied. 'But I just didn't want to take any chances.'"

I remember just after the 1964 campaign when my twelve-year-old son, Christopher, learned that his father was going to drive Barry Goldwater to the offices of *National Review* for a visit. He begged to be permitted to sit in the back seat of the car and promised to remain silent.

About halfway downtown there was a slight pause in our conversation, and from the back seat came the voice of a boy soprano.

"Senator Goldwater, do you want to hear a joke?"

Senator Goldwater said, "Sure, Christopher, what is it?"

"Well," said my son, "there was this Jew."

I froze at the wheel. Oh my God, I thought, my son doesn't know that our esteemed guest is half Jewish! I considered aborting his "joke," possibly anti-Semitic, by crashing the car into the nearest policeman; but it was too late. "Yes," said Goldwater, "so?"

"Well," said Christopher, "this Jew went to his father the rabbi and said, Father, I'm afraid I'm going to become a Catholic. So the rabbi said, Son, let's kneel down and pray. So they prayed, and soon they saw God come down, you know, like a cloud, and God said, Rabbi, *you* got troubles, *I* got troubles. You're worried about *your* son becoming a Catholic? How do you think I feel about *my* son?"

IT SEEMS ALTOGETHER too much that the political sponsor of modern conservatism in America should be in the company tonight of the foremost proponent of that philosophy in Great Britain. I know of no one better deserving of the tribute to be given tonight by the Goldwater Institute.

FROM WM TO WM

Remarks at a Memorial Mass for William F. Rickenbacker; St. Peter's
Catholic Church, Peterborough, N.H., April 1, 1995

A eulogy for a bird of paradise.

H E FIRST SURFACED for us at *National Review* when he
challenged the government of the United States. The
Census Bureau had gone to work collecting its data in
1960. Bill Rickenbacker had received what they called the "long
form," designed to elicit detailed information, the better to complete
the decennial inquiry into how many Americans were living where,
earning what, doing what, living how. Bill looked at the form, put it
in his wastebasket, and addressed one of his inimitable letters to the
secretary of commerce, whom he addressed as Dear Snoopchief,
denouncing the long form as an invasion of his privacy. C. Dickerman
Williams, *National Review*'s distinguished lawyer, undertook his
defense. He eventually lost and was fined $100 and put on one day's
probation: and at the end of the succeeding decade he tasted finally the fruits of his struggle when the Commerce Department announced that the long form would be completed only by those U.S.
citizens who wished to complete it.

Rickenbacker came to *National Review* as a senior editor, and
life was wonderful in his company. He retreated after eight years or
so, went into business for himself, wrote eight books, and continued
his studies of music, of languages, and of the canon of Western
thought.

But he never lost touch with us, and in 1991, with Linda Bridges,
he published the book *The Art of Persuasion*. A few years ago, re-
sponding to a rebuke for his failure to visit New York more often, he
wrote me, "I too wish I could move around a bit more, but I seem to
have simplified my life a good deal in recent years. Three or four
hours a day at the old piano will nail a fellow down good and hard. But

I have dreams, dreams in full color, not to mention aroma, of lunch at Paone's [the reference is to the restaurant around the corner, heavily patronized by *National Review*], which, by the way, why doesn't somebody burn it down and rebuild it up here in God's country?" The formulation of that last sentence is an inside joke, dating back to the opening sentence of an editorial written by the late Willmoore Kendall. It began, "Last week at Harriman House, which by the way why doesn't somebody burn it down . . ." There was some concern, not over the sentiments expressed but over the diction employed, until Bill relieved us by declaring that Kendall had used an anacoluthon, defined as "an abrupt change within a sentence to a second construction inconsistent with the first, sometimes used for rhetorical effect; for example, I warned him that if he continues to drink, what will become of him."

Bill, in his letter, went on about his schedule. "Now I'm moving steadily through the fifteen volumes of the collected utterances and effusions of Edmund Burke, and the more I see of him the less I trust him. He keeps reminding me of Everett Dirksen—not that Dirksen ever reminded me of Burke."

Bill was a professionally qualified pianist. "I've recorded," he wrote me, "to my satisfaction, four short pieces of our great teacher, the Bach of Bachs. Schubert comes next, and then a dollop of Chopin. I find this project far more difficult than it was twenty-five years ago. Two trends have been in play: my standards have risen, and my physical capacity has fallen. When I piled up my airplane and broke a dozen bones including my right wrist, I didn't advance the cause; my right hand, if I don't pay good attention, is still in danger of being shouted down by the unruly Bolshevik in my left—a faction that gathered its preternatural strength during ten years of intensive club-gripping on the golf course." He had been captain of the golf team at Harvard. And, like his father, Captain Eddie, he flew, until glaucoma stopped him.

His curiosity was boundless. "Did you see my Unamuno in the current *Modern Age*?" The reference was to an essay he had just published. "Next comes Ortega y Gasset. I've read twenty-one volumes of his and am now organizing my notes. I'll probably have sixty pages of notes in preparation for an eight-page piece. I don't think the name for that is scholarship; more like idle dithering."

It seemed endless, his curiosity. "I've been studying Hebrew very hard and loving it all the way. A wonderful language. Since college days I've wanted to read the Psalms in Hebrew; now I shall."

He was not altogether a recluse. A couple of years ago he consented to address my brother Reid's public-speaking school in South Carolina. Reid asked him if he had a particular topic in mind. He sent me a copy of Bill's suggested speech titles:

— How I Spent My Summer
— What the North Wind Said
— Counselor Said I Couldn't Eat Dinner till I Wrote Home
— Why I Hate My Sis
— Legalization of Crime: Pros & Cons
— Was Mozart Queer?
— The Bartender's Guide to the Upstairs Maid
— Merde! Golfing Decorum in Postwar France
— Are Lasers Protected under the Fourth Amendment?
— Public Speaking Minus One: A Tape Cassette of Wild but Intermittent Applause, with Stretches of Silence to Be Filled with Remarks by the Apprentice Orator
— Sexual Repression in Emily Dickinson's Punctuation
— Why I Am Running for President (applause)
— Why Dead White Males Don't Laugh
— Do Hydrogen and Oxygen Look like Water? I Ask You!: Chemistry Disrobed and Shown to Be the Fraud It Is

He kept in touch with his friends. When *National Review*'s expublisher Bill Rusher had his bypass operation, Rickenbacker wrote to me, "I heard from Claire [Bill Rusher's secretary] on Monday that his bypass was sextuple, which I thought pretty damned good for a bachelor, and look forward to sending him something cheerful as soon as they take the chopsticks out of his nostrils." And his concern for public affairs was alive as ever. "There has been some talk of flying the flag at half mast," he wrote me, "until the Court's decision [permitting the burning of the flag] is nullified, but I don't think a gesture of mourning is in order when the battle has hardly begun. Instead, I'm flying my own flag at full mast, but upside down, in the international signal of distress. A flag that has been abandoned by its own country is certainly in distress, and I intend to fly mine upside down until the Court turns right side up."

He enjoyed always the exuberant flash of muscle that interrupted, and gave perspective to, his serenity. "I have been a grandfather for five days now and I am growing crotchety. I have told both my boys and both my stepsons that the first one calls me gramps gets a knee in the groin but I doubt if I'll be safe much longer."

Though that was in 1990, he was right—not much longer. It was last fall that the cancer came. After the operation, he wrote to soothe me: ". . . my moribundity is no more serious than anyone else's of similar time in grade. The so-called treatment, which is in reality, as I need not tell you, . . . a form of Florentine poisoning, offers the advective cruelty of the absence of wine. Anyway I now have two Sanskrit grammars, a matched pair, and will present one copy to [his doctor] when next I see her, which I fear will be on Monday. My hope is that she with her wise Velázquez-brown eyes will find a way to administer my Sanskrit intravenously, with a dash of curry and the faintest after-aroma of popadams. (Do you remember when our mothers could buy popadams in large flat tins from India, the cakes packed between green tobacco leaves?)"

And, only a week later, a letter describing his doctor, whom he much admired. But halfway down the page, "EGGS ON FACE DEPT. When I sent you the copy of her letter, I failed to proofread her copy with care, and discovered only later that when she says she may extend a certain life span by two or three months, she means years. I double-checked her on this. So relax, mon vieux: it will be longer than you think before your life and property shall be safe."

The doctor was right the first time. But Bill went on with his work. "I've been having fun writing my study of three-letter words. Since the emphasis is on their history and not their definition or use, I have elbowroom in the definitions. 'Gun' for instance, which has a very peculiar etymology, I define as 'A metallic pipe through which missiles, which have been excited by chemical explosions in their fundaments, are hurled airmail to their recipients.' For the kind of people who like that sort of thing that's the sort of thing those people will like. And although I have made it a rule to exclude proper nouns, I couldn't resist 'Eli,' but I think I shall stay my mighty arm and not tell you how I defined Eli until Nancy [his wife] is rich and famous."

Bill had for a while been reading religious literature, and now he wrote, "I'm reading the pope's book. I bought a copy for each of my boys, gave one to Tommy, and held one back to read myself before giving it to Jamie. I should buy a third, because I want the book at my elbow always. It's so drenched in wisdom and experience and devotion that I can't take it in in one reading. I read sentence after sentence two or three times. What a man! Among the great souls of history, I say."

A month later I spoke with Nancy on the telephone. She had difficulty in speaking, but told me Bill had been given three or four days more to live. I asked whether I should write to him. Yes, she said, giving me the fax number. I had never before written or spoken to someone on his deathbed with whom circumspection was no longer possible. So I wrote to my dear and gifted friend:

"Wm, [this was our protocol, dating back three decades: all letters from one to the other would begin, Wm, and be signed, Wm]

"This is not the season to be jolly. Miracles do happen, Evelyn Waugh wrote in *National Review*, 'but it is presumptuous to anticipate them.' It will happen to us all, I brightly observe, but you should feel first the satisfaction of knowing that soon you will be in God's hand, with perhaps just a taste of Purgatory for the editorial you wrote when Bobby was killed, though I here and now vouchsafe you the indulgence I merited on declining to publish it. Second, the satisfaction of being with that wonderful Nancy in your tribulation; and third, the knowledge that those who have known you count it a singular blessing to have experienced you. I send my prayers, and my eternal affection. Wm"

In fact he lived three weeks more and, before losing the use of his writing hand, indited his own obituary, two paragraphs of biographical data, and the closing sentences: "A bug or two showed up last fall and began to do what a bug does best, namely, to make a joke out of life's spruce intentions, and to provide a daily wage or two for journalists, whose business it is not my duty as a Christian to inquire into. Sometime between when this ink and mine go dry the bugs will have had their day. He leaves behind him his wife and two devoted sons, two daughters-in-law, three grandchildren, a beloved sister, an unfinished manuscript or two, and a heart filled with blessings."

May he rest in peace.

O. J. SIMPSON AND OTHER ILLS

An Address at a Dinner Honoring Henry Salvatori, Hosted by Claremont-McKenna College; the Four Seasons Hotel, Los Angeles, May 7, 1995

The compendium of what isn't right in America includes now the trial of O. J. Simpson.

I MEAN TO TOUCH this evening on three current political concerns. The first is, How do we cope with the disparity between what we know and what we do? And, Are there political means of addressing that disparity? To give an example, if we can establish that steeply progressive taxation is unproductive, how is a self-governing society persuaded to alter its natural inclination to progressive taxation?

The second is, Can we, through politics, effect an evolution of the ethos, and if so, how? As a practical matter, how can we generate the spirit and the practices that have the effect of reducing poverty? Two factors that may contribute to the persistence of poverty have been isolated. The comprehensive effect of state welfarism on protracted poverty is in dispute, but Charles Murray has arrested our attention in concluding that welfarism generates attitudes and activity different from those once anticipated. What no one disputes is the contribution to poverty of single-parent families. A child growing up with a single parent is likelier, by a factor of six, to sidle towards illiteracy, crime, and drug addiction than the child raised by two parents. Are there political means by which we can at least arrest, at best reverse, the trend towards out-of-wedlock births?

And a third concern: Have we finally learned, from the ongoing O. J. Simpson trial, that we have edged towards travesty in the execution of justice, one of the three mandates of government acknowledged by Adam Smith?

ON THE FIRST point: Manifestly, some things aren't working. It is almost blasphemous to say that Oklahoma [the McVeigh bombing] is a vivid example. But at other levels also it is true: we are not deriving the advantages we ought to derive from the knowledge we have accumulated. This discontinuity is among other things a fundamental challenge to American idealism.

Consider the problem at the most basic level, which has to do with the plight of American education. The biological intelligence pool is there, and we know a great deal about effective pedagogy. And yet illiteracy prospers.

What is especially perplexing is the disparity between the amount of money being spent on education and the results achieved. Bear in mind that if we place the value of the dollar in 1960 at 100, then as of 1993, inflation had brought the general price level to 488. During that same period the cost of medicine rose to 908—and the cost of education to 1,360.

And yet 25 percent of U.S. high-school seniors identify Franklin Delano Roosevelt as the man who was president during the Vietnam War. Three-quarters don't know what Reconstruction was; and (my favorite) two-thirds can't place the Civil War within fifty years of when it took place. That means that two-thirds of our young adults are prepared to believe that the Civil War happened some time before 1811, or some time after 1915.

So what?

So what does that have to do with wages, wine, women, and song?

One young man, recently questioned by Mike Wallace on *60 Minutes*, wondered out loud why he should care to learn anything. The question is so majestic in its effrontery that one pauses, breathless, trying to come up with words that do it justice.

It wouldn't be hard to answer the petitioner's question if he were asking about purely practical knowledge. You can't carry a heavy load of material from one end of this hall to the other unless you know the uses of a wheel. You can't do plumbing without learning the tools of the trade: but a plumber, we are hearing it said in effect, need not know the difference between the Civil War and the Peloponnesian War, nor even which came first.

It is commonly urged on us that a shortage of money is the problem. But the highest SAT scores in the nation last year were earned by Iowa, South Dakota, North Dakota, and Minnesota. In dollars spent per student, these states came in respectively at twenty-seventh, forty-second, forty-fourth, and forty-ninth. The correlation regularly urged on us by the education lobby—give us more money and we'll give you a better-educated citizenry—becomes decreasingly persuasive. Not long ago, skeptical of the planted axiom about money and education, Senator Moynihan peered at a map of North America; located Iowa, South Dakota, North Dakota, and Minnesota; and suggested wryly that perhaps a safer correlation would be that a state's educational system is successful according to its geographical proximity to Canada.

Assign the blame as you like—on television, slothful parents, lazy children—still, the teachers are there to teach. We must assume a latent capacity to learn. But to enliven that capacity we need to communicate the value of learning. How is that done?

And what is the role of politics?

The knowledge was always available to Soviet officials that socialized agricultural production can't compete with production done by people who work their own land. Yet beginning in 1917, the government of the Soviet Union managed to record seventy-two consecutive annual droughts to account for the shortage in agricultural production. Meanwhile, demonstrations of the futility of socialized agriculture have been given to us in living Technicolor, as when only a year or so before the Berlin Wall came down, 6o *Minutes* did a documentary on two three-hundred-acre stretches of farming land separated only by the barbed wire of the Iron Curtain. One farm lay in East Germany, the other in West Germany. The yield of the western acreage was 6oo percent that of the eastern acreage, identically endowed.

Empirical evidence, in other words, does not automatically induce instructed conduct. Once burned is not always twice shy. A second marriage, Dr. Johnson mused, is after all the triumph of hope over experience.

Many problems are traceable to willful ignorance, which is different from lack of knowledge. Up until approximately 1982, users of unclean needles and practitioners of unsafe sex didn't know anything about the causes of a disease that proved mortal for so many of them. That knowledge is now all but universal. Even so, the disease continues to spread.

In contemplating ruefully such social problems as crime and illegitimacy we are forever being enjoined to look for "root causes," but it is never thought particularly useful to come triumphantly in from the fields and laboratories to report the discovery of original sin.

The cardinal human temptations, the so-called fleshly temptations, account for many of our problems, both personal and social, but hardly for all of them. It wasn't a fleshly temptation that drove Soviet planners for three generations to socialize agriculture, unless you call pride a fleshly temptation. What is the fleshly temptation that drives our teachers to look-say methods of teaching children how not to read?

The divide between the empirical knowledge we have accumulated and the dogged persistence of that extra ration of human affliction we might have been spared by the application of right and informed reason is our problem, is indeed the nightmare of conservatives. The dismay is all the greater for those who know what needs to be done, who know with the keenness of the man overboard who is separated from the lifeboat that the emancipating knowledge is there but, unaccountably, out of reach. It is as if one were standing by a great vat of vaccine as whole cultures succumb to the plague.

Attention accordingly focuses—my second point—on how a society undertakes to effect an evolution of the ethos. We have spoken about instrumental knowledge. The idea of a wheel to help move heavy material arrived in the awakened human imagination with its own palpability to recommend it. Instrumental knowledge meets resistance generated not by ignorance—the Russians knew how to increase the production of wheat—but by countervailing passions: ideological, as with socialism, or human, as with envy.

I somewhere wrote that in my lifetime I have seen only two absolutely discernible changes in the ethos we live with. The first has to do with ethnic prejudice. This was, in my childhood, an operative part of life, in low quarters and high—it was while I was at college that the first Jewish American received tenure on the Yale faculty. It is truly different today, whatever the lingering vestiges of the old prejudice.

The second has to do with a sense of responsibility to nature. When I was a boy we routinely dropped the garbage from our boat into the lake or sound. That simply is not done anymore. I believe that if every law on the books mandating fundamental ecological hygiene were revoked, and that if every law prohibiting racial prejudice were repealed, the ethos would sustain present attitudes. The law, Jefferson reminded us, is only a codification of public opinion.

How do we go about changing the ethos, or rather, re-establishing the tradition that enjoined us to acquire a humane education, and that curtailed procreation outside of marriage?

And—my third point—are we not provoked by the spectacle here in Los Angeles to raise other questions than that of whether O. J. Simpson killed his wife?

I recently heard the president of the American Civil Liberties Union tell an audience that her greatest regret was that not everyone accused of a crime has the same resources as O. J. Simpson.

But what we confront in that trial is evidence that the processes of justice are, if not universally stalled, significantly enough arrested to warrant asking whether justice is dying; and if so, whether it is perishing from the creeping immobilizations brought on in the name of civil liberties.

Certainly the traditional focus of the trial is altered. Leon Czolgosz assassinated President McKinley and seven weeks later, after trial and conviction, was executed. It is nowhere persuasively documented that he was in fact innocent. It is said over and over again but promptly forgotten that most convictions are based on circumstantial evidence. Leon Czolgosz was seen by a lot of people when he shot McKinley, but nobody saw Lee Harvey Oswald shoot President Kennedy, and Oswald was as surely the assassin as Czolgosz was. The long string of decisions by the Warren Court enhancing the rights of the accused buttress the idea of a trial as a game. More than a hundred years ago John Stuart Mill saw what the adversary system was heading towards. "People speak and act as if they regarded a criminal trial as a sort of game, partly of chance, partly of skill," he wrote, "in which the proper end to be aimed at is not that the truth may be discovered, but that both parties may have fair play; in a word, that whether a guilty person should be acquitted or punished may be, as near as possible, an even chance."

The criminal who gave his name to a famous decision of the Warren Court was acquitted and soon after resumed his occupation as a rapist, finally confessing his guilt. Judge Laurence Wren, who presided over the second trial, later reminisced, "When the verdict was finally in, I suddenly realized, with complete amazement and disgust, that we had not dealt at all during the nine-day trial with the basic question of guilt or innocence." Another way to put it is this: that the only obstacle to the establishment of the guilt of O. J. Simpson is legal. The whole epistemological apparatus of the modern world—psychology, science, logic, reason—establishes that he is guilty. Only the law, paradoxically, stands in the way of the application of justice.

So WHAT SHOULD conservatives do, who believe that politics must be put to the civilized use of adjusting practice to reality? What to do about shaping the ethos? About the evanescence of justice?

It is appropriate to recall the episode in the mid-1960s, after President Johnson refused to issue an executive order raising the pay of his speechwriters. Two days later he found himself in Austin, Texas, addressing a huge assembly. He turned the pages of his prepared speech one by one.

"Do you want to know the answer to the race problem?" he asked the audience. "Well, I have that answer."

He turned a page: "Do you want to know the answer to the problem of the proliferation of nuclear weapons? Well, I have that answer."

Again a fresh page: "Do you want to know how to bring peace and freedom to Vietnam? Well, I have that answer."

He turned the page and found himself staring at the words, "You're on your own, you son of a bitch."

But of course a conservative is never on his own, because we draw from very deep wells. They are not wells that bring up magic formulas that lead people to make always the reasonable choice. And they will not relieve a whole society of the temptation to sexual adventurism, or of the temptation to fanaticize such simple beliefs as that people must not be made to pay for crimes they did not commit. But they are wells which help us to resist the lures of ideology.

And even as we face problems that do not come at us with easy solutions standing by, we take some satisfaction from problems no longer acute. When I first met Henry Salvatori we were only a few years into the Cold War. It seemed that we were on a collision course with dystopia. It would be thirty-five more years before the Berlin Wall came down, signaling the end of the most highly organized threat to liberty in the history of the world.

During that period we relied on such inanimate objects as a nuclear repository. But we relied above all on sane thought and a clear and liberating determination. I know nobody who more strikingly incarnates the ideals of reason and liberty than Henry Salvatori. He did everything he could do as an individual to inspire the confidence and the devotion of the men and women who worked with him all those years. And then he took the fruit of his labors and put it at the disposal of men and women of a younger generation, charging only that they pursue the ideals he has so eloquently served since the day when at age six he got off the boat from Italy and began a lifetime of productive labor, leaving signs of his personal grace everywhere he lived and worked. I join you in honoring Henry Salvatori.

THE DRUG WAR IS NOT WORKING

A Statement to the New York City Bar Association; the Bar Association Building, New York, October 11, 1995

The audience was a panel of lawyers drafting a report for the New York Bar on the drug laws, concerning which I had frequently written. Present also, journalists and others especially interested in drug policy.

W E ARE SPEAKING of a plague that consumes an estimated $75 billion a year of public money, exacts an estimated $70 billion a year from consumers, is responsible for the incarceration of nearly 50 percent of those 1.3 million Americans who are today in jail, consumes an estimated 50 percent of the trial time of our judiciary, and occupies the time of four hundred thousand policemen—yet a plague for which no cure is in hand, or in prospect.

Perhaps you [gentlemen of the Bar] will understand it if I chronicle my own itinerary on the subject of drugs and public policy. When I ran for mayor of New York, the political race was jocular but the thought given to municipal problems was entirely serious, and in my paper on drugs and in my post-election book I advocated their continued embargo, but on unusual grounds. I had read—and I think the evidence continues to affirm it—that drug taking is a gregarious activity. What this means, as I see it, is that an addict will attempt to entice others to share his habit. Under the circumstances, I reasoned, it can reasonably be held that drug taking is a contagious disease and for that reason should invoke to the conventional protections extended to shield the innocent from Typhoid Mary. Some sport was made of my position by libertarians, including Professor Milton Friedman, who asked whether the police might legitimately be summoned if it were established that keeping company with me was a contagious activity.

I recall this reasoning today in search of philosophical perspective. Back in 1965 I sought to pay conventional deference to libertarian presumptions against outlawing any activity potentially harmful only to the person who engages in it. I cited John Stuart Mill and, while at it, opined that there was no warrant for requiring motorcyclists to wear a helmet. I was seeking, and I thought I had found, a reason to override the presumption against intercession by the state.

About ten years later, I deferred to a different order of priorities. A conservative should evaluate the practicality of a legal constriction, as, for instance, those states ought to do whose statute books continue to outlaw sodomy, which interdiction is unenforceable, making the law nothing more than print on paper. I came to the conclusion that the so-called war on drugs was not working, and that it would not work absent a change in the structure of the civil rights to which we cling as a valuable part of our patrimony. Therefore, if the war on drugs is not working, we should look into what effects that war has, a canvass of the casualties consequent on its failure to work. That consideration encouraged me to weigh utilitarian principles: a Benthamite calculus of the pain and pleasure introduced by the illegalization of drugs.

A year or so ago I thought to calculate a ratio, however roughly arrived at, in the elaboration of which I would need to place a dollar figure on deprivations that do not lend themselves to quantification. Yet the law, lacking any other recourse, every day countenances such quantifications, as when asking a jury to put a dollar figure on the damage done by the loss of a plaintiff's right arm, amputated by defective machinery at the factory. My enterprise became allegorical in character—I couldn't do the arithmetic—but the model, I think, proves useful in sharpening perspectives.

Professor Steven Duke of the Yale University Law School, in his valuable book *America's Longest War: Rethinking Our Tragic Crusade against Drugs* and in a scholarly essay, "Drug Prohibition: An Unnatural Disaster," reminds us that it isn't the use of illegal drugs that we have any business complaining about, it is the *abuse* of such drugs. It is acknowledged that tens of millions of Americans (I have seen the figure eighty-five million) have at one time or another exposed themselves to an illegal drug. But the estimate authorized by the federal agency charged with such explorations is that there are not more than one million regular cocaine users, defined as those who have used the drug at least once in the preceding week. There are (again, an informed estimate) five million Americans who regularly use marijuana; and, again, an estimated eighty million who once upon a time, or even twice upon a time, inhaled marijuana. From the above we reasonably deduce that the Americans who abuse a drug are a very small percentage of those who have experimented with the drug, or who continue to use the drug without any observable distraction in their life or career. About such users one might say that they are the equivalent of those Americans who drink liquor but do not become alcoholics, or those Americans who smoke cigarettes but do not suffer a shortened life span because of doing so.

Curiosity naturally flows to ask, next, How many users of illegal drugs in fact die from the use of them? The answer is complicated in part because marijuana finds itself lumped together with cocaine and heroin, and nobody has ever been found dead from marijuana. The question of deaths from cocaine is complicated by the factor of impurity. It would not be useful to draw any conclusions about alcohol, for instance, by observing that in 1931 one thousand Americans died from alcohol consumption if it happened that half those deaths were the result of drinking alcohol with toxic ingredients extrinsic to the retailed drug. When alcohol was illegal, the consumer could never know whether he had been given relatively harmless alcohol to drink—such alcoholic beverages as we find today in the liquor store— or whether the bootlegger's distillery had come up with paralyzing rotgut. By the same token, purchasers of illegal cocaine and heroin cannot know whether they are consuming a drug that would qualify for regulated consumption after clinical analysis.

But we do know this: that more people die every year as a result of the war on drugs than die from what we call, generically, overdosing. These fatalities include, perhaps most prominently, drug merchants who compete for commercial territory, but also people who are robbed and killed by those desperate for money with which to buy the drug to which they have become addicted.

The pharmaceutical cost of cocaine and heroin is approximately 1 percent of the street price of those drugs. A cocaine addict can spend as much as $1,000 per week to sustain his habit. The approximate cost of fencing stolen goods is 80 percent, so that to come up with $1,000 can require stealing $5,000 worth of jewels, cars, television sets—whatever. We can see that at free-market rates, $10 per week would provide the addict with the cocaine that, in this war-on-drugs situation, requires of him $1,000.

My mind turned, then, to auxiliary expenses—auxiliary pains, if you wish. The crime rate, whatever one made of its modest curtsey last year towards diminution, continues its secular rise. Serious crime is 480 percent higher than in 1965. The correlation is not absolute, but it is suggestive: crime is reduced by the number of available enforcers of law and order, namely policemen. The heralded new crime legislation, passed last year and acclaimed by President Clinton, provides for one hundred thousand extra policemen, for a limited amount of time. But four hundred thousand policemen would be freed to pursue criminals engaged in activity other than the sale and distribution of drugs if such sale and distribution were to be done, at a price at which there was no profit, by a federal drugstore.

So then we attempt to put a value on the goods stolen by addicts. The figure arrived at by Professor Duke is $10 billion. But we need to add to this, surely, the extra-material pain suffered by victims of robbers. If someone breaks into your house at night, perhaps holding you at gunpoint while taking your money and your jewelry, it is reasonable to assign a higher "cost" to the episode than the financial value of the missing money and jewelry. If we were modest, we might reasonably, however arbitrarily, put at $1,000 the "value" of the victim's pain. But the hurt, the psychological trauma, might be evaluated by a jury at ten times, or one hundred times, that sum.

And we must consider other factors, not readily quantifiable but no less tangible. Fifty years ago, to walk at night across Central Park was no more adventurous than to walk down Fifth Avenue. But walking across the Park is no longer done, save by the kind of people who climb the Matterhorn. Is it fair to put a value on a lost amenity? If the Metropolitan Museum were to close, mightn't we, without fear of distortion, judge that we had been deprived of something valuable?

Pursuing utilitarian analysis, we ask: What are the relative costs, on the one hand, of medical and psychological treatment for addicts and, on the other, of incarceration? It transpires that treatment is seven times more cost-effective. By this is meant that one dollar spent on the treatment of an addict reduces the probability of continued addiction seven times more than one dollar spent on incarceration. Looked at another way: Treatment for addicts is not now available for almost half of those who would benefit from it. Yet we are willing to build more and more jails in which to isolate drug users.

I have spared you, even as I spared myself, an arithmetical consummation of my inquiry, but the data here cited instruct us that the drug war is many times more painful, in all its manifestations, than would be the licensing of drugs combined with intensive education. We have seen a substantial reduction in the use of tobacco over the last thirty years, and this is not because tobacco became illegal but because a sentient community began, in substantial numbers, to apprehend the high cost of tobacco to human health, even as, we can assume, a growing number of Americans desist from practicing unsafe sex and using polluted needles in this age of AIDS. If 95 percent of the Americans who have experimented with drugs can resist addiction using their own resources and profiting from information publicly available, we can reasonably hope that approximately the same percentage would resist the temptation to purchase such drugs even if they were available at a federal drugstore at the mere cost of production.

Added to the above is the point of civil justice. Those who suffer from the abuse of drugs have themselves to blame for it. This does not mean that society is absolved from active concern for their plight. It does mean that their plight is subordinate to the plight of those citizens who do not experiment with drugs but whose life, liberty, and property are substantially affected by the illegalization of the drugs sought after by the minority.

I HAVE NOT spoken of the cost to our society of the astonishing legal weapons available now to policemen and prosecutors; of the penalty of forfeiture of one's home and property for violation of laws which, though designed to advance the war on drugs, could legally be used—I learn from learned counsel—as penalties for the neglect of one's pets. I leave it at this, that it is outrageous to live in a society whose laws tolerate sending young people to prison because they grew, or distributed, a dozen ounces of marijuana. I would hope that the good offices of your vital profession would mobilize at least to protest such excesses of wartime zeal, the legal equivalent of a Mylai massacre. And perhaps proceed to recommend the legalization of the sale of most drugs, except to minors.

LET US NOW PRAISE FAMOUS MEN

An Address to the Twelfth International Churchill Conference, Sponsored by the International Churchill Societies; the Ballroom of the Copley Plaza Hotel, Boston, October 27, 1995

At a conference commemorating the fiftieth anniversary of the end of World War II, I address the theme: Why is it that we praise famous men? And go on to praise one of our century's most famous.

WHEN I WAS a boy I came upon the line, "Let us now praise famous men." In succeeding decades I found myself running its implications through my mind. The evolution of my thinking is of possible interest to you under the auspices of this celebration.

Early on I found myself wondering why exactly it was thought appropriate, let alone necessary, to praise famous men. If such men were already famous, as the biblical injunction presupposes, then would they not disdain as either redundant, or immodest, the solicitation of more praise than they had already? It seemed, in that perspective, just a little infra dig to enjoin such praise.

Some time later I bumped into the melancholy conclusion of the historian who wrote that "great men are not often good men." That finding curdled in the memory. For a famous man to be praised, does it require that he be praiseworthy? And if he is not a good man, merely a man who became famous by inventing the wheel or invading Russia or writing *War and Peace,* should not the praise be confined to bringing to the attention of those who are behind in the matter that which the person being praised actually did that merits more vociferous admiration? Or is that obvious? Jack the Ripper was famous, but our praise of him, if such it is to be called, does not focus on his attainments, and the philosophical faculty comes to the rescue by suggesting the word infamous.

Then much later, much much later, I noticed a review of the life of Abraham Lincoln justified, or so it seemed, primarily by the author's diligence in bringing to light episodes in Lincoln's life, and aspects of his character, that work to diminish the myth. I found myself wondering at what point it is in the interest of civilization to devise a line between research designed to satisfy the curiosity, and research bent upon defacement, this last often an instinct of the egalitarian, who really thinks that all men should be equally famous, in the absence of which all men should be equally infamous. As in, If everybody can't be rich, then everybody should be poor. I am, at this stage in the development of my thought on that passage from Ecclesiasticus that tells us to praise famous men, more and more inclined to believe that the point comes when it is prudent, unless one's profession is in historical clinics, to accept that which has been legendary as legend, that which was mythogenic as myth; fortifying myth, ennobling myth.

When I was a junior in college and editor of the student newspaper I received an invitation to attend a speech at the Massachusetts Institute of Technology to be given by Winston Churchill, commemorating the midcentury. I drove with a fellow editor to Cambridge and awaited with high expectations the appearance of the great man, expectations made keener by the advance notices given by Mr. Churchill to the press, to the effect that the speech he would give at MIT would be an important historical statement.

Mr. Churchill's preceding visit to the United States had been to Fulton, Missouri, and we wondered excitedly whether he would go even further in characterizing the Soviet Union—perhaps as an evil empire? We watched him make his way, with some difficulty, to the stage—he was shorter than I had envisioned, less rotund. He guided a cane with his right hand, but even so needed help to rise to the lectern. Then the hypnotizing voice boomed in, and our attention was at tiptoe.

I remember rushing back to New Haven with some trepidation that the story I would write for the *Yale Daily News* might feature something Winston Churchill had said that was different from what the *New York Times* and the Associated Press and the United Press would agree was the major news story. In fact Mr. Churchill hadn't said anything very different from what he had said before, which was that the atom bomb, as we then called it, might prove to be the greatest humanitarian invention in history, making war so awful that wars would never again be fought. That hope did not prove prophetic, in that eighty million people have been killed in warfare since he gave it voice, but then it is true that most of them were killed in battles in which there was no general at hand with the atom bomb in his quiver.

But what mattered in 1949 was the sheer possession of the bomb. When Mr. Churchill spoke it was exclusively ours: copyright Los Alamos, U.S.A.; but the pirate paid no attention, and within months he would develop his own or, more exactly, succeed in transforming blueprints provided by U.S. and British spies into a nuclear bomb.

And then, of course, by the midcentury being celebrated by MIT, the real nightmare had already come to much of Eastern Europe, and only a year before had spread to Czechoslovakia. Mr. Churchill was to some extent on a diplomatic rein that night because he did not mention the name of Josef Stalin, referring instead to "thirteen men" in the Kremlin. But the image of Stalin was clearly in his mind when he reminded his audience that the Mongol invasion of Europe, well under way seven hundred years earlier, had been interrupted by the death of the Great Khan. His armies retreated seven thousand miles to their base to choose his successor before renewing their offensive; but they would never return to Europe. Might such a thing happen again after the death of Stalin? Churchill wondered.

Four years later, Stalin obliged us all by going, one hopes, to a world even worse than the one he created, assuming such exists; but it was not as when the Great Khan left this world without a successor: Stalin's successors would keep intact the evil empire for almost forty years. The plight of the captive nations, the dismaying challenges that lay ahead, the struggles in Berlin and Korea and Vietnam, the hydrogen bomb, the Cuban crisis, all unfolded with terrible meaning for those whose statecraft had failed us.

In October of 1938, a despondent Churchill had spoken in the House of Commons about the failed diplomacy of his colleague Neville Chamberlain. He said then, "When I think of the fair hopes of a long peace which still lay before Europe at the beginning of 1933 when Herr Hitler first obtained power, and of all the opportunities of arresting the growth of the Nazi power which have been thrown away; when I think of the immense combinations and resources which have been neglected or squandered, I cannot believe that a parallel exists in the whole course of history." But of course a parallel would come again, in Mr. Churchill's lifetime, and in that parallel he was a major player, if not, alas, the critical player.

In the same speech after the Munich conference in 1938 Mr. Churchill had ruminated on British history. Only an Englishman, surely, would be capable, except in parody, of the following commentary. "In my holiday," he said, "I thought it was a chance to study the reign of King Ethelred the Unready." (What did you study during *your* holiday, Neville?) "The House"—Mr. Churchill was addressing Parliament—"will remember that that was a period of great misfortune, in which, from the strong position which we had gained under the descendants of King Alfred, we fell very swiftly into chaos. It was the period of Danegeld and of foreign pressure. I must say that the rugged words of the Anglo-Saxon Chronicle, written a thousand years ago, . . . apply very much to our treatment of Germany and our relations with her. 'All these calamities fell upon us because of evil counsel, because tribute was not offered to them at the right time nor yet were they resisted; but when they had done the most evil, then was peace made with them.' That," Mr. Churchill said, "is the wisdom of the past, for all wisdom is not new wisdom."

Seven years later—and five years after England's, and his, finest hour had begun to tick, pursuant to England's denying to Herr Hitler the right to enslave Poland—Churchill prepared for the Yalta summit meeting. He confided to his private secretary, "All the Balkans except Greece are going to be Bolshevized. And there is nothing I can do to prevent it. There is nothing I can do for poor Poland either." To his cabinet he reported that he was certain that he could trust Stalin. The same man whose death he so eagerly looked forward to at MIT in 1949, in 1945 he had spoken of as a Soviet leader he hoped would live forever. "Poor Neville Chamberlain," he told Mr. Colville, "believed he could trust Hitler. He was wrong. But I don't think I'm wrong about Stalin."

His concluding experience with Stalin came just six months after he said this, at Potsdam, and by then Winston Churchill had come upon another historical force for which he was, this time, substantially unprepared. The first week in June 1945 he had gone on BBC to alert the voters against a domestic catastrophe which he was quite certain would never overpower even a country exhausted by the exertions of so fine an hour. "My friends," he said, "I must tell you that a socialist policy is abhorrent in the British ideas of freedom. . . . There can be no doubt that socialism is inseparably interwoven with totalitarianism and the abject worship of the state. It is not alone that property, in all its forms, is struck at, but that liberty, in all its forms, is challenged by the fundamental conception of socialism."

It was the fate of Winston Churchill to return again to power in 1951, yet resigned to a course of *not* fighting the socialist encroachments of the post-war years. He, and England, were too tired; and, as with Poland and the rest of Eastern Europe, there was nothing to be done. There was no force in Europe that could move back the Soviet legions, and no force in Great Britain that would reignite, until twenty-five years later, the visionary thunder Mr. Churchill displayed, speaking only to BBC microphones on June 5, 1945, since nobody out there was listening.

MR. CHURCHILL STRUGGLED to diminish totalitarian rule in Europe, which, however, increased. He fought to save the empire, which, nevertheless, dissolved. He fought socialism, which, his efforts notwithstanding, prevailed. He struggled to defeat Hitler, and he was victorious. It is not, I think, the significance of that victory, mighty and glorious though it was, that causes the name of Churchill to make the blood run a little faster.

In later years he spoke diffidently about his role in the war, saying that the lion was the people of England, that he had served merely to provide the roar.

But it is the roar that we hear, when we pronounce his name. It is simply mistaken to say that battles are necessarily more important than the words that summon men to arms, or that invoke the call to arms. The battle of Agincourt was long forgotten as a geopolitical event, but the words of Henry V, with Shakespeare to shape them, are imperishable in the mind, even as which side won the battle at Gettysburg will dim from the memory of men and women who will never forget the words spoken about that battle by Abraham Lincoln. The genius of Churchill was his union of the affinities of the heart and of the mind. The total fusion of animal and spiritual energy:

"You ask, What is our policy? I will say, It is to wage war, by sea, land, and air, with all our might and with all the strength that God can give us. . . .

"You ask, What is our aim? I can answer in one word: victory— victory at all costs, victory in spite of all terror, victory however long and hard the road may be."

In other days, from other mouths, we mocked any suggestion that extremism in defense of liberty was no vice. Churchill collapsed the equivocators by his total subscription to his cause. "Let 'em have it," he shot back at a critic of area bombing. "Remember this. Never treat the enemy by halves." Looking back in his memoirs on the great presidential decision of August 1945, he wrote, "There was never a moment's discussion as to whether the atomic bomb should be used or not." That is decisiveness we correctly deplore when we have time to think about it, but he was telling his countrymen, and indirectly Americans, that any scruple, at that time of peril to the nation itself, was an indefensible and unbearable distraction. Churchill was from time to time given to reductionism, and he could express frustration in searing vernacular. Working his way through disputatious correspondence from separatists in New Delhi he exclaimed, to his secretary, "I hate Indians." I don't doubt that the famous gleam came to his eyes when he said this, the mischievous glee—an offense, in modern convention, of genocidal magnitude.

But this was Churchill distracted from his purpose—the little warts Cromwell insisted on preserving; which warts lose their power to disfigure on such a face as Churchill's because of the nobility of his cause and his sense of the British moment. "Hitler knows that he will have to break us in this Island or lose the war. If we can stand up to him, all Europe may be free and the life of the world may move forward into broad, sunlit uplands. But if we fail, then the whole world, including the United States, including all that we have known and cared for, will sink into the abyss of a new Dark Age made more sinister, and perhaps more protracted, by the lights of perverted science. Let us therefore brace ourselves to our duties and so bear ourselves that, if the British Empire and its Commonwealth last for a thousand years, men will still say, 'This was their finest hour.'"

It is my proposal that Churchill's words were indispensable to the benediction of that hour, which we hail here tonight, as we hail the memory of the man who spoke them, gathered together, as we are, to praise a famous man.

THE UNDERPERFORMANCE OF THE PRESS

The Theodore H. White Memorial Lecture, at the Kennedy School of
Government, Harvard University; Cambridge, Mass., November 2, 1995

---

*The house was full, and I had been playfully introduced by my old friend
and adversary John Kenneth Galbraith. I address the question: Is there
a discernible bias, or delinquency, in the modern press?*

I NOTE FROM material so thoughtfully sent to me by Mr. Kalb that
my predecessors introduced their talks by recalling, where such a
link existed, personal experiences with Theodore H. White. I
happily do as much, because we were good friends.

I first met him in the fall of 1965. He had been commissioned by
Life magazine to do a piece on the mayoral campaign in New York
City, in which I was contending. With that total absorption for which
he was known, Teddy White scribbled in his notebook my replies to
his questions. At one point I introduced some levity. He raised his
hand, a rabbi's calm demurral. "Wait," he said. "Wait for that. We can
become friends later, at lunch. The next hour it's all business."

Not many years later a little club materialized in New York City,
its membership limited to seven people. It had a single function,
namely to convene for lunch every six weeks or so. I think we were
rather heady with the power we exercised. Teddy White was demon-
strably the most sought-after journalist in America. Oz Elliott ran
Newsweek. Abe Rosenthal ran the *New York Times*. Irving Kristol ran
the neo-cons. Dick Clurman ran the correspondents of *Time* magazine. John Chancellor ran NBC News. And, of course, I owned the
conservative movement.

We really did have a wonderful time, among other things exchanging professional intimacies without any fear of a leak. It was at
one of those lunches, in January of 1972, that Teddy described with
feverish anticipation the forthcoming trip to China of President
Nixon. He had applied, he told us, for one of the eighty-five seats

reserved for journalists, and he said he was confident—though in expounding that confidence he betrayed his apprehension—that given his distinctive history as a China specialist he would receive favorable consideration for one of the most coveted slots in modern journalism. I responded that, prompted by his enthusiasm, I too would apply to the White House. Teddy White paused, his eyebrows furrowed. He stared over at me brandishing contingent fear and loathing. "Buckley," he said, "if you are on that plane and I am not, I will never talk to you again!"

We were not only both on that press plane, but seated together. Teddy White was buddha-happy. He had a bulging satchel-load of books and magazine articles and clippings he worked over on those long, long flight legs, Washington to Hawaii, then to Guam, then to Shanghai, then to Peking. From his pile he would from time to time pluck out an anti–Red Chinese tidbit and offer it to me playfully in return for anything favorable to the Red Chinese I might supply him from my own pile, gentlemen's agreement. Now he beamed. "I have a clip here that says the Red Chinese have killed thirty-four million people. What will you offer me for that?" I foraged among my material and triumphantly came up with a clip that said the Red Chinese had reduced illiteracy from 80 percent to 20 percent, but White scoffed me down, like a pawnbroker. "Hell," he said, "I have that one already. *Everybody* has that one." I scrounged about for more pro–Chinese Communist data and finally told him, disconsolate, that I could not find one more item to barter for his plum; he smiled contentedly at this tactical victory, but I remember wondering whether in fact he had lost the war.

Books have been written about what happened in the ensuing ten days. I wrote ten columns and a long essay for *Playboy* magazine.

Teddy White came to grips with his disappointment, which in subsequent books he examined and re-examined with a conscientiousness that approached scrupulosity: but always he engaged the reader's attention, by his total commitment to the narrative excitement of what he was writing, heightened by his sense of theater and radiant with his concern for the language.

THE CHINESE EXPERIENCE in 1972 is useful in giving perspective to my thoughts on the curious underperformance of the press, and the bearing of its shortcomings on public matters. Some years ago I gave to Professor Galbraith the draft of an essay I was writing for *Foreign Affairs* on human rights and public policy. He advised me, with that ambiguity for which he is renowned, to put my conclusion up front, in the manner of the scholarly essay. Given that he has been so kind as to officiate over this assembly tonight and to give me shelter at his home when I am done, I oblige him here by saying, up front, that it is my premise that the politics of our free society suffer from the failure of the media to announce *verifiable* conclusions. Announce is perhaps not exactly the word I want. *Sustain* is better; an even better formulation, the failure of the media to correct factually inaccurate perceptions.

I say the Nixon trip to China gives us perspective. I was especially struck by an episode in Peking the day after we arrived. The banquet at the Great Hall of the People in Tiananmen Square had been hugely impressive, and the exuberance of President Nixon was such that following his after-dinner toast he raised his liqueur glass and circled the table, bowing, one after another, to each of the nine men and women who shared with him Chou En-lai's head table. I remember in my dispatch that night remarking that Richard Nixon's enthusiasm was at so high a pitch he'd have embraced Alger Hiss if he had been seated at that table.

The following day, those of us who had selected the academic option—our Chinese schedulers gave us three or four choices each day of what to do to instruct ourselves on the regime of Mao Tse-tung—were seated in the office of the rector of the University of Peking to learn about university life under the revolutionary government. Flanking the silver-haired rector, a scholar in his early seventies, stood two brachycephalic Red Guards, aged perhaps twenty or twenty-two, their faces grimly construed to suppress any temptation to geniality. The rector was addressing us in Chinese, his words interpreted by an official standing behind him. After a moment or two John Chancellor motioned to me and to Teddy White. He whispered, "I sat next to that guy last night. He speaks perfect English! He got his Ph.D. in chemistry from the University of Chicago!"

It transpired that the Red Guards were in effective control of the entire university system. They had forbidden the rector to speak to us in English because they did not themselves understand English and therefore weren't equipped to intercept any ideological error. This way, hearing the words in Chinese, one or both could, with a mere flick of the wrist, warn the translator, interdicting heresy, or inchoate heresy.

Later that morning, after surveying the ravaged university library, Teddy said to me, "The most unpretentious college in America with a China department could not make do with a library as sparse as this one."

Teddy White, the China specialist, was astonished by the lengths to which the Cultural Revolution had gone. The China of Owen Lattimore's time had been widely accepted as the flower of Chinese culture. The most widely read essays on contemporary China, devoured by every one of the journalists who traveled there in February 1972, had been published in two successive issues of *The Atlantic Monthly.* Professor Ross Terrill had described life in China, subsuming everything he saw in his reverie. He had concluded by asking, "Is China free?" and answering, ". . . but there is no objective measure of the freedom of a whole society. . . . At one point we and China face the same value judgment. Which gets priority: the *individual's* freedom or the *relationships* of the whole society? Which *unit* is to be taken . . . the nation, the trade union, our class, my cronies, me? This is the hinge on which the whole issue turns."

Now, in the office of the rector of the University of Peking, we had direct experience of what Professor Terrill had called the "hinge" on which the whole issue turns.

Yes, of course, we all acknowledge that ideology impinges upon the press, and even upon scholarship. But I am on my way to a different but related point, which is that the politics of a free society are influenced, sometimes even dominated, by impressions either created by a headstrong press or tolerated by an indifferent or collusive press, and that the result of this undereducation is that self-government is—what? led astray? corrupted? traduced?

Let me move, so to speak, to the other end of the inquiry, the political end. Some time ago I came across an observation—by a journalist, as it happens—to the effect that Great Britain is in several respects other than self-governing. He mentioned capital punishment. Capital punishment—hanging, in the British tradition—was abolished in 1965, notwithstanding that the polls established that more than 70 percent of Britons approved of the practice, public support that continues to this day. It was the journalist's point that members of Parliament, in this instance dominated by the sentiments of Oxbridge, opposed capital punishment, and, for this reason, capital punishment would not be restored. In respect of penology, Great Britain cannot lay claim to self-government.

What interests me more than the future of capital punishment in Britain is how to frame an explanation of this anomaly, an anomaly most graphically expressed in the syllogistic mode: (1) The British people are self-governing. (2) The British people wish to restore capital punishment. (3) Capital punishment is nevertheless denied. Whence we are required to shorten the pants of the major proposition, which now reads: The British people are in some respects self-governing. Or perhaps: The British people are self-governing for so long as they have the impression that they are self-governing. Let us suppose that Parliament, over the last thirty years, has quite simply understood itself as resisting mobocratic bloodlust. What draws attention is that I have never seen notice paid to this ongoing anomaly, save in that one lonely editorial. The rule seems to be: It is appropriate, when Parliament chooses to defy the will of the people, to distract attention from what it is doing. If the subject is brought up, change the subject. If you don't succeed, temporize. Stall.

Democratic hygiene, one would suppose, suffers from such impurities. The tablet keepers might be expected to speak out demandingly, saying some such thing as: *This is outrageous! The people want penological reform and Parliament refuses to give it to them.* A calmer way for the defenders of democratic rectitude to proceed would be to say: *Go ahead, go public with this business.* Parliament has the obligation to acknowledge the default. It should declare, in a public manifesto, that the people of England, in respect of capital punishment, are uncouth. The people desire of their representatives something their representatives cannot oblige them with, given that they are guided by more learned counsels, that they are blessed with a moral vision more farseeing, and therefore Parliament must most respectfully decline to reinstitute capital punishment. Edmund Burke and John Quincy Adams spoke such language and the electorate accepted it. This hasn't been done by the present Parliament, not explicitly, and the press is acquiescent.

Here is a relatively recent—and, in the context I speak of, utterly unnoticed—example, back here in the United States, of the phenomenon of press and politics passing each other on opposite sides of the street. This has to do with candidate Clinton, subsequently President Clinton, and the election of 1992.

Very soon after Mr. Clinton's inauguration, the *New York Times* published a series of articles by its Washington correspondent, David Rosenbaum. He undertook to give the reader what he called "the push and pull over taxes."

In the introductory piece Mr. Rosenbaum wrote, "One popular misconception is that the Republican tax cuts caused the crippling federal budget deficit. The fact is, the large deficit resulted because the government vastly increased what it spent each year, while tax revenues changed little."

You will have surmised that my question is, *Why* was there a "popular misconception"? How is it that the real picture of a subject so regularly reported on by the *New York Times* was so very different from what the American people had been led to believe?

The misperceptions go on. What about public spending on the infrastructure under Reagan-Bush? In *Newsweek,* early in March of 1993, we read reporter Robert Samuelson, who told us, "Clinton's basic rationale for more government is that investment in America has lagged. Actually, that isn't the case."

What? How so?

He went on, "Business investment has risen in every decade since World War II. In the 1980s, it averaged 11.5 percent of gross domestic product, up from 10.5 percent in the 1970s, 9.5 in the 1960s, and 8.9 in the 1950s. . . . Research and development spending—by business, government, and universities—jumped dramatically in the 1980s. The increase was 52 percent, compared with only a 12 percent gain in the 1970s. Even government investment has revived somewhat. Since 1980, highway spending (adjusted for inflation) has risen about a quarter. Contrary to popular impression, road conditions have gradually improved. Between 1983 and 1991, the share of urban interstate highways rated as poor dropped from 17 to 8 percent."

You will have surmised, again, that I wonder that the press declines a responsibility to illuminate that which is knowable in public controversy, and to maintain a spotlight on that which is known, when there are indications that the shadows of ignorance or of obfuscation threaten. Many years ago I wrote a book the subtitle of which was *The Superstitions of "Academic Freedom."* In it I deliberated on what is now pretty generally classified, and widely tolerated, as epistemological pessimism, the position that nothing is truly knowable. The premise of academic freedom, back in the 1950s, was that all ideas should be permitted to start even in the race, to use the phrase of Professor William Heard Kilpatrick of the Columbia School of Education. His position can be said to have stood on the shoulders of John Stuart Mill, who instructed us that no question can be deemed to be closed so long as a single person dissents from the common answer. One supposes that deconstructionism is the apotheosis of this position, which flowers everywhere, as among the jurors who freed Mr. O. J. Simpson.

It is a matter not of conjecture but of established knowledge that when taxes are raised or lowered, people will manage their financial lives differently; yet we continue to countenance economic projections based on static models. We know that inflation has devalued capital gains, but much of the press is given to a nonchalant silence when arguments against a capital-gains tax cut are advanced in the context of "fairness."

If it was knowable that the Maoists had totally eliminated freedom in the Chinese academy, that the British view on penology is routinely defied by Parliament, and that in the 1980s spending and taxes
and public investment moved differently from how the public
believed they did, why were all these facts not universally known?
Public ignorance in these matters happened because less-than-the-
truth suits the political strategies of ambitious office seekers and
because the press is willing, given congenial ideological circumstances, to defer noticing such anomalies. The alternative here was for
the press to accept responsibility for informing the public on what is
really going on, and not merely informing it but keeping it informed,
focusing on publicly ventilated misrepresentations as required to dis-
pel encroaching ignorance. On behalf of the Brookings Institution,
John E. Chubb and Terry M. Moe, respectively a senior Brookings
fellow and a political science professor at Stanford, conducted a rigorous statistical analysis of a massive schools-and-students database.
They reached the conclusion two years ago that school choice is
essential to the improvement of high-school students' scores on stan-
dardized tests. The great lobby on the other side, the teachers unions,
is just that: a lobby that is successful at the cost of relative American
illiteracy. Why is such a lobby safe from relentless public exposure?

Of course, the voucher question brushes up against constitutional interpretation, most conspicuously against the engulfing interpretation of the establishment-of-religion clause as forbidding any
grant-in-aid to religious schools. We arrive at a raw example of a
slothful press. Professor Eugene Genovese is a historian and political
scientist of some distinction, in political sympathies a socialist. In a
recent essay he remarked in passing on what he called the "monstrous" rulings of the Supreme Court at the expense of the freedom
of the community to specify the nature of religious instruction in the
local public school. Ad hoc, we get away with it: in Brooklyn the
schools close for Yom Kippur; here and there they close on Good
Friday; but such freedoms are exercised in constant fear of judicial
intervention. The ministers, priests, and rabbis of New York City
combined thirty-five years ago to formulate a prayer which in their

judgment was free of any denominational opportunism. That prayer—devised by religious leaders deputized to undertake that function by the men and women whose children attended New York City's public schools—was struck down by the Court as constituting an encroachment on the separation of church and state. The Court was not quite willing, in *Engel v. Vitale,* to opine that the saying of that prayer itself constituted the union of church and state. Rather, it relied, as most of the Court's votaries continue to do, on the slippery-slope argument, that if you admit common prayer or, as we would subsequently see, the exposure of the Ten Commandments on a school wall, you are risking a loss of constitutional gravity, auguring free fall into the arms of theocracy.

Now all this appears to me an assault on self-government that the press condones because the anti-religious sanctions appeal to secularist sensibilities. Probing the question with Mr. Ira Glasser of the American Civil Liberties Union I recently volunteered to make a major contribution to his organization if he would submit to a truth test that documented his genuine fear that the restoration of common prayer would risk the advent of a theocratic state. He laughed and changed the subject, but I knew that he was crying on the inside. Why does the press play dead on this point? Is it hypnotized? And if so, on what else is it hypnotized? Does it toss and turn over the spurious concern given to theocratic hobgoblins, or, like Harry Truman after he ordered the atom bomb dropped on Hiroshima, does it simply turn in for a good night's sleep?

The list of public misperceptions is pretty long. In October, grown senators and congressmen, including one or two who had served as college professors—including one who had served *here* as a college professor—were describing the proposed tax bill as "a rip-off for the rich." Let us suppose that every penny of the proposed capital-gains tax reductions would flow to the rich, never mind that this isn't so. Even then, capital-gains tax reductions account for only 25 percent of the proposed tax reductions. So that the defensible way to communicate one's opposition to the bill would be: "*One-quarter* of the tax reduction will flow to the rich, who are the predatory class." Now, politicians will take any provision they dislike, in any bill, and proceed to condemn the whole of it. My question isn't how do you get politicians to stop doing that kind of thing, because that would require reshaping human nature. But I wonder why the press doesn't require the politician to confront his distortions. In 1950, Senator Robert A. Taft, the primary sponsor of the Taft-Hartley Bill passed that year and denounced by all labor leaders and many Democrats as the "slave-labor act," ran for re-election in Ohio. His agents quietly distributed a poll among a valid sample of labor-union members itemizing a number of measures regulating union activity. The questionnaire asked which of those measures were approved by the union member filling out the form. The experiment established that fourteen of the seventeen provisions of the Taft-Hartley Slave-Labor Bill were popular with 80 percent of the slave laborers of the state of Ohio. But it was Senator Taft who brought that off, not Hearst, or Scripps Howard, or UP.

Self-government presupposes knowledge, at various degrees of intimacy, of what the public question is, and how it is proposed to deal with it. The dissemination of this knowledge is primarily the function of the press, which one supposes is the reason Jefferson once said he'd take a free press over government, if the choice had to be made. A mad current passion is increasing the size of the vote. We now receive a voter-registration card when applying for a driver's license, which card the applicant need not demonstrate his ability to read. This is a fetishistic extension of the democratic argument. It used to be that a voter needed to prove his literacy in English. First the trendsetters dropped the need for literacy, subsequently the need for English.

We are asked to assume that the vote is the important thing, not the information required to vote intelligently. But information, of course, is not enough. I repeat it here only because to fail to do so, in the context of my analysis, would seem strange to those who have heard it. What I wrote thirty years ago, pleading the necessity for political judgment to supplement sheer knowledge, was that I would sooner be governed by the first two thousand names in the Boston telephone directory than by the faculty of Harvard.

But for all the delinquencies of the press, there is out there a hard, inquisitive intelligence. Seven years ago I met with Professor Galbraith, on the *Today* show, the morning after the presidential election in which the Democratic challenger from Massachusetts received only the electoral vote of Massachusetts. Mr. Bryant Gumbel asked my reaction to the returns, and I said that the vote in Massachusetts had perhaps established that there is, after all, a need for federal aid to education, if only for this state. Mr. Galbraith interposed to remark that Massachusetts has always prided itself on being ahead of the general political culture.

Belatedly, I defer to Professor Galbraith's tribute. Yesterday, Governor Weld of Massachusetts proposed abolishing most state agencies here, to effect a $650 million saving. Those he would not eliminate, he would privatize. He was acting on recommendations made, at his invitation, by individual citizens who had.

The moment is clearly at hand first to thank Mr. Galbraith for his courtesies tonight, even as I thank you for yours, and then to congratulate him on his residence in the proud state in which the culture of our *Mayflower* forefathers has given us one more bloom.

THE MOTHER HEN OF MODERN CONSERVATISM

Remarks Introducing Lady Thatcher at the Golden Jubilee of the Foundation for Economic Education; the Waldorf-Astoria, New York, April 11, 1996

Wherein is recounted my first meeting with the guest of honor, and an ensuing social embarrassment.

THE YEAR THE Foundation was launched—1946—was the year I entered college. We would need the imagination of Oliver Stone to convey the stillness on the intellectual scene. It was rumored that F. A. Hayek was somewhere around looking for serfdom, and another mad Austrian was doing work on human action. But the postwar scene featured the consolidation of the New Deal in America, the renunciation of the Churchill government in Great Britain, the triumph of the Middle Way in northern Europe, and the need to reconstitute the infrastructure, brick by brick, in Germany and Italy.

Few of us would now question that a defining event of 1946 was the founding of a small, bookish think tank by the Hudson River where Leonard Read gathered a group of restive scholars and gave them nourishment from that huge libertarian literature he had collected and held to his bosom through that dark period of ignorance and indifference to the individual. We must flash way, way forward—a whole generation—to arrive at the year in which Margaret Thatcher was selected to lead her party with a mandate, no less, to revive the British spirit.

It was only three years ago that she published her memoirs, after serving over eleven years as prime minister. Much of the public and all of her critics were dismayed by the size of the crowds who lined up to purchase her book. Including young people! Young people, if they ever knew, tend to forget quickly, and it had been three years since Mrs. Thatcher ceased to govern; moreover, anti-Thatcher fever had run riot in critical circles. If she was so conventional, one critic observed, why did she not do the conventional thing that retired statesmen do—fade away?

Far from it. Margaret Thatcher fades away much as Elizabeth Taylor fades away. When last publicly observed, all of three weeks ago, Lady Thatcher was commemorating another anniversary, of Winston Churchill speaking at Fulton, Missouri: also fifty years ago. She gave sound counsel, as he had done. The tender for his warning was the atom bomb. For hers, the intercontinental ballistic missile.

The public reception given to her two volumes required one or two reviewers to acknowledge, however grumpily, that Mrs. Thatcher had transcended her politics. One has to struggle to remember exactly what "Gaullism" was, but not at all to remember who Charles de Gaulle was. It is of course so with Winston Churchill and, it gradually transpires, it is so with Margaret Thatcher. Loathe her though they do, they are left having to cope with these early signs of the lap-idary judgment of history, which is undeniable. We are coming to realize that she and Churchill and Lloyd George are the dominant political figures in twentieth-century British history.

Just a little while ago I heard Dr. Kissinger, at a private seminar, say, "Prime Minister Thatcher—I shall always refer to her as such, since there can never be her equivalent . . ." In which connection I remember an incident almost twenty years old.

I had resolved, just before my fiftieth birthday, that the time had come to abandon some of the more formal habits I had inherited from my father, principal among them, steadfastly to use surnames except among rather exact contemporaries. As I reflected on the question, it struck me that for the fifteen-year-old to address the twenty-five-year-old as "Mr. Templeton" was a deferential acknowledgment of a certain seniority. But as one got older, I analyzed, to abide by such a convention has the effect of a forty-year-old rubbing it in on Mr. Templeton that, at fifty, he is ten years older than his junior, leaving the impression that one is strutting one's relative youth.

And so I resolved when on *Firing Line*—or for that matter else-where—to change my ways, and to reciprocate the idiomatic infor-mality of my guests, the next one of whom, as it happened, was Mrs. Margaret Thatcher, a candidate for leader of the Conservative Party of Great Britain. Towards the end of the program, I heard the word "Bill" come out of her mouth, as she turned to me with that patient, importunate smile. I took a deep breath and resolved to embark on my new social protocols; and accordingly the following day, going through the receiving line at a reception in her honor, I beamed, "Hello, Margaret!"

She replied with a smile, "How are you, Mr. Buckley?"

The following morning, in a daze of mortification, I raced through the transcript of our program, only to discover to my horror that when I had heard her calling me "Bill," she was in fact making a ref-erence to the Bill of Rights. My trauma was total, and I instantly re-verted to my old habits, as I confessed in my column on the subject, which was published in the Paris *Herald Tribune*—resulting, a few days later, in a letter from London. It began, "Dear Bill." And was signed, "Margaret."

She is blessed not only by generous instincts toward the aggrieved who need balm. She is blessed also by a singular capacity to combine absolute firmness with sweetness of manner, attributes that have made her the formidable historical figure she is. True, one sometimes has the feeling that as soon as she mastered grammar and reason, she swung immediately into the mode—rhetoric—which the medieval teachers of the trivium told us it was the purpose of grammar and reason to inform. She loves the analytical gardens, and I have seen her visibly entranced by the same kind of poetical trenchancy in which she specializes.

But after she has listened, and weighed the arguments, her trademark is to stand up, and to take action. When philosophy is said and done, there has to be a political activist to make use of the accumulated knowledge. As she once put it, the cock can crow and crow and crow, but the hen has to lay the egg. Lady Thatcher is a mother hen of civilized thought and action. I know of no one better deserving of the tribute to be given tonight by the Foundation for Economic Education.

WHO CARES IF HOMER NODDED?

A Commencement Address at St. John's College; Annapolis, Md., May 19, 1996

My personal favorite.

YOU WILL NOT be surprised, I take it for granted, if a commencement speaker makes mention of his association, however attenuated, with St. John's College. Well, I mean to do just that—to invoke St. John's—and not to stop there but to deduce from the association a theme, my ambition being to catch your attention, however fleetingly, in competition with the fireworks that are so understandably a part of this day.

From quite early on, beginning when I was twelve or thirteen, I heard my father say that he hoped his sons, of whom I was the third, would attend St. John's. This did not happen, my brothers and I opting for the geographically expedient Yale, only an hour's drive from where we lived. But my father's reverence for the idea that animates St. John's lingers in the memory, and later on I would read references to this college in the work of my father's friend Albert Jay Nock. Mr. Nock was not given to ambiguity, and if I remember right, at one point he pronounced St. John's the only college in the United States where a student could still receive an education. As I think back on it, his views on education were more complacent than those of my father, who in a moment of exasperation with the modern curriculum told his ten children that, in America, either one could go to college, or one could receive an education.

Mr. Nock exaggerated, of course, but he would not be distracted from his main point, which was that any attempt at education that isn't grounded in Athens and Rome is quite simply evasive. Because, he said, every subject that challenges human curiosity and intimates the resources of the human mind is sitting there in the copious inventory left by ancient Greece and Rome. To ignore them, as most curricula now do, is to ignore the primary deposits of Western intellectual experience.

Most educators would classify any such claim as exorbitant, and many even deal with it condescendingly: this is easier to do now that Mr. Nock is dead, because he knew very well how to bite back, in any of the five languages he had mastered. Critics will cite the huge events in human thought and experience that came *after* the fall of Rome. No matter—St. John's is not here to deny the importance of what came later, which after all figures prominently in your own curriculum. Albert Jay Nock was insisting on the indispensability of root knowledge, of what is learned only, he insisted, by knowing first what was thought and done between the time of Homer and the time of Marcus Aurelius.

But our mind then turns to the other end of the scale, to the pro-liferation of knowledge.

How is it possible to keep up in today's world?

The answer is that it *isn't* possible to "keep up," in any actuarial sense.

Someone somewhere remarked that Erasmus was probably the last man on earth about whom it could more or less safely be said that he knew everything there was to know. By "everything" was meant everything in the Western canon. Probably that means that Erasmus was known to have read every book then existing in those Western languages in which books were written. Knowledge was finite in the fifteenth century, and so tightly packed that the entire Western library fitted into a single room in Salamanca. One still finds it, framed and hanging over the arched doorway through which one passes on leaving the library, a papal bull of excommunication automatically acti-vated against any scholar who departed that room with one of those invaluable volumes hidden in his habit.

Five hundred years later we are told that twice as much "knowl-edge" is charted with the passage of every decade. Suppose, by way of illustration, that at the end of every decade the penetrating reach of a telescope doubles. In that event you begin the decade knowing X about astronomic geography. At the end of the first decade, you know $2X$; at the end of the second decade, $4X$; and so on.

All this is so primarily because of the multiplier effect of com-puterized explorations. On *that* question skepticism is dead, very dead. It was only a hundred years ago that George Bernard Shaw was told that the speed of light had been ascertained to be 186,000 miles per second. He replied that such a finding was either a physicist's effrontery or a plain lie. But we know now that raw knowledge has to increase. Pol Pot made a titanic effort to bring about nescience in Cambodia. His undertaking, twenty years ago, was to kill everyone who was literate—excepting, presumably, those at his command who needed to decipher his instructions to kill everybody else who could read instructions. He tried very hard, killing almost one-third of the Cambodian population; but he did not succeed in his ambition, and no one will. The wonderful line from the Russian novelist Ilya Ehrenburg comes to mind here, that when all the world is covered by asphalt, somewhere a blade of grass will force open a crack, finding its ineluctable way through to sunlight.

The knowledge explosion, as we have come to refer to it, is philosophically accepted. With this acceptance comes a discreet resignation to living in relative ignorance, on a progressive scale.

So THEN THE question peeks in at us: What is it that we are expected to keep on knowing? And what are the prospects in the years ahead for the survival of a common cultural vocabulary?

If we mean to continue to talk to one another, don't I have to understand what you're saying if, to excuse an inattention, you remind me that, after all, even Homer nodded?

To know this is different from knowing that the earth is round, that a day comprises twenty-four hours, or that the seasons follow one another. But can we assume that the computer programmer, master of his own discipline, will in a moment of frustration console himself by reflecting that—even Homer nodded?

It is fair to ask, Why remember this formulation? To which the reply is that there is no design here to forsake others, merely to give an illustration. Besides, the defense avers, with the ascendancy of myth-breaking science, we should cherish a formulation that reminds us of man's fallibility. The impulse to self-government, along with the exercise of the scientific method, wore down many encrustations. The belief in the divine right of kings began to wither on the over-burdened wings of certitude. It was in the seventeenth century, the lexicographers tell us, that the phrase about Homer gained currency. If fallibility could catch up with Homer, how much likelier it is that we will err. Homer was the august poet universally regarded as unerring (the divine Homer). Yet it was before the time of Christ that textual explorations caught him up, in one case describing a ship in which he placed the rudder on the bow end. It was Horace who wrote that "even excellent Homer sometimes nods."

By documenting an imperfection in the excellent Homer, we are reminded of the comparative magnitude of our own errancy. A knowledge of individual fallibility nudges us on to accept the probability of collective fallibility, and—indulge me, please, my glide pattern—our mind then turns to such safeguards as government by laws, not men; checks and balances; human rights. And one is prompted to reflect that the knowledge of human fallibility may orient us to hunger after infallibility, which surely gives rise to the religious instinct. And this instinct acknowledges what some of us insist on calling "eternal verities."

Your curriculum takes you from Homer to Flannery O'Connor in literature, and from Plato to William James in philosophy. You have trod the great highways and byways of Western culture, and thus you have in hand the basic instruments of communication. Do not be overawed by what you have *not* learned. Everything over there in the high galaxies of experimental science and indeed social surmise is deracinated, except as it is rooted in what you *have* studied, and what you *do* know.

What so many of us experience, even those who have never laid eyes on St. John's, is the special lure of this campus, the serenity it continues to irradiate with its emphases on the initial struggle for knowledge, back when Thales first stated the quest for an understanding of man and his universe. You have every reason to be proud of what you have learned and to be grateful to those who taught it to you, and to the parents who expedited your passage first into the world, then to St. John's. You will not easily be surprised, standing on the shoulders of the giants; and, as you experience commencement speakers who come and go, you will be reminded, as today, that even Homer nodded.

How to Work, How to Read, How to Love

Remarks at the Memorial Service for Richard M. Clurman; Temple Emanu-El, New York, May 20, 1996

The deceased, who had served as chief of correspondents for Time-Life for thirty-five years and as cultural commissioner of New York City, was widely known and beloved. His widow specified no fewer than nine old friends to give two-minute eulogies. The room was crowded, but such was the self-discipline (the pros included David Halberstam, Barbara Walters—Clurman knew them all) that the ceremony, including the religious service, was concluded in less than one hour.

THREE YEARS AGO, one evening in July, he asked whether I'd consider crossing the ocean again in 1995, what would have been the fifth such venture, done at five-year intervals beginning in 1975. "I'm prepared to go," he told me.

I suppose I smiled; it was dark on the terrace when he spoke. I told him I doubted my crew could be mobilized for one more such trip, and just the right crew was indispensable. He had done with me two Atlantic crossings, one Pacific crossing. He was an instant celebrity for his ineptitudes at sea, done in high spirit with a wonderful, persistent incomprehension of what was the job at hand. He was the object of hilarious ridicule in my son's published journal—and he loved it all, even as Christopher loved him; even when, while discoursing concentratedly on matters of state, he would drop his cigarette ash into Christopher's wine glass, or very nearly set fire to the galley when trying to light the stove. He thrived on the cheerful raillery of his companions, but on one occasion he thought to say to me, in a voice unaccustomedly low, "I'm good at other things."

He hardly needed to remind me. Yes, and from everything he was good at he drew lessons, little maxims of professional and extra-professional life of great cumulative impact, instantly imparted to all his friends, at the least suggestion from them, or from their situation, that they needed help, or instruction. It is awesome to extrapolate from one's own experience of his goodness the sum of what he did for others.

When Oz Elliott, on Shirley's behalf, asked me to say something today I went right to my desk, but I found it impossible to imagine his absence from the scene. Was it true that there would be no message from him tomorrow on our e-mail circuit? That we would not be dining together during the week, or sharing a tenth Christmas together? In the strangest sense, the answer is, No, it isn't possible that we will not continue as companions, because his companionship left indelible traces: how to work, how to read, how to love.

It came to me last Thursday, when just after midnight my son reached me at the hotel, that I have always subconsciously looked out for the total Christian, and when I found him, he turned out to be a nonpracticing Jew. It will require the balance of my own lifetime to requite what he gave to me.

A Serene Gravity

Remarks in Honor of Walter Cronkite at the Museum of Television Broadcasting; New York, October 22, 1996

A tribute to a national institution.

I EXPECTED TO be dazzled by your Cronkite display, and I *am* dazzled by your accomplishments in celebrating his. I remember an evening in Phoenix, Arizona, when at the end of a sharp debate with a political innocent the whisper went around that *Apollo 13* was endangered. I went quickly to my hotel room and turned on Walter Cronkite. I stayed with him until about one in the morning, but there wasn't yet a prognosis—Would the astronauts live or die? Would the spacecraft return to earth or dissolve in ethereal matter? I wasn't sorry, when some time after one in the morning I turned off the set, that sleep was an alternative for me rather than more of a tension that, after three hours of watching, was very nearly unbearable. I set my alarm for six and, on waking, quickly turned on the set. And there he was; there he always was. He had not slept and would not until the crisis matured. He was apparently shaved, his shirt collar and tie in place, his expression grave but managing the serenity that captured the whole country.

He is a most awful left-winger. But so majestic is his poise, probably you didn't know that, and I wouldn't have known it except that I stumbled onto an interview he gave someone a year or so ago. Yes, one could reasonably assume that his inclinations were not such as would put off Frank Stanton or Mike Wallace or Bill Paley. But he seemed Solomonic in his judgment of most men and their doings. In the years that I have enjoyed him, the mere thought of any asperity has been inconceivable. Even when confessing to me a few months ago that such had been his misfortunes recently with his boat that he thought maybe he should give up sailing, he showed that philosophical equilibrium from which we all have so often profited.

We crossed on the *Queen Elizabeth* two years ago, the vessel packed with survivors of the Normandy landing, going now to France to celebrate the fiftieth anniversary of the event. Several of us had been retained to fill in idle hours. Ed Newman was there, and Andy Rooney, and we spoke about this & that. When it came time for Walter Cronkite to say his piece, he presented on the wide theater screen a documentary. What was its feature? Normandy. What was it celebrating? The twentieth anniversary of Normandy. Where was Walter Cronkite? Driving around Omaha Beach with a passenger. Who was the passenger? Who do you think? General Eisenhower. That's the way Walter always did things. It was only surprising that he didn't produce General Rommel.

I wish him many happy years, even if they are now all on land. And I join the company in complimenting you on your evening, which almost does justice to Walter Cronkite.

THE SPECIAL RESPONSIBILITY OF CONSERVATIVES

An Address to the First International Conservative Congress, Sponsored by the American Enterprise Institute, the Claremont Institute, the Heritage Foundation, the Hoover Institution, and *National Review*; the Mayflower Hotel, Washington, D.C., September 28, 1997

It was the heaviest concentration of (mostly) American conservative activists—political, journalistic, philosophical—in my lifetime, brought together by National Review *editor John O'Sullivan. After lunch on the Sunday, twenty-eight hours after the conference began, three addresses were scheduled. Speaker of the House Newt Gingrich went first; I followed him, and was followed in turn by Lady Thatcher. Later in the afternoon, Mr. Gingrich would conduct Lady Thatcher to the Capitol to unveil the portrait of her and Ronald Reagan that now adorns a caucus room. My emphasis was on the tough side of free-market life: Is it neglected? If so, who suffers most?*

W E ARE SATISFIED, after two days, that there are visions out there, some of them realized; some escaping or escaped; some gestating and fitful. My generation was fired by a threat at once strategic and philosophical. Josef Stalin was never easy for American fellow travelers to handle, though some attempted it and even found themselves defending the coup in Czechoslovakia in 1948. But it wasn't until Vietnam that the confusion became full-throated, especially in the academy. It was then, beginning in 1968, that Ho Chi Minh was likened to George Washington. The line blurred on why we should not persist in Vietnam. Our action there was deplored by reasonable critics on tactical and strategic grounds, an application of geopolitical prudence. But the opposition to the war became in many quarters first a fatalistic benediction of the Communist enterprise, finally an enthusiastic endorsement of it. *Ho, Ho, Ho Chi Minh / The NLF is gonna win.* Drawing deeply from the antinomianism of the time, some

Americans opined that there was no distinction between us and them; indeed that if we labored to parse the question, we'd draw back, embarrassed by our materialism, apprehended by history in a subordinate position on the idealistic ladder of politics. It was a time when serious derangement threatened, when some of our proudest universities gave over to mindless young philosophical terrorists control of their campus and the protocols of democratic exchange.

That ended, though not in a clear victory for the right-minded; the war's end finessed any moral resolution. In the larger theater, by and large we held fast. We can take pride in our steadfastness between 1945 and 1991. But there is a lesson here, and its implications should be with us always, especially as we find ourselves fretful, as so many yesterday and today expressed themselves as being. Kate O'Beirne wondered at lunch whether conservatives were expected to do nothing more than merely celebrate the tenure of the new Congress. At a gathering of the faithful in 1991 I remarked that I was nineteen years old when the Cold War was ignited at Yalta, and that the year the Communist empire crumbled I became a senior citizen. Thus the Cold War lasted throughout my adult lifetime, which meant that tens of millions lived *their* adult lifetimes in the bitter, seemingly endless cold of tyranny. The lessons are two. The first, that great strategic ends can take generations to realize. The second, that at least some element of impatience is owed to ideals envisioned and realizable.

A difficulty of American conservatives at this moment is that we are without a harnessing bias, which the Cold War gave us; and we are not completely comfortable with the metaphysics of democratic order. If our vision is unencumbered by conscientious qualifications or skepticism, then why can't we march forward? We did this a generation ago in the matter of civil rights. The vision of protection for Americans of all races was to be sure encumbered: there were those who saw and were deterred by constitutional reservations, which retrospectively we demote to constitutional niceties. No other grand vision can be said to have been realized in the succeeding generation. Not the elimination of poverty, not the universalization of literacy, not, I think, a tolerable subjugation of government. Having said this,

I vote with those who believe our objective is made more difficult by injections of fantasy, the dream of the blessings of statelessness. It is great sport to mock the state categorically, and I have in my lifetime engaged happily in ideological slapstick, as when lasciviously quoting H. L. Mencken's bracing law that the state is the enemy of all well-disposed, decent, and industrious men. Fun, but untrue. The sounding board of reason and experience harmonizes better with Jefferson's taunt, that the state cannot do anything for the people except in proportion as it can do something to the people. There is in Jefferson's formulation the sense of contingency that leavens with realism what is otherwise merely a cheerleader's incantation. The idea of abolishing the state is properly reserved for meditation in cloisters of ideological fundamentalism. The proper challenge of conservatives is to tame the state, and the question we most appropriately ask is, What is the proper tempo for such an enterprise? And if the tempo we wish for is incompatible with democratic practice—even as the liberation of Europe was for many years held to be incompatible with peaceful co-existence—at what point should impatience prevail over democratic docility? The aging prisoner of the Soviet Union who after forty years of waiting rebuked Western leadership, as Solzhenitsyn did, as preoccupied with avoiding military risk wins not only our sympathy but also our contingent understanding.

What satisfactions are we entitled to take from the vision itself? Charles Krauthammer told us yesterday we might try depoliticizing our perspectives. The Christian knows the rules of the game. Worldly approaches to the Christian vision are in the nature of things asymptotic. We can aspire to the goodness of Mother Teresa, but the realization of goodness is for another world. Meanwhile secular metabolism quickens the appetite for the achievement of earthly ends. Any confusion between the two visions runs the risk identified by Eric Voegelin when he warned against immanentizing the eschaton. History teaches us—or rather, fails to teach us—that political visions are slow to reify, as the American slaves would learn, and American women, on the long road to the voting booth. Much of what most American conservatives want can't be as niftily executed as the ratification of the Nineteenth Amendment. Much of what we want is illusory. How much of what we want is *properly* illusory? Perhaps the problem was explored in a seminar I didn't attend [the conference had included more than a dozen breakout sessions, as well as the major speeches], but in none that I did was emphasis placed on the besetting problem of illegitimacy. It is illusory to suppose the problem can be erased, but surely not illusory to suppose it can be reduced, and that American conservatives are best endowed to confront it.

ISN'T IT TIME to review the sanctions that might be used to make progress towards that which we seek that is not illusory?

Ten years ago, outraged by American life, George Kennan went so far as to ask whether we had anything to teach the Soviet Union. In America, he said, we were making no progress in removing our slums, in eliminating poverty, in containing pornography, restoring civility, nurturing the environment, reducing crime, or raising the level of literacy. Mr. Kennan was driven to ask, in 1987, Why do U.S. leaders speak condescendingly to their counterparts in Moscow?

This isn't an occasion to rub the nose of a gifted and industrious scholar in the differences between Soviet life as described, say, by Aleksandr Solzhenitsyn, and life in the United States as described by whomever. Still, it is true that we suffer the blights he enumerates. And the illegitimacy rate, in which so many other concerns are subsumed, is apparently uncontainable. What can conservatives contribute to alleviating a problem that generates an incidence six times as high, among children raised by a single parent, of crime, poverty, illiteracy, and drug addiction? Charles Murray argues persuasively against paying welfare benefits to unwed mothers, but he doesn't really convince us that this would mean an end to the fruit of unguarded sexual promiscuity. One wonders. Are we suffering from a failure of nerve?

The gravamen of the liberals' case against America has always had to do with the free-market society's disposition to let people make out on their own. We are preached to and cajoled and thundered at on what care we must take for those who do not learn to read and write, or to refuse drugs, or to resist criminal temptation or libertine sex.

Is it a special responsibility of conservatives to adopt correlative attitudes towards failures of a certain character? Elizabeth Taylor has dispensed with her eighth husband. We would have no reason to be surprised if tomorrow she married her ninth. Or to be surprised if that union were treated as simply one more glamorous event, with photographers from *People* magazine floating down in parachutes to capture the moment.

But what has to be the effect on the thinking and attitudes, indeed the behavior, of some whose values are unformed of the serial marriages of the most durably glamorous woman in America? If imitation is the highest form of flattery, might it be said that though Miss Taylor has had only eight husbands, she has given birth to millions of children?

We are free to outlaw disruptive behavior, but most sanctions are, happily, less than incarceration. What are these? And when and how is it appropriate to level them? And how might they be marshaled to make the public case against indiscriminate procreation?

When Bill Clinton was governor of Arkansas he proposed denying a driver's license to any sixteen-year-old who wasn't attending school. Examine the whole matter of sanctions. What favor do we confer on the student who, even though he has no learning disability, refuses to learn to read? Seventy percent of America's homeless are drug addicts or alcoholics. Do we really help them with comprehensive shelter? Why are we so determined to "understand" those whose behavior is anti-social, whether sowing disruption in classrooms or seeds of life in lackadaisical engagements? A good society needs to be hospitable to virtue, which is the easy part; but shouldn't it also be inhospitable to dereliction?

It is for another forum, perhaps the Second International Conservative Congress, to explore suitable rewards and acceptable tribulations. Let's leave it that as long as the behavior of Elizabeth Taylor merely amuses, we cannot generate stigma. A man who fathers a child whom he proceeds to ignore is a second-class citizen. How should we discourage second-class behavior? Isn't this a fruitful concern of conservatives, whose stake is so large in the preservation of the family and the diminution of activity by the state?

MR. SPEAKER, HOWEVER illusory some of our most extravagant dreams, we do take pleasure, most though not all of it wholesome, from choice historical episodes, when providence seems to smile down on us. One such was the great social and economic validations Mrs. Thatcher midwived for us. I remember as a boy wondering what exactly it was that Mr. Jefferson had in mind when he spoke of our rights as including the pursuit of happiness. What, I wondered, was the nature of what we were pursuing? In the rivers in California the prospectors sought gold, a readily identifiable substance. The pursuit of it was, or was not, successful; even as you did, or did not, find oil after drilling that hole.

I know now that it is the pursuit itself that brings happiness, which is why, in our own way—for some of us obsessive, for others secondary—we pursue that deliquescent happiness. Happiness can be very concrete, like electing Ronald Reagan, or turning Congress over to Newt Gingrich. What first intimidates, and then frightens, is the prospect of pursuit deflected, or profaned, or become counterfeit. Where the objective is absolutely tangible, one's progress can be reliably tabulated. If my objective is to count the number of people I have persuaded to cast their ballots for Margaret Thatcher, I can at the end of the day measure the fruit of my work.

We are engaged in the continuing attempt not merely to crystallize our goals, but to reanimate our enthusiasm for the pursuit of them. In two days we have heard illustrious performances by the Knights Templar of our amorphous but not disfigured movement, and the blood stirs, and the rush reminds us of the intoxicating joys of liberty, in a country of our making, and of our fathers' and mothers' making, in which we revere our freedom and labor for our goals, yes, with democratic punctilio, but hearing also the drumbeat of excitement that reminds us insistently that we were born free and urges us on in our determination to die freer yet, so help us God.

The Personal Grace of J. K. Galbraith

Remarks in Celebration of a Ninetieth Birthday; Cambridge, Mass.,
October 15, 1998

The party was held at the Kennedy Center at Harvard. The nine speakers included John Kennedy Jr., Arthur Schlesinger Jr., George McGovern—and the dissenter, a devoted personal friend.

EVER SINCE I had the good fortune to meet Professor Galbraith, which is to be distinguished from the jolt some of us get from reading the things he writes, I have found him an omnipresence, in books, articles, and columns; as in the op-ed that hit us all as recently as last week, in the *New York Times.* Galbraith-speak goes on all the time. Yesterday I received a volume entitled *Proceedings, 1994–1995,* from the Churchill Center in Washington, and lo! in an introduction, mind you, to me—*me*: my own essay on Churchill—what do I run into? John Kenneth Galbraith.

Introducing me, the editor wrote, "In 1975, when Mr. Buckley first sailed the Atlantic, the *New York Times* reported that he had arrived in the Azores 'accompanied by John Kenneth Galbraith, celebrating his retirement from the Harvard faculty, as part of the crew.' Mr. Buckley immediately wrote the *Times,* 'The Galbraith on board was not my friend the 6-foot-11-inch emaciated Menshevik John Kenneth, but my friend the chunky 5-foot-10-inch Manchesterist Evan, ambassador to France; and anyway, surely it was Harvard, not Professor Galbraith, that had reason to celebrate?'"

Professor Galbraith, the narrator continues, "had meanwhile *also* written the *Times*: 'William F. Buckley Jr. was boasting as usual when he told you that I'd sailed to the Azores as a member of his crew. He is not that brave; nor, may I say, am I.' But later," the introducer concluded that part of the story that involved our guest of honor, "on reading Buckley's book-length account of the voyage, he wrote of it, 'Buckley takes me to sea, makes me part of the whole adventure. Mr.

Buckley should give up politics and concentrate on writing. He cannot afford to have serious people think he is a failed politician when he is a master of a higher craft.'"

That is a fine mix, pure Galbraith, the mordancy intact, the generosity making a cameo appearance. The careful hand of Mr. Galbraith in regulating the activity of his critics was never better dramatized than when, five years ago, I was invited by his publishers to be one of seven speakers at his eighty-fifth birthday party here in Boston. Our talks, quite understandably, were limited to four minutes per speaker. When my turn came I got up in the vast Boston Public Library and had got through the first half of my tightly woven remarks when the master of ceremonies brusquely pushed me to one side, grabbed the microphone, and called out, "Is there a doctor in the house?"

There was one, and after a minute or two he was located, and oriented in the direction of the afflicted. The microphone was replaced in my hands, but, of course, the beautiful sonnet I had crafted was entirely fractured; like starting off *Hamlet* with the death of Ophelia.

The next day I mailed a copy of my remarks to Professor Galbraith. I said, in the covering sentence, "Ken, you may not have heard my talk"—the acoustics are very bad at the Boston Library—"so I send along a copy."

A week later I received his acknowledgment. It read, "Dear Bill: That was a very pleasant talk you gave about me. If I had known it would be so, I would not have instructed my friend to pretend, in the middle of your speech, to need the attention of a doctor."

I am here of course for very personal reasons. John Kenneth Galbraith quietly, discreetly, engages us, as no doubt many in this room have found out for themselves, by his concern for his friends and students, a concern that he takes so far as to tell us what to think and say. I suspect that he is unaware that, however silently, there are those of us who observe him in deeds he continues to think of as invisible, unremarked, unremarkable. Maybe there is a market explanation for this: Personal grace is inelastically noticeable?

There are many here, and many not here, who have been encouraged by him and elevated by his example, when he is not wearing his war paint. He can be deadly serious when acting simply as a friend. And in such moments he detaches himself from workaday perspectives, philosophical and literary: the irony and the handling of paradox which in his hands make readable even abstruse thought and polemics.

As I contemplate the company in which I am thrust tonight I can only think that this is Ken's ironic contribution to that part of the First Amendment that guarantees against an establishment of religion: a common political religion that binds the speakers here tonight, save for one invincibly ignorant contrarian, who, while rejecting Galbraith's mission, happily acclaims a great scholar and writer, and a beloved personal friend.

A MAN WHO LOOKS THE BEGGAR IN THE FACE

Remarks at the Inaugural Herman Kahn Award Dinner, Sponsored by the Hudson Institute; the Rainbow Room, New York, December 7, 1998

A toast to William E. Simon.

WHEN I WAS a sophomore in college competing for election to the *Yale Daily News* I called on the dean for a comment on that season's burning question: Should there be preferential treatment by the admissions office for promising football players, or should admission be purely on merit? The wise Southern dean smiled over the contention between alumni on the one hand thirsty for athletic triumphs, on the other hand proud of their policy on fair and open admissions. Dean De Vane explained to me that La Rochefoucauld understood the problem three hundred years ago, when he enunciated his maxim, *Sad is the lot of the woman at once violently inflamed, and inflexibly virtuous.*

I have that problem with Bill Simon here tonight, because there is at this moment, pending, an application for a grant from the Olin Foundation by one of my enterprises. If what I was now to say about him sounded stingy and mean-spirited, would that not affect the disposition of *any* philanthropist? On the other hand, if what I was to say sounded oleaginous and fulsome, it would earn the silent contempt of a discerning and unbribable man of honor.

Well, you see, my problem is that Bill Simon is exactly that: an overwhelming human being, in honor, grace, intelligence, and generosity, but I am afraid of putting it in those words, lest I be thought self-serving. So I'll need to resort to a device. If there were absolutely nothing pending with the Olin Foundation, I would tell you that in the last twenty years I've been frequently in the company of the honoree, I and often my wife. We met once at the Reichstag to discuss the consequences of the great fire of 1933. We sailed the Baltic and explored the historical flora and fauna of the Scandinavian world, including the Ferris wheel at the Tivoli Gardens in Copenhagen. We were fellow penitents at Lourdes, begging forgiveness for our sins and further blessings for ourselves and our families and our country.

I thought I already knew the measure of his care and generosity until I saw last year in a journal a full profile of it, a detailed accounting of what he has actually done for so many, so vastly outdistancing the modest biblical tithe imposed on us. But in this brief champagne toast I'll single out only one aspect of his grace, which is the language of his missives, whether their content regarding your application is positive or negative. It is the difference between the man who looks the beggar in the face when giving alms, and the man who drops the coin as he might a token in a subway turnstile.

In his letters, you can see Bill Simon experiencing the joys and enduring the tribulations of the man who leads a pivotal life, on whom so many depend, even as so many continue to benefit from the fruits of the mind of Herman Kahn [the social philosopher and founder of the Hudson Institute], who'd have been proud to honor this first recipient of the award named after him. Let us, then, toast to Bill Simon.

FORGIVING THE UNFORGIVABLE

A Lecture to the Annual Dinner of "The Moles"; the New York Hilton,
New York, January 27, 1999

---

*Ever since the previous January, speakers had been unable safely to neglect
the raging question of the day, which centered on President Clinton and
Monica Lewinsky and Paula Jones. The night of this talk, the Senate
was debating a motion (finally voted down) to dismiss the impeachment
case. Two weeks later, the Senate would vote to acquit Mr. Clinton. I
attempted here to condense the relevant arguments and to surface a moral
point. The audience: a society of underground and underwater engineers.*

W E FACE, TONIGHT and seemingly every night, the problem faced in 1945 by General Anthony McAuliffe. He
was the hero of the Battle of the Bulge, fought out bitterly fifty-four years ago, in the closing yet desperate months of the
world war. In Belgium in December 1944 the American fighting divisions were encircled. The Nazis sent their ultimatum to the com-
manding American general. It seemed that all of America was trans-
ported to his celebrated reply to this demand for surrender. His answer
was, "Nuts."

Very nice; but a month or two after General McAuliffe had
returned to Washington, he had got as tired of hearing the word *Nuts*
as Rachmaninoff had become of hearing the C-sharp minor prelude,
which he had composed at age nineteen and was required to perform
as an encore every time his fingers touched the keyboard.

So what happened was one more party given in the general's
honor, by a celebrated Washington hostess. She was delicately approached the night before by the general's aide and told, "Please,
Mrs. Witherspoon, do not mention the Nuts business; it drives the
general crazy."

She promised, and the party went swimmingly, and as the general prepared to depart he gave his thanks to the hostess, who smiled
graciously and said, "I was delighted to meet you, General McNuts."

So it is. Here I am—substituting for Senator Bradley, who is in New Hampshire showing young voters how to use snowballs as basketballs—addressing representatives of the construction and engineering industry on what subject?

Nuts.

There is no way to avoid the subject. Even then one runs the risk. I am writing these words on Tuesday night. I postponed their composition as long as I could. But who knows what is happening this very evening, disorienting these thoughts? How will the Senate vote on two critical motions? Though, come to think of it, whatever contributions I have to make on the subject can't really be disoriented. They are a part of the story, moral and historical.

The Lewinsky matter and its implications are overwhelming in their demand for attention. At the most dramatic political level it is asked, Should the United States Senate convict the President of the United States on charges brought by formal impeachment proceedings by the House of Representatives, removing him from office? At the most dramatic public level, we ask, What in the way of behavior does the American public, in the year of Our Lord 1999, expect of its president? Or, perhaps more accurately, What in 1999 will the American public settle for in the behavior of its president?

I have endeavored to formulate a few propositions, the first being that *The Paula Jones case should have been aborted for reasons not always put forward.*

Nine members of the Supreme Court ruled almost two years ago that the suit brought against the president by Mrs. Jones should stay on the trial court's calendar. The offenses complained of—sexual harassment and intimidation—had been committed before the defendant became President of the United States. No special immunity, therefore, attached to him. Moreover, there was no reason to assume—the Court implicitly argued—that Mr. Clinton could not simultaneously defend himself at trial and conduct the nation's business. It was suggested in effect that if it happened that the trial were to fall on the very same day as a projected bombing of Iraq, the trial judge could reasonably be expected to put off the proceedings for a week or two.

There is a sense in which this lawsuit crept up on the American public substantially unnoticed, rather like the lazily apprehended knowledge that the way things were arranged, computers were destined to crash at midnight at the end of the day that brings on the next millennium. On the computer front, we simply have assumed, or at least I have, that the wizards of Silicon Valley will find the right plug to pull at some point before midnight, and the cyberworld will continue to hum. Though I do recall an Austrian intellectual who years ago pointed out the difference between builders and theorists. "The engineers," he said, "build the Brooklyn Bridge. The scientists buy it." In the same way, something—it was generally thought, until the appearance of Miss Lewinsky—would happen and Paula Jones would go away and Mr. Clinton would continue on through his term.

I proposed, three years ago in my newspaper column, that Republican and Democratic leaders agree for the sake of the public tranquillity to view Paula Jones's challenge as a bipartisan problem. Back then, Mrs. Jones was asking for damages of $700,000 and for an apology from the president.

If she had persisted in demanding an apology, we'd have needed to see a display of diplomatic statesmanship in Mr. Clinton. Even if entirely innocent, he might have been counseled to go ahead and authorize an apology written as if he might only conjecturally have been guilty. Every day people in commerce sign consent decrees in which they acknowledge the hypothetical possibility of guilt even when absolutely convinced of their innocence. Mr. Clinton could have reasoned that his concern for presidential decorum outweighed any appearance he might permit of hypothetical guilt. He could have said, "Whatever I did that gave offense to Mrs. Jones, I regret."

That and $700,000 could have rescued us all from a long life in the trough ahead.

And of course the question is left with us now, Was the failure to settle, back then, an early warning sign of defective presidential leadership? Our Chief Executive is also our First Politician. Expert politicians are expected to avoid unnecessary crises. Mr. Clinton is every day proving—most notably a week ago with his State of the Union address—that he is a politician who can survive crisis, but that's different. The best governors are those who don't permit crises to generate, hugely easing the problem of surviving them.

My next proposition is that *Many Americans seemed to be saying that public servants can be expected to be—casual—in the matter of conjugal morality.*

The editorial writer of the *Orlando Sentinel* expressed his views on the subject: "In our hearts, most of us know that few (if any) among us could pass such scrutiny [as Bill Clinton is being subjected to]. . . . But the success of our system is based on its ability to recruit normal people for extraordinary service. If we exclude the normal, we invite the extreme."

The paper went on to urge, beginning with the next presidential inauguration, the following reform, patterned on the marriage ceremony. At weddings, the editor reminds us, words such as the following are spoken: "Let all those who oppose this union speak now or forever hold their peace." The editor proposes a law that would grant "blanket immunity" from criminal or civil prosecution to the president and to every officeholder who is in the line of succession to the president under the Constitution.

Very interesting. What is a normal person? It isn't safe to assume that the Orlando editor thinks entirely "normal" a man who has dropped his pants—literally—in front of a subordinate, as an invitation to dalliance. A distinction appears to be asserting itself on the matter of sexual promiscuity, the shorthand of which would read: If it's about sex, it's okay.

The May issue of *Playboy* magazine carried an editorial by founder-philosopher-rake Hugh Hefner, who joyfully welcomed Bill Clinton into the fraternity of the enlightened. "President Clinton," Hef wrote, "has become a sort of sexual Rorschach test. I," he observed proudly, "have been in a similar position for more than 40 years." The founder of the Playboy Philosophy was willing to share his crown. "The sexually charged atmosphere of the White House," he wrote, "has lit a thousand points of lust—around watercoolers, on the Internet, in bedrooms, on telephones—and a thousand points of tolerance." These points of tolerance are now telling us in effect that illegal behavior is a tolerable thing, if its purpose is merely to pull down the shade on what was going on.

My next proposition is that, *Granted what actually did happen, Mr. Clinton's administration during those long months made the public learning process difficult.*

It finally required a DNA test done on the stain on a woman's dress to catalyze Mr. Clinton's repentance of August 17. That reluctance to speak candidly is a difficulty which his closest associate, Vice President Gore, also seems to suffer from. Your friendly family lawyer will advise you that what Mr. Gore did a year earlier, when accosted with his fund-raising meeting at the Buddhist temple in California, was "to plead in the alternative." Here is how pleading in the alternative goes: (1) My client didn't do it. (2) If my client did it, it was legal. (3) Even though it wasn't legal, it should have been. And (4) my client won't do it again.

But then suddenly, in February, Mr. Clinton, speaking through his wife, Hillary, explained that the entire business was the working of a "vast right-wing conspiracy."

Well of course it's true that there are extremists on the Right as on the Left. The kooks go on. There are the wild militiamen of the Right in Idaho, and, from the Left, every now and again we hear such things as that Wall Street is planning another depression, the Pentagon another war; or that AIDS was an invention of the CIA to arrest the growth of the black population. But it was never plain that the extremists were in charge of the investigation, at the judicial or legislative level.

Motives are always mixed. It is wrong to deny that certain satisfactions are taken from adversities that affect certain others. Our disagreeable neighbor, our unspeakable cousin, Notre Dame if you're rooting for Army, Army if you're rooting for Notre Dame.

Sometimes this human weakness goes as far as Schadenfreude, the pleasure that people can get from the miseries of others. This is human nature. Suppose that a fairy with the proverbial magic wand had volunteered early in June 1972 to waft down upon the Oval Office just when President Nixon was about to give orders to call off the

FBI on the grounds that Watergate was a CIA-related affair. Pffft!! The smoking gun would have been undischarged!! Richard Nixon would never have uttered his fateful, mortal words, words which his tape machine would spit out in July 1974, ejecting him from the White House.

Would the American Left have been pleased that this subversive latency in American history had been aborted? Let's face it, no. What the Left most wanted was to discredit Nixon and get rid of him. If the same magic lady were to appear tomorrow and offer to restore Miss Lewinsky's virginity, do we suppose that the right wing would be happy about it? One more virgin, in exchange for the exposure of a defective Democratic president?

So grant that some of the ill will is entrenched and opportunistic. Does it all reduce to mere political factionalism?

My next proposition is that *Whatever the concerns for morality and integrity, the political consideration inevitably figures.*

What would happen if Clinton were removed? Al Gore would become president. Gore's agenda is to the left of Clinton's. If Mr. Clinton were gone, President Gore would be there to pursue his own visions. He'd be unencumbered by the bedraggled Clinton, who no matter what the Senate does in the days ahead will not be able to sneeze during the balance of his term without the body-language people wondering what his real motives are. Why should a Republican Congress, looking out for itself, prefer President Gore to President Clinton?

Another thing: If Clinton were removed, Gore would run for election in the year 2000 with the bouncy launch of a sitting president. Why should Republicans prefer an opponent who would be running with all the advantages of the White House working for him?

If I were a consultant to the GOP, instead of spending my life as an expert on engineering and construction, and if I were concerned exclusively with the fruits of power, I would beg the leadership to just drop the whole thing, kick in a little censure motion for appearances' sake, and go on to things like Iraq and Social Security. Let Clinton stay where he is, I'd advise. Let his presence in the White House fray the Democratic rhetoric about integrity and family values.

My next proposition is that *The heat of the rhetoric of this period is itself informative.*

Even as Senator McCarthy aroused huge and hysterical fears fifty years ago about subversion of government by Communists, we hear now, at about the same pitch, suspicion of subversion of government by conservatives. There was, for instance, that meeting last week. There was Harvard law professor Alan Dershowitz, who protests everything on earth except the guilt of most of his clients, advising everyone that a vote for impeachment was a vote for bigotry, for fundamentalism, against environmentalism, and against choice by incipient mothers. Nobel Prize–winning author Toni Morrison saw Dershowitz and raised him one: The Hyde people in Congress, she said, are "an arrogant theocracy genuflected at the knees of a minority." Author Blanche Cook dismissed the congressional majority as "filthy mean-minded swiny people." Elizabeth Holtzman, the former congresswoman, gave a judicious explanation: "What is at stake is the right of the American people, by majority vote, to elect a President of the United States and not have it undone by moralizing, sanctimonious—" but the reporter notes that the roar of approbation from the crowd drowned out her last words, leaving us to wonder that Ms. Holtzman is so enthusiastic about the strategic wisdom of the same American voters who chased her out of office.

There is the other position, namely, that Republican legislators who voted to impeach, and senators who incline to convict, are upholding their oaths to act according to their understanding of the Constitution. Will the voters, in protest, commit a Republican genocide in November of 2000?

How will the Republicans, on the defensive, protect themselves? What will they say it was that motivated their pursuit of Mr. Clinton?

Well, they might begin by quoting Mr. Clinton's most eloquent defender, former senator Dale Bumpers, who brought the whole country to a standstill last week in admiration of his speech pleading with the Senate not to convict his old friend. How did he characterize what Mr. Clinton actually did? The words used by Senator Bumpers were that President Clinton's conduct was "indefensible, outrageous, unforgivable, and shameless."

Before he was through, it became clear that Senator Bumpers means by indefensible, something which you can defend—after all, Clinton was only trying to cover up a sex thing. And Bumpers means by "unforgivable" something you can forgive. After all, Clinton was only, well, only trying to cover up a sex thing. That leaves us with only "outrageous" and "shameless." And what do you do about conduct that is outrageous and shameless? Why, you . . . transcend it.

Time magazine asks its readers a question in the current issue: "All things considered, twenty-five years from now do you think Bill Clinton will be remembered for: (1) His accomplishments as president?"—that got 18 percent. "Or (2) Controversies over his personal life and financial dealings?"—that got 72 percent.

Twenty-five years from now people will remember his presidency not for what he accomplished as president, but for his personal conduct. If that is so, are Republicans really expected to worry in November, twenty-two months from now, about the time they have given to reflection on his conduct?

Here is a measure of the frustration felt by those who do really believe that what Mr. Clinton did was indefensible and outrageous. It is that in our culture it is not possible to give a president authority simply to proceed as a detached political technician. It is a part of human nature to admire and even to love people who exercise great power. Ivan the Terrible was cheered by the crowds and beseeched not to give up his crown. Stalin and Hitler and Perón and Huey Long received thunderous public approval. One day after Mr. Clinton's State of the Union address, one week after twenty hours' enumeration of the deeds and words that caused Senator Bumpers to assert the need to forgive the unforgivable, Clinton was in Buffalo, speaking at a great rally. The minister who gave the invocation called him "the greatest president for our people of all time." Yesterday he was exchanging ruminations on virtue with the pope.

Will the Republicans who believe they are standing by the moral and constitutional imperatives be assaulted, in November 2000, for having kept open the question of Mr. Clinton's removal? But what will the opponents of the GOP incumbents say? "There were those," Whittaker Chambers once wrote me, "who, at the great nightfall, took loving thought to preserve the tokens of hope and truth."

My final proposition is that *America is correctly proud of its capacity to forgive, but also we are aware that forgiveness is a joint exercise.*

Forgiveness presupposes contrition.

There is something continuingly provocative in Mr. Clinton's personal appearance. He doesn't—ever—look guilty. When he gave his State of the Union speech last week his expressions recalled the face of Winston Churchill on V-E Day. His manner was as triumphant as if he had single-handedly accomplished the rape of all the Sabine women. Good old Tricky Dick Nixon never let the public down in these matters. He *always* looked guilty, never more so than when he was facing the public and averring his innocence. His face was a polygraph. Clinton's face is that of the freshly minted altar boy. He is Oscar Wilde's Dorian Gray. We have looked at that face through the corrosive mists of Gennifer Flowers, draft evasion, platonic experiences with marijuana, through Vincent Foster, Webster Hubbell, the Lincoln Bedroom, through Huang, FBI files, Mrs. Willey on *60 Minutes,* and what we see is something in the nature of incredulity. For that reason, a convincing apology from him is as inconceivable as a sex change. Bill Clinton couldn't bring it off. The Church made Henry II march over to Canterbury and get himself flogged publicly to atone for the assassination of Becket. Clinton has no comparable recourse, besides which we have the separation of church and state, and he would veto the proposal.

But the public does not seem to be determined to exact convincing contrition. We might ask: What is the matter with the public? Why does it not understand the gravity of what is happening? Can it be that there is something missing at the other end of the democratic scale, as between the governor and the governed? W. B. Yeats wrote a letter, back in the 1930s, to a Dublin daily newspaper which had published serial criticisms of the Lord Mayor, the most recent of which had asked, "What has the Lord Mayor of Dublin done lately to commend himself to the people of Dublin?" Yeats's letter read, "What have the people of Dublin done lately to commend themselves to the Lord Mayor?"

From time to time it is, perhaps you will agree with me—some of you, anyway—appropriate to wonder about the judgment of the majority. Whatever happens in the days ahead, the questions touched upon in the last year will be pondered for many years, by historians of course, but also by moralists. There will be those who applaud the presidential denials. La Rochefoucauld is endlessly relevant. Remember, he wrote that hypocrisy is the tribute that vice pays to virtue. If you heatedly deny having stolen from the collection plate, we can at least take satisfaction from your implicit position, which is that it is wrong to steal from the collection plate.

Mr. Clinton can, in the sense we speak of, be set down as in favor of virtue, even if he didn't inhale it. What the moral tribunals will say of America's behavior during the long year since last January is again difficult to predict. Perhaps they will say that America showed a great sophistication in separating private conduct from public conduct. Or they might say that the United States was so waterlogged with good times and good interest rates and no wars to fight that we lost our capacity for moral refinement.

Or they might say this—the question that most interests me—they might say that for most Americans, conduct, unless it directly affects them, is no longer evaluated by what were once publicly acknowledged as public standards. That would be the triumph of what some would call personal detachment. Ayn Rand's followers would call it the triumph of self-concern. Others would wonder about solipsism, the theory that the self is the only thing that can be measured, that, indeed, matters.

That would be bad news, and I reject it. The task ahead is to reconstruct our basic allegiance to what is right. Come to think of it, where best to launch that movement than at a conference of engineers and constructors? I wish you Godspeed. Keep America intact, and keep your eyes on the infrastructures we all rely on. Good night.

THE ANIMATING INDISCRETIONS OF RONALD REAGAN

The Keynote Address at a Symposium in Honor of an Eighty-Eighth Birthday; the Ronald Reagan Library and Museum, Simi Valley, Calif., February 4, 1999

My talk at the banquet was very personal (as had been requested). "Dutch," of course, was not there, and I was sad that he would never hear this tribute from an old friend.

I RECALL THAT Henry Mencken described an introduction to him on a celebratory occasion as having evoked "a full moon, the setting sun, and the aurora borealis." In this perspective, if all the generous things Mark Burson has said really belong to me, how am I expected even to intimate the achievements of Ronald Reagan? Well, I can do that, really, in one sentence.

He succeeded in getting Nancy Reagan to marry him.

The country is familiar with the legend of Nancy, familiar with her accomplishments as companion, aide, monitor, wife, and lover. There was never anyone who more devotedly served a husband. She has renewed for us all the meaning of the pledge to stand by in sickness and in health.

This being a convocation of friends and admirers, in celebration of his birthday, I propose as keynoter to dwell a while on a long friendship. It began in the spring of 1960. Ronald and Nancy Reagan, whom I hadn't met, were seated at one end of the restaurant, my sister-in-law and I at the other end. We were out of sight of one another. Both parties were headed, after dinner, across the street to an auditorium in a public high school. There I would be introduced, as the evening's speaker addressing an assembly of doctors and their wives, by Ronald Reagan, a well-known actor and currently the host of a television series sponsored by General Electric; moreover, a public figure who had taken an interest in conservatives and conservative writings.

We bumped into each other going out the door. Ronald Reagan

introduced himself and Nancy, and said he had just finished reading my book *Up from Liberalism*. He quoted a crack from it, done at the expense of Mrs. Roosevelt, which he relished. I requited his courtesy by relishing him and Nancy for life.

He distinguished himself that night—and dismayed Mrs. Reagan—by what he proceeded to do after discovering that the microphone had not been turned on. He had tried, raising his voice, to tell a few stories. But the audience was progressively more impatient. Waiting in vain for the superintendent to unlock the door to the tight little office at the other end of the hall, in which the control box lay, he sized up the problem and, having surveyed all possible avenues of approach, climbed out the window at stage level and, one story above the busy traffic below, cat-walked, Cary Grant style, twenty or thirty yards to the window of the control room. This he penetrated by breaking the window with a thrust of his elbow; he climbed in, turned on the light, flipped on the microphone, unlocked the office door, and emerged with that competent relaxed smile of his, which we came to know after Grenada, Libya, Reykjavik, and Moscow; proceeding with the introduction of the speaker. And all that was thirty years before bringing peace in our time!

In later years I thought his movements that night a nifty allegory of his approach to foreign policy: the calm appraisal of a situation, the willingness to take risks, and then the decisive moment: leading to lights and sound—and music, the music of the spheres.

We stayed friends.

Twenty years later he was running for President of the United States. Early that winter the Soviet military had charged into Afghanistan, beginning a long, costly, brutal exercise. A week or two after he was nominated in Detroit I wrote him. I told him I thought he would be elected. And told him that, on the assumption that on reaching the White House he might wish to tender me an office, I wished him to know that I aspired to no government job of any kind.

He wrote back that he was disappointed. "I had in mind," he said, "to appoint you ambassador to Afghanistan." Over the next eight years, in all my communications with him, I would report fleetingly on my secret mission in Kabul, where, in our fiction, I lived and worked. In his letters to me he would always address me as Mr. Ambassador. The show must go on, where Ronald Reagan was involved.

Soon after his election I was asked by the Philadelphia Society to speak on the theme "Is President Reagan doing all that can be done?" It was a coincidence that my wife, Pat, and I had spent the weekend before the Philadelphia Society meeting as guests of the president and Mrs. Reagan in Barbados. I recalled with delight an exchange I had had with my host on the presidential helicopter. We were flying to our villa the first evening, before the two days on Easter weekend reserved for bacchanalian sunning and swimming on the beach in front of Claudette Colbert's house. I leaned over and told him I had heard the rumor that the Secret Service was going to deny him permission to swim from that beach on the grounds that it was insufficiently secure. I asked him whether that was so, that he wouldn't be allowed in the water.

Helicopters, even Air Force One helicopters, are pretty noisy, but I was able to make out what he said. It was, "Well, Bill, Nancy here tells me I'm the most powerful man in the Free World. If she's right, then I will swim tomorrow with you."

Which indeed he did.

I recall also that during one of those swims I said to him, "Mr. President, would you like to earn the *National Review* Medal of Freedom?" He confessed to being curious as to how he would qualify to do this. I explained, "I will proceed to almost drown, and you will rescue me." We went through the motions, and that evening I conferred the medal on him, in pectore.

I REMEMBER TELLING the Philadelphia Society that the most powerful man in the Free World is not powerful enough to do everything that needs to be done. Retrospectively, I have speculated on what I continue to believe was the conclusive factor in the matter of American security against any threat of Soviet aggression. It was the character of the occupant of the White House; the character of Ronald Reagan. The reason this is so, I have argued, is that the Soviet

Union, for all that from time to time it miscalculated tactically, never miscalculated in respect of matters apocalyptic in dimension. And the policymakers of the Soviet Union knew that the ambiguists with whom they so dearly loved to deal were not in power during those critical years. So that if ever the Soviet leaders were tempted to such suicidal foolishness as to launch a strike against us, suicidal is exactly what it would have proved to be. The primary obstacle to the ultimate act of Soviet imperialism was the resolute U.S. determination to value what we have, over against what they, under Soviet dominion, had; value it sufficiently to defend it with all our resources.

Ronald Reagan, in my judgment, animated his foreign policy by his occasional diplomatic indiscretions: because of course it was a diplomatic indiscretion to label the Soviet Union an "evil empire." But then, quite correctly, he would switch gears when wearing diplomatic top hat and tails. He did not on those occasions talk the language of John Wayne—or of Thomas Aquinas. But how reassuring it was for us, every now and then ("Mr. Gorbachev, tear down this wall"), to vibrate to the music of the very heartstrings of the leader of the Free World, who, to qualify convincingly as such, had after all to *feel* a total commitment to the Free World. When in formal circumstances the president ventured out to exercise conviviality with the leaders of the Soviet Union, the scene was by its nature wonderful, piquant: What would he say that was agreeable, congenial, to the head of the Evil Empire? The summit conferences brought to mind the Russian who, on discovering that his pet parrot was missing, rushed out to the KGB office to report that his parrot's political opinions were entirely unrelated to his own.

THE ENSUING CHAPTER in the life of Russia presents its own problems. They are internal problems, with a surly outer face. You can hear the words framed on the mouth of the few remaining statues of Lenin. His lips are saying, *So much for your capitalism!* Russia poses no strategic threat to the Free World, to which Russia, de jure, now belongs. But the contemporary experience of Russia is a devastating rebuke to facile universalist ideas about what needs to be done to nurture advances towards prosperity.

One key, of course, an indispensable key, is human freedom. When West Germany was liberated from fascist tyranny, and Japan from imperialist militarism, well-wishers of freedom cheered the results as life began its dramatic turn towards self-rule and a market economy. But in Russia the old brew didn't mix, did it? It isn't hard to compile a list of the missing elements. We know now about the profound corruption, and know how corruption conjoined with industrial satrapies can defy the benevolent ministrations of a free market. The causes of the wealth of nations heralded by Adam Smith cannot make their way in the absence of a reasoned mobility of a nation's resources and a receptive theater for the entrepreneurial energies of its people.

There will be many books written about what happened in Russia in the decade beginning with liberation. The inquests will be various and prolonged and they will all be sad; but they will make vivid lessons we need to absorb, as we project the economic future of other nations, to be sure, but also of our own. The overarching lesson is that the elements of a good society oriented to the improvement of life aren't all disembodied, inanimate—weight scales at a free-market counter. There is the live component.

And it is not just formal self-rule. Democracy is a mantra, but it isn't an amulet. We can chant the benefits of democratic arrangements and cheer democratic practices; but these practices do not always lead to enlightened policies. One-third of the Duma in Moscow are Communists. The freedom the Russians had, for the first time, to vote very nearly returned a Communist president in the election of three years ago. The popularity of the democratically elected president of Russia today is given as 1 percent. (He should try poking an intern.) A substantial number of Russians would exchange life as it is today for life as it was yesterday. Thirty million Russians have not been paid for weeks of work, in some cases for months of work. What is a Russian gravedigger supposed to do if he is not paid? Dig his own grave?

At the other end of the world we have the dismaying spectacle of Japan, recently referred to as the Land of the Setting Sun. "It is quite amazing," Larry Kudlow recently opined. "They haven't managed to do *anything* right." Eight consecutive years of mismanagement by the second wealthiest country in the world, a democratic society whose people are demoralized, seemingly lost.

The lesson for our students of political economy is that we cannot fully depend on autopilots to do what is necessary. The framers of our own Republic said it again and again: that in the absence of virtue, no government could vouchsafe to its people a life of liberty and order. There are technical questions to solve and others that aren't at all technical. What Japan needs to do, its governors are not doing, in part because of ignorance, in part because pride and stubbornness and fear prompt them to preserve decadent enterprises. The Russians despair of reform, and the social festering continues, awaiting almost inevitably what sadly we think of as another revolution, one that might make dominant a class of leaders willing to adjourn their own fleeting interests today, for enduring gains tomorrow.

The problem is theirs, and our concern is limited to geostrategic questions. At our blessed geographical remove from Tokyo and Moscow, we have the benefit of a little insularity. But the Atlantic Ocean and the Pacific are finite comforts, only as reassuring as the distance between where midrange missiles land and strategic missiles land, a distance that time is battering away at, progressively diminishing the security we feel in our little snuggery here. The words "from sea to shining sea" used to evoke an almost infinite distance. It is now a mere stretch of space, traveled by missiles in about eighteen minutes.

The Reagan years accustomed us to a mood about life and about government. There were always the interruptions, the potholes of life. But Ronald Reagan had strategic vision. He told us that most of our civic problems were problems brought on or exacerbated by government, not problems that could be solved by government. That of course is enduringly true. Only government can cause inflation, preserve monopoly, and punish enterprise. On the other hand it is only a government leader who can put a stamp on the national mood.

One refers not to the period of Shakespeare, but to the period of Elizabeth. Reagan's period was brief, but he did indeed put his stamp on it. He did this in part because he was scornful of the claims of omnipotent government, in part because he felt, and expressed, the buoyancy of the American Republic.

We have now the paradoxical situation, a leader whom 75 percent of the American people don't wish to disturb, and whom 75 percent of the American people do not trust. It is comforting to tell ourselves that what this means is that we live in an age in which the long arm of government is so discredited, it can't really do us much damage. If Mr. Clinton were indeed powerless, then he would be a threat only to maidens passing by. But leaving aside the power he wields as commander-in-chief, he has the power, and has exercised it, to cultivate a cynicism whose final effects we cannot appraise, nor even imagine. If what he has done is trivial, then much of what we think of as the infrastructure of civil society is also trivial: our commitments to truth, to the processes of justice, to the sanctity of oaths. It is possible that in future years, if there should be a return to wholesomeness of habits of thought and deed, the cloud that will hang over the last year of the twentieth century won't be the memory of a year spent on impeachment, but the memory of a year in which no action was taken after impeachment.

It is fine that the Ronald Reagan Library, Museum, and Center for Public Affairs, which serves as our host, will collect President Reagan's papers and ambient literature, permitting generations of scholars to explore and linger over those happy years which augured the end of the Soviet threat, the revitalization of our economy, and a great draft of pride in our country. To the library I'll convey in years ahead my own collection of letters from Ronald Reagan. The very last one written from the White House, the day the Soviet Union announced that it would withdraw from Afghanistan, began:

"Dear Mr. Ambassador:

"Congratulations! The Soviets are moving out of Afghanistan. I knew you could do it if I only left you there long enough, and you did it without leaving Kabul for a minute."

He closed by saying, "Nancy sends her love to you and Pat." That was eleven years ago, and we cherish it today, and, through her, convey our own love and gratitude to the president, on his eighty-eighth birthday.

Preserving the Heritage

A Lecture to the Heritage Foundation; the Pierre Hotel, New York, October 20, 1999

A lecture on the topic "Heritage," the last in the Heritage Foundation's two-year-long Leadership for America series, celebrating the Foundation's twenty-fifth anniversary. I was introduced by my son, Christopher Buckley, and I reproduce his introduction here:

I first met William F. Buckley Jr. in September 1952. I was struck by his considerable . . . height. From the first moment I set eyes on him, I found myself looking up to him. Over the years, I reached his approximate height in feet and inches, but I have never stopped looking up to him.

The theme tonight is "Heritage." Your honoree [receiving the Clare Boothe Luce Award] is well suited to talk about that. His own roots go deep in the American soil. His grandfather was a Texas sheriff. The family does not widely advertise that, owing to the fact that he was a Democrat. The sheriff's son became a Texas oilman, from which point on the family's voting registration remained staunchly Republican.

William F. Buckley Sr., the father of tonight's honoree, was by all accounts a remarkable man. Self-made, devoutly Catholic, a risk taker. He once talked Pancho Villa out of shooting a train conductor for committing lèse-majesté. He indignantly refused to become the American governor-civil of Veracruz after Woodrow Wilson trained the U.S. Navy's guns on the city. A few years after that, having lent his support to the losing side in that week's revolution, he was obliged to depart Mexico under sentence of death. He came home to America, married a young Catholic beauty from New Orleans, and raised ten children, not one of whom grew up speaking English as a first language. It was said of him that he worshiped three things: God, his family, and education . . . in that order.

That was the heritage that William F. Buckley Jr. inherited. Not a bad one. Like his father, he grew up devout, risk taking, and occasionally supporting the losing side, though ultimately, as intellectual godfather to the movement that produced the election of Ronald Reagan, he was a very big winner. Yet even when he was on the losing side, he managed, unlike his father, to stay on the right side of the firing line.

At Yale, he made a glorious pain in the ass of himself with an administration and faculty that in his view had turned its back on that college's heritage. His first book—of some forty, at last count—sought to reassert that heritage and those principles, which he held sacred, then as now. It was Act One in a remarkable public life.

He served in the CIA and founded a magazine whose stated mission was to "stand athwart history, yelling Stop!" He has written a thrice-weekly column for almost forty years. He ran for mayor of New York, making the Conservative Party safe for James L. Buckley and Alfonse D'Amato. He became host of Firing Line, *the most substantive dialogue ever produced on television. Two months from now he will tape the last show, and enter the record books as the longest-running single host of a television program in history.*

He was delegate to the United Nations, where for a brief shining moment he made life intolerable for so many deserving tin-pot potentates who up to then had viewed that forum as a dumping ground for their latest grievances about the United States, enemy of humanity.

At fifty he became a best-selling novelist and sailed himself across the first of many oceans. Concert pianist at sixty. Ex–concert pianist at sixty-one.

He has been there, done that. Flown in the cockpit of an F-4 Phantom jet, and dived three miles deep to peer into the skeleton of the Titanic. *One March day in Long Island Sound after an accident, he dragged a drowning friend a half mile through freezing water and saved his life, an incident that should excite his biographer, if trends in current biography are any indication.*

I've watched the President of the United States hang a medal around his neck and call him a hero. I've listened as Cardinal O'Connor—who is in our prayers tonight—addressed him in a room crowded with important prelates and called him "the jewel in the crown of American Catholicism." And I have heard my mother say one thousand times, "Your father is impossible."

And you know, they were all *right.*

To those voices I can only add my small prayer of gratitude tonight to providence for being so bountiful that day in 1952 in the matter of my own heritage.

Ladies and gentlemen, William F. Buckley Jr.

M Y FATHER WAS a friend of Albert Jay Nock, who, silver-headed with the trim moustache and rimless glasses, was often at our house in Sharon, Connecticut. There, at age thirteen or fourteen, I scurried about, going to some pains to avoid being trapped into hearing anything spoken by someone so manifestly professorial. Most of what my father would relate about him—relate to me and my siblings—was amusing and informative, not so much about such Nockean specialties as Thomas Jefferson or Rabelais or the recondite assurances of the Remnant; but informative about him. I remember hearing that Mr. Nock had made some point of telling my father that he never read any newspapers, judging them to be useless and, really, infra dignitatem. But one day my father stopped by at the little inn Mr. Nock inhabited in nearby Lakeville, Connecticut, to escort Mr. Nock to lunch, as arranged. Inadvertently my father arrived a half hour earlier than their planned meeting time. He opened the door to Mr. Nock's quarters and came upon him on hands and knees, surrounded by the massive Sunday editions of the *New York Herald Tribune* and the *New York Times.* My father controlled his amusement on the spot, but not later, when he chatted delightedly with his children about the eccentricities of this august figure, this great stylist—my father preferred good prose to any other pleasure on earth, if that can be said credibly of someone who sired ten children. He thought Mr. Nock the most eloquent critic in America of, among other things, President Franklin Delano Roosevelt and his shortcomings.

My father's disapproval of Mr. Roosevelt engaged the collaborative attention of my brother Jim. He was sixteen and had a brand new rowboat. He launched it after painting on its side a prolix baptismal name. He called it *My Alabaster Baby, or To Hell with Roosevelt.*

When father heard this, he instructed Jimmy immediately to alter the name. "He is the President of the United States," my father said, no further elaboration on FDR's immunity from certain forms of raillery being thought necessary; besides which, my father observed, his days in the White House were numbered.

Because that summer Wendell Willkie ran against President Roosevelt. My father went to the polls and voted for Willkie, thinking him a reliable adversary of America's march towards war. A year later, in conversation with Mr. Nock, my father disclosed that he had voted for Willkie, thus departing from a near-lifelong resolution, beginning in his thirties, never to vote for any political candidate. He now affirmed, with Mr. Nock's hearty approval, his determination to renew his vows of abstinence, Willkie having been revealed—I remember the term he used—as a "mountebank."

"They are all mountebanks," Mr. Nock said. It was about that time that I began reading Albert Jay Nock, from whom I imbibed deeply the anti-statist tradition which he accepted, celebrated, and enhanced. One of his protégés, who served also as his literary executor, was Frank Chodorov. He became my closest intellectual friend early in the 1950s. Chodorov accepted wholly the anarchical conclusions of Mr. Nock, though when we worked together, on *The Freeman* and at *National Review,* Mr. Chodorov temporized with that total disdain for politics that had overcome his mentor. Mr. Chodorov permitted himself to express relative approval, from time to time, for this or another political figure, notably Senator Robert A. Taft in 1952.

I remember, in the work of Nock and in the work of American historical figures he cited, the felt keenness of that heritage, the presumptive resistance to state activity. It was very nearly devotional in character. It was in one of his essays, I think, that I first saw quoted John Adams's admonition that the state seeks to turn every contingency into an excuse for enhancing power in itself, and of course Jefferson's adage that the government can only do something for the people in proportion as it can do something to the people. The ultimate repudiation of the institution was pronounced by a noted contemporary of Albert Jay Nock, his friend H. L. Mencken. He said apodictically that the state is "the enemy of all well-disposed, decent, and industrious men." I remember thinking that that formulation seemed to me to stretch things a bit far, and so began my own introduction into the practical limits of anarchy.

But the American legacy—opposition to unnecessary activity by the state—was from the start an attitude I found entirely agreeable, in my own thinking and in my student journalism. And when *National Review* was launched I found myself in the company of thoughtful and learned anti-statists. Our managing editor, Suzanne La Follette, had served as managing editor of the original *Freeman,* of which Mr. Nock was the founder and editor. That magazine, after several years, failed in the 1920s. In his memoirs Mr. Nock reported fatalistically that it was a journal that had had its day on earth and should be, after four years, ready to phase out, even as, a generation later, there were those who thought it appropriate that the Mont Pelerin Society, after twenty-five years, should end its life uncomplaining. And then too, Mr. Nock conceded retrospectively, there might have been failures in his own administration of the enterprise. "As a judge of talent," he wrote in his recollection, "I am worth a ducal salary. As a judge of character, I cannot tell the difference between a survivor of the saints and the devil's ragbaby."

Max Eastman was also with us in 1955. Now a heated enemy of the state, the poet-philosopher-journalist had been a fervent Communist. James Burnham, who was by this time questioning even the authority of government to outlaw Fourth of July fireworks in private hands, had been a leading Trotskyist. Frank Meyer was for some years a high official of the Communist Party in Great Britain and in America. His newfound antipathy to collectivist thought stayed with him to the very end. He was suffering terminally from cancer, on that last Friday I visited with him in Woodstock. He told me hoarsely that he hoped to join the Catholic Church before he died but was held back by that clause in the Creed that spoke of the communion of saints, which he judged to be a concession to collectivist formulations. He overcame his misgiving the very next day and died the following day, Easter Sunday, at peace with the Lord who made us all equal, but individuated. And of course Frank Chodorov came to us after the resurrected *Freeman* folded. He had just published a book. Frank chose a subtle way of making his point about the undesirability of collectivism: he called his book *Two Is a Crowd.*

How MIGHT WE reconcile the American heritage of opposition to distorted growth in the state with the august, aspirant movement in which the Founding Fathers plighted their trust? The impulse to categorical renunciation, in the language of Mr. Nock and Frank Chodorov, ran up against what we at *National Review* deemed a sovereign historical responsibility in those postwar years. It was to protect the American people and their government: to protect the state, yes, from threats to its existence. After the Soviet leaders had acquired the atom bomb, all the while reiterating a historical commitment to imposing dominion over the whole world, the primary responsibility of our own state became at the very least co-existence, at best liberation. In the vigorous anti-Communist enterprise we were joined by the most categorical anti-statists of the day, including Milton Friedman and Ayn Rand, even though to achieve our purposes meant alliances, military deployments abroad, and, yes, wars.

There would be no denying the relevance of John Adams's monitory words, because even as we developed the military and institutional strength necessary to face down, and eventually to cause to collapse, the Communist aggressor, unrelated branches of government swelled. It was not only our defensive capabilities, military and paramilitary, that prospered. The contingencies of which Mr. Adams warned were everywhere inducing public-sector growth and government intervention, as, for instance, in university life after the first Soviet satellite was launched. It was as if only federal dollars could expose twenty-year-olds to science. The country evolved statist programs that all but took over graduate education, and we issued regulations in the tens of thousands, regulations that direct much of what we do, or that keep us from doing what we otherwise would do. And today, while our military requirements are met with less than 4 percent of the gross national product, 22 percent of what we produce is commandeered by the federal government, in its feverish application of more and more lures and wiles, the better to seduce the voting public. There are those—I think of the late Murray Rothbard—who cried out against the politics of co-existence and liberation, but his perspective was so much the captive of an anti-statist obsession that his eyes squinted, and at the end he was incapable of distinguishing— he loudly professed—between the leaders of the Soviet Union and the leaders of the United States. On this matter, in those frenzied days, I counterpreached that the man who pushes an old lady into the path of an oncoming truck, and the man who pushes an old lady out of the path of an oncoming truck, are not to be denounced even- handedly as men who push old ladies around.

IN COLLEGE, in the late 1940s, I remarked a general conformity by the majority of our faculty on the matter of state enterprise. Almost uniformly the scholars urged its expansion. I noted also what I thought the parlous direction of religious intellectual life, conde- scendingly treated when it wasn't actively disdained. Was there—is there—a nexus? Mr. Nock began his professional life as an ordained minister of God; but then, I remembered irreverently, at age forty he suddenly (by contemporary account) left his wife and two sons to pursue his famous career as a dilettante scholar. The state got in his way, and we don't know whether God ever asserted himself. Although not combative on the religious question in his writings, Mr. Nock left the discerning to suppose that he had abandoned his sometime com- mitment to Christian dogma, though not to the secular transcription of the Christian idea, which is that all men are equal and born to be free. Whittaker Chambers said in passing that liberal democracy was a political reading of the Bible. Certainly we were cautioned very early, in theological thought, against coveting our neighbors' goods.

    In my published reflections on the neglect of religion at Yale I remembered, of course, the heritage of Christianity in the life of the country and of the university I had attended. That heritage was boldly proclaimed in the inaugural address of the scholar-historian who was president of Yale when I studied there. Charles Seymour had said in 1937, "I call on all members of the faculty, as members of a thinking body, freely to recognize the tremendous validity and power of the teachings of Christ in our life-and-death struggle against the forces of selfish materialism."

It appears to me now, sixty years after he spoke those words, that we can lay claim to having defeated the immediate threat to which Mr. Seymour pointed (when he spoke, Hitler had only eight years to live). But what he called selfish materialism is something we need always to pray about, if we remember to pray.

In hindsight I note what may have been a careful circumlocution when the president of Yale, an American historian, spoke of the validity and power of the teachings of Christ in our life-and-death struggle. There is pretty wide support for the teachings of Christ, if we subtract from them that teaching which he obtrusively listed as the pre-eminent obligation of his flock, namely to love God with all our heart, soul, and mind. Most of the elite in our culture have jettisoned this injunction. We're taught in effect that what's important in Christianity is the YMCA, not the church.

I wonder whether this truncation—the love of God's other teachings, the love of one's neighbor, dismembered from the love of God—is philosophically reliable. The old chestnut tells of the husband leaving the church service after hearing the rousing sermon on the Ten Commandments with downcast countenance. Suddenly he takes heart. "I never," he taps his wife on the arm, "made any graven images!" But there are graven images here, and worship of them best describes some communicants.

The Founders sought out divine providence in several perspectives, as they gathered together to mint the American legacy. They staked out a claim to the "separate and equal station to which the Laws of Nature and of Nature's God" entitled them. This tells us that, in their understanding, to assert persuasively the right of a people to declare its independence, something like a divine warrant is needed. The specific qualifications for such a warrant are not given— the signers weren't applying for a driver's license. Were they supplicants, appealing for divine favor? Or is it a part of our heritage that they posited a transcendent authority, whose acquiescence in their enterprise they deemed themselves entitled to? We do not find any answer to that in the Constitution. But the Declaration is surely the lodestar of constitutional assumptions.

The second invocation asked "the Supreme Judge of the world"—they were not referring to the Supreme Court—to aver the "rectitude" of the fathers' "intentions." The appeal was to forgive the drastic action they were now taking, a declaration not only of independence, but of war. War against the resident authorities, with the inevitable loss of human lives.

And, finally, the signers were telling the world that they proceeded to independence "with a firm reliance on the protection of Divine Providence." This was Thomas Jefferson's variation on the conventional formulation, "Thy will be done."

We had, then, (a) an appeal to transcendent law, (b) an appeal to transcendent modes of understanding national perspective, and (c) an appeal for transcendent solicitude. We are reminded of the widening gulf between that one part of our heritage, thought critical by the signers, and the secularist transformation; the attenuations of it today in the feel-good Judeo-Christianity which, however welcome its balm, gives off less than the heat sometimes needed to light critical fires. We read the speeches of Martin Luther King Jr., whose life we celebrate while tending to ignore the essence of his beliefs, acclaimed by him (as by Abraham Lincoln) as the ground of his idealism. A bizarre paradox in the new secular order is the celebration of Dr. King's birthday as a national holiday acclaimed as the heartbeat of articulated idealism in race relations, conscientiously observed in our schools, with, however, scant thought given to Dr. King's own faith. What is largely overlooked, in the matter of Dr. King, is his Christian training and explicitly Christian commitment. Every student is familiar with the incantation "I have a dream." Not many are familiar with the peroration. The closing words were ". . . and the glory of the Lord shall be revealed, and all flesh shall see it together." The sermon Martin Luther King preached at the Ebenezer Baptist Church three months before he was killed was selected by his votaries to be replayed at his funeral. It closed, "If I can do my duty as a Christian ought, then my living will not be in vain." George Washington would not have been surprised by Dr. King's formulation. Washington admonished against any "supposition" that "morality can be maintained without religion." "Reason and experience," he commented, "*both* forbid us to expect that national morality can prevail in exclusion of religious principle." Two centuries before the advent of Dr. King, George Washington wrote with poetic force a letter to the Hebrew congregation of Savannah on the divine auspices of intercredal toleration. "May the same wonder-working Deity, who long since delivered the Hebrews from their Egyptian oppressors . . . continue to water them with the dews of heaven and make the inhabitants of every denomination participate in the temporal and spiritual blessings of that people whose God is Jehovah."

The infrastructure of our governing assumption—that human beings are equal—derives from our conviction that they are singularly creatures of God. If they are less than that—mere evolutionary oddments—we will need to busy ourselves mightily to construct rationales for treating alike disparate elements of humanity which anthropological research might persuasively claim to be unequal. A professor newly appointed to Princeton has no problem with infanticide. Those who believe in metaphysical equality will resist any attempt to extend homo sapiens to homo sapienter by saying, What have such findings to do with the respect, civil and spiritual, that every American owes to every other American? The political turmoil of this year left us in moral incoherence. The most eloquent escapist summoned to make the case against removal following the impeachment vote was former senator Dale Bumpers, who proceeded to defend what he had designated as "indefensible." In the absence of durable perspectives, language loses its meaning and reality slips through the mind's grasp.

It is reassuring that our heritage, having finally excreted slavery and apartheid, appears to be in lively acquiescence on the matter of equality. We no longer suffer from civil encumbrances to the freedom to seek happiness, the search for which was held out to us in the Declaration as a birthright of the new Republic. The American Revolution was done entirely without the ideological afflatus that, a dozen years later, launched another revolution, this one symbolized by the guillotine. It never occurred to any of the signers to doubt the distempers Hamilton spoke of as an inevitable part of the human experience. On the most dramatic eve in American history, the night of the third of July 1776, John Adams was, as usual, writing a letter to Abigail. He had zero illusions about human frailty. On the contrary, his words seethed with both excitement and trepidation. "The furnace of affliction," he wrote solemnly, "produces refinement in states as well as individuals." But to inaugurate the new regime would require, as he put it, a "purification from our vices, and an augmentation of our virtues, or there will be no blessings." In France it was postulated that with the elimination of a social class, the wellsprings of human virtue would repopulate the land with a new breed. The succeeding revolution to that of the Jacobins came in Russia in the twentieth century. Its lodestar was the elimination of property, an end of which would bring on an end to the causes of human friction.

The Founders had no such categorical illusions about the causes of human strife. James Madison cherished the prospect of a favorable *balance* in human performance, but a balance it would always be: "As there is a degree of depravity in mankind which requires a certain degree of circumspection and distrust, so there are other qualities in human nature which justify *a certain portion* of esteem and confidence." Note, a certain portion of esteem and confidence. He went on: "Republican government presupposes the existence of these [last] qualities in a higher degree than any other form. Were the pictures which have been drawn by the political jealousy of some among us"— he meant by the term "jealousy" a resentful desire for others' advantages—"faithful likenesses of the human character," then "the inference would be that there is not sufficient virtue among men for self-government; and that nothing less than the chains of despotism can restrain them from destroying and devouring one another."

The harvest of "jealousy," to use Madison's term, is everywhere, as he expected. In contemporary language, there is romantic jealousy; at street level, there is rivalry; at the national political level, jealousy strives to make public laws and practices.

Here, I think, susceptibility to the vices John Adams pleaded that we guard against is critically encouraged by the amendment that authorized unequal taxation, giving constitutional rise to jealous appetites that have taken redistribution to the level of confiscatory legislation. Mr. Nock described what he considered the single most ominous institutional development of his lifetime, namely, as he put it, the "substitution of political for economic energy as a means of self-aggrandizement." It is tempting to build your house by enticing the legislature, rather than the market. Professor Hayek, looking back on the century he so singularly adorned, pointed to progressive taxation as the Achilles' heel of self-government. Even as a consensus flourishes that property should be protected, a consensus withers on the definition of property, which becomes now that much of a citizen's earnings as are left to him, or to his estate, by sufferance of Congress. The towering irreconcilability is between the constitutional amendment that promises equal treatment under the law, and the successor—one-sentence—amendment that, fifty years later, authorized discriminatory taxation.

IN THE 1950S, young American adults had the routine experiences— at college, after college, in the professional schools engaging business, law, medicine, the humanities. Those who got around to lifting their sights in search of perspective in politics had reason to wonder whether the infrastructure of marketplace thinking had been quite simply abandoned by the productive sector of the American establishment.

In the years immediately after the war the productive community, browbeaten by twelve years of the New Deal, by four years of dirigiste policies in a military-minded economy, by the socialist emanations of postwar Europe, was listless in the defense of its own values. Men of affairs are—men of affairs. They tend not to linger over brewing consequences of intellectual and polemical torpor. I remember in senior year of college the excruciating experience of seeing in public debate an American businessman trying hopelessly to contend against hardwired enthusiasts for statist activity. It was so also with the polished academic establishmentarians, who held out hoops at every trustees' meeting, through which our men of affairs would jump, as if trained to do so from childhood. With distressing frequency those who upheld the heritage left the stage or studio exposed to humiliation by the poverty of their resources. It's different now. We have substantially to thank for it the institution whose anniversary these lectures celebrate. What began as tinkertoy research grew in twenty-five years into the dominant think tank in the country.

The aim of the Heritage Foundation is to heighten economic and political literacy among those men and women whose decisions affect the course of the Republic. In pursuit of this aim the Foundation had an exhilarating hour when Ronald Reagan was elected president in November of 1980. The new president found waiting for him in the White House three volumes of material designed to help him chart the course to take the nation back in the right direction. Sixty percent of the suggestions enjoined on the new president, I am advised, were acted upon (which is why Mr. Reagan's tenure was 60 percent successful).

The broader community of journalists, opinion makers, and academics is hardly ignored. The masses of material generated by Heritage flow out into the major arteries of American thought. We rest more comfortable in the knowledge that high ideals have intoned their enduring pitch in the tumult of a century that strove mightily to inter the heritage of American idealism.

We have come, Mr. Chairman, to the end of your two-year-long inquiry into the roots of American order, begun by Lady Thatcher, who, in her talk on the theme of courage, could hardly avoid autobiography. Clarence Thomas spoke about character, which he has helped to define. Bill Bennett about truth, which he arrantly acknowledges the existence of. And Steve Forbes about enterprise, and who, without that spirit of enterprise supercharged, would undertake to compete for the presidency?

So it has been: Michael Joyce on self-government, which he encourages in practical measures, year after year; Peggy Noonan on the subject of patriotism, which flows in hot poetry from her pen. And on with Midge Decter, George Will and James Q. Wilson, Ed Meese and

Father Neuhaus; Václav Klaus celebrating liberty and the rule of law, and Gary Becker the spirit and the fruits of competition; Jeane Kirkpatrick and Newt Gingrich clearly distinguishing between authority and authoritarianism, between responsibility and officiousness.

We comfort ourselves that right reason will prevail, that our heritage will survive. I close by summoning two injunctions. The first, the concluding sentence of a letter from George Washington, again to a Hebrew congregation, in Newport, Rhode Island: "May the father of all mercies scatter light, and not darkness, upon our paths, and make us all in our several vocations useful here, and in His own due time and way everlastingly happy."

Two hundred years after Washington wrote these words, an American president, Ronald Reagan, closed his second inaugural address by describing what he called "the American sound." It is, he said, "hopeful, big-hearted, idealistic—daring, decent, and fair. We sing it still," he said. "We raise our voices to the God who is the author of this most tender music."

We hear that sound, and call back to say that the attritions notwithstanding, our heritage is there. To the end of its preservation, with reverence and gratitude, we dedicate ourselves.

INDEX